Shaping the Network Society

Shaping the Network Society

The New Role of Civil Society in Cyberspace

edited by Douglas Schuler and Peter Day

The MIT Press
Cambridge, Massachusetts
London, England

This book was set in Stone Sans and Stone Serif by Integra Software Services Pvt Ltd., and was printed and bound in the United States of America.

Library of Congress Cataloging-in-Publication Data

Shaping the network society : the new role of civil society in cyberspace / edited by Douglas Schuler and Peter Day.
    p.   cm.
"An outgrowth of the Seventh DIAC symposium held in Seattle in 2000"—Introd.
Includes bibliographical references and index.
ISBN 0-262-19497-X (hc : alk. paper)
1. Information technology—Social aspects. 2. Computer networks—Social aspects. 3. Social participation. 4. Civil society. I. Schuler, Douglas. II. Day, Peter, 1954– III. DIAC (Conference) (7th : 2000 : Seattle, Wash.)

HM851.S43   2004
303.48′33—dc22

2003065170

10   9   8   7   6   5   4   3   2   1

Contents

Introduction

Douglas Schuler and Peter Day

In 1987 Computer Professionals for Social Responsibility (CPSR) sponsored its first "Directions and Implications of Advanced Computing" (DIAC) symposium, intended to help raise issues related to the social implications of computing. The symposium was built on the premise that academics do not necessarily have to be "merely" academic but can play a vital role in society. It was also intended to provide a forum for the nascent and relatively unorganized group of academics concerned about the uncritical adoption of computers in society.

Of course, since those early days there has been an immense increase of interest among academics and other researchers in a multitude of issues surrounding the use of computers in society. Unfortunately much of this work is divorced from the "real world," including all the messy issues, perplexing threats—and opportunities—that it provides. Information and communication technology (ICT) has been, and increasingly is being, marketed in the service of efficiency, speed, progress, and, of course, profitability. The more flesh-and-bones aspects of life—neighborhoods, emotions, resistance, fallibility, accidents, carnivals, play, smells, death, and so on—play little part in the antiseptic aura spun by the high priests and priestesses of computerization. The message is this: computers are for people in control, not for people who are under control. In other words, computers are to be used to maintain the status quo, not to perturb it.

In much of the "developed" world, especially the United States and Europe, "research" in computing, unless it is devoted to "e-commerce," is rarely applied (excepting, again, disciplines devoted to business, such as management information systems). If the communities using the systems are not businesspeople, research in that area is often at the margins of acceptability. The reasons for this are numerous and beyond the scope of this book. But the upshot is that people (both inside and outside academia) who are interested in research related to real-world issues may be tolerated but are rarely championed.

This situation raises a number of important questions in urgent need of consideration. Why is research that is socially shaped so important in the network society? What can/should academics do? Why do they need to work with people and communities? How could this be a win-win situation? This book illustrates how research that focuses on people in their natural social environments, that uses common language, and that is flexible and pragmatic and nonetheless receives little support from national and international funding agencies can and is being successfully undertaken around the world. Partnerships based on a spirit of mutuality, reciprocity, and trust are emerging between some spheres of academia and a diverse range of action/advocacy networks and local communities. From these alliances new research paradigms and orientations are emerging: a "new pact" that engages with the rest of the planet, where everything is connected to everything else!

The contributors to this book assume that ICT represents important opportunities and threats that cannot be ignored. Ideally we would like to envision and develop sociotechnical systems that help humankind deal with our environmental crises, curb militarism, and promote social and economic justice, but how can such a social vision be achieved? The collective message from the chapter authors provides us with some hope for the future of a network society. By working together in a collaborative and cooperative manner, by sharing experiences and knowledge through discussions that legitimize actions, and through communicative action that enables citizens to engage in shaping local community initiatives and enterprises, great strides can be made. Finally, by demonstrating courage and dedication, sometimes in the face of enormous odds, hugely significant social advances can be made locally that impact at the global level.

This book is an outgrowth of the Seventh DIAC Symposium, held in Seattle in 2000. We have been working with several of the attendees at this symposium (and one or two others) to help bring out the message that computer professionals have a critical role to play in the ongoing deployment of computers. We also began a discussion of how civil society should engage with the United Nations on the issue of ICT for the common good. In that meeting, we started work on a collective "pattern language." Since that time, the Eighth Symposium was convened.

We believe that people interested in the other side of computing should read this book. This includes community and civil-society practitioners, teachers and students, journalists, artists, policymakers, and—most important—citizens. This book tells at least part of the new story that is emerging about how computers might be used more effectively by people in communities, by activists in social movements, and by citizens interested in a better future.

Computer professionals need not confine themselves to the bits, bytes, algorithms, theoretical musings, and so on that have traditionally defined computer science. (Interestingly, while some would narrowly define computer science as a type of engineering, many departments have ushered in new programs in e-commerce and entrepreneurism.) Enterprises with less potential for generating income in the short term—such as preventing and recovering from environmental catastrophes, strengthening the digital commons, or developing civic intelligence—are frequently neglected by the private sector and the government as well. The work here—and elsewhere—demonstrates that important research can be conducted in partnerships with civic and community activists in ways that vastly expand the scope, and relevance, of their practice.

We have been fortunate while preparing this book to work with such a creative, dedicated, and engaged group of authors from around the world. While we feel that this group is exceptional, we are happily aware that they are not unique in their concerns. If the ideas expressed in this book (and the related ideas issuing from all over the world) are to become influential in a broad sense, it will be due to the efforts of the hundreds of thousands of people who are working—generally with little fanfare and fewer resources—on all of these issues. We wish you—and all of them—good luck. We are hoping to be able to work with you in the future in the ongoing struggle to *shape the network society*.

We also would like to thank a few people. Our families, first and foremost—wives Terry and Denise, and children, Reed, Zoe, Nadine, and Katie—for putting up with our absences, even when we were physically present. Jessica Smith put in hours on the more thankless chores, formatting, alphabetizing, and so on. We would also like to thank The MIT Press, Bob Prior, and Catherine Innis for supporting this project and working with us to see it through. Finally, of course, this work would not even be possible without the great authors, those who assisted them—and the people from around the world who are currently engaging with communities so that they participate in shaping the network society.

The Social Dimensions of Engineering, Science and Technology (SDEST) division of the National Science Foundation helped support this work through grant 0138149. We would also like to thank the Creativity and Culture program of the Rockefeller Foundation for its generous support.

1 Shaping the Network Society: Opportunities and Challenges

Douglas Schuler and Peter Day

Global civil society is best expressed in the global non-governmental movement. As a group, non-governmental organizations (NGOs) are diverse and multifaceted. Their perspectives and operations may be local, national, regional or global. Some are issue-oriented or task oriented; others are driven by ideology. Some have a broad public-interest perspective; others have a more private, narrow focus. They range from small, poorly funded, grassroots entities to large, well-supported, professionally staffed bodies. Some operate individually; others have formed networks to share information and tasks and to enhance their impact.

—"Our Global Neighborhood," the Report of The Commission on Global Governance

That an explosion of information and communication technology (ICT) is helping to restructure the world's economic, political, and cultural systems is not news. What is news, however, is the strong role—largely unacknowledged—that global civil society is playing in shaping the "network society" (Castells 1996). Too often people regard the current work in technology development as an arena in which millions of dollars of venture capital are required in order to participate. Yet, on every continent, through countless experiments and projects, teachers, social activists, researchers, community organizers, and concerned technologists are writing their own rules. These people are working to establish an information and communication infrastructure that is in marked contrast to that desired by the dot-coms and the technolibertarians—an infrastructure that truly meets the disparate and critical needs of the world's citizenry.

The directions taken by practitioners of civil-society ICT are too numerous to be explained exhaustively in this chapter, or even in this book. These projects have yet to be cataloged in their entirety. They may be changing and growing too fast for analysis and may be too far-ranging for a single book. The sociotechnical environment of those systems is also complex and dynamic. Yet in a very real sense, these projects need to be considered as elements of a broader "movement," however unorchestrated that movement may be. It is our modest hope that this book will help weave these related, though largely disparate, strands together into a more coherent, cohesive, and useful fabric for researchers, practitioners, policymakers, and citizens.

The purpose of the book is to lay some of the initial groundwork for understanding the actuality and potentiality of new, generally Internet-based, forms of information and communication for social amelioration and social change. Because these forms are, after all, "media" (albeit new, nontraditional, less established and supported, and dedicated to different ends), and because their competition is also "media" and because our society is increasingly mediated, this book also considers other types of media, especially new global-media empires. John Thompson, writing in *The Media and Modernity: A Social Theory of the Media* (1995), underscores the critical importance of media systems, including both the vast global leviathans and the grassroots upstarts we consider in this book:

We can understand the social impact of the development of new networks of communication and information flow only if we put aside the intuitively plausible idea that communication media serve to transmit information and symbolic content to individuals whose relations to others remain unchanged. *We must see, instead, that the use of communication media involves the creation of new forms of action and interaction in the social world, new kinds of social relationships and new ways of relating to others and to oneself.* (p. 4; our emphasis)

Although the systems and projects in our book are not *grafted* onto the existing world, instead being *integrated* into existing systems and projects, their effects—consolidating existing power and/or empowering a plethora of socially ameliorative and decentralized forces, for example—may be profound.

Local Skirmishes/Global Forces

On the first night of the Seattle ministerial meeting of the World Trade Organization in November 1999, with the steady howl of police sirens in the background, a civic encounter had been convened at the nonprofit "Town Hall" to look into root causes of the disagreements and, hence, of the chaos outside. Three proponents of the WTO were squared off in a debate against three opponents. The themes of the meeting were intensified by the noise from outside; the somewhat abstract themes of world trade were made concrete and urgent because of the struggles outside the enclave. The "Battle in Seattle" and subsequent clashes in Genoa and other places highlight a rift, a growing fault line. So does the September 11, 2001, attack on New York and Washington, D.C. In the WTO debate in Seattle, a curious point of agreement emerged from those on both sides of the issue: over the past twenty or so years the rich had indeed gotten richer, the poor poorer. Several such rifts are strongly apparent and widening further: rural and urban, secular and fundamentalist, global and local. The gap between rich and poor is perhaps the most obvious and the most grievous, for not only does it lead to misery and hardship for the poor, but to war, disease, and environmental degradation for everybody.

The scope of these concerns is becoming increasingly global; our social (political, cultural, economic) systems are linked in an interdependent web that is complex and largely incomprehensible. At the same time the environmental cocoon on which we all depend for life is increasingly being marred and abused by humankind's misdeeds. Collective and basically unchecked use of fossil fuels can eat away at our atmospheric mantle, changing climatic factors unpredictably and sending environmental—and thus social—shock waves throughout the world, unmooring habitual behavior and provoking a cascading imbalance that may yet undo us. Homer-Dixon, Boutwell, and Rathjens (1993), for example, demonstrate the clear link between the loss of renewable resources and deadly conflicts worldwide.

Solutions may come about through dialogue, discussion, deliberation, and debate. These forms of communication—and democracy in general—presuppose the existence of a public sphere.

What Is a Public Sphere and Why Is It Needed?

In 1962 the philosopher Jürgen Habermas, of the renowned Frankfurt School in Germany, used the term *Öffentlichkeit* ("public sphere"), where information exists and communication occurs in a public way, where public discussion and deliberation take place, a "space," in other words, within which public matters are settled, on which democratic systems must rely. Although his influential book on this subject was not translated into

English—as *The Structural Transformation of the Public Sphere: An Inquiry into a Category of Bourgeois Society*—until 1989 (Habermas 1989), the concept of a public sphere soon became one of the most important concepts in communication studies. In contrast to other concepts in communication studies (like cultural imperialism or media monopoly), the concept of public sphere is posited as a *positive* one, a mode of communication that represents a desirable state of affairs. It is an idealized communication venue (or "theater," to use Nancy Fraser's (1988) term) into which everyone can freely enter. Important civic decisions are made through the discussions in this "public sphere," rendering it a fundamental aspect of democratic systems. A public sphere is a "mediating structure," albeit an abstract one, like political parties, representative governments, the media, and so on. A mediating structure is a *linking* mechanism; it is intended to connect disparate viewpoints, to give voice to all, to prevent the escalation of grievances into desperation or lethal conflict.

A public sphere seems to be characterized by three main features. First, it presents communication opportunities in a broad sense. Thus coffee shops, public hearings, town meetings, and other venues where people interact with one another face to face fit under its conceptual umbrella. Forms such as newspapers, broadcast media, and the Internet can also fit— under some circumstances. Second, public spheres are "public" in two ways: people can enter the "spaces" without undue hindrances, regardless of their ethnicity, religion, sexual preference, gender, or economic status, and the spaces themselves are visible; the discussions and decisions do not take place behind closed doors, gated neighborhoods, or private intranets. Third and finally, a public sphere mediates between people and institutions, between those that may be powerless and those that may be extremely powerful. Without this linkage or engagement, conversations would take place in walled-off zones and be ineffectual; the conversations may be full of "sound and fury" but if they are unheard and unheeded, they ultimately signify nothing.

As it turns out, Habermas's concept was flawed in many respects, as he himself has acknowledged. For one thing, the one instance of a public sphere (namely, liberal European bourgeois society during the 1800s) that Habermas brought to light was not really a *public* sphere at all. The poor were excluded, as were migrants, workers, and women. The public sphere that Habermas identified was more of a "gentlemen's club," according to one observer.

The concept of the public sphere, moreover, is imprecise; people do not agree on its meaning. Habermas himself did not explain exactly what he thought one was, nor did he offer a theory of how to build one. Is there a single, central public sphere that everybody in the world would or could use? Maybe there are dozens, hundreds, or millions of spheres, as some have suggested. And are there needs for *alternative* public spheres whose raison d'être is to *challenge* the assumptions and specifics of the more orthodox public spheres? What are the consequences of these limitations? Do they render the concept useless, or can it be salvaged in some way? And—more important for us—how can we use the concept effectively to help steer technology to make it better serve human needs? How, for example, does it help us think about the Internet and its ongoing evolution? Can it be used to spur activism on a large scale? A global scale?

A public sphere must be inclusive in several respects. First, everyone should be able to participate on an equal basis; those with more money than others should not be able to purchase more influence with their money, either directly or indirectly. For example, weapons makers should not determine foreign policy; prison-guard unions should not develop "three strikes you're out" laws, computer and media conglomerates should not define proper use of public airwaves, and software billionaires should not determine whether a city needs a new football stadium. This means that society needs to closely examine the ways people participate in public decision making (at community meetings, for instance) and help ensure that those mechanisms do not favor the privileged.

Second, there must be ways citizens can place their concerns on the public agenda. If the public agenda is monopolized and manipulated by corporations, politicians, or the media, the public sphere is seriously imperiled.

Third, the public sphere requires a deliberative public process in which all voices are equal—at least at decision points. This point entails the following critical ideas:

• *Deliberative*. Adequate time must be allotted for hearing and considering multiple points of view.

• *Public*. The discussion should take place openly, where it can be observed by all.

• *Process*. The procedures through which concerns are brought up, discussed, and acted on should be clear and widely known.

Since the concept of public sphere is abstract and imprecise, its best use may be as an indicator for direction and as a metric for criticism and action. The idea of a public sphere helps us to critique existing systems and imagine better ones. The preceding observations will serve as a useful backdrop for all the forthcoming chapters.

Structure of the Book

The major themes of the book are reflected in its structure. The broad context for ICT and civil society is discussed in part I, "Civilizing the Network Society." A variety of case studies from around the world offer rich and textured exemplars of local cyberspace-based civic projects in part II, "Global Tales of the Civil Network Society." Part III, "Building a New Public Sphere in Cyberspace," provides theoretical underpinnings, empirical findings, and other intellectual support for the development of the next generation of civic applications of ICT.

Civilizing the Network Society

Part I provides useful context for the chapters that come after. It introduces the critical elements of the opportunities and challenges offered by new ICT capabilities. This part also provides theoretical frameworks that are employed later. The chapters in this first section present most of the key conceptual elements related to communication technology deployment and social forces that are then woven together throughout the book.

Oliver Boyd-Barrett's contribution, "U.S. Global Cyberspace" (chapter 2), is grounded in the sociology of cyberspace. The goal of the chapter is to provide critical contextual information for understanding the evolving character of cyberspace and the prospects for an accessible and effective public sphere. Boyd-Barrett's work does not invalidate grassroots efforts— all great social movements have started as small, quixotic, uncertain impulses. It does, however, provide valuable educational grounding for the utopian among us while pointing to the vast challenges ahead.

The portrait he paints of cyberspace is one of exclusivity. Corporate and state bullies of immense proportions take advantage of—and promulgate— ideological forces that allow them to control an interconnected and powerful web of ICT assets in all spheres of broadcast and digital communications. We should thus be suspicious, Boyd-Barrett cautions us, of any attempts by these corporate and state entities to get on the bandwagon of grassroots democracy.

Gary Chapman, in "Shaping Technology for the 'Good Life': The Technological Imperative versus the Social Imperative" (chapter 3), explores the idea of technological imperative in the current context of a rising "technoglobalist tide" and various countermovements, predominantly the "slow food" cultural movement that originated in Italy in 1986. Chapman places "Moore's law," an intellectual cornerstone of today's global technologists, under particular scrutiny. In 1965 Intel cofounder Gordon Moore predicted with uncanny accuracy that microprocessor power would double approximately every eighteen months until 1975. Remarkably, this trend persisted well beyond 1975 and is still holding true, some twenty-five years later. To some people, this suggests that Moore's observation/forecast is, in fact, a physical "law" manifested independently in nature, rather than describing a set of technological opportunities that could be fruitfully exploited with the proper (immense) investment of time, money, and human resources. Accepting Moore's law *as a law*, consciously or unconsciously, can lead one to believe that the future is preordained and that technological innovations themselves (with no social intervention) are the motor behind an inexorable unfolding of tomorrow.

Enter the slow food movement, which Chapman proffers as an alternative paradigm (among many others) that challenges the global-technological imperative. Far from being simply a glib rejoinder to the American fast food orientation, the slow food ideology offers a middle ground, mediating between antitechnology anarchists and technoglobalist true believers. Instead of focusing on technology or on corporate capitalism—either for or against—the slow fooders (and advocates of other new paradigms) turn back instead to more basic questions: What is the good life ("il buon vivere"), for example, and how do we get there? Beyond this, there is a conscious attempt to do the hard work of organizing and building new institutions that can help propel the new work forward.

Chapman then applies his analysis to the realm of a network society. He believes that global-technological forces are acting to shape the Internet into the media equivalent of fast food. He believes that "fast media" are not preordained and that human values and human aspirations must reassert themselves over a putative global-technological imperative.

The prominent Dutch communications researcher and activist Cees J. Hamelink has contributed "Human Rights in the Global Billboard Society" (chapter 4), which contrasts the onslaught of global marketing and merchandising with universal values. He discusses the latter largely through the lens of the United Nations' "Universal Declaration of Human Rights" and the U.N.'s plans for the first "World Summit on the Information Society."

Hamelink discusses how four rights from the U.N. Universal Declaration—the right to free speech, the right to a democratic order, the right to equal participation in social life, and the right to cultural identity—are specifically threatened by the "billboardization" of society. He contrasts the political preferences of the "global billboard society" with those of the International Human Rights Regime (IHRR), which he believes to be on a collision course. As a longtime U.N. watcher, contributor, and gadfly, Hamelink fears that the U.N. is likely to side with the forces of the global billboard society to the detriment of the IHRR and other socially ameliorative communities worldwide. Although the development of collaborative civil-society networks raises complex questions, Hamelink believes that the mobilization of civil society is necessary to strongly remind the U.N. of its mission and the people worldwide for whom it claims to act.

Global Tales of the Civil Network Society

The case studies in part II provide a sampling of actual projects from all over the world that have developed in response to, and in the context of, powerful social and technological forces. These case studies are intended to be interdependent with the writings in the rest of the book. Their evolving and experimental nature will be stressed: What do they accomplish for their users? What are their objectives? How do they relate to other similar efforts and to the orienting ideas from part I of this book? Where are these projects going and what obstacles—of both an internal and an external nature—do they face? Additionally, setting the stage for the ideas in the rest of the book, these chapters discuss best practices as well as new social and technological directions.

In "A Census of Public Computing in Toledo, Ohio" (chapter 5), Kate Williams and Abdul Alkalimat attempt to identify every public computing facility in Toledo, Ohio, a medium-sized American "Rust-Belt" city. They explore three main settings in which citizens have access to networked computing—three possible "bridges across the digital divide": the home where *personal computing* occurs, the workplace where *private computing* occurs, and other places, where access is more open-ended and inclusive, especially in but not solely confined to libraries, schools, community centers, churches, and storefronts, which the authors call *public computing*. They are concerned with what will happen to democracy in the transition to an information society, and they scrutinize Toledo as a possibly typical "dual city" (Castells and Hall 1994) with this in mind. From the observations of Toledo's ninety-nine public computing sites, Williams and Alkalimat show that government sites are more or less randomly located around the city, community sites are generally located in economically rich or poor (but not middle-stratum) neighborhoods, while commercial and university sites correspond most closely to market forces and are located in close proximity to upper-income and student populations. If these findings are generally valid, the implications for democracy—particularly in relation to poor and working people—are profound.

In "A Polder Model in Cyberspace: The Contemporary Amsterdam Public Digital Culture" (chapter 6), two Amsterdam Internet developers and critics, Geert Lovink and Patrice Riemens, discuss developments in Amsterdam's new-media culture since its beginnings in the early 1990s. They especially focus on Amsterdam's community network, the Digital City (De Digitale Stad). Roughly paralleling the Seattle Community Network and Blacksburg Electronic Village (both Silver, chapter 14, this volume) and Rete Civica di Milano (De Cindio, chapter 10, this volume), the Digital City project as a product of Amsterdam's new-media culture was a vibrant and utopian digital project offering free services to tens of thousands of people. But in retrospect, it was on a collision course due to its own internal contradictions (conflicting management and user objectives and strategies) and the all-consuming ideological Zeitgeist of the "new economy's" get-rich-now mentality. Analogous to David Silver's "historical archaeologies," Lovink and Riemens depict a rich and volatile sociotechnico-historical landscape in which idealism bloomed and was, to a large degree, frustrated. Lovink and Riemens point to what they consider the particular "Dutchness" of the project, including its exclusive use of the Dutch language (the only policy decision along these lines made by management), the radical-squatter and "new-media-culture" movements, and the "Polder model" of social/political interaction characterized by "endless rounds of meetings." Some of the issues they raise are more universal: the lukewarm (at best) and indifferent or hostile (more commonly) attitudes shown by municipalities and other government units toward utopian public-sphere projects in cyberspace, like the Digital City. They also underscore the inability of those harboring more idealistic visions, to successfully organize, to articulate compelling visions, and to garner support and effectively work toward common goals.

The main goal of Susana Finquelievich's "Community Networks Go Virtual: Tracing the Evolution of ICT in Buenos Aires and Montevideo" (chapter 7) is to evaluate the social impact of ICT uses in local contexts, on both sides of the River Plate in South America. She focuses on local governments and their communication with citizens, as well as on the practices of civic networks trying to increase their impact on public issues. ICT uses and effective reach were studied in the local government's internal management practices, as well as in their attempts to assimilate the population to the information society. Finquelievich traces how some of the region's historical factors as well as the sociotechnical infrastructure have had a powerful influence on ICT development. Although the main focus of the chapter is on earlier data, Finquelievich discusses how the current crises in Argentina are shaping and are being addressed by existing citizen networks and ICT infrastructure.

Veran Matic's chapter "Civil Networking in a Hostile Environment: Experiences in the Former Yugoslavia" (chapter 8) is a chronicle of steadfast media resistance in a hostile environment over a period of five or so years in the former Yugoslavia. As such it highlights the critical—and dangerous—role of journalists and media institutions in securing human rights and democratic reform while fostering a critical and informed citizenry in the face of fascism and totalitarianism.

Matic's chapter performs the valuable service of highlighting particular issues and ideas that may be applicable in a variety of other situations, not only in fascist states and systems, but also in the West, as a corrective response to current methods of media operations. Experiences in the former Yugoslavia remind us that media can be used creatively and energetically in pursuit of higher goals, a principle unfortunately ignored or forgotten to a large degree by media producers (and consumers) all over the world.

Scott S. Robinson, in his chapter "Rethinking Telecenters: Microbanks and Remittance Flows—Reflections from Mexico" (chapter 9) focuses on a different geographic region. Robinson casts a critical yet hopeful eye on the nascent telecenter movement in Mexico and the other countries of the global South and on the particular set of historical forces in which these telecenters are spawned. He calls telecenters "cybercafés with a social conscience," and he sees them as an institution for the new "Second World" of refugees and migrants that could serve as the nucleus of a wide range of potential socially ameliorative functions. Robinson views them first as possible centers for microbanking in villages (which currently lack any formal financial institution), and secondarily as centers for training and for the use of (and production of) new electronic extension services.

Robinson is particularly interested in the new Second World of migrant populations who, of necessity, routinely traverse the First and Third Worlds. Since migrants often lose a substantial percentage of the money they send home, he proposes to combine community telecenters with microfinance institutions and offer cost-plus communication and basic financial services to migrants and their families at home. The savings could not only pay for the telecenters on both ends, but once the human and technical infrastructure is in place, other services could be provided and scaled to networked migrant communities, North and South.

Fiorella de Cindio's chapter, "The Role of Community Networks in Shaping the Network Society: Enabling People to Develop Their Own Projects" (chapter 10), is in large part the oral history of the Milan Community Network (Rete Civica di Milano or RCM in Italian), one of the world's most prominent community networks. By using the words of people who developed purposeful social venues within RCM's sociotechnical framework, De Cindio tells a meaningful story of social engagement in the hands of ordinary citizens, deftly illustrating the main tenet of this book—that civil society should be allowed and encouraged to play a role in shaping the network society.

De Cindio performs two additional services for us. First, she discusses four "genes" (academia, computer-supported cooperative work, participatory design, and civil engagement) or philosophical and methodological orientations that provided foundations that helped steer RCM into a useful platform for Milan's citizenry. Second, she relates how social actions nominally confined to a single community can have repercussions beyond the local context.

Building a New Public Sphere in Cyberspace

Part III, "Building a New Public Sphere in Cyberspace," focuses on the future: What do the case studies suggest? In what ways do they constitute new opportunities for civil society? How might a more democratic, community-centered information and communication infrastructure help steer humankind in directions that may be at odds with those suggested by the ubiquitous neoliberal, corporate media? What should be done?

Craig Calhoun's contribution, "Information Technology and the International Public Sphere" (chapter 11), is a wide-ranging explication of issues and prospects related to the development of information technology and the emerging network society. Calhoun's focus is on Habermas's idea of a public sphere and its possible relevance in today's world of "culture, capitalism, and inequalities" in a new mass-mediated, globalizing environment.

Calhoun is emphatic in his belief that a global public sphere is essential to the democratization of the global order. He is realistic, however, about the actual prospects. He argues that global public sphere in which critical public discourse trumps propaganda, commercialism, threats, and violence may indeed be possible—but that its future is by no means certain.

In "What Do We Need to Know about the Future We're Creating? Technobiographical Reflections" (chapter 12), Howard Rheingold embarks on a personal odyssey of his expectations and experiences with emerging computer technology. Using his own personal story, Rheingold starts with his grade school lectures on "Howard and the Atom" and progresses to his present-day work on "smart mobs" as a parable. To some degree Rheingold's own somewhat-diminishing infatuation with technology echoes the view that he expects the rest of humankind to now be adopting: that technology—and the Enlightenment worldview that engendered it—while being extremely powerful intellectually as well as materially, is not up to the task of solving the problems the world is currently faced with. (Although many of the problems we are faced with now are not new, it was generally easier to dismiss them as transparent or superficial—not deep, systemic, and persistent—in previous generations.)

Rheingold's continuing fascination with, and everyday use of, online communication naturally leads him where other people looking for ideas for new paradigms and technologies have also been led: to questions related to the "public sphere" in traditional Habermasian terms and to new possibilities as well. Without forswearing technological opportunities in general, but through a consideration of possibilities opened up by new sociotechnical systems, Rheingold believes that new information and communications systems can play an important role. If they are thought about—and *shaped*—with this in mind, they can help our species to better prepare for—and shape—the future and to help develop a more enlightened stance toward world stewardship.

Nancy Kranich's chapter, "Libraries: The Information Commons of Civil Society" (chapter 13), explores the role of the public library in the current era, in which print-based, broadcast, and new digital media all coexist. She builds a compelling case for libraries as a cornerstone of democratic society. She describes libraries as an abiding public institutionalized force for equitable and readily available information. Lost in the dot-com hysteria is the intriguing story about increasing library usage and the increase in the number of titles published each year.

At the same time, libraries have not let the online, digital boom—and its likely long-term effects on future information and communication spheres—escape them. Libraries have been busily providing access to the Net and to digital information while engaging in political and legal battles to maintain—and possibly strengthen—these rights in the future. For democracy to flourish in the digital age, the public will need a commons to exchange ideas and interact with fellow citizens. Libraries promise to provide such a public space, but citizens need to pick up the gauntlet and fight to ensure equitable access to information in their local communities.

David Silver's chapter, "The Soil of Cyberspace: Historical Archaeologies of the Blacksburg Electronic Village and the Seattle Community Network" (chapter 14), compares two influential community networks in the United States. The first, the Blacksburg Electronic Village (BEV), was amply endowed with millions of dollars (thanks to Bell-Atlantic, the Virginia State Legislature, the U.S. Department of Commerce, and others) and received many commendations, at least in its early days. The second, the Seattle Community Network (SCN), the product of progressive computer scientists, software developers, librarians, and homebrew computer nerds, relied on volunteer labor and virtually no funding. Silver performs the gritty genealogical detective work of analyzing the *soil*—the sociotechnical milieu—that shaped and nurtured the development of the two community networks.

Now the environment for both systems has changed dramatically; access to the Net (at least in Blacksburg, Seattle, and much of the United States) is ubiquitous, and the collapse of the dot-coms has taught sobering lessons. The community and civic potential for systems such as BEV and SCN has not gone away (nor has their need), although their proponents may have been chastened by the way things have turned out. Can BEV and SCN developers free themselves to some degree from the bonds of the history that they have helped write (and that Silver elucidates)? The environment in which they emerged has changed. Can the form they have created evolve accordingly, while they continue to strive toward the ambitious community and civic goals they have espoused?

Douglas Morris's chapter on "Globalization and Media Democracy: The Case of Indymedia" (chapter 15) explores one way the sociotechnical milieu that the Internet offers has been quickly and creatively embraced by people with a radical critique of contemporary neoliberalism. The Independent Media ("Indymedia") Center (IMC) movement is being propelled by a growing but widely distributed, loose-knit group of antiglobalist activists worldwide. These activists have stitched together a remarkable communications network using a common technological infrastructure, a more or less shared philosophy and strategic orientation, and few economic resources. Launched in anticipation of the major protests surrounding the World Trade Organization's meeting in Seattle in 1999, the network has grown to over 130 nodes worldwide.

The case of the IMC is critical to our present inquiry for two main reasons. We are concerned with the issues that the IMC has helped put on the public agenda. Is a corporate, top-down, rationalized, homogeneous philosophical orientation going to be the single ideology that guides our thoughts and actions, or will there be space for alternative viewpoints and ideological diversity? Who makes the rules and (more important?) the news?

We wonder, particularly, about the alternative and independent use of cyberspace. Can sustainable models of civic, noncommercial enterprises, including those that rely substantially on volunteer labor, be found? Can they gain legitimacy and influence in a sea of well-funded commercial enterprises? Finally, can the social, political, and economic functions that the IMCs strive to provide, coalesce with other efforts, including less confrontational efforts, like, for example, those of the public library? How do the arguably more traditional civil-society institutions support or detract from the militant calls for social change that the IMC and other, more radical groups demand?

The concluding chapter, "Propects for a New Public Sphere" (chapter 16), by Peter Day and Douglas Schuler, has two major objectives. The first is to take stock of today's sociotechnical milieu and the issues raised by the book's contributors. Currently there is urgent and widespread interest in developing new models, services, organizations, and ways of thinking around the world. It is possible that this work may blaze brightly for a time and burn out just as quickly as the novelty fades or the obstacles become insurmountable. On the other hand, this work may signal the beginning of new social forces that could significantly alter the paths humankind takes in the future.

The second objective is to propose and evaluate efforts for a new public sphere that effectively employs the medium of cyberspace for social and environmental progress. The protean nature of the medium and its potential for inexpensive and ubiquitous access to information and communication suggest a rich potential for civic uses, but will these aspirations be realized? Do Basalla's (1988) conditions for technological innovation exist? Part of the reason for including views from around the world, of course, has been to demonstrate the commonality (as well as the diversity) of the efforts to create new systems.

Day and Schuler discuss a number of the challenges these systems are likely to face. They come in two basic varieties: internal and external. Internal challenges result from the necessity of responding flexibly and effectively to changing and possibly inhospitable conditions. Externally policies can change, as can institutions, the general Zeitgeist of the era, and the technological foundation on which we create these systems. Will the systems be able to adapt to change?

Advancing "utopian" schemes is always risky, yet it may be that new historical circumstances are setting the groundwork for rapid change. Once the technological pieces were in place the World Wide Web grew (and continues to grow) at an unprecedented rate. Do these new developments signal something profound historically, or will they be known ultimately merely as historical footnotes?

The final chapter concludes with a number of suggestions—both practical and somewhat speculative—on how an effective, equitable, and durable public sphere can be advanced in the years ahead. We have attempted to weave relevant strands of critique, analysis, case studies, and policy considerations into a coherent story of a powerful yet diffuse movement. Although many of the authors are academics (who are burdened with at least some of the deficiencies that the label implies), most, if not all, of them infuse their work with human values and hope for positive social change.

The world offers a nearly infinite number of opportunities, challenges— and *surprises*. While some of these circumstances may change from moment to moment, others may stubbornly persist. How we interpret and act in response to the circumstances we encounter constitutes the business of living. Although we must play with the cards we are dealt, we may decide to change the rules of the game from time to time.

I Civilizing the Network Society

2   U.S. Global Cyberspace

Oliver Boyd-Barrett

This book explores the contributions of cyberspace toward a better world. My skeptical position is rooted in the sociology of communications, a challenging source for assessing media contributions to democracy. Between the first and final drafts of this chapter the global economy moved from threat of mild recession to something darker, exacerbated by the September 11, 2001, attacks on the World Trade Center and Pentagon. The computing, Internet, and telecommunications sectors led the way into recession, after years of boom, bubble, and disproportionate, hyperbolic news coverage. Market decline and "9-11" do not challenge the U.S. lead in information technology (IT) (whose response will likely be further concentration and convergence), nor its significance for global development and U.S. foreign policy.

Computing and the Internet incontestably benefit many people. I argue that benefits disproportionately accrue to the wealthy and powerful, within and between nations, and that corporate interest is an ever-present threat to public interest in an equitable system of governance, use, and accessibility of global cyberspace. In this chapter I attend to the global context of the evolving cyberindustry—its contributions to and implications for the balance of power and, in particular, U.S. interests.

I place the "digital divide" in a broader context of threats to global security, environment, and human development. How does this guide us to strategic reforms for all communications media? Long-term actions need to address the structure of the world economic order, whose outstanding feature is U.S. dominance of global business, including communications. I examine U.S. leadership of the global computer industries and their infrastructural underpinning of an information-entertainment complex. U.S. dominance of global communications is part cause, part outcome of a dialectical interplay between macrostructural trends over several decades. Evolution of these trends parallels a transitional epoch that began with ex-colonial calls for a "new world economic order" (NWEO) and "new world information and communication order" (NWICO). These were savaged by the Reagan administration's neoliberal "new world order." I assess how communications media contribute to the contemporary process of U.S.-led economic "globalization" and argue that the relationship between communications and globalization contributes to continuing U.S. world dominance.

From Digital Divide to Human Development

In May 2000, BBC News Online reported that 50 percent of the U.S. population had home Internet access. In Europe as a whole (despite high distribution in Scandinavia, Britain, and elsewhere) the proportion was as low as 4 percent, and only 3 percent in Russia. In China the figure was not much above 1 percent, and in Africa it was 0.016 percent. Subsequently, these figures have grown, in some cases dramatically, but large disparities will persist for the foreseeable future.

It is right to extend the benefits of computing and computer interconnectivity to as many people as possible. Such efforts need to take account of the broader political and cultural contexts in which the computing industries operate. If our end goals are economic growth, amelioration of economic inequality, protection of human rights, and liberation from both political and corporate oppression, we should ask whether computing really is the appropriate place to start or on which to focus. Whose interests are served by so doing—those of the people, or those of the corporations that produce computer hardware and software? Are these interests compatible? Is this a new digital age, or an old age digitized?

The *Human Development Reports* by the United Nations Development Program (UNDP) for 1999 and 2000 show that there were over six billion people on earth, of whom *half*, three billion, subsisted on less than $2 a day. Worse yet, 1.2 billion people subsisted on less than $1 dollar a day. One dollar a day as the benchmark borderline between poverty and non-poverty is bizarre, to say the least. Worldwide, many families experience poverty on annual incomes of many thousands of dollars.

There have been improvements: reduction in malnutrition, improved access to safe water, more employment, less income poverty, increased life expectancy, more democratic institutions, increased literacy, reduction in armed conflict, and advances in the opening of national markets to trade. But in 2000, 790 million people were malnourished; a billion people in developing countries lacked access to safe water; 2.4 billion people had inadequate sanitation. Ninety million primary-age children were out of school. Twenty-five percent of all adults were illiterate. Thirty thousand children died daily from mainly preventable causes. Forty countries were without a multiparty electoral system. Global policymaking institutions (IMF, World Bank, G7), dominated by large, rich countries, gave poor countries and poor people little influence or voice. Over 150 million workers were unemployed (as of 1998); there were ten million refugees and five million internally displaced persons. As many as 1.2 million women and girls trafficked in prostitution. There were 250 million child laborers; 100 million children lived or worked on the street; 300,000 children were soldiers. Six million children were injured in armed conflicts during the 1990s.

Global income inequalities have rapidly accelerated. Income disparity between richest and poorest countries, 3 to 1 in 1820, was 44 to 1 in 1973, 72 to 1 in 1992, and 74 to 1 in 1997. Inequality invites such problems as migration, environmental pressure, conflict, instability. Average annual income growth per capita in 1990–1998 was negative in fifty-five countries. Eighty countries in 1999 had per capita incomes lower than a decade or more previously. Tax revenues declined in poor countries from 18 percent of GDP in the 1980s to 16 percent in the 1990s, reducing governments' capacity for response to inequalities.

In 1997, the richest 20 percent of the world's population living in the highest-income countries enjoyed 86 percent of world's GDP, 82 percent of exports of goods and services, 68 percent of foreign direct investment, 74 percent of world telephone lines, 93 percent of Internet usage. The bottom fifth had just 1 percent of world GDP, 1 percent of export markets, 1 percent of foreign direct investment, 1.5 percent of telephone lines, and less than 1 percent of Internet usage. OECD countries, with 19 percent of the global population, accounted for 71 percent of global trade in goods and services, 58 percent of foreign direct investment, and 91 percent of all Internet users. The world's 200 richest people had assets of over $1 trillion. Assets of the top three billionaires surpassed the combined GNP of *all* of the least developed countries and their 600 million people. By 2001, the world had 7.2 million people with "investable" assets of at least $1 million, controlling a third of global wealth. Additionally, there were 425 billionaires, of whom 274 lived in the United States. (Bishop 2001). In 1993, ten countries accounted for 84 percent of global research and development expenditures and controlled 95 percent of U.S. patents granted in the previous two decades. More than 80 percent of patent grants in developing countries belonged to residents of industrial countries.

One in ten people was an Internet user in 2001. Approximately 30 percent of persons in urban areas of China, India, Russia, and the rest of the developing world had even to hear of the Internet (Ipsos-Reid 2001). The poor do not buy many computers. In 2001, a computer cost the average Bangladeshi over eight years' income, the average American one month's wage. Sixty percent of the world's population lived in rural areas in 2000, yet 80 percent of the world's main telephone lines served urban areas; relatively few had even made a phone call. Teledensity in India was 1.5 percent and narrowband; less than 1 percent of adults had personal computers. Even if people in the rural, developing world could access the Internet, its usefulness would be hindered by illiteracies, cost, and insufficient access. In 2001, 70 percent of Internet users lived in the United States, Western Europe, and the remainder of the English-speaking world. Forty-eight percent of websites were in English; worldwide, one in ten people speak English (many fewer read it).

Maps exist for those who would apply digital solutions to global problems. The 1999 UNDP *Human Development Report* called for global governance by a framework of values prizing ethics, equity, inclusion, human security, sustainability, and development. Good governance required strong commitment to global ethics, justice, and respect for universal human rights; human well-being as the end, with open markets and economic growth as means; respect for the diverse conditions and needs of each country; and accountability of all actors. The report outlined a plan to strengthen policies and actions for human development, and adapt them to the global economy. Measures included the reduction of financial volatility and associated human costs; efforts to tackle global threats to human security; technology innovation for human development and poverty eradication; reversal of the marginalization of poor, smaller countries; and the creation of an inclusive, coherent, democratic architecture for global governance.

The *Human Development Report* for 2000 identified freedoms that require widespread adoption. These included freedom from discrimination, want, fear, injustice, and violation of the rule of law; freedom of thought and speech; freedom to realize one's human potential, participate in decision making, and form associations; and freedom for decent work without exploitation.

The 2000 report recommended key strategies to secure human rights. Every country should strengthen social arrangements for securing human freedoms—with norms, institutions, legal frameworks, and an enabling economic environment. Legislation alone was not enough. The fulfillment of all human rights required democracy that is inclusive—minority rights, separation of powers, and public accountability. Elections alone were not enough. Poverty must be eradicated—an issue of development and of human rights equally. Human rights required global justice. The state-centered model of accountability must be extended to the obligations of nonstate actors and to the state's obligations beyond national borders. Improvements in information and statistics were needed for a culture of accountability and realization of human rights, one that could smash barriers of disbelief and mobilize changes in policy and behavior. Achieving all rights for all people in all countries would require action and commitment from major groups of every society. Human rights and human development could not be realized universally without stronger international action to support disadvantaged people and countries and counter global inequalities and marginalization.

Media's role would be to offer what the report identifies as more connectivity, community, capacity, content, creativity, collaboration, and cash. In the case of computing, the United States is leader, standing to benefit most from its expansion. Computing is vital to global knowledge industries, of which a few wealthy countries are principals. Computing and communications companies are significant players among, and contribute to the power of, the world's leading transnational corporations (TNCs), principal drivers of contemporary globalization. To be sanguine about this, one must believe that TNC interests are global interests.

Core Features of Contemporary Globalization

World business is led by a handful of major economies. These are primary hosts to most TNCs, which mainly benefit the same host countries. The world economy was worth $33 trillion in 2000, led by the United States, whose economy was twice as large as that of all of Europe combined (Kahn and Andrews 2001); the economies of the United States, Europe, and Japan accounted for over half of global economic activity. Fifty percent of the world's 1,000 largest corporations in a 1999 *Business Week* compilation were U.S.-based. The United States, Britain, and Japan accounted for 942 of the 1,000. Of the FT Global 500 (ranked by market capitalization) top corporations in 2001, the U.S. accounted for 239 (48%). North America and Western Europe together accounted for 80 percent.

In 1999 the world's approximately 60,000 TNCs controlled 500,000 foreign affiliates. Eighty-five percent of TNCs were based in developed (OECD) countries. TNCs primarily benefited their host countries, corporate managers, and shareholders. They accounted for two-thirds of global exports in 1999 (of which one-third were intrafirm transfers); they typically employed two-thirds of their workforce in, and produced more than two-thirds of their output in, primary host countries. Much American trade was TNC intracompany, accounting for $563 billion (47%) of U.S. imports and $246 billion (32%) of U.S. exports in 2000 (O'Connell 2001). In 1998, sales by foreign subsidiaries of U.S. firms totaled some $2.4 trillion, substantially more than exports of merchandise (worth $933 billion).

The United States accounted for two-fifths of world GDP growth in 1995–2000 while tying the world's economies to America through trade, global supply chains, and TNCs (*The Economist*, 2001), a factor contributing to global recession in 2001. American imports in 2000 were worth 6 percent of the GDP of the rest of the world. Two-fifths of the growth of non-Japan Asia in 2000 was due to an increase in IT exports to America.

U.S. knowledge-based industries are strongly represented among TNCs. In OECD countries they accounted for half of business output in the mid-1990s. Of the world's top 1,000 companies, by market value as ranked in *Business Week* in 1998, over 11 percent were in information and communication technology (ICT), a category that accounted for one-third of the top 100, and one-half of the top 10. Of the top 200 best-performing public, ICT companies rated by *Business Week* in June 2001 by revenue growth, size, shareholder return, and return on equity, 129 or 64.5 percent were based in the United States, followed a long way behind by Japan with 25 (13.5%) and Taiwan with 7 (3.5%). Of the FT Global 500 in 2000, some 20 percent were ICT.

An August 2001 *Business Week* ranking of the world's 100 most valuable brands, based on future projected earnings among brands with significant nondomestic sales, 62 percent originated in the United States, 29 percent in Europe, and 7 percent in Asia. Over one-third of all brands were significantly related to ICT industries. Commerce in cultural products alone accounted for more than 7 percent of U.S. GDP in 1999, when U.S. copyright-intensive industries like film, television, and music exported goods worth almost $80 billion, more than any other sector (even chemicals, aircraft, and agriculture) (Vaidhyanathan 2001). The 1999 UNDP report noted that the single largest export industry for the United States was entertainment, led by Hollywood (grossing $30 billion worldwide in 1997).

The annual growth rate of the ICT sector in the United States in the 1990s was twice that of the overall economy, peaking at one-third of economic growth. I conclude that the U.S. economy, both in terms of GDP and international trade, relies considerably on knowledge-based industries.

Globalization and the Communications Media

Globalization is not new, but assumes a defining form in each epoch, and also shapes the epoch. There are at least three defining characteristics of contemporary globalization (Boyd-Barrett 1999). First is the relative inclusivity of the global economic order: it embraces almost all countries. Second, this era of globalization has been driven by predominantly Western-based TNCs. Their number will be joined by state, military, and private enterprises based in China. TNC activities outstretch and outsmart the will or capacity of regulatory agencies. Contemporary globalization, third, is dependent to a high degree on the ICT sector.

Communications industries contribute to globalization in four principal ways. They create profit, first, from global sales of hardware, software, telecommunications services, computing, broadcasting, cinema, print, public relations, and advertising. Indirectly, profit comes from sale of licenses protected by proprietary patent and intellectual property rights (IPR), mostly of benefit to interests located in the large, wealthy countries. Piracy of intellectual property is estimated to cost billions of dollars each year, yet IPR are increasingly enforced by countries that accede to WTO membership and its disciplines, or subscribe to conditions imposed on applicants for funding assistance from the IMF or World Bank.

Second, many communications products and services are vehicles for the carriage of advertising. Advertising is critical to the transnationalization of product and service sales, both directly, through paid-for advertisements and promotions, and less directly, through the representation, paid-for or incidental, of products, services, and lifestyles in media content. Paid-for representation of cigarette smoking in Hollywood films, or submission of screenplays to federal agencies to attract financial support, count among the worst of known practices. Advertising is the economic basis for much broadcasting, print, and Internet revenue. Trends toward deregulation and privatization in media industries increase media dependency on advertising, promote neoliberal regulatory practices designed to reduce state subsidy, and increase dependency on advertising and commercial revenue.

Third, ICTs have become essential facilitators of global trade and finance. Basic and enhanced telecommunications services are related to the economic development of states and enterprises alike. The availability and quality of such services help to determine how TNCs functionally differentiate their activities in time and space, and how they interact with providers and clients. Many content services are tools for trade and finance, sometimes structuring the marketplace for the buying and sale of services. Examples include web-based, print, and audiovisual services provided by Reuters, the Associated Press, Bloomberg, Dow Jones, CNNf, and the *Wall Street Journal*.

Fourth, communications industries contribute to the "semiotic construction" of the world—that is, the ways images of the world, nations, institutions, people, and activities are designed, packaged, and disseminated, *or not*, as the case may be, by the media, or by influences that act on the media. Images signify meanings and values that are related to globalization processes and have implications for how these processes are understood, supported, or contested. It should never be assumed, in the absence of evidence, that given media contents have particular "effects"—human consciousness is often too fluid to be impacted permanently by given media "messages." But the patterns of representation and expression thus formed are a matter of concern, not least because they privilege some voices, ideas, and interests and exclude or marginalize others (Boyd-Barrett 1998).

Trends in Global Communication

Several interacting trends in recent decades have enhanced the contribution of communications media to globalization (I have built on six trends identified by Hamelink in 1994): digitization, convergence, fusion (the merger of common-carrier and gatekeeper models), deregulation, privatization, concentration, "competitivization," commercialization, internationalization, Americanization, and democratization.

Digitization speaks for itself. Its impact coincides with the history of computing and of the transition from analog to binary communications. It is a precursor to new forms of *convergence*, the coming together of what were once discrete technologies for the delivery of communications. The Internet, a dramatic example, can deliver data; text; voice, natural sound, and music; still and moving images. Much delivery is interactive in ways not previously possible. Bandwidth permitting, the Internet can deliver content that was once separately associated with newspapers, magazines, posters, books, radio, telephone, fax, photography, television, and cinema. It has weakened boundaries between previously discrete industries, while older interdependencies associated with advertising, music, celebrity coverage, and so on have been enhanced.

Some predigital differences between delivery systems resulted from regulatory agreements, not technological necessity. For example, early telegraphic cable companies were also news agencies; telephony was once a broadcast medium. What is sometimes called *convergence* may be *reconvergence* (see Winseck 1998). A form of (re-) convergence in telephony is the merger or fusion of different regulatory orders, notably *common-carrier* and *gatekeeper* models of control. In the common-carrier model, telecommunications companies (telcos) agreed to restrict their activities to delivery of content, not its *production*. In return, governments protected their monopoly status, which the telcos alleged was necessary for system rationality and 'universal service' irrespective of place or status of client communities. Adopting the alternative gatekeeper model, telcos have acquired direct influence over what gets communicated over their lines, much as television channels determine their own programming portfolios. This happens, for example, when telcos move into cable or broadcasting (such as AT&T's acquisition of MediaOne—later acquired by Comcast—in the United States).

Technology developments and applications result from human choices, often in the service of institutional goals, subject to regulatory controls. Formal regulatory structures for communications are powerful. In the United States, issues subjected to the regulatory control of the Federal Communications Commission (FCC) have included restrictions on mergers between print and broadcast interests within the same communities, the local or national proportion of households that may be captured by any single cable network, and the provision of airtime for political candidates. Processes of deregulation promoted during the 1980s' Reagan administration have had immense impact, nationally and internationally. *Deregulation*, however, is a confusing term. It suggests a reduction in quantity of regulation, but really signifies a *change* from one kind of regulation to another, from a system that protects the public interest, toward a system that referees competition between major corporations—a shift that was ratified by the 1996 Telecommunications Act (Babe 1997). Deregulation does not necessarily nor permanently increase competition. Five years after the 1996 Telecommunications Act, most cable markets were still monopoly markets, and Baby Bells exercised monopoly control over 95 percent of local telephony in their respective regions.

In countries that had supported "public-service" media, controlled or protected by the state, deregulation took the path of *privatization*, the sell-off of state communications properties to private interests, and/or the exposure of state media to the discipline of a competitive marketplace. Privatization has been prevalent in broadcasting and telecommunications worldwide. Stated rationales had to do with technology and efficiency. With expansion of available bandwidth, it was argued, the state no longer needed to control all communications space. The privatization argument took strength from, but predates digitization. The BBC-dominated U.K. television market was opened to market forces after the introduction of independent television in 1962, a measure lobbied for by advertising and other commercial interests. It has also been argued that state media enterprises were too bureaucratic, insufficiently responsive to the needs of consumers and advertisers.

Convergence facilitates a century-old trend toward industrial *concentration*, both horizontal and vertical. An important countervailing influence— boosted by free-trade politics—has been the opening of domestic and international markets to greater competition. I call this *competitivization* to distinguish it from mere competition, signifying that new competition is often induced unnaturally, or is simply a phase defining the boundary between one pattern of concentration and another. In telephony, private interests avoid servicing poor, rural areas until special government inducements stimulate a competition that the market by itself did not. Some broadcast services, including interactive television, reflect "industry push" more than "market pull"; industry hopes that video on demand can be packaged with other interactive services for which consumers show less enthusiasm.

Competition is often the short-lived product of technological innovation, and of sudden expansion in market size that innovation may cause. Such developments create opportunities seized on by entrepreneurs, whether existing players, other industries, or "out of nowhere." Numbers are later pruned in an ensuing crisis of oversupply, falling prices, and mounting debt obligations (as in the dot-com and telecommunications collapses of 2000–2001). Intensification of global competition may be the pretext for loosening domestic impediments to concentration, on the grounds that domestic industry must be "strengthened" so that it can better compete internationally. Alternatively, deregulation may lead to greater diversity on the domestic market following the local appearance of foreign corporations. This same "diverse" range of corporations, meanwhile, stitches up the international or regional market. As local telco monopolies are privatized in the developing world, the ex-monopolies of the developed world—enterprises such as Deutsche TeleKom, France Telecom, British Telecom, (Spain's) Telefónica, and others—pounce in search of booty.

Such trends intensify *commercialization* and *internationalization* of media markets. Deregulation and privatization of broadcast media reduced the influence of state-controlled communications systems, whose raison d'être was public interest more than profit. In their place came institutions driven by shareholders to maximize advertising and audiences, reduce costs, and transform news and documentary to tabloid "infotainment" (see Thussu 1998). Deregulation forms part of the neoliberal project for world trade, involving the progressive (selective) dismantling of trade barriers and constraints on capital flows. These facilitate international sales of communications products as well as transfers and accumulations of capital, and they make it difficult, ideologically and in terms of business strategy, for governments to engage in cultural protectionism. Even where ownership and content are predominantly local, the business model for communications is increasingly western in terms of advertising, competition policy, program formatting, and genre. This has implications for content and audience address, and creates products that function like the commercial Western products they imitate.

There has been increasing evidence of "reverse flow"—that is, of foreign capital investing in the United States. The leading communications exponents of this tendency, such as Bertelsmann (Germany), Pearson (U.K.), Sony (Japan), Vivendi (France), and News Corporation (Australia), come to depend on the United States for a substantial part, even most (80 percent for Bertelsmann) of their global revenues. In the process, their business strategies, media contents, and mode of global address become "Americanized." They increasingly demonstrate the characteristics of neoliberal capitalistic con-glomerates everywhere—enslavement to shareholder expectations of profit, narrowness in business practice, product range, and genre.

This eager supply of foreign capital simultaneously helps reinforce American hegemony and *reduces* rather than enhances diversity. Munoz (2001) notes that Hollywood increasingly looks to foreign investors, mainly from Europe and Japan, who prefer casts with European-Americans as leading characters. Japanese investors are uninterested in financing films with African-Americans. International box office sales show that dramatic stories with ethnic leads do not sell as well as movies that star white talent. Stories about African-Americans or other "ethnic" groups are not thought likely to sell well abroad. Films with white male stars tend to be the biggest sellers abroad. Perceived marketability, Munoz (2001) notes, has a major effect on casting decisions and has limited opportunities for ethnic actors in dramatic roles. The core of the argument here is a seeming paradox, namely, that both the export of U.S. cap-ital and the import to the United States of foreign capital contribute to a global process of *Americanization,* a form of loosely regulated capitalism that threat-ens to homogenize and standardize business practice, cultural commodities, and social behavior worldwide. Efforts to "localize" cultural commodities superficially disguise a ruthless singularity of corporate greed.

The issue of democratization reflects the growing number of countries that have adopted electoral representation as the basis of government. This includes Central and Eastern Europe, the Russian republics, much of Africa, and South America. By 1997, between two-thirds and three-quarters of the people in developing countries lived under relatively pluralist and democratic regimes. Nearly all countries now have universal adult suffrage, and between 1974 and 1999 multiparty elections were introduced in 113 countries. Democratization has typically been followed by a liberation and proliferation of media outlets, both print and broadcast, whose numbers have later contracted as market forces exercise their customary push to external and internal buyouts and concentration. In many countries, the relationship between government and media continues to be very tense. Chinese media, though certainly more pervasive and liberal than hitherto, are essentially government controlled. Independent TV in Russia finally disappeared in 2003.

Democratization is a long-term improvement when contrasted with the regimes that it succeeds. But the ten-year period of chaos suffered by Russia following the ouster of Communist Party reformist Mikhail Gorbachev, and his replacement first by Boris Yeltsin and later by Vladimir Putin, as well as the sheer magnitude of economic upheaval and political and criminal disruption of that period, should at least give optimists some reason to pause. This chaos should also be seen to have contributed to a reversal of some of the freedoms that were initially gained. Many of the new democracies are born into a neoliberal world of diminishing state sovereignty, interventions by global institutions and multinational corporations, reductions in job security, social security, and social services, and a marked widening in the divisions between rich and poor. In all these processes, communications media have had a part to play, often through uncritical acceptance of neoliberal utopias.

CyberLeader

I will look briefly at the structure of the computing industry in the period 1999–2000. Subsequent changes have not challenged the relative strength of the U.S. lead in ICT. There is insufficient space here to deal with the broader context of U.S. dominance of the information and entertainment industries. I do not argue that U.S. or even Western communications influence is all-pervasive. On some dimensions, communications systems are very national or local in terms of regulatory structure, ownership, and feel.

In summary, my thesis is fivefold. First, I maintain that communications capital and control are accumulating and concentrating, first and foremost in the United States, and then in some of the advanced economies. I believe that the true scale and impact of these processes, already dramatic, has scarcely reached "liftoff" (note FCC liberalization of media regulations in 2003).

Second, the processes of globalization, in particular relating to movement of capital and product, are further enhancing the already considerable transnationalization of communications activity.

Third, transnationalization, which further contributes to the world hegemony of the United States and other leading powers, is first manifested at a subcontent level, in relation to sources of capital, technology, patent, formatting, business models, and so on. Through computing, in particular, the United States provides the digital infrastructure on which global industry and services in general, and communications in particular, come to depend.

Fourth, notwithstanding my third point, some countries of the world, including some developed, Western countries, are indisputably the targets of overt media imperialism; I would include Canada, New Zealand, and Eastern Europe among these.

Fifth, within national borders, there is near universal evidence of the colonization of communications space by massive concentrations of communications capital and power.

By 2000, American companies—Microsoft, Hewlett-Packard, Sun Microsystems, Oracle, Intel, IBM, Compaq and Dell, AOL Time Warner, Cisco, and Lucent—dominated the global markets for operator systems, computer chips, computer and PC hardware manufacture, Internet access, computer server systems, and telecommunications equipment. At the time of writing Hewlett-Packard and Compaq are scheduled to merge. (Much of what follows is drawn from *Hoovers Online* business data and the *Financial Times* FT Global 500 report. Figures predate the 2001 market crisis, but reflect relativities of power.)

Microsoft ranked fifth in the FT Global 500 in 2001, with market capitalization of $258 billion, annual revenues of $23 billion, and assets of $52 billion. Microsoft controls almost all the global market for operating systems of personal computers. In 2001 it anticipated sales of 160 million new personal computers with Windows software. Its MSN was the second most popular Internet portal after Yahoo!, with fifty million hits; MSN web access, with five million subscribers, was a distant second to AOL. One hundred million customers enjoyed free Microsoft e-mail; thirty million used instant messaging. Microsoft share values in 2000 increased by 60 percent. Microsoft had significant ownership interests in other large communications enterprises, including AT&T and AOL Time Warner.

Intel ranked ninth in the FT Global 500 in 2001. Its profits far exceeded those of other semiconductor manufacturers, commanding over 80 percent of the world's PC microprocessor market, with market capitalization of $227 billion and annual profits of $34 billion. Microsoft's operating system software is written for Intel chips. Demand for servers exploded in the late 1990s due to the popularity of the Internet and of corporate networks linking employees, customers, and suppliers. Primary customers for Intel include computer manufacturers Compaq and Dell, both U.S. companies. Way behind Intel, the number 2 slot is held by U.S. company AMD, most of whose sales are exports, with revenues of $5 billion in 2000.

The leading global provider of computer hardware was New York–based IBM. IBM was number 11 in the FT Global 500 in 2001, with a market capitalization of nearly $203 billion and annual turnover in 2000 of $88 billion. IBM claimed the number 2 position in software, after Microsoft. Another U.S. company also claimed title to that position, namely Oracle, a database specialist ranking 14 in the FT Global 500 in 2000, with market capitalization of over $182 billion and annual revenues of $10 billion. The database market is dominated by Oracle and Microsoft. Databases are platforms for "enterprise resource planning" (ERP) applications. Oracle dominated the Unix market, and provided over 40 percent of the databases running on Microsoft NT. Oracle claimed that 87 percent of Fortune 500 companies had an Oracle database, and that the ten most-visited consumer websites, including Yahoo! and AOL, were powered by its databases, as were the ten biggest business websites (*The Economist*, March 18, 1999).

Another major U.S. software producer is Sun Microsystems, based in San Francisco, and using its own chips and operating system. Its programs include JAVA. It ranked 35 in the FT Global 500, with $101 billion in market capitalization and nearly $16 billion in sales. During 1999, Sun Microsystems had become the premier maker of server computers for the Internet and e-business, in competition with IBM and Hewlett-Packard. Eighty-four percent of its sales were made over the Internet, and more than 80 percent of customer queries were answered online (*The Economist*, April 6, 2000). The world's three leading manufacturers of PCs in 2001 were Dell (13 percent market share), Compaq (12 percent), and IBM (7 percent) (*Business Week*, August 3, 2001).

The world's largest purveyor of technology services was IBM: "It counsels customers on technology strategy, helps them prepare for mishaps, runs all their computer operations, develops their applications, procures their supplies, trains their employees, and even gets them into the dot.com realm" (Sager 1999, 132). Sixty percent of IBM's revenues came from outside the United States. Hewlett-Packard (San Francisco) was the number 2 manufacturer of computers after IBM, earning 85 percent of is revenue from computing and imaging, and in the process of becoming an Internet specialist. Fifty-five percent of its sales came from outside the United States. It ranked 68 in the FT Global 500 in 2000, with market capitalization of $68 billion and annual revenues of $49 billion. Houston-based Compaq was the third largest computer company after Hewlett-Packard. It ranked 181 in the FT Global 500 in 2000, with market capitalization of $38.5 billion and annual sales of $42 billion. Texas-based Dell Computer Corporation was the number 1 direct-sales computer vendor, with 75 percent of its revenues from sales of desktop and notebook PCs. It ranked 104 in the FT Global 500 in 2000, with market capitalization of $50 billion and annual sales of $32 billion.

As these data indicate, computer production had become an increasingly U.S. activity. Siemens of Germany withdrew from the PC market in 1998; in Japan, NEC, following Fujitsu, gave up the fight to maintain a proprietary PC system in its own home market and decided instead to sell machines built to Wintel standards. NEC's market share in Japan slid from about 70 percent to 35–40 percent (Schiller 1999, 83). Indeed, Japan grew increasingly dependent on U.S. computer technology during the 1990s.

The number 1 company for the growing market of data routers was Cisco, based in San Francisco, ranking number 2 in the FT Global 500 in 2000, with market capitalization of $305 billion and annual revenues of $19 billion. Cisco controlled two-thirds of the global market for routers and switches that link networks and power the Internet. It remained the clear market leader in the broadband DSL access concentrator market, and maintained the top market-share position in the cable head-end market. Its competitors were U.S. companies Juniper Networks, Lucent Technologies, and (Canadian) Nortel. Juniper, also based in San Francisco, was number 2 in this market, with a ranking of 131 in the FT Global 500 in 2000, market capitalization of $556 billion, and annual revenues of $679.5 million.

AOL Time Warner ranked seventh in the FT Global 500 in 2001 and had a market capitalization of $214.5 billion. AOL in 2000 had services in sixteen countries and eight languages. Including the 2 million subscribers of CompuServe Interactive Services, Inc., which AOL owned, AOL served more than half of all the wired homes in the United States. Only three other companies in the United States had passed the 1 million mark (AT&T WorldNet with 1.7 million, EarthLink with 1.3 million, and MindSpring with 1.2 million). Jupiter Research reported that the top 50 popularity ratings for portals in February 2001 were led by AOL Time Warner Network with 69 million unique visits, followed by Microsoft sites' nearly 60 million and Yahoo!'s 57.5 million (Newsbytes.com, March 14, 2001).

The leading U.S. companies were also active in overseas markets. AOL and Microsoft were leading rivals in the Internet messaging (IM) market that allows users to "chat" in real time. Nearly 90 million people used IM services in 1999, and roughly 80 percent of them were AOL customers; users generated an estimated 760 million messages a day, twice as many as the letters handled daily by the U.S. Postal Service. Such a huge audience was highly attractive to advertisers. (Pan and Arora 1999). AOL has subsequently merged with Time Warner, whose access to Hollywood-related properties enhanced AOL sites.

Internet content services were dominated by U.S. corporations. Leading news sources accessed through major portals AOL, Yahoo!, and countless other websites included the Associated Press, CNN, MNBC, and Dow Jones. Reuters (U.K.) and Bloomberg (U.S.) were leaders of online financial news services for business and investment communities. The global leader in digital rights management transaction services was Reciprocal (U.S.). The principal Internet market researcher was Forrester (U.S.).

The U.S. telecommunications market, heavy consumer of ICT technologies, was the world's largest. The process of capital concentration, the crisis of 2000–2001 notwithstanding, produced economic powers of great aggressive potential on world markets. AT&T was the nation's number 1 long-distance provider, ranking 54 in the FT Global 500 in 2000, with market capitalization of $79 billion and earning $66 billion annual revenues. Verizon was the number 1 local telephone company and number 2 telecommunications provider in the United States, ranking 21 in the FT Global 500, with market capitalization of $148 billion and earning annual revenues of $65 billion. The two other major players were Sprint (with both fixed-line and wireless arms) and WorldCom MCI, operating in sixty-five countries.

U.S. leadership in computing and telecommunications gave the United States a foothold in almost every industry worldwide, including other communications industries. Film and broadcasting production and distribution were increasingly digitized. Computing industries were integrated with communications industries on a larger and larger scale. A prime example of convergence was the alliance forged in 1999–2000 between AT&T (telephony; with 60 percent of the U.S. residential long-distance calls in 2000), Microsoft (with a 2.6 percent share of AT&T in 1999, software supplier for AT&T set-top boxes), TCI (cable), Time Warner (video content and local phone), and wireless communications. AT&T owned 10 percent of Time Warner. By acquiring the third largest U.S. cable company, MediaOne, in 2000, AT&T acquired a 25 percent ownership of Time Warner Entertainment, now part of AOL Time Warner. Ownership of MediaOne gave AT&T co-control of web-access service Road Runner, one of the two principal suppliers of high-speed Internet access by cable. AT&T already owned the other principal operator, @Home. AT&T now had control over delivery and content—for example, AT&T could give a high profile to the Excite web portal that @Home also owned.

By 2001 AT&T Broadband was the nation's largest broadband services company, providing analog and digital television entertainment services in English and Spanish to over sixteen million customers in the United States. AT&T also partnered with British Telecom in acquiring a third of Japan Telecom, number 2 telcom in Japan after NTT, and had bought into Telewest, one of Britain's largest cable companies, owned by BT rival, Cable and Wireless. AT&T and British Telecom between them controlled half of global business telecommunications, and half of the lucrative North Atlantic communications traffic.

Wireless telephony demonstrated a significant confluence of telephony, computing, and Internet. European corporations, notably Nokia (Finland) and Ericsson (Sweden), led the world in application and marketing of wireless technology, a lead that looked fragile in face of potential U.S. demand (160 million U.S. cellphone users anticipated by 2005) that could hand dominance to U.S. providers like Motorola. In any case, Ericsson, Nortel, Siemens, and other original-equipment manufacturers contracted out work to giant U.S. companies such as Flextronics International and Celestica Inc. with worldwide networks of factories, suppliers, and just-in-time delivery systems (Einhorn and Keliher 2000).

Telecommunications also converged with computing through the "Internet backbone" networks routing Internet traffic. In 1997, four leading backbone suppliers, together handling 80 percent of U.S. Internet traffic (the rest being accounted for by twenty-five smaller companies), were owned by major telecommunications carriers, including InternetMCI, Sprint IP Services, GTE Internetworking, and WorldCom's UUNet. Fears of monopoly control of the backbone inspired regulator resistance to a planned merger between Sprint and MCI in 2000 that would have reduced competition in many markets, combining the world's number 1 Internet backbone, MCI, carrying 50 percent of worldwide traffic, with Sprint's network, carrying 18 percent. The top three U.S. telecommunications providers, WorldCom, Sprint, and AT&T, commanded 80 percent of markets for U.S. residential customers, U.S. Internet backbone service, U.S. international long distance with fifty foreign countries, U.S. international private lines with sixty foreign countries, and data network and custom network services to large U.S. business customers (Associated Press, June 27, 2000).

U.S. computing strength impacted many countries' economies. In 1990, 95 percent of India's software industry revenues came from the United States. The United States accounted for 62 percent in 2000, followed by Europe (24 percent) and Asia. Indian production in 2001 was damaged by the technology downturn of 2000–2001 (Joseph 2001). Ireland also prospered from U.S. investment in the technology boom of the 1990s. The largest foreign investor was Intel. Microsoft sales alone accounted for 3 percent of Irish GDP in 2000, and for 4 percent of exports. Other major investors include IBM and Dell. In a total workforce of 1.7 million the computer/electronics sector employed, in 2001, some 44,000 people, accounting for 22.8 percent of total exports. But 2,500 jobs were lost in the first months of 2001 (*Business Week*, August 3, 2001). Non-U.S. manufacturers and suppliers of computer chips around the world, some of them government protected, were heavily impacted by the slump and its ensuing overcapacity and falling prices: South Korea's Samsung electronics and Hynix Semiconductor, Japan's Toshiba, Taiwan's Semiconductor Manufacturing Company, Singapore's Chartered Semiconductor Manufacturing, and Europe's Infineon. East Asia had been overreliant on exports of IT equipment to the United States (*The Economist*, August 9, 2001).

The Politics of World Domination

These trends worked to consolidate U.S. global power, in general and in communications, even while the global pitch was readied for intensified economic competition between the United States, the European Union, and

China. This point deserves further contextualization. The 1970s represented a difficult period for the United States. The country had survived the Cuban missile crisis of the 1960s, stalemating relations between the Soviet Union and the United States. Fearful subsequent reaction to the perceived "domino effect" of communism trapped the United States ever more tightly in the Vietnam quagmire, leading to military standoff, then surrender to the North Vietnamese. Castro and communism were spurious justifications for U.S. support of various despotic and undemocratic regimes, even to the point of usurping democratically elected regimes deemed too left-wing, as in Chile. Its power notwithstanding, the United States was vulnerable to the maneuvers of its Cold War opponents, the Soviet Union and China, and to backlash from its own military interventions (Iran, Angola, Guatemala, Nicaragua, El Salvador, and so on).

The United States was also vulnerable ideologically, in forums such as the United Nation and the Non-Aligned Movement (NAM), during an era of decolonization and postcolonialism. Emerging new nations, after decades of struggle, aspired to a political-economic sovereignty they soon discovered was elusive. Through the United Nation, whose membership they had swollen, came their demands for a "new world economic order" (NWEO), challenging U.S. interests. NWEO strategy involved import substitution, national control over TNCs, and cartelization of Third World raw materials suppliers (Ryan 1998), as in OPEC's decision to restrict oil and raise prices (leading to worldwide recession).

Then came a parallel call for a new world information and communication order (NWICO) (see Boyd-Barrett 2001) to redress one-way, unregulated, and biased flows of news and information from First to Third worlds. Nations could not control how foreign media covered them, nor how other countries were represented in the imported First World media on which governments and media depended for world news. This had political and economic implications. Hence the Third World call for free and *balanced* information exchange between sovereign nations, and for national sovereignty over inward and outward information flows.

Early in his administration, President Reagan took the United States out of UNESCO (followed by the U.K.), a major U.N. agency that had endorsed NWICO. These were signs of a major shift in U.S. thinking about the global economy. NWICO was scarcely a practical contender in a global capitalist system. As for the vaunted economic order, import substitution was mostly impossible for impoverished nations, unable to compete with First World providers. Nationalization of TNCs, augmenting the state's economic power, fostered inefficiency and corruption. Scarce available resources were exhausted by debt payments, not least those incurred for payments to Western arms suppliers in Third World struggles to consolidate borders and establish control. OPEC undermined the West temporarily, but OPEC-style consensus among supplier nations was less likely for nonoil products that Western nations found easy to substitute.

The United States intensified its global defense of capitalism and pursued its national interest through agencies over which it had control, such as the World Bank, International Monetary Fund, G7. Retaliating against UNESCO calls for NWEO and NWICO, the United States proposed a "new world order" of free flows of goods and capital, regulated by the powerful nations, while resubscribing to precrisis concepts of information "free flow" that would allow Western media corporations to grow bigger and gave free reign to a U.S. military–incubated "secret weapon"—computer microprocessor technology.

U.S. policy presumed an age of digital plenty that would eliminate older rationales for regulation based on ideas such as scarcity, universal service, and separation of carrier from provider. The new world order dismantled trade barriers, enhanced trading activity, and strengthened TNCs, thus heralding global economic boom. The boom provided ideological and physical resources that undermined the communist regimes of Europe and Soviet Russia. But they did not undermine the Chinese communist regime, whose cheap, controlled labor, party centralization, and military muscle created a long-term competitor to the United States. The economies of China and India comprised one-sixth of global GDP in 2000, while Russia's economy was likely to be less than one-fifth the size of that of the United States even in 2015.

A December 2000 CIA report noted that economic dynamics, the WTO, and the spread of ICT made globalization an increasingly important driver of global trends. Workshops sponsored by the Department of State and the CIA in 1999 identified four future scenarios for globalization. In the *Inclusive Globalization* scenario, a virtuous circle was envisaged between technology, economic growth, demographic factors, and effective governance, enabling a majority of the world's population to benefit from globalization. In the *Pernicious Globalization* scenario, global elites would thrive while the majority of the world's population failed to benefit from globalization. In the *Regional Competition* scenario, regional identities would sharpen in Europe, Asia, and the Americas, driven by growing political resistance in Europe and East Asia to U.S. global preponderance and U.S.-driven globalization and by each region's preoccupation with economic and political priorities. In the *Post-Polar World* scenario, U.S. domestic preoccupation would increase as the U.S. economy slowed, then stagnated. Europe would turn inward; national governance in Latin America would destabilize; national rivalries would intensify in Asia, with potential conflict between China, on the one hand, and Japan and the United States on the other.

This *Global Trends 2015* report argued that U.S. global influence would be unparalleled among nations and regional or international organizations, casting the United States as the key driver of the international system. The United States would be identified throughout the world as the leading proponent and beneficiary of globalization. The United States, with its decisive edge in information and weapons technology, would remain the dominant military power for fifteen years. (Of international arms sales worth $36.9 billion in 2000, half were accounted for by U.S. corporations, whose sales of $18.6 billion doubled those of the next major supplier, Russia, and exceeded the sales of the six largest non-U.S. international arms suppliers. Two-thirds of these arms went to developing countries (Shanker 2001).) Access to space was critical to U.S. military power (and to the proposed missile shield), although this would be increasingly countered by competitors and adversaries (evidenced sooner than expected by the "9/11" low-technology attacks). Further bolstering U.S. strength were its unparalleled economic power, its university system, and its investment in research and development—half of the total spent annually by the advanced industrial world.

But CIA future scenarios all forecast a waning of U.S. influence (which may help explain the Bush policy of U.S. global hegemony as articulated in September 2002 and U.S. invasion of Iraq in 2003). Governments would have less control over transborder information and other flows. The networked global economy would require rapid, largely unrestricted flows of information, ideas, cultural values, goods and services, and people. ICT would build international commerce and empower nonstate actors, integrating increasingly with other technologies such as biotechnology. Increasing urbanization of the world's population—more than half by 2015—and a growing middle class, already two billion strong, would further expand ICT. The United States would maintain a strong edge in IT-driven "battlefield awareness" and in precision-guided weaponry. It would lead the technological revolution from information to biotechnology and beyond. China would lead the developing world in utilizing ICT.

Growth of the U.S. population and economic activity would require a 61 percent increase in energy imports, in turn requiring more political and military intervention abroad to ensure supply. U.S. strategy would require access to key overseas supplies of petroleum by pressurizing foreign governments to open up their energy sectors to significant investment by U.S. energy firms, ensuring "political stability" in producer countries so that U.S. companies could safely operate, promoting reduced barriers to trade and investment, and improving the "investment climate." Countries likely to be targeted for attention in relation to U.S. energy needs included Azerbarjan, Columbia, Georgia, Kazakhstan, Nigeria, the Persian Gulf countries (the United States invaded and occupied Iraq in 2003), and countries of the Caspian Sea basin (many of these figuring ominously in the 2001 "war against terrorism").

U.S. ICT preponderance was not everywhere reflected in media content, arguably the least important indicator of ultimate control and benefit. Rather, it was reflected multidimensionally, through choices of business model, sources of capital, sources of advertising, control over the global "Internet backbone," dominance of satellite supply and launch, supply of computer hardware, server, network, database management and software, program format, and audience address. These were paralleled by the control of global media such as Hollywood films; Disney; AOL, CNN, and *Time*—these three all belonging to AOL Time Warner—Dow Jones and the *Wall Street Journal*, and so on.

The cyberrevolution may be a triumphal phase in the trajectory of an otherwise much-touted decline of "U.S. media imperialism." This would correspond to consolidation by America's elite of its central role in the global polity and economy through the WTO, NAFTA/FTAA, World Bank, and G7, while protected by a continent-wide missile defense system against the consequences of a potential long-term waning of relative power. The achievements of cyberspace and its sophisticated networking opportunities, and the expansion of resources and sources that it represents, should be evaluated against this backdrop of the concentration of world power by the United States and its allies.

Conclusion

In this chapter I traced the links between trends in the communications industries, particularly computing and telecommunications, and the global balancing of power around a governing neoliberal framework of value of which the U.S. elite—its government and corporations—are the principal guardians and beneficiaries. My analysis left open the question as to what fissures may exist for the formation of a global public sphere, and what role in this the Internet may or may not have. Any such public sphere must, by definition, show itself sufficiently independent of state and corporate influence to contest features of the governing framework that might constitute a threat to global security, environment, and human development. This task must involve an assessment of how far the Internet, in particular, affords such spaces for contestation and under what conditions. This book as a whole is a contribution to such an assessment.

3 Shaping Technology for the "Good Life": The Technological Imperative versus the Social Imperative

Gary Chapman

Since the collapse of the Soviet Union and the communist Eastern bloc at the beginning of the 1990s, technology and economic globalization have become the chief determinants of world culture. Indeed, these two omnipresent features of modern, civilized life in the postindustrial world are so intertwined that they may be indistinguishable—we may speak more or less coherently of a "technoglobalist" tide, one rapidly engulfing most of the world today.

A significant point of debate raised by this phenomenon is whether, and to what extent, the rapid spread of technologically based global capitalism is inevitable, unstoppable, and even in some vague sense autonomous. There are those who believe that there is in fact a strong "technological imperative" in human history, a kind of "technologic" represented both in macro-phenomena such as the market, and in individual technologies such as semiconductor circuits or bioengineered organisms. It is not hard to find evidence to support such an idea. The prosaic description of this concept would be that technological innovations carry the "seed," so to speak, of further innovations along a trajectory that reveals itself only in hindsight. Moreover, the aggregate of these incremental improvements in technology is an arrow that points forward in time, in a process that appears to be accelerating, piling more and more technologies on top of one another, accumulating over time to build an increasingly uniform and adaptive global civilization. There often appears to be no escape from this process. As the allegorical science fiction villains of the TV series "Star Trek," the Borg, say in their robotic, repetitive mantra, "Resistance is futile. You will be assimilated." Stewart Brand, the *Whole Earth Catalog* guru and author who turned into a high-tech evangelist, put it this way: "Once a new technology rolls over you, if you're not part of the steamroller, you're part of the road" (Brand 1987, 22).

The growing and vocal antiglobalization movement, on the other hand, is questioning such assumptions and challenging the idea of a necessary link between a "technological imperative" and human progress. The protesters at antiglobalization demonstrations typically represent a wide range of both grievances and desires, so it is difficult to neatly characterize a movement that is repeatedly drawing hundreds of thousands of protesters to each major demonstration. But the one principle that seems to unite them—along with many sympathizers who choose not to participate in public demonstrations—is that the future is not foreordained by a "technological imperative" expressed via global corporate capitalism. There is the hope, at least, among antiglobalization activists that human society might continue to represent a good deal of diversity, including, perhaps especially, diversity in the way people adopt, use, and refine technology.

Who wins this debate, if there is a winner, will be at the heart of "shaping the network society," the theme of this book. The outcome of this ongoing debate may determine whether there are ways to "shape" a global technological epoch at all. If the concept of a "technological imperative" wins out, over all obstacles, then human beings are essentially along for the ride, whether the end point is utopia or apocalypse or something in between. Human consciousness itself may even be shaped by surrender to the technological imperative.

If, on the other hand, technology can be shaped by human desires and intentions, then the critics of the "autonomous technology" idea must either explain or discover how technologies can be steered deliberately one way and not another. Neither side in this debate has a monopoly on either virtue or vice, of course. Letting technology unfold without detailed social control is likely to bring many benefits, both anticipated and unanticipated. Setting explicit goals for technological development could, on the other hand, help us avoid pitfalls or even some catastrophes. It will be the search for balance that is likely to characterize our global discussion for the foreseeable future, a balancing of the "technological imperative" with what might be called our "social imperative."

The Technological Imperative Full Blown—Moore's Law and Its Distortions

In 1965, Gordon Moore, the cofounder of the Intel Corporation and a pioneer in semiconductor electronics, publicly predicted that microprocessor computing power would double every eighteen months for the foreseeable future. He actually predicted that the number of transistors per integrated circuit would double every eighteen months, and he forecast that this trend would continue through 1975, only ten years into the future. But in fact this prediction has turned out to be remarkably accurate even until today, more than thirty five years later. The Intel Corporation itself maintains a chart of its own microprocessor transistor counts, which have increased from 2,250 in 1971 (the Intel 4004) to 42 million in 2000 (the Pentium 4) <http://www.intel.com/research/silicon/mooreslaw.htm>. The technology industry is nearly always preoccupied with when Moore's Law might come to an end, especially as we near the physical limits of moving electrons in a semiconductor circuit. But there always seems to be some promising new technology in development that will keep Moore's Law alive.

Moore's prediction has so amazed technologists, because of its accuracy and its longevity, that it has become something close to a natural law, as in Newtonian physics. Of course, there is bound to be an end to the trend that makes the prediction accurate, which means that Moore's Law will someday become a historical curiosity rather than a "law." But the prediction has taken on a life of its own anyway. It is no longer regarded as simply a prediction that happened to be fulfilled by a company owned and controlled by the predictor, a company that spent billions of dollars to make sure the prediction came true and profited immensely when it did come true. Moore's law is regarded by some technophiles as "proof" that computers and computer software will increase their power and capabilities forever, and some computer scientists use the thirty five-year accuracy of Moore's law as evidence that computers will eventually be as "smart" as human beings and perhaps even "smarter" (Kurzweil 1999; Moravec 1998).

There is no connection between transistor density on a semiconductor chip and whether or not a computer can compete with a human being in terms of "intelligence." It is not even clear what constitutes intelligence in a human being, let alone whether or not a computer might match or surpass it. Intelligence is an exceedingly vague term, steeped in controversy and dispute among experts. Computers are far better at some tasks than humans, typically tasks that involve staggering amounts of repetitive computation. But human beings are far better at many ordinary "human" tasks than computers— indeed, an infant human has more "common sense" than a supercomputer with billions of transistors. There is no evidence that human beings "compute," the way a computer processes binary information, in order to cogitate or think. Nor is there evidence that the von Neumann computer model of serial bit processing is even a simulacrum for human information processing.

This is not to say that Moore's law is insignificant or irrelevant—the advances in computer processing power over the past thirty five years have been astonishing and vitally important. And the fact that Gordon Moore was prescient enough to predict the increase in a way that has turned out to be amazingly accurate is fascinating and impressive. But as others have pointed out, the semiconductor industry has spent billions of dollars to make sure that Moore's prediction came true, and it is worth mentioning that Moore's own company, Intel, has led the industry for all of the thirty five years Moore's law has been tested. Nevertheless, if the prediction had failed we would not be talking about it the way we do now, as a cornerstone of the computer age, and for this Moore deserves credit. But there is nothing about Moore's law that points to the kinds of future scenarios that some authors and pundits and even engineers have attributed to it. There is nothing about Moore's law that makes it a true "law," nor is there any imperative that it be accurate indefinitely, except the industry's interests in increasing transistor density in order to sell successive generations of computer chips. In any event, there are trends now that suggest that this measure of progress, of increasing chip density, is gradually losing its significance (Markoff and Lohr 2002).

Moore's law is an example of how a thoughtful and interesting prediction has been turned into an argument for the technological imperative, that society must invest whatever it takes to improve a technology at its maximally feasible rate of improvement—and to invest in a specific technology, perhaps at the expense of a more balanced and generally beneficial mix of other technologies. Advocates of the semiconductor industry argue that semiconductor chips are the "seed corn" of the postindustrial economy, because their utility is so universal and significant to productivity. But so is renewable energy, or human learning, or sustainable agriculture, all things that have experienced a weakness in investment and attention, at least in comparison to semiconductors and computer hardware.

In April 2000, Bill Joy, vice president and cofounder of Sun Microsystems—a very large computer and software company in Silicon Valley—published a provocative essay in *Wired* magazine titled "Why the Future Doesn't Need Us" (Joy 2000). Joy raised some troubling questions for scientific and technological researchers, about whether we are busy building technologies that will make human beings redundant or inferior beings. Joy's article created a remarkable wave of public debate—there were public discussions about his thesis at Stanford University and the University of Washington in Seattle, he was invited to present his ideas before the National Academy of Sciences, and he appeared on National Public Radio. His warnings were featured in many other magazine articles.

Joy refers to the arguments of two other well-known technologists, Ray Kurzweil and Hans Moravec, who have both written extensively about how computers will one day become "smarter" than human beings. Humans will either evolve in a way that competes with machines, such as through machine implants in the human body, or else "disappear" by transferring their consciousness to machine receptacles, according to Kurzweil and Moravec. In his *Wired* article, Joy accepts this as a technological possibility, perhaps even an inevitability, unless we intervene and change course. "A technological approach to Eternity—near immortality through robotics," writes Joy, "may not be the most desirable utopia, and its pursuit brings clear dangers. Maybe we should rethink our utopian choices" (Joy 2000).

But the question then becomes, Can we rethink our utopian choices if we believe rather thoroughly in a technological imperative that propels us inexorably in a particular direction? Can Moore's law coexist with a free ethical choice for technological ends? Joy says that perhaps he may reach a point where he might have to stop working on his favorite problems. "I have always believed that making software more reliable, given its many uses, will make the world a safer and better place," he notes, adding that "if I were to come to believe the opposite, then I would be morally obligated to stop this work. I can now imagine such a day may come." He sees progress as "bitter sweet": "This all leaves me not angry but at least a bit melancholic. Henceforth, for me, progress will be somewhat bittersweet" (Joy 2000).

There is a great deal to admire in such emotions; these are the musings of a thoughtful and concerned person, and, given Joy's stature and reputation in his field, such qualities are welcome precisely because they seem so rare among technologists.

But behind such ideas is an unquestioned faith in the technological imperative. Joy suggests that unless we simply stop our research dead in its tracks, on ethical grounds, we may create dangers for which we will be eternally guilty. This is certainly possible, but it is distinctly one dimensional.

Could we not redirect our technological aims to serve *other* goals, goals that would help create a life worth living rather than a life shadowed by guilt and dread? Joy begins to sound like Theodore Kaczynski, the "Unabomber," whom he quotes with some interest and intrigue (as does Kurzweil). Kaczynski also believed the technological imperative is leading us to our doom, hence his radical Luddite prescriptions and his lifestyle, not to mention his deadly attacks on technologists for which he was eventually sent to jail for life. Kurzweil, Joy, and Kaczynski all portray technology as an all-encompassing, universal system—Joy repeatedly uses the phrase "complex system"—that envelops all human existence. It is the "totalizing" nature of such a system that raises troubling ethical problems for Joy, dark fantasies of doom for Kaczynski, and dreams of eternity, immortality, and transcendence for Kurzweil. But might there not be another way to adapt technology to human-scale needs and interests?

The Slow Food Movement in Italy

The Italian cultural movement known as "slow food"—not a translation, it is called this in Italy—was launched by Roman food critic and gourmand Carlo Petrini in 1986, just after a McDonald's hamburger restaurant opened in Rome's magnificently beautiful Piazza di Spagna (Slow Food, 2002). Petrini hoped to start a movement that would help people "rediscover the richness and aromas of local cuisines to fight the standardization of Fast Food." Slow food spread very rapidly across Italy. It is now headquartered, as a social movement, in the northern Piedmont city of Bra.

Today there are 65,000 official members of the slow food movement, almost all in Western Europe—35,000 of these members are in Italy. These people are organized into local groups with the wonderfully appropriate name *convivia*. There are 560 *convivia* worldwide, 340 of them in Italy (Slow Food, 2002). Restaurants that serve as "evangelists" of the slow food movement display the group's logo, a cartoon snail, on the front door or window. If one sees this logo displayed by a restaurant, one is almost guaranteed to enjoy a memorable dining experience.

Slow food is not just about sustaining the southern European customs of three-hour lunches and dinners that last late into the night, although that certainly is part of the message. Petrini very cleverly introduced the idea of a "Noah's ark" of food preservation, meaning a concerted effort to preserve nearly extinct natural foodstuffs, recipes, and, most of all, the old techniques of preparing handmade foods. From this idea, the slow food movement has broadly linked gastronomy, ecology, history, and economics into a benign but powerful ideology that nearly every southern European citizen can understand. Slow food, in addition to being an obvious countermovement to American "fast food," has developed into a movement that promotes organic farming and responsible animal husbandry, community-based skills for the preservation of regional cuisines, and celebrations of convivial, ceremonial activities such as food festivals and ecotourism. The Slow Food organization has even sponsored a film festival, featuring films with prominent scenes about food, and plans to award an annual "Golden Snail" trophy, the slow food equivalent of an Oscar.

Slow food is thus one of the more interesting and well-developed critiques of several facets of globalization and modern technology. Specifically, it is a response to the spread of globally standardized and technology-intensive corporate agriculture, genetic engineering, high-tech food preparation and distribution, and the quintessentially American lifestyle that makes "fast food" popular and, for some, even imperative. Italian proponents of slow food and their allies in other countries—*convivia* are now found in other European countries as well as in the United States—view this as a struggle for the soul of life and for the preservation of life's most basic pleasures amidst a global trend pointing to increased competition, consumerism, stress, and "hurriedness":

We are enslaved by speed and have all succumbed to the same insidious virus: Fast Life, which disrupts our habits, pervades the privacy of our homes and forces us to eat Fast Foods. . . .

Many suitable doses of guaranteed sensual pleasure and slow, long-lasting enjoyment preserve us from the contagion of the multitude who mistake frenzy for efficiency. (Slow Food, 2002)

In 1999, the slow food movement spun off a new variation of itself: the slow cities movement. In October of that year, in Orvieto, Italy, a League of Slow Cities was formed, a charter was adopted, and the first members of this league elected as their "coordinator" Signor Paolo Saturnini, the mayor of the town of Greve in Chianti (Città Slow, 2002).

The Charter of Association for the slow cities movement (which in Italian does have the Italian name "città slow") has a rather sophisticated and subtle view of globalization.

The development of local communities is based, among other things (sic), on their ability to share and acknowledge specific qualities, to create an identity of their own that is visible outside and profoundly felt inside.

The phenomenon of globalization offers, among other things, a great opportunity for exchange and diffusion, but it does tend to level out differences and conceal the peculiar characteristics of single realities. In short, it proposes median models which belong to no one and inevitably generate mediocrity.

Nonetheless, a burgeoning new demand exists for alternative solutions which tend to pursue and disseminate excellence, seen not necessarily as an elite phenomenon, but rather as a cultural, hence universal fact of life (Slow Food, 2002).

Thus, slow cities are those that

• Implement an environmental policy designed to maintain and develop the characteristics of their surrounding area and urban fabric, placing the onus on recovery and reuse techniques

• Implement an infrastructural policy that is functional for the improvement, not the occupation, of the land

• Promote the use of technologies to improve the quality of the environment and the urban fabric

• Encourage the production and use of foodstuffs produced using natural, ecocompatible techniques, excluding transgenic products, and setting up, where necessary, presidia to safeguard and develop typical products currently in difficulty, in close collaboration with the Slow Food Ark project and wine and food Presidia

• Safeguard autochthonous production, rooted in culture and tradition, which contributes to the typification of an area, maintaining its modes and mores and promoting preferential occasions and spaces for direct contacts between consumers and quality producers and purveyors

• Promote the quality of hospitality as a real bond with the local community and its specific features, removing the physical and cultural obstacles that may jeopardize the complete, widespread use of a city's resources

• Promote awareness among all citizens, and not only among inside operators, that they live in a Slow City, with special attention to the world of young people and schools through the systematic introduction of taste education. (Slow Food 2002).

Slow food and slow cities are thus *not* neo-Luddite movements; both acknowledge the importance of technology, and they specifically mention the benefits of communications technologies that allow a global sharing of ideas. But both movements are committed to applying technology for specific purposes derived from the values of the "slow" movement as a whole: leisure, taste, ecological harmony, the preservation and enhancement of skills and local identities, and ongoing "taste education." The subtleties of this worldview are typically lost on most Americans, who have no idea where their food comes from, nor would they care if they did know (this applies to most, but not all, Americans, of course). Many Italians and French are concerned that this attitude might spread to their countries and wipe out centuries of refinement in local cuisines, culinary skills, agricultural special- ties, and other forms of highly specific cultural identity. As the Slow Cities Charter of Association straightforwardly asserts, "universal" culture typically means mediocre culture, with refinement and excellence reserved in a special category for people with abundant wealth. The "slow" alternative is to make excellence, identity, and "luxury" available "as a cultural, and hence univer- sal fact of life," something not reserved for elites but embedded in daily life for everyone. This will require "taste education," something meant to offset the damage of mass marketing and the advertising of mass products.

Slow food might be dismissed as a fad among the bourgeoisie, a cult of hedonists and effete epicureans. It is certainly a phenomenon of the middle class in southern Europe, but it may serve as a kind of ideological bridge between more radical antiglobalization activists and older, more moderate globalization skeptics. The slow food movement is not thoroughly opposed to globalization, in fact. It is concerned with the negative effects of global- ization and technology, which have prompted the movement's appearance and its eloquence—with respect to the leveling of taste, the accelerating pace of life, and the disenchantment with some of life's basic pleasures, such as cooking and eating.

In this way, the "slow" movement is an intriguing and perhaps potent cri- tique of modern technology, which is otherwise widely viewed as propelling us toward the very things the "slow" movement opposes. In the United States, for example, bioengineering is typically regarded as inevitable, or even promoted as the "next big thing" for the high-tech economy. In Europe, by contrast, genetically engineered crops and foodstuffs are very unpopular, or, at best, greeted by deep skepticism, even among apolitical consumers. In the United States, there is widespread resignation in the face of the gradually merging uniformity of urban and especially suburban spaces. Shopping malls all look alike, and even feature the same stores; many Americans look for familiar "brand" restaurants and attractions such as those associated with Disney or chains like Planet Hollywood, indistinguishable no matter where they are found; a "successful" community is one where the labor market is so identical to other successful communities that skilled workers can live where they choose; suburban tracts of new homes are increasingly impossible to tell apart. Critics of this universal trend in the United States bemoan the appearance of "Anywhere, U.S.A.," typified by the suburban communities of the West, the Southwest, and the Southeast. These communities are often characterized by a sort of pseudo-excellence in technology—they are often the sites of high-tech industries—but mediocrity in most other amenities of life. Such trends are not unknown in Western Europe—Europeans are starting to worry that these kinds of communities are becoming more and more common there too—but there is at least a vocal and sophisticated opposition in the slow food movement and its various fellow travelers.

At bottom, the slow food and slow cities movements are about the dimensions of what Italians call "il buon vivere"—the good life. For Italians and many other Europeans (as well as many Americans and people in other countries, of course), the "good life" is one characterized by basic pleasures like good food and drink, convivial company and plenty of time devoid of stress, dull work, or frenzy. The advocates of slow food see the encroaching American lifestyle as corrosive to all these pleasures. The American preference is for convenience and technology that replaces many time-intensive activities, rather than for quality and hard-won skills. Plus, the American style is one of mass production aimed at appealing to as many people (or customers) as possible, leaving high-quality, customized, and individualized products and services reserved for the wealthy. In the United States, this trend has now taken over architecture, music, films, books, and many other things that were once the main forms of artistic and aesthetic expression in a civilized society. Many fear this American trend toward mass appeal, mediocrity, and profit at the expense of quality, excellence, and unique identity is now taking over the Internet as well.

It must be mentioned that the orientation toward local communities, the preservation of skills, skepticism about globalization and technology, and so on is not without its own pitfalls. At the extreme ends of this perspective are dangerous and noxious political cauldrons, either of nationalism and fascism on the one hand or neo-Luddite, left-wing anarchy on the other. There are already discussions in Italy about the similarities in antiglobalization sentiments shared by the extreme right and the extreme left, which in Italy represent true extremes of neofascism and full-blown anarchism. At the same time that these two forces battled each other in the immense antiglobalization protests in Genoa in the summer of 2001—when neofascists on the police force allegedly beat protesters to their knees and then forced them to shout "Viva Il Duce!," a signal of the fashionable rehabilitation of Mussolini among the Italian right wing—intellectuals on the right of Italian politics were musing in newspapers about how much of the antiglobalization rhetoric of the protesters matched positions of the neofascist parties.

The slow food movement has nothing to do with this dispute—the movement is capable of encompassing the entire political spectrum, except perhaps the extreme left wing. Nevertheless, there is the possibility that an emphasis on local and historically specific cultural heritage, even limited to cuisines, could become a facade for anti-immigrant or even xenophobic political opinions, which are discouragingly common in European politics today. Moreover, there is a long history of skepticism and outright opposition to technology among right-wing extremists, who often try to protect nationalist and conservative traditions threatened by technologies such as media, telecommunications, the Internet, and reproductive technologies, to name a few.

So far, it appears that the slow food and slow cities movements are admirably free of such pathologies, at least in their public pronouncements and in the character of their concerns, such as environmental, agricultural, and water quality in developing nations. Both movements argue that technology has a place in their worldview, especially as a tool to share ideas globally, and as a means of protecting the natural environment. Far from being tarred with the neofascist surge in Italy, or with the anarchist tactics of French activist Jose Bove—who has smashed a McDonald's in Provence and burned seeds of genetically altered grain in Brazil—slow food and slow cities have been linked to the concept of "neohumanism," a phrase used by Italian poet Salvatore Quasimodo in his acceptance speech when he received the Nobel Prize for Literature in 1959. "Culture," said Quasimodo, "has always repulsed the recurrent threat of barbarism, even when the latter was heavily armed and seething with confused ideologies" (Quasimodo 1959).

This seems to me the idea of culture that the slow food and slow cities movements represent, using cuisine and urban planning as vehicles, like Quasimodo's poetry, to both repulse barbarism and strengthen "il buon vivere." It seems no mere accident that slow food has been born in the same country that gave us humanism and the greatest outpouring of art and aesthetic beauty the world has ever seen, roughly 500 years ago. Now, in an age of high technology, "neohumanism" seems like our best course for the future.

Lessons for the Networked Society

Just as Carlo Petrini presciently identified a trend in food preparation and consumption that threatens some cherished traditions of southern Europe, numerous commentators have pointed out that the Internet is now confronted by the media equivalent of "fast food": the immense and increasingly concentrated "infotainment" companies that are clearly aimed at dominating the Internet and turning it into a global consumer service, a medium of sales, profit, and mass appeal. These companies are rapidly absorbing various other equally concentrated media such as music and movies, and all the companies focused on this "new economy" of services over the Internet are exploring ominous ways to protect intellectual property, methods that may turn much of cyberspace into a "pay-per-view" environment, squeezing the medium's public space into irrelevance.

I have called this, in the past, the "suburbanization" of the Internet, a process led with great diligence by AOL Time Warner, which now accounts for about a third of the Internet users in the United States. The model is nearly identical to what is happening in real American suburbs. In many if not most suburban developments in the United States, public space is sacrificed for private space, or spaces that are deliberately configured to contribute to profits. Identities are privatized, rather than shared communally, since most suburbs look and feel the same. American suburbs are notorious for their attachments to nearly all facets of mass culture: music, fashion, design, political attitudes, and so on. While "deviant" ideas can be found in both suburbs and on AOL, they are typically lost in the noise, overwhelmed by the large numbers of people who gravitate to the mediocre median of culture described in the Slow Cities Charter. This description appears to fit much of the Internet as well. AOL staked its corporate future on being the brand name on the Internet with the most mass appeal. Microsoft set its goals on the same target with its software applications and its Windows operating system, and has also succeeded with nearly complete market dominance worldwide.

What concerns many people today is the economic viability of alternatives to this model of corporate gigantism, with its many economies of scale and its market power. Wal-Mart in the United States has used its market power to drive out of business many small stores that were once cornerstones of small communities, and chain bookstores and restaurants have devastated their small-business counterparts. There is growing alarm over the effects of similar concentration in Internet services and information, despite the promise that the Internet would foster the emergence of millions of new voices that had previously never been heard.

Slow food activists are frightened about the survivability of small farms and independent grocers and restaurateurs, and with good reason—the state subsidies in Europe that have propped up many small farmers are threatened by new trade-equalization rules, not to mention the dire economics of small farming that have killed thousands of family farms in the United States. Just five to seven years ago, someone could start a new website and hope to acquire an audience with relatively low investments. Now it often costs millions of dollars to program a website with the latest technologies and then market it enough that it penetrates the cacophony of calls to "look at me!" Plus, the survivability of the best of the web has been called into question over the past two years, as many showcase web ventures died, along with the "dot-coms," such as the sites of FEED magazine, the Word, Suck.com, and many others. Widely admired sites of quality journalism, like Salon.com, are barely hanging on and may yet go under.

Under such conditions what are even more in jeopardy are efforts, like slow food, meant to preserve skills and knowledge that are by their nature *difficult to acquire*. It is not just cheaper prices at chain stores and supermarkets that threaten smaller businesses, it is a lack of knowledge about quality that is an obstacle for people who truly wish to preserve what is best about civilization, or else improve what we already have. There is the combined threat of economic efficiency (whose costs are often hidden) and of convenience, of immediate presence, and of not caring enough to do better. These are the signals that slow food has tried to point out as corrosive, long-term threats to good living.

The same must be done for the Internet. Right now, the Internet is rapidly, inexorably beginning to resemble and imitate television, another case of a technology that has fallen far short of its potential. Turning the Internet away from the trajectory of television requires not only intervention but the difficult work of convincing people that doing better might involve thinking more and working harder. This runs up against the current, common sales pitch for the Internet (for online services, for example) that the Internet will make life easier and more fun.

There are many facets to the struggle to preserve quality, identity, and skill on the Internet, and there are some laudable groups and intellectuals dedicated to these values. Below are just a few of the key battlegrounds for shaping the networked society.

Skills

There is a lamentable pressure in the Internet business to confine the skills of users to the bare minimum necessary to pay for a service; very often these days what passes for "computer literacy" is the most rudimentary collection of skills like pushing a cursor around a screen, using menus, and finding websites. Commercially, the only complex skills encouraged by service providers are for playing byzantine computer games.

Internet activists must strike a balance between giving users the tools they need to understand how computers work and making it easy for people to do what they want to do. The fundamental premise should be that Internet users should be producers, not just consumers of information. The skills needed to produce information are not supported as well, or even encouraged, by most large Internet services. It will take a guerrilla movement of people interested in hearing the voices of users online to turn this around. The "blog" movement[1] that appears to be gaining momentum is encouraging in this regard, and new software tools are appearing to make it easier for individual users to get their ideas online without having to learn complex scripting or programming languages. More of this is needed, as is universal and ubiquitous access to Internet services that support information producers, instead of just consumers.

Open, Free Information

The "copyright wars" are just beginning, despite the fate of Napster.[2] There will be incessant pressure to "monetize" information, or make it profitable, and thus there must be constant pressure to keep some information free, openly circulating, and protected from appropriation. Stanford Law School Professor Lawrence Lessig has done yeoman's work in keeping this idea alive in the United States, but he must be joined by a broad and vocal coalition of people who understand the value of an "information commons" (Lessig 2002).

One idea, proposed and pursued by media policy veterans Lawrence K. Grossman and Newton N. Minow, is called the Digital Promise Project

(Digital Promise, 2002). Grossman and Minow have proposed a new federal agency for the U.S. government, to be modeled on the National Science Foundation, that would support educational and public-domain digital information, funded by revenues generated by the Federal Communications Commission's auctions of spectrum rights for telecommunications. Such auctions could produce up to $18 billion over the next five to seven years, according to Grossman and Minow, a portion of which could be used for public investments in information resources. In April 2002, Senator Chris Dodd of Connecticut introduced the Digital Opportunity Investment Trust Act, which will instruct the National Science Foundation to investigate the Digital Promise idea (Digital Promise, 2002).

Open Source, Free Software

The Open Source and free-software movement has exploded in recent years, thanks to a growing and enthusiastic base of Linux users worldwide. Open Source software like Linux has even transformed companies like IBM, which is now essentially a Linux company. While Open Source software development has slowed, it is still an exciting and hopeful alternative to the Microsoft Windows monopoly and to expensive software in general. Open Source software may be of particular advantage in developing nations, where it can be used without fear of violating new international intellectual property laws, and a lot of Open Source software is the right price, too: free. The fact that Open Source software is often more difficult to use than commercial software may actually be of some benefit. People who become good at using and improving Open Source software are likely to know a lot more about computers than their counterparts who use commercial software with secret code. Open Source software can be used on everything from huge supercomputers to handhelds, and it does not add anything to the price of a component. Sun Microsystem's chief researcher, John Gage, has proposed to the World Economic Forum that the international digital divide be addressed using cheap Sony Playstation 2 game machines running Linux with a satellite connection for Internet connectivity, a device that costs about $300 (Evers 2001).

The real benefits of Open Source software, however, are similar to the benefits of slow food's *convivia*—Open Source is a model of collective competence, of building community, of sharing and improvement for the common good. In some utopian future, one could imagine a universal environment of software development standardized enough to foster ubiquitous compatibility, but configurable enough that even modestly skilled computer users might configure computers for their own individual needs and share their programs with others. Open Source is a step in that direction. Of course, free software is troublesome for commercial software vendors, which is why Microsoft has put so much energy into fighting the free-software movement. Microsoft offers its own products as more convenient and less taxing to use, which again raises the issue of whether a little work and skill on the part of computer users might actually pay off in the long run, just as if everyone learned how to cook well or speak a second or third language.

Open Source software should improve, in terms of its ease of use and its array of software applications, and volunteers can help these things happen. There should be pressure applied on schools to consider using Open Source software as a legitimate alternative to Microsoft or Apple software, or at least with equal status. Public institutions like government agencies should be willing and able to use Open Source software and become part of the user community of Open Source. Ways should be developed to help educate the public about the Open Source alternative—most people have never heard of Linux or other Open Source programs. Right now, Linux is reserved for "geeks" and "techies"—and, it should be added, for gifted students. There are plenty of reasons why Open Source software should become a mainstream phenomenon, but with enough diversity to nurture excellence and innovation.

Fostering Identities and Excellence through Communities

Just as the Slow Cities Charter of Association argues that excellence comes from communities' ability "to create an identity of their own that is visible outside and profoundly felt inside," so must we foster such qualities in the online world. Pioneers of "virtual communities" have observed that such associations really thrive when the online communication can be supplemented by face-to-face communication, either in groups or one-on-one. While virtual communities do not have to be groups that are geographically proximate, it helps, and thus there is a connection between online communication of interests and desires and the development of real community ties. Such associations can help build collective purpose and both group and individual identities. That in turn helps develop self-confidence, which is a prerequisite to excelling at anything.

The alternative model is of atomic and anomic consumers who share little online except the vague and unremarkable experiences of shopping, "surfing," or communicating via e-mail with the typical list of family and friends. Such experiences are valuable but can also add up to a lot of wasted time. What benefits society most is the practical and deliberate development of "social capital," that phrase made famous by Harvard sociologist Robert Putnam (2000b), meaning the networks of trust and self-sufficiency that are the backbone of democracy, particularly the concept of democracy as friendship. This concept is intimately, historically connected to the tradition of humanism, yet another intersection of humanism and the "good life" in cyberspace.

Closing the Digital Divide

The term *digital divide* was invented to describe the disparities in access to the Internet between income strata and racial and ethnic groups in the United States. It has now acquired global reach—the term is used around the world to refer, for example, to the disparities between entire continents. In the United States, the idea has taken on more complexity and subtlety than just disparities in access to the Internet. Researchers now speak of gaps in skills, relevancy of information, gender, age, and various other dimensions of inequality.

There is controversy in the United States over whether the digital divide is closing or not. The administration of George W. Bush has never been a cheerleader for eliminating the digital divide the way the Clinton administration was, and Bush's 2003 budget eliminated most of the Clinton-era programs created to address the issue. The argument of Bush-administration officials is that the growth in Internet use among former target populations is now greater than the growth of Internet use among white and affluent groups, and therefore the digital divide is disappearing (National Telecommunications and Information Administration (NTIA), 2002). Critics of this argument point out that the rate of change is less important than the fact that poor Americans are still vastly underrepresented on the Internet, and for a variety of reasons this is something we need to fix (Digital Divide Network, 2002).

This political dispute is likely to continue in stalemate for the foreseeable future. What is more important is that Internet activists simply figure out ways to help close the digital divide, with government help or not, and that they come to understand the disadvantaged populations starting to use the

Internet as users with their own needs and interests, just like everyone else. The deficits that affect affluent populations are strong in low-income communities too—lack of skills, a rising tide of information that requires paying a fee, a lack of understanding of the Internet as something more than just an information-delivery or an e-mail system, and so on. In other words, people who work on the digital-divide issue should have—must have—a vision of what the Internet can and should be, rather than just pushing the Internet as it exists, with all its crass and increasingly expensive content. The "vision thing" should encompass and make room for ideas contributed by new users just coming to the Internet, too.

Tying It All Together

It is fortuitous, but no accident, that all of the tasks for building an Internet that serves the "good life" seem to fit together into one alternative vision that can be communicated, refined, and advocated. All of the elements described above require *action*, both individual and collective, as opposed to the passive behavior that allows an (alleged) technological imperative to take its course. These elements require understanding and consideration, and in some cases active seeking of information, connections, and ideas, all activities that go against the grain of current trends on the Internet. A basic premise is that technological development is not in fact inevitable, or that a particular outcome of a technology's trajectory is not foreordained. Making appropriate choices thus becomes not only possible but of paramount importance, and it helps a lot if multiple choices work together to enhance and promote values worth defending.

Slow food, for example, has admirably linked culinary enjoyment to environmental protection and responsibility as well as to a critique of economic forces that push people into a harried life. The Slow Cities League has extended this idea to the cultural identity of towns, cities, or regions, and then in turn to the desire for excellence and distinctiveness among individuals. The Open Source and free-software movement is clearly linked to grassroots struggles over intellectual property laws and to the challenge of balancing hard-won skills and ease of use. So far, technology activists attracted to the Open Source and free-software movement have had less sympathy with addressing the digital divide, although there are many activists who have made this bridge. This is simply an area where more work needs to be done.

It is obvious that there is not yet a completely realized "consciousness"—for lack of a better word—about the new paradigm described above, a way of thinking about the world that is not only opposed to the negative, dehumanizing aspects of globalization but that recognizes globalization's positive features and incorporates them into a worldview that both embraces technology and shapes it to different ends. Many young antiglobalization activists are—unfortunately—opposed to all aspects of globalization, and some are even opposed to modern technological development in general (even though antiglobalization organizations are very effective users of the Internet, by and large). Some young anarchists mistakenly want to preserve cultures and forms of social organization that are guaranteed to be stuck in poverty and ignorance indefinitely. Among the most visible antiglobalization activists—for example, those who are willing to resort to violence and overt confrontation with the police—there is hardly more intellectual content than an inchoate rage or the thrill of rebellion, which are useless for building alternative visions of good living.

The antiglobalization movement, on the other hand, has tapped into some powerful feelings, and not only among young rebels. Thoughtful people who simply see a world with intensified forms of current trends—including industry concentration and gigantism; a magnetic pull toward blandness, sameness, and mediocrity; a life chock-full of advertisements; and the replacement of authentic and free culture with ersatz and "pay-per" "experiences"—have reasons to be both alarmed and angry. People whose Internet experience stretches back to the years before the dot-com frenzy of the 1990s are often appalled at what the Internet has become. There is a sense that when commerce touches anything these days, it either dies or is transformed into something artificial and alien, a poor substitute for the "real." This may continue indefinitely, but not without resistance and friction.

Conclusion: A New Bipolarity?

During the decades of the Cold War, the "intellectual frame" of the world was organized around a competitive bipolarity between the capitalist West and the communist East, with other parts of the world judged on their orientation to these two poles. For historical and political reasons, the bipolarity of the Cold War was both ideological and geographic, symbolized by the phrase—and the reality of—the "Iron Curtain." This experience predisposed many of us to think of cultural and political bipolarities in geopolitical terms.

Globalization has not only ended this way of thinking about the world, but it has introduced the potential, at least, of thinking about competing worldviews that have no geographic "map"—that is, there are different social movements representing different goals for culture and history that transcend nation-states or regions. Since the tragedy of September 11 there have been speculations about a colossal and terrifying "clash of civilizations" between the secular West and the Muslim crescent that stretches from the west coast of North Africa to Indonesia. Such scenarios typically leave out the fact that there are millions of Muslims in Western countries, largely an epiphenomenon of globalization. The September 11 terrorists themselves spent years outside of Islamic countries. The old framework of geopolitical rivalries representing alternative views of how society should be organized and governed is no longer as relevant as it once was. People with any particular political orientation that claims to be relevant to the entire world can cheaply and easily find allies and surrogates around the globe by using the Internet and other communications technologies. The impact and significance of "memes"[3]—or germs of cultural ideas—have been increasing in a dramatic fashion because of these developments. Even the Zapatistas, the political movement of the impoverished and largely illiterate population of southern Mexico, have used the Internet in such effective ways that their conflict in Mexico has been described as a form of "information warfare" (Ronfeldt and Martinez 1997). The use of the Internet by antiglobalization protesters around the world has become a key component of their success in organizing massive and repeated demonstrations at the meetings of world leaders (Tanner 2001).

But it is the slowly emerging threads of a different vision of how to live life—and how to think about technology—that are most interesting, especially as they begin to interweave and create a positive, attractive, and feasible alternative to large-scale corporate organization and mass consumerism. Slow food and slow cities are two examples, and the Open Source and free-software movement is another. The growing opinion that biotechnology is a distraction from addressing the world's crisis in biodiversity is yet another example. The tumultuous politics in the Middle East are supplying new urgency to questions about postindustrial societies' dependence on fossil fuels for energy. There are other examples. So far, these "alternative" views, or challenges to the status quo, have yet to cohere into a complete ideological framework that might appeal to large numbers of people, enough people to transform political agendas. But this could happen. The antiglobalization protests are large enough and frequent enough—particularly in Western Europe—that they may begin to have sweeping effects on political discourse and elections. In the United States, there is growing evidence of a widening gulf between the two main political parties. The activists of each party, the Democratic Party and the Republican Party, are increasingly polarized; even the leadership of the Democratic Party is often viewed by its own supporters as too timid and compromised by deals with wealthy donors and corporations. Moreover, the two ends of the political spectrum are coming to represent not just political choices but entirely separate "lifestyles," or two distinct cultures, as intellectuals on both the right and the left now admit.

The familiar strategy of reigning in capitalism when its excesses need to be checked, typically through state institutions with regulatory powers, is losing its appeal among many people who are looking for completely new ways of reconfiguring economic sectors such as agriculture, communications, entertainment, and health care. We seem to be in the process of creating two cultures that will coexist but with constant friction, especially because of the economic fragility of small-scale enterprises in comparison to their more powerful global counterparts. If French farmers are put out of business because of world-trade agreements and the French lose their cherished traditions of regional culinary specialties, a lot of French people will be looking for ways to fight back. If the Internet turns completely into a pipeline for junk e-mail, pop-up web ads, online scams, garish "infotainment" sites, and pornography, with little material of quality and excellence as compensation, there will be a backlash. If all these things happen at more or less the same time—say, within the next twenty years—and enough people see this trend as folly and tragedy, a new, nongeographic bipolarity, may develop, one between people who care about such things and those who do not, or between people who have one vision of the good life and a competing group who see their vision as being fulfilled by contemporary capitalism. This is already happening in one form or another in most modern countries. Global capitalist culture is already uniting the interests of billions of consumers. What we are only starting to see is the merging of interests of people who have reservations about that particular fate for the world. Pieces of an alternative global culture are beginning to appear, but are not yet meshed into a coherent picture.

The world has many problems and not all of them will be solved by "alternative" ways of thinking. We are likely to see more wars, more anguish among entire peoples, perhaps even more terrorism, and there will be responses to all of these things that will shape history in important ways. There has certainly been a dramatic reinforcement of conventional security institutions in the United States since September 11, 2001, for example. The big global problems like poverty, illness, and violence will still need to be addressed by institutions with consensual powers of authority.

Nor will we see complete harmony and a convergence of ideas and goals among people who deliberately oppose the status quo. So many degrees of difference among such people may persist that they will continue to look like a chaotic, cacophonic mob rather than a historic force of change. It may only be over the course of many years that we come to recognize an emergent, new way of thinking, which is likely to take different but related forms all over the world. The common thread that may unite many disparate but like-minded efforts, from food activists to digital rights activists, is thinking about technology as malleable, as capable of serving human-determined ends, and as an essential component of "il buon vivere," the good life. It is only by working with that premise that the idea of shaping the network society makes sense.

Notes

1. The word *blog* is a shotened version of the word *Weblog*, a recent phenomenon on the World-Wide Web. Weblogs are typically online journals or diaries, and also typically the work of a single author. But the capabilities and features of blogs are expanding very quickly. Blog software allows blog authors to "subscribe" to each other's online content, creating a networked web of like-minded or thematically linked diarists. Other interactive features include posting readers' comments on blog entries, creating hyperlinks to other Web sites that include commentaries on a blog's entries, and so on. These features have led to the conceptualization of a new class of Internet applications, so-called social software.

2. Napster—originally a file-sharing software application created by Shawn Fanning, then (1999) a college freshman at Northeastern University in Boston—eventually became the name of a company that facilitated music file-sharing over the Internet. A series of lawsuits agaisnt Napster, for copyright violations, led to a court ruling in July 2000 that set in motion Napster's shutdown as a company and as a service. In 2003, Napster was relaunched as a commercial music-downloading service.

3. The word *meme* is defined by *The Merriam-Webster Dictionary* as "an idea, behaviour, style, or usage that spreads from person to person within a culture."

4 Human Rights in the Global Billboard Society

Cees J. Hamelink

Arguably the least well known of all the provisions in the Universal Declaration of Human Rights is Article 28, which states that "everyone is entitled to a social and international order in which the rights and freedoms set forth in this Declaration can be fully realized."

The present chapter explores the extent to which the standard Article 28 sets is met in the process of shaping the network society. The orientation of the chapter reflects my conviction that the world is contending at present with the emergence of a global billboard society, not a global network society. This position does not ignore the fact that networks are increasingly crucial to the functioning of contemporary societies. It proposes, however, that these networks consist primarily of commercial messages.

Utopian Expectations for Network Societies

New information and communication technologies are often introduced as the carriers of revolutionary social change. This was certainly the case with the transistor, the cassette recorder, and the television satellite. In reality, however, these technologies have predominantly become the carriers of commercial messages! Again today many utopian visions assure us that the emerging network technologies are guiding societies toward fundamentally new times. Commentators are offering numerous variations on the visions that Marshall McLuhan projected in the 1960s onto the electric and electronic future. At the core of his thinking was the notion that the global network society—through all its linkages—would constitute a global mind comparable to Teilhard de Chardin's "noosphere." According to McLuhan, electricity would liberate human beings from war and violence. He saw electricity as a metaphysical force freeing human society from the bonds and restraints that modernity has imposed. In a similar way, the electronic media would lead humanity toward a fuller and more spiritual life.

In the same utopian tradition, Alvin Toffler proposed visions of direct democracy, decentralization of power, and liberation from conventional constraints. In his conception of digital life, Nicholas Negroponte predicted that digital network technology would create a new and superior mode of living. Former U.S. Vice President Al Gore (1994) has suggested that a global information infrastructure—the mother of all networks— would create full employment, better education and health care, a safe environment, and a new age of Athenian democracy.

Such utopian visions seem to suggest that the emerging network technologies are creating a more humanitarian society, whereas current social realities suggest that around the world these technologies are mainly being used by commercial interests to usher in a global billboard society. The key concern in this chapter is that in this process the essential normative standards of the international human rights regime are coming under serious threat.

The Global Billboard Society

As the 1998 United Nations Development Program (UNDP) report claims, "Globalization—the integration of trade, investment and financial markets—has also integrated the consumer market" (UNDP, 1998, 62). The opening of markets for consumer goods, mass production, mass consumption, and advertising has both economic and social dimensions. The latter imply that "people all over the world are becoming part of an integrated global consumer market—with the same products and advertisements." As a result, they are beginning to share the same standards of the "good life" (UNDP, 1998, 62).

However, the increasing visibility of consumer goods is not the same as their availability: "While the global elite are consumers in an integrated market, many others are marginalized out of the global consumption network" (UNDP, 1998, 62). On the global consumer market most people are merely gawking. As markets open worldwide and more advertising for consumer products arrives to promote the expansion of a global "fun-shopping" culture, an explosive disparity develops between visibility and availability of goods around the world. The global shopping mall saw some $24 trillion in consumer expenditures in 1998. Over 80 percent of this was spent by 20 percent of the world's population (UNDP, 1998, 62). Propagating the "good life" worldwide is happening against the backdrop of globalizing poverty.

Poverty has been increasing steadily around the world (for example, in Eastern Europe it has risen sevenfold since 1989), so that the richest 20 percent of the world's population had 86 percent of the global GDP in 1989. The ratio of the richest 20 percent of the world's population to the poorest 20 percent rose from 1:30 in 1960 to 1:74 in 1997. As the 1999 UNDP reports warns, "Global inequalities in income and living standards have reached grotesque proportions" (p. 104). The potentially explosive conflict between rich and poor is reinforced by today's global media.

More than anything else, media audiences get commercial messages. This is the heart of the global media market, and it is expanding. Advertising expenditures per capita are steeply rising worldwide. At an average of 7 percent per year, this increase is more than the GDP growth rates in many countries. The worldwide advertising market represents an over $400 billion business. The general expectation is that spending for advertising will continue to rise. McCann-Erickson predicts an increase from $335 billion in 1995 to $2 trillion in 2020. Growth is projected to be especially steep for Asia (in particular China) and Eastern Europe. If this process continues, many countries will spend more on advertising than on education in the future.

Even the African continent reports that the six largest advertising agencies in African countries had in 1995 billings for over $360 million. These agencies were Young & Rubicam, McCann-Erickson, TBWA International, Ogilvy & Mather, Ammirati-Puris-Lintas, and FCB.

Global advertisers and marketing firms are in hot pursuit of new targets. Children are becoming major audiences for commercials. The average child in an affluent country—at the age of seven—sees over 20,000 commercials a year. At the age of twelve, most children have complete consumer profiles in the databases of the major marketers. This is not so unexpected, once one realizes that in the United States alone, children between ages four and twelve spent some $25 billion (in 2000). Even more staggering, they are thought to have had a major impact on the buying habits of their parents, accounting for some $188 billion in sales. Children have enormous commercial clout, and though the International Code of Advertising Practices of the International Chamber of Commerce forbids the use of "pester power," advertisers are reaching out to children worldwide more and more as kids spend more time online. Teens constitute an especially fast-growing market segment and a fast-growing proportion of the Internet community. When young people cannot be reached through the Internet or TV, the billboard society knows to find them through the educational system. Advertising in textbooks and other forms of education-advertising mixtures (such as corporate sponsorships) now occur in many countries.

The central role of advertising is obvious in the number of deals advertisers are making with media companies. Examples include the cooperative arrangements between the Disney studios (owner of ABC News) and McDonald's, or between the NBC TV network and IBM. The result is an unprecedented influence of advertisers editorial policies. There is a good deal of empirical evidence to demonstrate this worrisome development, as well as other similar developments. One such practice involves the blurring of the difference between selling and informing through "advertorials," "infomercials," or sponsored messages. The launching of these new forms of advertising is important, since many markets are saturated and the overproduction characteristic of advanced capitalism needs to be sold.

In 1998 the trend emerged to offer more outdoor advertising. Large advertisers began spending an increasing proportion of their budgets on billboards. The American Outdoor Advertising Association estimated that in 1998 over $2 billion was spent on open-air ads. Using digital and holographic technologies, the billboards are rapidly becoming more spectacular and their production less expensive and faster. Per 1,000 people who can be reached with a commercial message, digital billboards cost half what newspaper advertisements cost. As a result, there is a proliferation of billboards along highways, as well as in sports stadiums and schools, in many countries. There is also a rapidly increasing number of mobile billboards: cars wrapped in ad messages as vehicles for outdoor advertising.

The new developments include the expansion of product placement in feature films and TV programs as well. Whereas only brief exposures to products used to occur in films, now they can be seen through most of the movie. In this way films help to advertise products, and advertisers promote films worldwide. Moviegoers are not only entertained but are also sold products. For example, fashion designer Tommy Hilfiger's products represented 90 percent of the wardrobe of the teen science fiction horror production *The Faculty*. Hilfiger funded half of the $30 million budget for the promotion of the film. The general expectation in the advertising industry is that product placement and entertainment will blur as part of the merger between advertising and the entertainment industry. Since journalism is increasingly moving toward forms of info-tainment, the production of news is also becoming more vulnerable to the blurring of formats and to the growing impact of advertising.

It is worth noting that the advertising industry has increasingly usurped a central role for itself in modern society. Advertising and marketing personnel often describe their enterprises as philanthropic missions. Because advertising is less and less about products than about brands, these are elevated to the status of gods. Magazines such as *Advertising Age* and *Advertising Age Global* refer to advertising executives as "missionaries on a messianic mission" in the "battle for the souls" of consumers. In March 2001, *Advertising Age Global* published an article titled "Are Brands Our New Gods?", proposing that "the most powerful gods of this age are those that come with more than just a product to sell—they have a message in their marketing". In February 2001 a report by the ad agency Young & Rubicam announced that brands have become the gods of a new age: "Our faith in religious institutions has been replaced with a belief system that revolves around the brands that help give our lives meaning". As the article argues, it is particularly the so-called belief brands (like Calvin Klein, Ikea, MTV, Yahoo!, Nike, Virgin, and Microsoft) that are now more influential than institutions such as churches and schools. These brands represent the values that shape people's views of the world. As people aspire to these values, they worship at the altar of these brands (*Advertising Age Global*, March 2001).

The prevailing neoliberal political climate is reinforcing the expansion of the global billboard society. Its aspiration to open up and expand markets around the globe will require the growth of global advertising. This implies, among other things, the need for more commercial space in conventional media and on the Internet and for more public places to advertise in.

Human Rights Implications

Basic to the concept of human rights is the notion that human beings have the inalienable right to respect for their intrinsic dignity. This means that people must be treated in accordance with certain basic standards. The recognition of the dignity of the human person implies that human beings cannot treat each other however they see fit. The standards of human conduct have evolved over a long period of time and under the influence of different schools of religious and philosophical thought. The novelty of the international human rights regime—as it has been established after 1945—has been the codification of these standards into a catalog of legal rights.

Human rights standards have been formulated in the United Nations Charter of 1945 and in the International Bill of Rights (the Universal Declaration of Human Rights, the International Covenant on Economic, Social, and Cultural Rights, and the International Covenant on Civil and Political Rights). Human rights standards have also been covered by a series of international human rights treaties, by regional instruments—such as the European Convention for the Protection of Human Rights and Fundamental Freedoms (1950), the American Convention of Human Rights (1969), and the African Charter on Human and Peoples' Rights (1981)—and in the Islamic declaration of human rights, prepared by the Islamic Council of Europe in 1980 and presented to UNESCO in 1981. Earlier human rights declarations included the Magna Carta of 1215, the British Bill of Rights (1689), the American Declaration of Independence (1776), and the French *Déclaration des droits de l'homme et du citoyen* (1789).

In 1945 this long history of the protection of human rights acquired a fundamentally new significance. First, the protection of human dignity (earlier mainly a national affair) was put on the agenda of the world community. The defense of fundamental rights was no longer the exclusive preoccupation of national politics but became an essential part of world politics. Judgments on whether human rights had been violated were no longer the exclusive monopoly of national governments. Second, the enjoyment of human rights was no longer restricted to privileged individuals and social élites. The revolutionary core of the process that began in San Francisco—with the adoption of the U.N. Charter in 1945—is that "all people matter." There are no more nonpersons. Basic rights hold for everyone and exclude no one. Third, the conventional view that individuals can only be objects of international law gave way to the conception that the individual is the holder of rights and bearer of duties under international law. The individual can appeal to international law for the protection of his or her rights, but can also be held accountable for violations of human rights standards.

The recognition of individual rights under international law was thus linked with the notion that individuals also have duties under international law. This was eloquently expressed in 1947 by Mahatma Gandhi in a letter to the director of UNESCO on the issue of human rights. Gandhi wrote, "I learnt from my illiterate but wise mother that rights to be deserved and preserved came from duty well done."

In the International Bill of Rights we find seventy-six different human rights. In the totality of major international and regional human rights instruments (see appendix I), this number is even greater. With the tendency among human rights lobbies to put more and more social problems in a human rights framework, the number of human rights is likely to further increase.

But it is questionable whether this proliferation of rights strengthens the cause of the actual defense of human rights. Various attempts have been made to establish a set of core human rights that are representative of the totality.

One effort led to the identification of twelve core rights (Jongman and Schmidt 1994, 8). These are:

1. right not to be discriminated against
2. right to education
3. right to political participation
4. right to fair working conditions
5. right to life
6. right not to be tortured
7. right not to be arbitrarily arrested
8. right to food
9. right to health care
10. right to freedom of association
11. right to political participation
12. right to freedom of expression

The shaping of network societies should be measured against principles that derive from these core rights, such as the right to free speech, the right to a democratic order, the right to equal participation in social life, and the right to cultural identity.

The Right to Free Speech

As a result of the growing pressure on editorial policies by advertiser interests, the human right to freedom of expression has come under serious threat. In the global billboard society the dependence of information media on advertising income tends to invite this interference. The world's largest advertisers need to secure ample and permanent access to global audiences, so that they have a strong interest in controlling media content.

The Right to a Democratic Order

The commercialization and globalization of the information media pose a serious threat to democracy. Citizens are primarily treated as consumers at the disposal of global advertisers. The global info-com conglomerates do a better job of informing people worldwide about better ways to fun-shop than of providing information on democratic practices.

The Right to Equal Participation in Social Life

The global billboard society promotes a world society in which a small proportion of the population consumes most of the world's resources. This approach effectively discriminates against the world's majority, which is invited into the global electronic shopping mall but only to gawk, because they have no purchasing capacity of any significance.

The Right to Cultural Identity

Global advertising—in spite of an occasional nod to such local offerings as the Indian vegetarian burger and Chinese rock on MTV—promotes a single cultural standard for its worldwide audiences. As the global billboard Society subjects the world's cultural differences to the dominance of a consumption-oriented lifestyle, people's essential identity is to be a consumer and their most important cultural activity is fun-shopping. Advertising also teaches children around the world the values of materialism and the practices of consumerism. This promotes a cultural uniformity that is fatal for the development of diverse identities in multicultural and multilingual societies.

Table 4.1

Collision course between the global billboard society and the international human rights movement

Global Billboard Society Preferences	International Human Rights Preferences
Maximizing corporate profits	Optimizing public welfare
Treating people as consumers	Treating people as citizens
Privately appropriating public space	Safeguarding public space
Prioritizing trade-law principles	Prioritizing human rights
Treating culture as a commodity	Treating culture as a public good
Ignoring inequality in market transactions	Aspiring to equality in human interactions

The global billboard society and the international human rights regime represent different political preferences that are on a collision course. Table 4.1 summarizes the issues of confrontation.

Governance for the Network Society

Whatever happens in the wake of technological developments is more determined by the quality of technology governance than by specific technical characteristics or innovative technological applications. With respect to the network society, there are currently two conflicting governance agendas, neoliberal and humanitarian. In the field of advertising, the humanitarian agenda proposes—counter to the prevailing neoliberal agenda—that public space be reclaimed from commercial communications. It recommends creating ad-free zones in local communities, in the media, and in public spaces. It suggests developing—across the globe—initiatives such as the law adopted by the Swedish parliament, which prohibits TV advertising directed at children. It proposes protecting editorial policies in news media against deals between media owners and advertisers. The humanitarian agenda demands that the international community match the commercial funding available for efforts to teach people how to become consumers with public funding to teach them how to become citizens.

At present, the battle between these conflicting agendas is being fought on an uneven playing field. The commercial agenda is supported by a strong constituency of the leading members of the WTO and powerful business lobbies (such as the Software Business Alliance and the Global

Business Dialogue). Much will depend, however, on the outcome of the confrontation between the forces of economic globalization WTO-style and those who contest the globalization process.

At present, the humanitarian agenda (although increasingly active in the world arena, as the protests in Seattle, Prague, and other places since 2000 have demonstrated) is still in search of an active constituency in the world communications arena. The development of such a constituency and its active participation in global policy will raise complex substantial and logistical questions.

The U.N. World Summit on the Information Society (WSIS; <www.wsis.org>), held first in 2003 in Geneva and scheduled for 2005 in Tunis, will be a major forum for testing the viability of an effective role for a civil constituency in the global governance of information and commu- nication. For the third time in fifty-five years, the international community will address in a major way information and communication issues. The first time was the 1948 U.N. Conference on the Freedom of Information in Geneva. The second was the debate in the 1970s on a New World Information and Communication Order.

These earlier attempts were rather unsuccessful. They created strong antagonism between factions and offered no real solutions to the prob- lems they confronted. The 1948 conference, in particular, suffered from the emerging Cold War ideological confrontation. It produced numerous resolutions and three draft treaties on Freedom of Information (proposed by the British delegation), the Gathering and International Transmission of News (proposed by the U.S. delegation), and the International Right of Correction (proposed by the French delegation). Only the Right of Correction draft entered into force in 1962 and has since been ratified by eleven U.N. member states.

The debate in the 1970s produced similar ideological confrontations between East/West and the Third World. It produced the UNESCO-sponsored *MacBride Report* with many useful recommendations, most of which were not implemented, and it established an underfunded development assistance pro- gram, the International programme for the Development of Communication (IPDC). It also inspired the departure from UNESCO of two major member states, the United States and the United Kingdom. The greatest political challenge facing the international community as it again attempts to address information and communication issues (via the WSIS) will be the question of whether the summit can genuinely allow public intervention in matters of global governance.

A series of recent U.N. world conferences have dealt with a range of critical social issues such as gender, environment, and population. The WSIS is different in the sense that it addresses society as a whole. This summit is about the shaping of future societies! The way the summit does this will send a strong signal to the world community about the democratic quality of future information societies.

For the WSIS to be effective, citizens need to feel that they are coproprietors of the eventual outcome: the final declaration and the plan of action. An outcome that cannot be appropriated by civil society since it had no part in the decision-making process will have no credibility for many citizens around the world. The risk is also fairly real that without adequate and sufficiently forceful pressure from civil society, the WSIS may end up with a U.N. blessing for the global billboard society.

It seems obvious that civil society should be mobilized to safeguard the public interest. In much of the literature and debates one finds the tendency to romanticize civil society by viewing it as inherently good and homogeneous. In reality, civil society is neither. In many genocidal conflicts (such as in Rwanda), members of civil society have played a major role, and sociopolitical and economic interests are strongly divided among various citizen groups.

As a result, it may be unrealistic to hope for constructive intervention in the global forums by a permanent, homogeneously oriented entity that represents civil society. It seems more useful to adopt a flexible approach, because different forums and issues require different intervention modalities. For example, public-interest intervention in intellectual property rights negotiations may need a different coalition from the intervention in the proceedings of the International Telecommunication Union, when the organization deals with tariffs and accounting rates.

It will be necessary to establish changing ad hoc coalitions that focus on specific issues and that put pressure on the decision makers to take public-interest motives into account. These ad hoc coalitions should be crossborder in nature—not only in the geographic sense, but also in terms of discipline and orientation. They should not only involve civil movements active in the info-com field, but should stretch beyond this community to include public-interest groups in fields such as human rights, environmental concerns, peace and security matters, and so on. Actually, since the political and business domains are also divided, there could be alliances—on certain issues—with representatives of business and diplomatic communities as well.

The inevitable question is how realistic the prospect of an egalitarian democratic arrangement for the governance of the network society is. Given the formidable power of the driving forces behind the new world order and the associated belief systems, this prospect would seem dim, to put it generously. The fundamentalist market forces behind the new world order and their often equally fundamentalist Islamic opponents are dividing our planet through endless repetitions of us versus them conflicts. The most effective remedy is probably to achieve a level of distance from our own sectarian interests that allows us to see "everyone's life as of equal worth and everyone's well-being and freedom as equally valuable" (Lukes 1993, 36).

But the political reality of the world is not very encouraging for those who adopt this egalitarian perspective. It seems unlikely that we could mobilize counterforces against a world order that provides uneven access to the world's communications resources and that reinforces a growing gap between knowledge-rich and knowledge-poor nations and individuals. Even so, one could argue in support of this mobilization that the current arrangement can only continue as long as most people believe a social and international order that is inegalitarian, insecure, and undemocratic is in their best interest. Can we bank, however, on the achievement of "globalization-from-below," as opposed to "globalization-from-above" (Falk 1993, 39)? The key component of an egalitarian, democratic social and international order is a vibrant, active, self-mobilizing world civil society. Although the current political climate may not be encouraging, it should also be noticed that: "Twenty years ago many despaired that global problems were spinning out of control. But slowly, inexorably, communities have shown that global change is within their power. They have cut the world's problems down to manageable size and exerted influence far in excess of their numbers. They have ended wars, freed political prisoners, cleaned up the global environment, rebuilt villages, and restored hope" (Shuman 1994, 91).

Today millions of people around the world are involved with forms of local community-based activities that focus on global problems. A new type of world politics is emerging through these initiatives. This new approach represents a departure from conventional international relations mainly conducted by the foreign-affairs elites consisting of statesmen, diplomats, and politicians toward a world political arena in which people in local communities are becoming directly involved in the world's problems, often bypassing their national officials. As these local communities begin to network and cooperate, a formidable new force in the shaping of world politics is emerging.

In this process, globalization of the local is countered by local communities going global. Local communities have begun to assume responsibility for problems outside their boundaries and have put world problems on their policy agenda. Local initiatives provide people with the opportunity to assume this responsibility and to make a significant contribution to political life. People in local communities are aware that the fundamental obligation to take the future into their own hands is implicit in the democratic ideal. Just as local communities around the world are presently engaged in such areas of activity as economic development, the environment, and human rights, it could be argued that the goal of achieving a democratic world *communications* order should also be put on their agenda. After all, this too will decisively shape the quality of life in the third millennium.

Guidelines for Future Governance

Basic guidelines for the public-interest agenda in relation to governance of the network society can be found in the standards for the evaluation of technological developments that the international community has adopted in a series of international instruments. These standards point to the right of protection against the harmful effects of technical applications, the right of access to and enjoyment of technological progress, and the right of participation in decision making about technological development. With regard to the protection against harmful effects, there are provisions such as:

• *The right to human dignity (e.g., in the Universal Declaration of Human Rights, 1948, Articles 1, 5, 6, and 29).* This is pertinent when technologies in general, and information and communication technologies in particular, are deployed for surveillance, decision making by electronic systems, automation in business and government, censorship of information, restriction of the access to information, or the divulging of "disinformation."

• *The right of access to technology*. This right is provided for in Article 27.1 of the Universal Declaration of Human Rights, which contains the provision that "everyone has the right to . . . share in scientific advancement and its benefits." This right is inspired by the basic moral principle of equality and the notion that technology belongs to the common heritage of humankind.

• *The right to participate in choices about technology*. The idea of human rights has to extend to the social institutions (the institutional arrangements) that would facilitate the creation of fundamental standards. Human rights cannot be realized without involving citizens in the decision-making processes about the spheres in which freedom and equality are to be achieved. This moves the democratic process beyond the political sphere and extends the requirement of participatory institutional arrangements to other social domains.

It also underscores the point that technological choices should be subject to democratic control. This is particularly important in light of the fact that current institutional processes tend to delegate important areas of social life to private rather than to public control and accountability. Increasingly large areas of social activity are withdrawn from public accountability, from democratic control, and from the participation of citizens in the decision-making process.

Conclusion

The essential question is whether these standards will—as usually happens—be balanced against other pressing interests. This common strategy reflects what could be termed the trade-off approach to human rights. In this approach much lip service is paid to human rights standards, but they are conveniently negotiated away and traded in for such interests as national security, the battle against terrorism and crime, commercial advantages, the privileges of the elite class, and so on.

However, once human rights standards are negotiable, they no longer represent intrinsic values but values relative to other norms. Intrinsic value is not the same as absolute value, and the option always remains of limiting the rights of some to advance the rights of others, for example. However, if rights are intrinsic values, every attempt to limit their effectiveness puts a heavy burden of proof on those who would propose limitations. It is not impossible that under extraordinary circumstances the interest of national security justifies limits on the exercise of essential rights, but very strong arguments would be required to prioritize the value of—for example—national security against the intrinsic value of—for instance—privacy. With human rights standards as guidelines, the sweeping expectations of those who project digital utopias for the network society may not be necessarily be realized. However, the implementation of these standards would—at a minimum—give the network society a chance to be shaped in the spirit of Article 28 of the Universal Declaration of Human Rights.

II Global Tales of the Civil Network Society

5 A Census of Public Computing in Toledo, Ohio

Kate Williams and Abdul Alkalimat

This chapter reports on research designed to identify every public computing site in the city of Toledo, Ohio. In addition to describing these sites, we analyze their social environment. Our goal is to explore how different social processes are influencing the informatization of society and the persistence (or not) of the digital divide.

Three Bridges across the Digital Divide

The digital divide is a concept about inequality that has grabbed the imagination of scholars, activists, policymakers, and all varieties of hardware and software producers. (A good overview might include Norris 2001, the Benton Foundation's http://www.digitaldividenetwork.org, the Pew Internet and American Life reports at http://www.pewinternet.org, and Williams 2001.) Being wired started out as an interesting innovation for scientists and the military but now has become a systemic norm for social and economic life. Moreover, social and technological change makes the digital divide a moving target. The digital-divide concept, explicitly or not, is now at the heart of most discussions about workforce development, architectural and urban planning, youth and social welfare, and all levels of education (Schön, Sanyal, and Mitchell 1999). The fundamental assumption is that computer literacy is a requirement for being a first-class member of society (National Research Council, 1998; Williams 2003).

The most frequently cited measures of the digital divide focus on access (by ownership or some other means) and use. There are multiple and related conceptions and measures (National Telecommunications and Information Administration (NTIA), 1999a, 2002; Loader 1998; DiMaggio and Hargittai 2001). Elsewhere we advanced the concept of cyberpower, a measure of to what extent individuals, groups, or institutions are able to wield power with information and communication technology or ICT (Alkalimat and Williams 2001).

There are three ways people bridge the digital divide to access and use information and communications technologies and even have the possibility of cyberpower. They may use a computer (with or without the Internet) at home; we call that *personal computing*. They may use ICT on the job; we call that *private computing*. Market forces drive personal and private computing, involving individuals as consumers or as workers, respectively. But there are many other places where people can access and use computers and the Internet: universities, schools, libraries, cybercafés, and so on. New ICTs are being introduced as well. On one block in Boston, several shops and cafés offer free wireless access to anyone who has a laptop and wireless network card (Bray 2002). On New York City streets as well as in many airports, a public telephone–like booth offers web browsing and e-mail (Emling 2002). As part of its plan to combat the digital divide, the city of Atlanta is rolling out a mobile computer lab on a bus (Holsendolph 2001), building on earlier rolling computer labs in Indianapolis (Drumm and Groom 1998) and elsewhere. All these settings for using ICT apart from home or work we call *public computing*.

Public computing is a major aspect of how space is and will be allocated in society. This is a collaborative process involving professionals such as architects, urban planners, social-service agencies, librarians, and educators as well as advocates or activists, be they politicians, community interest groups, or social movements. This process of designing public computing into urban spaces is one theme running through a stream of books emanating from MIT over the last decade or more by a set of public intellectuals of the information revolution, scholars and cheerleaders for their versions of the future. (Thus from MIT's departments of architecture, artificial intelligence, computer science, and the Media Lab, in chronological order, we saw Brand 1987; Mit●hell 1995; Negroponte 1995; Dertouzos 1997; Gershenfeld 1999; Mitchell 1999; Dertouzos 2001; Brooks 2002.) Magazines from MIT's own *Technology Review* to the trade-oriented *Archi-Tech* (Turkel 2002) address this problem of designing smart spaces.

Figure 5.1 compares personal, private, and public computing using data from U.S. federal surveys (Williams 2001, using data from Kominski 1999; NTIA, 2000). By 1990, more than half of K–12 students had ICT access in

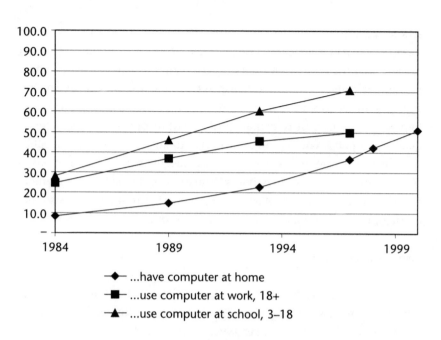

Percent of U.S. households that...	...have computer at home	...use computer at work, 18+	...use computer at school, 3–18
1984	8.2	24.6	28.0
1989	15.0	36.8	46.0
1993	22.8	45.8	60.6
1997	36.6	49.8	70.8
1998	42.1		
2000	51.0		

Figure 5.1
Operationalizing personal, private, and public computing: Percent of U.S. households that . . . *Source*: Williams 2001, using data from Kominski 1999; National Telecommunications and Information Administration, 2000.

school. By 1997, more than half of adults had access at work. By 2000, more than half of American households had a computer at home. Figure 5.1 suggests that the greatest and certainly the earliest equality of access might be found in public computing. The quality of that access—part of which is expressed in the social environment of a given public computing site—is an important determinant of digital equality. But before we can evaluate the quality of a public computing site we have to know it exists. Many public computing sites are invisible even to their neighbors and thus overlooked at the many levels of research, policy formation, and practice. Our method, explained below, can be applied to bring these sites into plain view so that research, policy, and practice can be more informed.

Two Social Processes

We are concerned with how democracy will fare in the transition to the information society, and this has been another thread through the literature (Toffler and Toffler 1995; Schuler 1996a; Lévy 1997; Miller 1996; Lee 1997; Perelman 1998; McChesney 1999; Walch 1999; Rifkin 2000; Hodges 2000). The early adoption of ICT followed the dynamic of the marketplace, taking place at high income levels and in occupations related to the military, science and technology, banking and finance, and the media.

But two social processes are at work. Society functions with and within the world's markets and also depends on a democratic tradition. This tradition, encoded in laws and cultural practices, can complement or counterbalance the impact of the market on national policy and on the life chances of those with the least—people with marginal or no employment or dependent on low incomes. We are accustomed to the interplay between these two traditions of social life and social change, the market and the democratic public sphere.

The strength of the market is that innovation in search of profit drives change. With regard to ICT, new hardware and software, new uses and applications, are being produced constantly and prices tend to fall. While not a natural law (see Chapman, chapter 3, this volume), Moore's law— every eighteen months, chip capacity doubles and chip prices fall by 50 percent—is holding true into the twenty-first century. The problem with the market is that we see persistent and even worsening inequalities that threaten the fabric of society (Kelly 1998; Schiller 1999; Gilder 2000).

The strength of the democratic tradition is that its emphasis on equality mediates against alienation and social conflicts. But at the same time, poverty nurtures the legacies of intolerance and authoritarianism that undercut the trust and stability necessary for democracy to be sustained.

From the earliest public computing projects—Community Memory in Berkeley, California, Playing to Win in East Harlem, New York, and the Cleveland FreeNet in Ohio, for example (Schuler 1995)—to the relatively recent federal eRate legislation, the United States has seen considerable democratic activity designed to provide ICT access for all. As we will see, public computing itself expresses the interplay and contradictions between forces of the market and forces for democracy. This can help us to understand prospects for the digital divide.

The Social Environment of Public Computing

People enter virtual space—to browse the web or play a game of virtual Solitaire—via technology located in actual space (Lévy 1997, 1998, 2001). That space is a social environment, the result of a confluence of social forces, institutions, and histories. People negotiate their way through and into social spaces when entering a public computing site, and operate in social space when online.

The social environment of public computing includes four aspects. The first is the hardware and software configuration. The second is the institution that hosts a given public computing site. The third is the immediate surrounding community. The fourth is the larger territory or macroenvironment—a city, country, and region—in which each community is located. This social environment in turn impacts and shapes our use of ICT and of cyberspace.

Castells (1989, 1996, 1997, 1998, 1999; Castells and Hall 1994) has categorized various macroenvironments according to their position in the global transition to the networked society. Relying on Castells, we see three categories: the technopole, the unconnected areas, and the dual city.

In the technopole, almost everyone is connected to and with ICT. In the world's unconnected regions, almost everyone is generally delinked from ICTs. In the dual city, some communities and strata of people are connected, and other communities and strata are not. Most of the world's industrial cities in transition to the information society are dual cities. So are most national capitals, even if the only ICT-connected are the armies, the NGOs, the state and supranational institutions, and the inevitable business and luxury hotels.

Castells and Hall (1994, 10–11) discuss four kinds of technopoles: industrial complexes, science cities, technology parks, and certain regions with a comprehensive technopolis program for regional development. Their summary points to three main functions of these cities: reindustrialization, regional development, and synergy for innovation. Castells (1998) also advances the concept of the Fourth World, the world's delinked regions and countries. He explores (1999) how the typical "informational city" is a dual city and asks whether and how the digital and other social divides in such a place can be reversed. Many empirical measures are discussed in these works, but it appears that public computing is not in the picture.

Examining Toledo, Ohio, as a dual city, we have pursued two research questions. What are the public computing sites? What is the social environment of public computing?

Public Computing: The National Picture

There is a growing body of research literature on the process of informatization of U.S. society. Here we scan this literature with four questions in mind:

1. To what extent are people using ICT?
2. What has been the impact of government policy on public computing?
3. What has been the contribution of the community technology center?
4. What trends provide leading models for change?

People Using ICT

The U.S. Department of Commerce released its latest digital divide report in 2002, summarizing findings from a September 2001 survey. At that time, the number of people using the Internet in the United States was increasing by two million people per month. Overall, 66 percent of individuals use computers, 54 percent use the Internet, and 45 percent use e-mail. Among children age five to seventeen, 96 percent use computers (NTIA, 2002).

Table 5.1, shows data from the Department of Commerce report (NTIA, 2002) to summarize trends among selected population strata. Each of these population strata increased its use of computers and the Internet between 1997 and 2001. The digital divide between men and women practically vanished. But the other paired strata show a different trend, as the bold-face numbers in the table highlight. For white/black and college degree/no high school, the digital divide in both computer use and Internet use widened. For employed/unemployed and >$75,000 income/<$15,000 income, the computer-use gap narrowed, but the Internet-use gap widened. Eventually, all strata could be on par. But the widening divide in the interim is troubling because late adopters have a different relationship than early adopters with the technology—and with the economy and society that are structured around this technology.

Government Public Computing Policy

Government policy with regard to public computing has resulted in expanding funds for schools, libraries, and community centers. Where there is quantitative data, we see different rates of ICT availability across the population within the overall trend of increased ICT availability to all.

The eRate, which provides technology funds for schools and libraries, has amounted to a $6 billion investment in public computing since it was implemented as part of the 1996 Telecommunications Act. In 1994, 35 percent of U.S. schools were connected to the Internet; by 2001 99 percent were. Table 5.2 Kleiner and Farris 2002 summarizes trends among selected types of schools. Each of these types of schools has more school Internet and more classroom Internet in 2001 than in 1994. But as the boldface numbers in the table indicate, certain gaps widened: between high and low minority-enrollment schools and between schools with high and low percent of students receiving free lunches (the most measured indicator of student poverty). In minority/poor schools, Internet access tends to be more limited to libraries, computer labs, or computers used only by teachers and administrators.

Library provision of computers and Internet is nearly universal, with 95.7 percent of the country's libraries having Internet connections, 94.5 percent making Internet connections available to their patrons, and an average of 8.3 workstations per library location (Bertot and McClure 2000, 25). The Gates Foundation has set out to boost public computing in library branches located in low-income communities, and in a study of

Table 5.1

Percent of U.S. population using computers and the Internet

		Computer use		Internet use	
		October 1997	September 2001	October 1997	September 2001
Gender	Men	53.8	65.5	24.3	53.9
	Women	53.3	65.8	20.2	53.8
	difference	0.5	(0.3)	4.1	0.1
Employment	Employed	61.7	73.2	28.5	65.4
	Unemployed	24.8	40.8	12.4	36.9
	difference	36.9	32.4	**16.1**	**28.5**
Household income	$75,000 and above	80.8	88.0	44.5	78.9
	Less than $15,000	29.8	37.3	9.2	25.0
	difference	51.0	50.7	**35.3**	**53.9**
Ethnicity	White	57.5	70.0	25.3	59.9
	Black	43.6	55.7	13.2	39.8
	difference	**13.9**	**14.3**	**12.1**	**20.1**
Education	College degree	74.3	84.9	41.4	80.8
	No high school diploma	7.9	17.0	1.8	12.8
	difference	**66.4**	**67.9**	**39.6**	**68.0**

Source: National Telecommunications and Information Administration, 2002

Table 5.2
Percent of schools and classrooms with Internet access

| | | Schools with Internet | | Classrooms with Internet | |
		1994	2001	1994	2001
Minority	6% or lower	38	99	4	88
enrollment	50% or higher	27	98	2	81
	difference	11	1	**2**	**7**
Percent of	35% or lower	39	99	3	90
students	75% or higher	20	97	2	79
receiving free lunch	*difference*	19	1	**1**	**11**

Source: Kleiner and Ferris 2002

Toledo libraries, we found that each library branch did provide public computing. But the branches with more ICT were located in communities that were more white, with higher incomes, and more educated. So our small local study of libraries suggests a trend similar to the school situation and to ICT use across the population (Williams 2000).

The Pew Public Internet Project has been issuing a stream of empirical reports that include data on public awareness of public computing. They report that 51 percent of the adult population know of a public place to use computers and get on the Internet (whites 53%, blacks 44%). Among computer users, awareness increases to 63 percent. Of various sites they mention libraries (42% aware of these), schools (2%), cybercafés (1%), and copy centers (1%) (Horrigan 2001, 26). Gordon et al. (2002) report a survey in which 76 percent of Americans agree that "public access to computers and the Internet will help to narrow the gap between the haves and have-nots in our society," and a "substantial majority" of those surveyed are willing to pay to guarantee public-access computing.

Community Technology Centers and Community Networks

The community technology center (CTC) is a more varied category than schools and libraries and has so far included technology centers in community centers, apartment complexes, churches, and trade unions. A combination of grassroots efforts and federal funds (Department of Education, Commerce, Housing and Urban Affairs, and NSF), state funds (in Ohio, for instance, via settlements against Ameritech as part of its agreements with the state's public utilities commission; see Children's Partnership, http://www.techpolicybank.org/ohdesc.html, and Ohio Community Computing Network, http://www.occcn.org/history.html), and private funds has resulted in the proliferation of these organizations. Today a number of CTCs are organized on the national, state, and local levels. The Community Memory project mentioned above, where computer hobbyists installed a public-access terminal outside a shop in Berkeley, is perhaps the earliest community technology site (Farrington and Pine 1997). Community networks, which originated before the Internet to network home computer users together, were early originators of CTCs, placing terminals in laundromats and elsewhere to broaden access beyond computer owners (Bishop 1993; Agre and Schuler 1997).

Ohioans work in active CTC associations at all three levels. CTCNet (more than 650 members; http://www.ctcnet.org) was launched in 1994 based on the experience of the early CTC Playing to Win, established by Antonia Stone in New York City. Ohio Community Computing Network (more than sixty-six members; Angela Stuber, personal communication, 2002; see also http://www.occcn.org) formed in 1995 to oversee the allocation of funds for community technology projects from a settlement against Ameritech for unequal phone-service provision across the state. CATNet, based at the Urban Affairs Center of the University of Toledo, formed in 1996 and has a current membership of forty centers (http://www.uac.utoledo.edu).

Model Cities for Public Computing
The national projects mentioned above could certainly be taken as models. But on a smaller scale, a number of cities have taken the initiative to overcome a digital divide identified between communities and organizations. These cities have set out to create and shape public computing. Some are technopoles and other are readily identifiable as dual cities:

- Technopoles such as Austin, Seattle, and Portland, Oregon
- Government cities such as Nashville, Atlanta, and Washington, D.C.
- University towns such as Blacksburg, Virginia, and Urbana-Champaign, Illinois
- Diversified cities such as New York and Boston

(S. Levy 1998 and Sassen 2002 provide two among many approaches to categorizing and ranking cities with respect to informationalization.)

Noteworthy among these cities is Seattle, where public computing is a major thrust for city government. The city department of information technology is implementing Citizens Technology Literacy and Access programs, providing funds, and conducting research aimed at making Seattle a "technology healthy city" (http://www.cityofseattle.net/tech/). Seattle is the home of Microsoft Corporation and also of the highly successful Seattle Community Network, which played an early role in public computing by advocating and/or providing technical support, e-mail accounts, and web space for public computing in libraries, laundromats, and other public locations.

The city has created an online directory that links to 132 Seattle CTCs (http://www.cityofseattle.net/tech/techmap/). In a recent survey, 82 percent of residents reported having access to the Internet and 72 percent as having home Internet access. The 10 percent reporting access only outside the home report using the Internet at work (81%), school (76%), an Internet café (62%), a community center (39%), or a public library (34%) (Information Technology Indicators Residential Survey, 2000, 24).

Method

Our method depends on surveys, key-informant interviews, statistical analysis, and keeping our eyes open as involved actors in the city under study. But in order to recruit students to responsible positions within the research project, we reconceptualized our method as the D6 method. This served to orient inexperienced young people both to what scientific research is about and to the specific tasks of researching public computing in Toledo. Several of the students then used the D6 method in their master's theses (Hamilton 2002; McGreevy 2002; Zelip 2002).

We call the method the D6 method because it has six parts, each beginning with the letter D: definition of the problem, data collection, digitization, discovery, design, and dissemination. Table 5.3 describes the basic activities associated with each concept.

D1, Definition of the Problem

Our definition of the problem came as much out of experience as it did from the research literature. Dealing early on with technology as a potential solution to social problems, and with technology as ubiquitous on

Table 5.3
D6 method

Definition	Defining the problem, summing up the relevant literature, and formulating the research question and/or hypothesis
Data collection	Operationalizing the variables, drawing a popualtion sample, collecting data regarding the variables
Digitization	Inputting, scanning, otherwise putting the data on the computer, organized in a useful way
Discovery	Analyzing the data to test the hypothesis or answer the research question
Design	Laying out the data and the analysis in text, tables, and figures in order to convey the findings to various audiences
Dissemination	Sharing the findings with the various audiences as widely and effectively as possible

major campuses but hard to find off campus, we experienced the importance of public computing. We searched constantly for places where people could get online, and eventually became involved in a community technology center (Alkalimat and Williams 2000). The large datasets such as the NTIA surveys have not placed much emphasis here, but the literature close to everyday practice with technology tells many tales that suggest its value to people seeking work, social connections, even political impact (McKeown 1991; Mark, Cornebise, and Wahl 1997, Chow et al. 1998, 2000; Williams 2001).

D2, Data Collection

We collected data in the setting of an academic department and a community technology center, using students who worked in both. The students were paid by the federal work-study program and/or were earning academic credit through enrollment in the University of Toledo course "Cyberspace and the Black Experience" (Africana Studies 4900, 2002). Data collection included a phone survey, visits to sites, and the use of various digital devices—camera and tape recorder.

We created a list of all of the potential sites for public computing that we could find. Our starting point was the telephone as a near-universal feature of organized public life. In the United States nearly 90 percent of the entire population has at least one telephone at home, or lives within a few blocks of a public phone. We assumed that organizations would have a phone, and used the phone directory as the starting point in our enumeration.

We constructed a list of organizations to contact using the hardcopy yellow pages, an online yellow pages then available for free at www.555–1212.com, several local directories, news clippings, and personal leads. We identified ninety-six yellow-page categories as relevant to our search, based on personal familiarity and on our review of the research and policy literature about community computing and other forms of public computing (available from the authors). The daily newspaper, for example, mentioned a children's hospital providing computers for patients to use, so for that reason alone we included hospitals as a category for potential sites. We called coffee houses because we knew of at least one cybercafé in town.

After compiling a list of more than 1,578 organizations that might host public computing sites, we began canvassing them by telephone to find out who actually did provide computers for nonstaff to use. Students made most of the calls. Each call began as follows: "Hello, I'm calling from the University of Toledo researching computer use in the area. Do you have any computers for (the public/your members/parishioners/students/or other relevant term for that institution) to use?" We made on average three attempted calls before recording the site as a no response. These calls were made over eighteen months during 2000 and 2001. As we made the calls, we also located the addresses and verified that exactly 1,578 of the organizations were actually within Toledo city limits. Those outside the city were omitted from the dataset. We also contacted institutions that we estimated would host multiple sites (the public library, public schools, Catholic schools, and so on) and gathered data from them in person.

D3, Digitization

Digitization began when we used the online yellow pages to build our call list and continued building a database of our call data. We also used geographic information systems software for geolocating the possible and actual sites.

D4, Discovery

Discovery proceeded using GIS software (ArcView) to map the location of the public computing sites and the demographics of Toledo, and using a statistical package (SPSS). We made use of class sessions and team meetings to discuss results periodically.

D5, Design

Design involved writing this chapter and producing a website (http://www.communitytechnology.org/toledo) that will provide information about the public computing sites in a searchable database. The University of Toledo Urban Affairs Center plans to publish our findings.

D6, Dissemination

In addition to disseminating the book and the website via academic and online channels, we will present findings to a growing network of business and community leaders who are interested in a technology plan for Toledo to advance new-technology-related local industries and boost the skills and connectivity of the local and future workforce.

Enumeration and Analysis of Data

Our search for public computing in Toledo found 253 sites hosted by a variety of institutions, as shown in table 5.4. We coded these 253 public computing sites as government, community, commercial, and university, according to their host institutions. *Government* public computing sites are those located in public institutions, a direct reflection of public policy and political forces. *Community* public computing sites are those hosted by nongovernmental, not-for-profit organizations. These represent the diversity of civil society. *Commercial* public computing sites are those operating for a profit, in response to market opportunities. *University* public computing sites are those established at colleges and universities. While they will always be fewer in number, they will likely be the most technology-intensive public computing facilities in any community. Each type of public computing has its own economic imperatives, social dynamics, and spatial realities or demographics.

As table 5.4 indicates, schools represent the largest number of sites in each of the four categories. So government sites are primarily schools and libraries. Community sites are primarily schools, churches, and community centers. Commercial sites are primarily schools and apartment complexes.

Table 5.5 provides an overview of the response rates that led to the enumeration in table 5.4. We can use these figures to estimate the actual count of public computing sites in the city. Of the 1,578 potential hosts we sought to ask, we got yes or no responses from 761, or 48 percent. Of these,

Table 5.4

Public computing in Toledo, Ohio, by host institution

Schools—K–12 public	92
Public libraries	14
Apartments, hotels, and other group residences—public	2
Government offices	1
Total government	109
Schools—K–12 private	29
Schools—preschools and child care—nonprofit	8
Schools—other	1
Churches and temples	29
Civic organizations—other	12
Civic organizations—youth	4
Civic organizations—seniors	6
Apartments, hotels, and other group residences—nonprofit	4
Civic organizations—unions	3
Museums and parks	2
Hospitals and health care centers	1
Total community	99
Schools—preschools and child care—for profit	13
Schools—trade—for profit	10
Apartments, hotels, and other group residences—for profit	15
Copy shops, cybercafés, stores	4
Total commercial	42
Schools—universities and colleges	3
Total university	3
Grand total	253

253 (33%) reported that they do host public computing. The 817 sites we could not contact may or may not host public computing. So we calculate that between 16 percent (253 out of 1,578) and 33 percent (253 out of 761) of the institutions on our list of 1,578 do host public computing. We believe the sites we could not contact are less likely to host public computing. As a result, we chose to settle on a rate of 20 percent, and estimate that Toledo is likely to have 316 public computing sites.

Toledo is a "Rust-Belt" industrial city, historically connected to the auto and glass industries. The 2000 U.S. Census (http://www.census.gov) reports its population as 313,619, 23.5 percent African-American. The distribution of the population is similar to other Midwestern cities: the African-American

Table 5.5

Contact data on public computing in Toledo, Ohio

	Potential host institutions	No, do not host public computing	Yes, host public computing	Yes as percent of all responses	No response	Response rate, percent
Government	138	21	109	84%	8	94%
Community	935	270	99	27%	566	39%
Commercial	501	216	42	16%	243	51%
University	4	1	3	75%	—	100%
Grand total	1,578	508	253	33%	817	48%

population is concentrated in the inner city and people with higher incomes live near the periphery or in the suburbs. Toledo also has a working-class east side, home to many Latinos and to a concentration of Toledoans of Hungarian descent. This demographic pattern allows us to identify four areas: East Toledo, a commercial downtown, the inner city, and the outer city. Toledoans call the outer city the North, West, and South Sides. The map in figure 5.2 shows these four areas. Shaded areas represent poverty rates of greater than 25 percent. With this in mind, we can examine the four types of public computing uncovered in our enumeration.

Government Public Computing

Of the 109 government public computing sites mapped in figure 5.3, 92 are public schools and 14 are public libraries. There are also two computer labs operated by the county's public housing administration, and one county tax assessor's office. This office provides computers for the public to use to search the county's real estate databases.

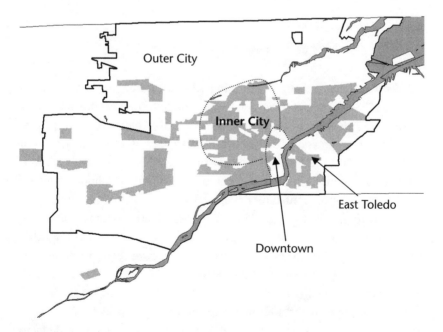

Figure 5.2
Four areas of Toledo, showing census block groups of 25 percent or higher poverty rates.

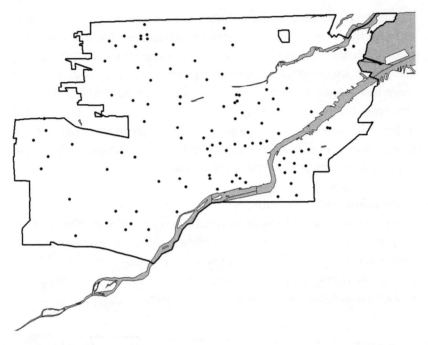

Figure 5.3
Government public computing sites.

Toledo is a city with six overlapping school systems: the Toledo Public Schools (TPS), Washington School District (an autonomous district wholly within the Toledo district), the Catholic schools, charter schools, private schools, and an emerging but tentative statewide virtual school system of online schools. Except for the virtual high schools, all of these are sur- rounded by suburban school systems. In Toledo Public Schools there are eight high schools, eight junior high schools, and forty-four elementary schools (http://www.tps.org). There are over 37,000 students, of whom 46 percent are African-American and 7 percent are Latino. On the other hand the staff is only 20 percent black. The legacy of segregation persists, such that the high schools fit into three groups. One school is mainly black (95% black), three schools are in the middle (blacks making up 61, 56, and 51% of enrollment), and four make up the third group (26%, 24%, 19%, and 13% black enrollment). Thus the school system suffers from de facto segregation based on class and race. The Supreme Court of Ohio has ruled that the current arrangement of school districts in Ohio is unfair because it produces major inequities in funding levels for different school districts, especially ones like Toledo (DeRolph v. State, 2000, 88 Ohio St.3d, http://www.catalyst-cleveland.org/06–00/DeRolph.htm).

The technology transformation of the public schools got a boost when a bond issue passed in 1994 provided additional funding. A technology commission was set up within TPS that also included telecommunications industry representatives. The period from 1995 into 2001 was a period of rapid technological development. The State of Ohio invested over $800 million in K–12 technology. A TPS official reported that the system grew from about 4,000 client computers to its current size of 10,000 clients, and the figure would rise to 15,000 within a year and a half ("Toledo Public Schools: NetApp Scores an A+ for Improving Content Delivery," 2000). As of early 2001, every elementary classroom had about five networked computers, and almost every school has at least one computer lab for the entire school.

Many organizations are attempting to expand technology access in the schools and enhance training. The State of Ohio has SchoolNet and SchoolNet Plus, which offer funding and training (http://www.osn.state. oh.us/home/). They fund support for Tech-Prep programs for students going into technical careers, but this functions primarily in the suburbs of Toledo. Federal and state funds are channeled through the University of Toledo to other programs like Prep-Tech, Excel, and Gear Up, which are designed to enhance the educational achievement of either at-risk or minority students.

The public schools' computer labs service the student body of each school. In the past the Toledo Public School System has had an open-door policy— for example, the lighted-school concept involved having an open school for community use one night a week. This is no longer commonplace, and would certainly not involve the use of the computer labs. In contrast, some of the suburban schools do exactly this, running computer classes in the evening for the public. Another important feature of the computer labs is that Toledo Public Schools invested in reading- and math-drill software (Computer Curriculum Corporation, http://www.ccclearn.com) and have avoided providing Internet access in the labs in order to drive teachers to make full use of the software. However, many TPS teachers are not trained to use the diagnostic powers of the software to customize test questions to the strengths and weaknesses of the individual student. The district runs free classes on the software in the summer, but few teachers take the course.

The public-library sites are all part of the Toledo-Lucas County Public Library (http://www.toledolibrary.org). In addition to the fourteen sites in Toledo, there are four branch libraries in the suburbs. Approximately 250 computers in the system dedicated to Internet and/or database access, children's software, or word processing functions are available. The library sought and won several grants from the Gates Foundation to acquire computers to equalize the access of lower-income communities, and these computers were allocated primarily to the neediest branches, as mentioned above (Williams 2000).

The library has a part-volunteer, part-paid program of Web Wizards who assist patrons in using the Internet. Printing was free until September 2000, at which time the library introduced a fee of 10 cents per page. In general, the Wizards and the general library staff help anyone who comes in with this technology. In response to the state's requirement that libraries have a plan to protect children from pornography, children have to have their parent's signature and be issued a card before going online at the library.

Public schools and public libraries are located in all neighborhoods of the city. They are government agencies and fall under the mandate of the Four-teenth Amendment, requiring equal access under the law for all citizens. Our sense is that this government mandate, even supplemented by private initiatives, is not yet enough to overcome the disparities of race and class.

Community Public Computing

There are a total of ninety-nine community computing sites. These are mapped in figure 5.4. The host institutions are nonprofit organizations, nei-ther commercial nor government, although they may receive public funds. There are thirty-eight schools and preschools, twenty-nine churches, twenty-eight community facilities or centers of various kinds, and four apartment complexes.

Of the thirty-eight schools, twenty-two are part of the Catholic Diocese of Toledo. As elsewhere in the United States, many of the European immigrant populations were Catholic and built churches in what was a smaller city. In a sense, the Catholic schools (http://www.cyss.org/Schools/SchoolPage.html) are a parallel system to Toledo Public Schools as well as a link to their respective churches. But these schools are tuition based, so they represent a form of community schooling oriented to those who can pay. As such, they are more friendly to parents, community, and congregation.

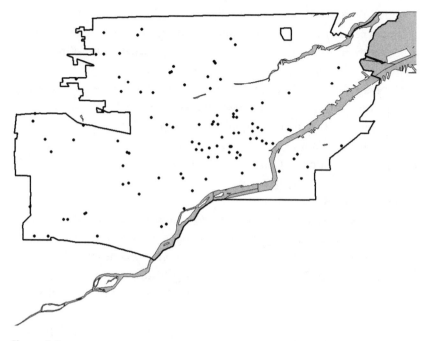

Figure 5.4
Community public computing sites.

In most Northern U.S. cities, about 10 percent of students attend Catholic schools; for Toledo the rate is an unusually high 20 percent (Patrick McGuire, personal communication, 2002).

The twenty-nine churches include seventeen different Christian denominations. The highest representations are Lutheran (ten), Baptist (seven), and Catholic (three). In many cases these are churches with affiliated schools, but they have computer access for church use.

The rest of the community public computing sites consist of community centers oriented either to the general public or a specific constituency. They include community centers for the general public (e.g., Wayman Palmer YMCA, W. J. Murchison Community Center, Adelante), for seniors (e.g., Alpha Community Programs, Eleanor Kahle Senior Center), for youth (e.g., Boys and Girls Clubs, Black Data Processing Associates), for union members (Farm Labor Organizing Committee, Toledo Federation of Teachers, Police Patrolmen's Association), for museum visitors (Center for Science and Industry and the Toledo Museum of Art), and the Medical College of Ohio hospital. The last two are unusual: the museum has a computer in its K–12 resources center that is used by children and teachers, and the hospital has a PC set up in a lounge near its physical therapy department for inpatients to use.

The map shows a concentration of community sites in the inner city along with sites in higher-income areas near the northwest suburbs. The community centers with computers are primarily dedicated to poorer central-city populations, and the remainder of the sites are located in communities that can afford computer labs.

Commercial Public Computing

There are forty-two commercial public computing sites in Toledo. Of these, twenty-three are commercial schools and preschools, fifteen are apartment complexes, three are Kinko's copy shops, and one is a cybercafé. The map in figure 5.5 makes it clear that these public computing sites are either in the downtown area or in the outer city, especially in the western part of the city.

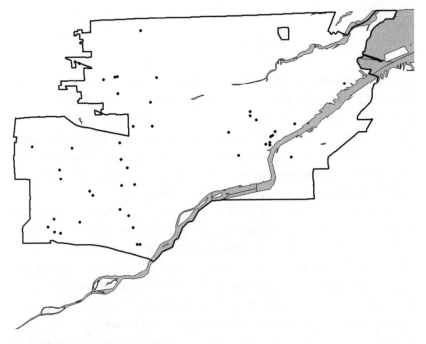

Figure 5.5
Commercial public computing sites.

Several of the apartment complexes belong to the same owner, who won a Department of Housing and Urban Development grant to set up computer labs and thus improve his apartments. He has helped to grow the CTC association in town, CATNeT.

Kinko's is a copy shop that developed a business model and a reputation around public computing. Their sites are near the suburbs and the University of Toledo campus. The cybercafé is also near campus.

Commercial sites are far fewer than government or community sites. This might reflect a lack of effective demand from the local population, or a lack of imaginative capital from Toledo entrepreneurs.

University Public Computing

Three universities and colleges in Toledo provide computer labs for their students: the University of Toledo (UT), the Medical College of Ohio (MCO), and Mercy College of Northwest Ohio, a nursing and allied health college. Each of these institutions is oriented toward educating professionals and technical workers. UT and MCO are located in outer Toledo, and Mercy College is located in the inner city near what was once a hospital complex. (See figure 5.6.)

Their computer facilities are open only to students or rare one-time public events, with two important exceptions. Mentioned above is the computer available for patients at MCO hospital. UT's women's studies program operates a women's computer lab as part of their support for un- or underemployed women in Toledo.

The university and college facilities are possibly the most advanced public computing sites in the city. For instance, the UT business school is a wireless zone for laptop access to the network. Many departments provide specialized hardware and software. UT also teaches computer classes of all kinds in several off-campus labs downtown.

The university is an important partner for public computing. UT faculty helped start and continue to work with CATNeT, the local association of community technology centers. A larger group of faculty is also proposing a sociology minor in social informatics. This program would link with public computing across the city in order to place interns for potential future employment, conduct research, and collaborate for advocacy and policy formulation.

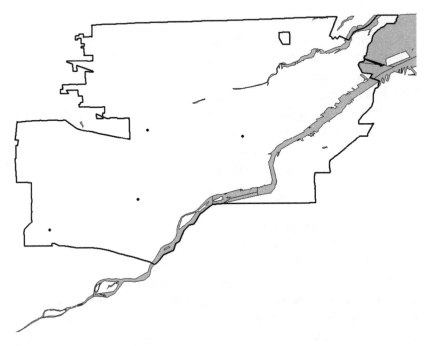

Figure 5.6
University public computing sites.

Social Environment of Public Computing

We hypothesize that the four kinds of public computing fit three patterns in relationship to the social environment:

• Government sites are randomly located, in the same proximity to rich and poor.

• Community sites are located close to the opposite ends of the social spectrum, the rich and the poor having community sites but not the middle strata.

• Commercial and university sites are located according to market demand, closer to upper-income groups and students.

As the maps indicate, our data suggest this pattern, but weakly. We expect that a broader dataset would make a more compelling case.

The marketplace has a direct impact on the location of commercial and university sites. There are however, two important particularities. University sites combine upscale owner-occupied single-family homes with low-cost apartment complexes for students. Further, a large concentration of ICT users live in relatively affluent suburbs (Sylvania, Perrysburg, Maumee, and so on), which transforms this urban pattern into a metropolitan one.

The U-shaped pattern of the predicted community public computing sites may prove to be the best countermotion to the market as a foundation for democratic traditions. The role of the church and other institutions that represent bonding social capital is to give poor and working populations a basis for collective consciousness and action, including self-empowerment projects with ICT.

Government public computing sites are a result of public spending that reflects increasing commitment to an ICT transformation of education at all levels. As figure 5.7 indicates, the informationalization will be equal, but the level of access and use is a matter of available state revenue and relative level of commitment. In times of expanding revenue, an egalitarian state is a major factor, but in dire times the impact can be relatively negligible.

In general, changes in hardware and software will dramatically impact what we mean by public computing, especially the increasing use of wireless, voice recognition, broadband, and technology convergence (phone, computer, TV, music, camera, and so on). But we will still have the basic four categories of public computing. In each case, we are interested in the rate of adoption and pattern of use, and then in what cyberpower—people's ability to use ICT to achieve their goals—results in. (Alkalimat and Williams 2001

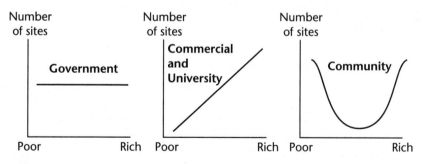

Figure 5.7
Modeling the distribution of public computing. Government computing sites distributed equally across poor and rich communities, commercial and university sites distributed more to rich, community sites distributed more to poor and rich, leaving out middle income.

elaborates on the concept of cyberpower as an outcome of a community technology center.)

We are arguing that the stream of technical innovation is a force banging against society, and like the beginning of a game of billiards, the balls are scattering. Each type of public computing expresses a structural force—an aggregation of institutions, people, and spaces—constituting a power dynamic. It is the configuration of all the power dynamics of a society that determines the likely course history will take.

We envision two stages of future research. The first stage involves confirming this description of public computing and measuring variation in different urban and rural areas, as well as in different countries. In the second stage, we and others will examine what is going on in public computing sites, what users are doing, and what forms of cyberpower emerge. The stakes are high; we believe they extend to the nature of democracy in the information age.

Note

The authors acknowledge the support of the Alliance for Community Technology at the University of Michigan, The W. K. Kellogg Foundation, and the Urban Affairs Center and Africana Studies program at the University of Toledo.

6 A Polder Model in Cyberspace: Amsterdam Public Digital Culture

Geert Lovink and Patrice Riemens

This chapter is part of an ongoing participatory action research endeavor into the Digital City (DDS), an Amsterdam-based free community network. The DDS is the most famous of a motley collection of initiatives that came collectively to be known as the Amsterdam Public Digital Culture. Launched in January 1994, this community-network project got off to a lightning start and attracted in a short span of time tens of thousands of users, making it the largest "free net" in the world. Thanks to the publicity it generated, it was also to a great extent instrumental in the introduction of the public use of the Internet in the Netherlands. The aim of its founders was to democratize the use of the Net and create a "digital public domain."

In the first part of this chapter we will look at the origins of and the premises underlying the Digital City project within the broader Amsterdam new-media culture that existed at the time. The second part focuses on internal developments within DDS in the late 1990s, since they exemplify the evolution of this culture under the influence of a totally changed and greatly expanded new-media landscape. Five years after DDS's founding, the displacement of the early forms of the Internet by the speculative new economy at the height of its frenzy altered—fatally—the character of the Digital City, and of grassroots media initiatives in general. We will devote an afterword to DDS's privatization by way of a management buy-out, the determination of the new owners to discontinue the public-domain functions of the Digital City, and the resistance by users, (former) DDS employees, and various concerned groups to these policies. In late 2000 a newly founded users association (www.opendomein.net) tried unsuccessfully to salvage the public-domain sections of the Digital City, while other parts were either terminated or sold off. In August 2001 the Digital City was relaunched as a commercial DSL broadband reseller—a sad end to one of Europe's biggest and most interesting community networks.

Let's be clear from the beginning. The Digital City Amsterdam did not intend to be a representation of the real city. Nor was it expressing a need to catch up with the global economic dynamics. In this case the city concept was used as a metaphor.[1] Ever since the rise of computer networks there has been a desire to "spacialize" virtual environments. The cyberspace concept is a prime example. In this case, the name *Digital City* appealed to the imagination of thousands of users. Although maps were made to help navigate the Digital City web space, the city metaphor was used in a restrained way. The spatialization was neither a representation of a computer network nor a simulation of an actual city. The reference to the urban environment here is to the concept of city as the "house of culture." *City* referred to a conceptual density that results in diversity and debate. The collective mapping of complex community spaces was seen as an act of culture-in-the-making. The city experience made operational for the Internet context was that of a cosmopolitan flair, ready to ignore the all-too-obvious dichotomies of real-virtual and local-global. What kind of Internet culture would result from this choice of metaphor remains up to its players and users and is the topic of this chapter. But let's go back in time first.

Squatting the Media

By the early 1990s, the (in)famous Amsterdam squatters movement, which had dominated the sociocultural (and law-and-order) agenda in the previous decade, had petered out in the city's streets, but its autonomous, yet pragmatic, mode of operation had infiltrated the more progressive cultural institutions. It was a time in which cultural centers like Paradiso and De Balie, which were in the vanguard of local cultural politics, embraced the theme of "technological culture" in their programming. In the beginning, this took the form of a critical, if somewhat passive, exploration of the technologies surrounding us, and of their risks and opportunities. This lecture-based approach was, however, soon replaced by more do-it-yourself, from-below methods, whereby various Amsterdam groups and the public joined in making an event happen.

The shift, which also involved a shift in generations, came when (information) technology was no longer seen as the preserve of science, big business, or the government. It could also be accessible to ordinary people or groups. Mass availability of cheap electronic hardware and components had created a broad user base for definitely low-tech applications, something that in turn spawned a profusion of video art, pirate radio, and public-access television initiatives, besides well-attended festivals where technology was rearranged in a creative and playful manner. It was a time when the self-appointed vanguard of Amsterdam's progressive cultural sector did not want to merely reflect on the impact of technology on society but opted in favor of active involvement. In this post-Thacherite but pre–Third Way era of ongoing deregulation and privatization, with brutal and repetitive budget cuts in the arts and culture sectors, it no longer seemed to make sense to expect the state to become architect and caretaker of a public domain in cyberspace. Its creation and management were going to be the responsibility of the public itself. And it was time to act before major media corporations could move in and, in close collaboration with various governments, seal off the new electronic spaces in order to gain control of what they primarily saw as an economic opportunity presented by the accessibility of a broad consumer base.

Going back to the beginning of that decade, the magic period around 1989 was not only marked by the fall of the Berlin Wall. It also witnessed the emergence of computer networks. Such networks had already been adopted by the military, financial institutions, and academia, but their use was restricted to a few well-defined activities. Meanwhile, a number of grassroots computer enthusiasts had also been building a patchwork of so-called bulletin-board systems (BBS) for some time, but it was the hackers' repeated and much-publicized intrusions in the big network known as the *Internet* that put electronic communications on the political agenda for the general public. And thus the demand for public access was born, in the Netherlands at least.

What made the Amsterdam situation even more special was the degree of organization among the hackers and their willingness to structure themselves as an open ("new") social movement. This enabled them to communicate with a wide audience and to negotiate their acceptance in society at large through journalists, cultural mediators, some politicians, and even a few enlightened members of the police force. After a whirlwind performance in Paradiso by the already-notorious German Chaos Computer Club (CCC) in the fall of 1988, the stage was set for the Galactic Hackers Party, the first open, public, and international convention of hackers in Europe. This took place in August 1989, again with Paradiso as the venue. From then on, hackers deftly positioned themselves in a cultural landscape dominated by artists, intellectuals, political activists, and cultural workers in general. They were even getting kudos from some segments of the computer industry.

By then, the concept of public media in Amsterdam was also familiar, thanks to the unique distribution of cable broadcasting: cable radio and television were reaching over 90 percent of households by the mid-1980s. These forms of media were operated by the KTA Corporation, set up and owned by the municipality. The corporation was run as part of the provision of public utilities services, and the choice of channels it transmitted and its tariff rates were set by the city council. The council had also mandated that one or two channels be made available to various constituencies, such as minority and artists' groups. This was intended to curb the wild experiments of TV pirates, and so various programs began to be broadcast on the local channel, whose bill of fare, to put it mildly, was distinctly different from mainstream television.[2]

Besides radio and television, there was also a proliferation of small, specialized, and noncommercial outfits in the realm of electronic music—like Steim, Montevideo, and Time Based Arts—devoted to both general and more political video art as well as to technoculture magazines such as *Mediamatic*. All this resulted in a politically (self-) conscious, technically fearless, yet financially modest and hence unassailable atmosphere and constituency, which went a long way toward fostering a media culture in Amsterdam that was neither shaped by market-oriented populism nor informed by cultural elitism. The various players and the institutions in the field did obtain some support from the usual funding bodies and government agencies, but managed to retain their independence, thanks in part to a mostly voluntary mode of operation and a low-tech and low-budget approach. The shift in funding practice, moving away from recurrent subsidies to one-of project-linked disbursements, in keeping with the ruling market-conformist ideology of the time, also left its mark on the format of these activities. Many small-scale productions had thus emerged, but the establishment of more permanent structures remained constrained. This in turn led to the prevalence of a hands-on, innovative attitude, an ingrained spirit of temporariness, and the deployment of "quick-and-dirty aesthetics" by groups such as TV 3000, Hoeksteen, Park TV, Rabotnik, and Bellissima (all active in the public broadcasting space provided by the cable channel SALTO). This edgy climate also resulted in the relative absence of direct linkages between the new-media culture and the political establishment, diluting the influence of the latter. Such a media culture was therefore seen as a buffer, an intermediary, not an expression of or an appendage to representative democracy. This is what the Adilkno collective has termed "sovereign media," liberated from the statutory obligation to serve an audience and benefit shareholders.[3]

In the meantime, electronic activists were poised for the next phase: the opening up of the Internet for general use. The hacker movement, operating under the banner of the Hacktic group (which was also publishing a magazine by the same name, full of technical "disclosures" that annoyed the telecom managers to no end), staged a coup by obtaining from the Dutch academic network permission to officially hook up to the Internet and resell the connectivity. What no one had anticipated, least of all the budding hackers-turned-entrepreneurs themselves, was that all 500 accounts that formed the initial offering of the Hacktic Network would be snapped up the very first day. Access to the Internet through nontraditional service providers was henceforth established as a norm of sorts in the Netherlands. Combined with the technological expertise of the hackers, this created a situation in which commercial enterprise would follow and benefit from the existing creative diversity rather than riding the waves of the Internet hype and making quick money without any incentive to innovate or to show concern for public participation.[4]

These developments did not escape the smarter elements in the government, who were on the lookout for ways of modernizing the social and economic infrastructure of the country in the wake of the globalization process. Since electronic communication was also perceived as posing all sorts of possible threats on the law-and-order front, a two-pronged approach occurred, meant to contain the "menace" on the one hand, and to co-opt the whiz kids on the other. Comprehensive and fairly harsh computer-crime laws were approved by parliament in 1993. The second big hackers' convention in the Netherlands, "Hacking at the End of the

Universe" (HEU), in the summer of 1993, responded to this potentially repressive climate with a public relations offensive. By stressing the civil liberties aspect, a coalition was formed between computer activists and various media, culture, and business players who did not want to be reduced to mere consumers of the agenda set by big corporations. The idea was that programmers, artists, and other concerned parties could, if they moved early enough, shape, or at least partially influence, the architecture and the content of the networks. This is often the characteristic stance of early adopters, since it enables one to gain ideological ascendance when influential projects are taking shape, a move suitably, if somewhat cryptic-ally, called in German "to take the definition of the situation into one's own hands" ("Die Definition der Lage in die Hand nehmen"). A form of citizens' activism emerged that in the late 1990s would be identified and relabeled as the "spirit of entrepreneurial leadership."

Elected politicians meanwhile struggled with another situational prob-lem: that of their own position amidst rapidly dwindling public support and sagging credibility. Not surprisingly, this problem was blamed on a "communication deficit" for which a substantial application of new media suddenly appeared to be an antidote. The cue was not lost on the De Balie cultural center, which approached City Hall with a free-net-based proposal to link up the town's inhabitants through the Internet so that they could engage in dialogue with their representatives and with the policymakers. The system itself was to be set up by the people at Hacktic Network, the only group of techies readily available—or affordable—at that time. The Digital City (De Digitale Stad, DDS) of Amsterdam was launched in January 1994 as a ten-week experiment in electronic democracy to coincide with the municipal elections to be held in mid-March of that year. The public response was overwhelming. And in no time, "everybody" was communi-cating with everybody else. With one exception, though: the politicians themselves never made it to the new medium.

It is unquestionable that the DDS functioned as a catalyst for Internet acquaintance and usage in the Netherlands. For many it represented their first contact with the world of the electronic networks, whether because they participated themselves or because they read, or watched television programs, about it. But the Digital City also grew rapidly into an interna-tional symbol of the public domain in cyberspace. Even though the DDS did not bridge the gap between politicians and the electorate—which had been one of its prime stated objectives, and the reason the government put money in the experiment—it did have an exemplary function in the ongoing debate about the information society. The DDS system grew in no time into Europe's largest and most famous public computer network, or "free net," as Americans called this model of free community servers. In practice, this meant scores of dial-in phone lines, a free e-mail address for every user, and later disk space for a home page, lots of opportunity to make contact and gather and/or disseminate information, and above all, the freedom not to be bothered by censorship and surveillance.

Liberty of the Sovereign User

By mid-1998 DDS had over 70,000 "inhabitants"—that is, registered users—and many more visitors, or "tourists." Even more people were willing to join, but in fact the limits of the current system's capacity had already been reached much earlier. It is a sad truth that most European Community Internet and web projects that followed up on the DDS's initial success remained fairly empty and virtual indeed, and attracted far fewer users. For example, Berlin's "Internationale Stadt" initiative, the DDS's most direct clone, never had more than about 300 users, and soon moved in the direction of content provision and software development. It closed down in early 1998. By that time, the Amsterdam Digital City had managed to spawn a diverse and lively Net culture. On the other hand, its system had grown so big, and so intricate, that hardly anybody—least of all the DDS management—had a complete grasp of it. The Digital City had grown into a huge networked community facility—but without becoming a community in itself.

One of the main reasons for this peculiar, but not idiosyncratic, state of affairs is that DDS never attempted to solve, or even to properly address, the contradictions in objectives and hence in methods of operation that have resulted from the clash between the local and the global inherent in the digital age. Within the DDS, as in many other free-net-inspired initiatives, "The driving interest in the organizing group was divided between those who wanted a focus on local information, communication, and networking, and those who wanted access to the global Internet" (Cisler 1993). Apart from the decision to stick to the Dutch language in external communications and all administrative matters, the DDS simply let itself be overrun by the onslaught of the Internet (especially in its World Wide Web manifestation). From then on, like elsewhere, most "inhabitants" used the DDS as a free way to reach content hosted all over cyberspace, and could hardly be bothered by the alleged Amsterdam connection of their provider.

The prime cause of the Digital City's success and reputation, however, was the freedom granted its users from the very beginning. This is not trivial, in view of the amount of control over Net use exercised by universities and businesses, especially outside the Netherlands. For instance, the Digital City had refused to become a public relations channel for City Hall under the usual pretense of "bringing politics closer to the common people thanks to information technology." The DDS system was not the property of the municipal corporation, even though many people assumed this to be the case. In fact, apart from an initial grant, the DDS never received any direct subsidy from the local (or national) authorities. The fairly obvious fact that politics constitute only a small fragment of our daily lives has also proved true on the Net. Besides, it appeared rather quickly that politicians were neither able nor willing to familiarize themselves with the new medium, because efforts made in the beginning of the DDS to bring them online and start a dialogue with their constituents proved a waste of time. And the citizens were far more interested in dialoging among themselves than in engaging in arcane discussions with close-minded and self-important politicos.

To take more of an insider's view of the workings of the Digital City, we will now let a few of the actors directly involved speak for themselves about their experiences. For this purpose we collected interviews with a number of (former) DDS employees over a period of time. Here we will go into the stories of Nina Meilof (formerly in charge of community relations and of the local broadcasting and streaming-media wing of DDS operations) and Hapee de Groot (previous systems administrator of the Digital City). These interviews were conducted in 1996 and 2000 respectively.

Meilof has a background in local television (another flourishing sector of the Amsterdam culture). She was hired by DDS back in 1995 to organize discussions about local political issues, such as the—failed—attempt to restructure the municipality into an "urban province," the controversial house building drive into the Y-lake artificial island IJburg, the even more controversial north-south underground railway project, or the extension of Schiphol Airport, which had the whole environmental community up in arms. The main goal was to find a way of transcending the unproductive state of current political rituals.

According to Meilof, "A major advantage of DDS remains its anarchic character. There are a lot of secret nooks and crannies, such as cafés in out-of-the-way places. Then you may look into home pages and find the history of that particular café, replete with the club jargon, a birthday list, and a group snapshot. There is a Harley-Davidson meeting place, for instance, which coalesces around one particular café, and it brings a newsletter out. This kind of subculture is of course far more thrilling than the mainstream sites maintained by big corporate or institutional players. No way do those sites ever rock." Hence the DDS's policy of looking for a balance between private interests and those of the general public, whereby this type of subculture would still grow optimally, but without "politics" being discarded altogether.

A precondition for this was the system's independence. But that did not come cheap. DDS had increasingly grown into a business, albeit by default rather than by design, while wishing to retain its not-for-profit character. At the time, the management was pursuing a policy of courting a handful of major potential customers who would be able to bring some serious financing in. The catch was to attract projects compatible with the DDS philosophy, however vague, and that was not a totally smooth process. On the practical plane, the DDS organization came to be divided into three components: a commercial department going after the money, an innovation wing that developed new technologies for paying customers, and the community itself, which DDS wished to represent as a social laboratory of sorts. But the image of a virtual community, as Howard Rheingold (1993) has called it in his book by that name, was not really appropriate here. DDS had grown instead into a multifaceted amalgam of small communities, who shared among themselves the intention of perpetuating the DDS system as an "open city."

Out of that, a somewhat Faustian, and in any case unwritten, "social contract" was hatched between the inhabitants and the management of the Digital City, whereby the DDS would keep facilitating the activities of the users free of charge, and otherwise leave them alone. Users, in turn, would let the management manage and would not interfere in the daily operations of the DDS business, thereby acquiescing in the "democracy deficit." As a consequence, general meetings of users and management were discontinued, and the discussion list "dds.dds," having lost its role as a platform for bipartite dialogue, withered away into a quaint digital equivalent of the Hyde Park Corner soapbox.

Metaphors and Interfaces

The central interface also played a key role in the evolution of the community identity of the Digital City. It was originally designed to provide within a fully text-based environment an overview of the mass of information available. In keeping with the metaphor implied in the system's name, the DDS interface is built around the notions of squares, buildings/homes, and (side) streets. But it does not show pictures of or simulate the actual (Amsterdam) cityscape, as many people would have expected. Rather, the arrangement is intended to be thematic, so as to attract communities of (shared) interests. There are, for instance, "squares" devoted to the themes of the environment, death, sports, books, tourism, social activism, government and administration, and so on, but the interface was never able to provide a full representation of the underlying activities. News features, and the DDS's own newspaper, the *Digital Citizen*, attempted to fill this lacuna. But how did an insider keep abreast of current developments? Meilof (who was also the editor of the *Digital Citizen*) again:

I was getting the "logstats" of the most popular "houses" (= home pages), so I would go and look into them from time to time. We had, for instance, a network of male homosexual "houses" springing up at some juncture. These exhibited pictures of attractive gentlemen. Those were very popular sites. Yet it was all fairly down to earth, in fact. Cars, substances, "how to grow your own weed" advice, music sites with extensive libraries, and that sort of thing was on offer. There was also a extensive circuit where you could obtain or exchange software, and some of these "warez-houses" would be up for one or two days only and vanish again. And of course, you had Internet games, those were an evergreen. But it may also have been a home page on some very rare bird, becoming an internationally famous site attracting ornithologists from all over the planet. Then other people freaked out on design or on JavaScript. You got the links samplers. And don't forget the joke sites . . .

Thus there was in the DDS a gigantic alternative or underground world, but there was also something like the "official" Digital City on the surface and in the public eye. The subject matter most often brought to the fore in that context was of the "democracy and the Internet" variety. For six months in 1996–1997 an experiment was conducted with a "Digital Square on Traffic and Transport Issues," sponsored by the Dutch Ministry of Public Works, Roads, and Waterways. Registered DDS "inhabitants" could react to such statements as: "If we don't pull together to do something about congestion, traffic jams will never go away," or "Aggressive driving does pay: it gets you there faster," or "The automobile is the most marvelous invention . . . of the nineteenth century." The experiment even boasted the luxury of a professional moderator, journalist Kees van den Bosch, who would invite another high-profile politician to stir up the discussion every month. And the government was footing the bill.

Van den Bosch was satisfied with the degree of participation. Yet it was easy to fall prey to an overoptimistic estimate. Just a handful of participants generated an impressive quantity of statements. Genuinely new ideas and arguments were few and far between. The evaluation report also stated that little use had been made of the opportunity to obtain background data on the problems discussed. A large majority (about 75%) of the participants only made one contribution and disappeared from view, leaving the discussion to a vocal minority. The report also mentioned the high occurrence of very personal traffic experiences being recounted, whereby senior bureaucrats in the ministry let themselves be quick-started into direct action. The typical hierarchical routine, with a minister making decisions at the top would be temporarily disregarded.

Nonetheless, Meilof always had faith that the new media would influence public opinion indirectly rather than directly. A good example was the toning down of the referendum instrument by the local body politic. A few weeks before our interview, Amsterdam had introduced the hitherto politically tricky concept of a "corrective referendum" in matters of local decision making by the municipal council. The idea had not really taken off, because City Hall tried almost immediately to restrict its scope while at the same time upping up its threshold. Meilof notes that: "politicians were constantly tinkering with the rules, in order to give the impression that voters had a say, while in fact everything stayed the same. Every referendum was getting comprehensive coverage in the DDS, but it was clear every time that politicians did not want to be bothered." She concludes that it is far more interesting and rewarding to do your own thing on the Net and let the old media report about them in their usual feverish fashion. This way you do exert some influence, however indirectly. She adds: "You may even hope that some day politicians would be wanting to make contact with their constituencies." So in Amsterdam too, even if the Internet's growth has been exponential, it is still taking quite some time for political institutions and practices to adapt to the new realities.

Indeed, a great deal has happened over the past few years in the field of ICT development. And ever since its hackers' phase, it had been the custom at DDS to give entirely free reign in computer-related matters to the techies. Because DDS was also a relatively big but underfunded network in the fast-growth lane, crisis was a permanent feature at system operations. Technical problems and glitches were an everyday occurrence, as the system's hardware and software was constantly pushed to its operational limits—and beyond. Added to this was an overriding ambition to be on the cutting edge in technology, and to take a similarly innovative position on the knowledge frontier. This has been a game at which DDS has been remarkably successful up to fairly recent times. Meilof again:

At some point we got heavily into RealAudio and RealVideo—that is, combining Internet with radio and TV (streaming media). It would be great if we could provide home-page TV for our users. To achieve this, you must be well aware of the latest technical developments and must also nurture a good relationship with the owners of bandwidth who are going to carry out this fancywork. We wanted to avoid the situation in which normal citizens have to go to big corporate players if they want to put television on the Net—and pay their price. We felt that streaming media too should be readily available to the greatest number, so that any private person could start web TV at home.[5]

This technical-innovation push did not always square well with some users' expectations regarding content and regarding the quality of public discussions. In the early days of DDS, there was that idea that the Digital City was some kind of empty shell that would be filled up by users and customers, without much intervention from the DDS organization itself. But that formula turned out to result in a very static system. Not very much changed in the content structure of DDS over the years. Some felt that users' creativity had to be rewarded somehow. After all, that is what had kept the social going (DDS did "reward" outstanding home-page developers in the end, with extra bandwidth and technical support, but these had to be pretty spectacular achievers). And as far as the DDS's role as a platform for public discussion is concerned, it is still not clear whether the Net is really a good place, let alone the premier place, to conduct a meaningful, in-depth discussion. The first hurdle is, of course, the issue of moderation. Or to put it differently: Was the DDS a medium like others with editors who would organize and edit (and hence censor) the discussion, or was it some digital remake of the Hyde Park Corner soapbox?

One format that attempted to put more structure and coherence into the presentation of the system's content was the online newspaper, the *Digital Citizen*. This publication also carried a line of supplements, which you could opt to receive (or not). This made for an interesting forum to which people might address contributions, which were filtered by an editorial board. This was the case with the "best-house" contest, for which one had to register beforehand—thus it was a mixed format, where the content was being coproduced by the users. In addition, web-ring technology was made available, where sites were automatically beaded together and visitors could be taken on an organized tour of sorts by the editors.

Two models are competing here. One might be called anarchistic, where things began to fall into place only after a period of time, if ever. The other model was a more organized one, with editors surfing the place on the lookout for those really interesting sites. A web ring was seen as a nice compromise between the two. However, DDS never implemented all the models discussed here, nor did it change its interface very much. In fact, a few years after its inception, and while it was still growing at a fast pace, it became obvious that the city had come to a conceptual standstill.

Another often-raised question had to do with the much-vaunted urban metaphor of the Digital City. Would the city idea die at some point, and with it the DDS, having achieved its emancipatory task? What about its strictly local role; would that dwindle into insignificance also? Around 1998 no more than a quarter of the "inhabitants" were actually living in the town of Amsterdam.[6]

One of the very few policy decisions that the DDS management made was to retain Dutch as the official language of the Digital City. Many users, for instance, were unwilling or found it difficult to express themselves in English. Generally it was felt that sticking to our own tongue was one of the few areas where the Digital City could claim some local anchorage. In itself, however, this said very little about the local or global character of the system. That was something for the users to decide, and for their net usage to show. Hence, successful home pages usually ended up having an international exposure, and thus making, at least partially, use of English. But at the same time it turned out that the Internet was also being used more and more in a very local or regional context. One could now go online to check out the program of the culture club next door. On a more practical level, the question arose about how much longer such typical metaphors as "houses" and the "post office," which had been the hallmark of DDS, would retain any relevance. But then, fortunately, the Digital City never tried to impose its own metaphors on the users. As it turned out, it was mostly outsiders, looking at the DDS on their PCs but not being "inhabitants" themselves, who took the Digital City name too literally, and then started bashing the city metaphor as inadequate.

To recapitulate at this point, critical mass was eventually reached by the DDS when its user base had become so variegated that it could both go for decentralized diversity—which it did to a great extent—and for near-total independence, even immunity vis-à-vis-attempts by the management to govern its activities. This peculiar variant of the "network effect" could only be achieved because the infrastructure was operated as a facility and not as a compelling framework, and because the existence of competing and sometimes contradictory sets of values among the user base was accepted, whether by design or by default. This situation in fact quickly became normative in the DDS organization, where semiautonomous units proliferated up to the management level. This created a climate that could be repressive, but that surely also produced tolerance and led to all sorts of initiatives, ranging from the very obscure to the highly flamboyant, quite reminiscent of the "Islands in the Net" setup (Bruce Sterling). Another outcome was the absence of a dominant DDS scene as such, an endemic feature of the mainstream Amsterdam cultural circles (even though there are many smaller coteries, based on chat channels, cafés, MOO environments, and so on). Incidentally, this was also the prevalent mode of operation of the whole new-media culture at that time. But it also failed to set standards of accountability and decision making from below, and hence to establish a truly democratic tradition in the realm of nonprofit, public digital culture.

Yet the greatest difficulty is how to define *public* in the phrase "public digital culture." It should be clear at the outset that this "public" element does not necessarily form the same constituency as that of the traditional media, the occupants of the public domain in real space, or the franchised electorate in general. Even if some of the basic tenets of the public domain (and especially its ethics) can be transferred to cyberspace, their mode of implementation is for the most part yet to be invented—and put into practice. Another thing the Amsterdam example seems to demonstrate is that the barrier of computer literacy was, and still is, very real, and this had a great deal of influence on the actors involved in the DDS situation as well as on their actions. Thus, the digital culture of the late 1990s remained to a great extent the preserve of geeks/hackers, students, media professionals, and a smattering of people who had gone to the trouble of becoming conversant with computers.

In the search for alternatives to this state of affairs, we find ourselves still being hampered by the founding myths of the network. Those myths refer to a rumored golden age when "everybody" was an active participant and "everything" was in the public domain. Freeware and shareware were the rule then, a near-perfect gift economy existed, and the absence of authority was in itself a safeguard for privacy and a guarantee of ethical conduct. This lore naturally glosses over the fact that users at that time had of necessity an extremely high level of computer competence, and were even less representative of the population in general than now. Such an "Athenian-democracy" model automatically generates its own story of inevitable decline. It cannot deal in a positive way with the consolidation of the user base, even though it was the very thing it had propagated in the first place.

Most Amsterdam digital initiatives had, more or less consciously, tried to escape this predicament. This policy was successful to the extent that it built on a well-entrenched pragmatism in organizational matters and issues connected with a media environment that was traditionally run on a nonprofit basis. In keeping with Dutch values, pluriformity was taken for granted, high expectations were conspicuous by their absence, and benign neglect by the powers that be was the rule. These are still the basic premises of the current situation.

Community Networks in the Age of Dot-Com Greed

To return to our case study, we have seen that the Digital City had evolved from an amateur, low-tech, nonbudget and grassroots initiative into a fully professionalized, technology- and business-driven organization. And this process seems to have been carried to its logical conclusion: corporatization.

In December 1999, the astonished "inhabitants" learned that the directorate of the DDS had shed the foundation status in favor of a private-enterprise framework, within a so-called management buyout. They also learned that whereas community building and support remained noble aims, they were no longer the paramount objectives of "Digital City PLC." Incorporation took place with the assent of the Digital City Foundation's board, which laid down a number of conditions under which privatization would occur.

The way was paved for this metamorphosis by the prevailing craze surrounding e-commerce-oriented Internet start-ups, which mobilized surrealistic amounts of venture capital on the basis of the flimsiest of business plans and previous experience. In that respect, DDS's prospects looked more promising, yet the incorporation came too late. Far from rescuing the Digital City, it throw it into even greater turmoil.

By the late 1990s the provision of complimentary access and facilities the DDS had pioneered a few years before had become much more generally available. Scores of commercial free-access providers and hosting services were popping up all over, offering the same kinds of services as—or in many cases more and better ones than—the DDS was able to provide. These providers sponsored massive advertising campaigns, and they were addressing a potential customer base far removed from the idealistic concerns that had informed the original Digital City. This almost immediately resulted in a substantial erosion, both quantitative and qualitative, of the DDS's own user base—and the process is accelerating. (The same developments threatened xs4all, too, but they countered it with an extremely smart public relations campaign.)

Even if the absolute number of accounts rose to an alleged all-time high of 160,000 "inhabitants" in early 2000, an analysis of the use patterns showed that most of these accounts could no longer be related in any way to the concept of community building or even to sociopolitically relevant information exchange. Interest in home-page building and upkeep, for instance, long the hallmark of DDS "citizenship," declined. The once-valuable DDS real estate—its web space—had turned into empty lots as fewer and fewer inhabitants claimed ownership of an electronic homestead. The Digital City was fast losing its attractiveness for common users and got caught in a downward spiral. But the question of whether privatization was a cause of or a response to this erosion of credibility is complex, and we will not attempt to answer it here.

The Digital City had also lost ground as a platform for discussion of local issues, despite various—and genuine—efforts to trigger debates around important political events, as we have seen. Unfortunately, these efforts took place in isolation from the rest of DDS's operations. As a result, the DDS had basically been turned into a facilitation structure providing the usual ICT services to its "clients," with the fee-paying ones (organizations, institutions, and businesses) getting priority at the expense of the non-paying community of individual inhabitants. Most clients, in fact, saw the DDS as a convenient channel for Dutch-language interchange, and cared little for the community as a whole.

This left sponsorship by the corporate sector as the only remaining avenue of resource mobilization, together with some consultancy and hosting jobs for various public and semipublic bodies. This mode of operation, besides not sitting well with those who placed a priority on community building and community service, gave rise to an increasingly obfuscating rhetoric of public-private partnership masquerading as policy. As could be expected, both approaches proved elusive in the end, and this lack of direction left the DDS both politically vulnerable and seriously, and permanently, underfinanced.

The growing number of users, with a host of individual requirements and little patience for idealistically induced technical deficiencies, as well as the need to deliver better performance to the paying (institutional) customers, made this predicament even more acute. The lack of substantive political, and hence financial, support—as opposed to gratuitous encouragement, which was never in short supply—compelled the DDS to turn even more to the market, but its status as a foundation precluded it from attracting investors' money.

Last but not least, something needs to be said about the "postdemocratic" management culture and management choices, which, either by design or by default, presided over this unhappy evolution of the DDS's fortunes. Very early on, the opportunity to turn the Digital City into a truly self-governed networked community had been put aside in favor of an allegedly more efficient, but in the end messy and contentious, executive model of governance. Before long, the "inhabitants" grew tired of the paltry participation opportunities given to them.

As far as the decision to go corporate was concerned (and parallel to similar developments, such as the sellout of geocities.com, Multimania, and so on), it is obvious that the DDS's management must have had the value of individual accounts and brand visibility firmly in mind. "Properties" of this nature had generated absurd multiples of thousands of dollars per unit worldwide at the height of the dot-com mania that characterized the last half of 1999. The actual realization of these dreams by DDS, however, had to wait until the complex conditions pertaining to the new ownership structure had been sorted out. They were, but not in time.

Ironically, like most of the new-media initiatives described in this chapter, the Digital City lacked internal democracy. It may have been a backlash against the democracy overkill of previous decades, with all the collectives and workers' councils, that led to the pragmatic, sometimes domineering governance of these initiatives (often by people who came from alternative movements themselves). Since the cultural sector does not carry much economic weight, general interest in (and scrutiny of) that sector was, and remains, deficient. Management and employees alike appear not to be overly concerned with building up a democratic structure. According to De Groot, "After a decade of activism a lot of people, still having a lot of energy in them, were looking for new opportunities. Some of them joined the NGO community, often under some kind of workfare employment scheme. Other joined media projects such as the Digital City. They became so involved, not to say obsessed, with their jobs that they completely identified with the organization they were working for, and completely cut off the opportunity for others to unfold their own ideas."

In these exciting years, when everyone seemed to be participating in the construction of the network, raising questions about ownership, power relations, and work conditions was not the thing to do. Critiques of management, and demands for more participation or even for better pay, were rarely expressed. If they were, prompt categorization under any of the headings "old economy," "losers' whining," "cultural pessimism," "negative attitude," "maladjustment," or even "sabotage of the organization's constructive work atmosphere" was sure to follow. One either had to endorse the parameters of the future, as defined by New Age business gurus, with enthusiasm, or become an instant casualty. Looking through the lens of this proprietary claim to the Internet, start-up personnel even felt pity for those left behind and interpreted any critique as a sign of spitefulness or resentment. Dissent came to be seen as an echo of a chaotic past that had been expelled from the realm of successful ideas. Only innovators and entrepreneurs were endowed with creative ideas and possessed the unique knowledge of how to implement them.

This discussion, however, leaves the fundamental problem untouched: no precise blueprint for an open, public domain in cyberspace has emerged yet. In fact, this public domain has not even been precisely defined—despite numerous and sometimes outlandish fantasies and speculations. The big questions remained unanswered. For instance, who is going to take responsibility for noncommercial culture in cyberspace? Even more important, who will own the concept, content, and finally the space itself? It is clear—in the Netherlands, at least—that political parties have been avoiding this debate, and effectively left the Digital City to operate in a vacuum.

DDS and the Quest for Network Democracy

What is also crucial is the actual ownership of the cables, or "pipes." Legislation is a contentious issue as well, yet is highly relevant to what people, as potential producers of content, will be able to achieve with regard to the design and maintenance of a new public domain in cyberspace. One thing should, however, be clear: it serves no purpose to wait for governments or corporations to implement, or even facilitate, the emergence of a public digital culture. The Amsterdam example shows that it is not the big visions, models, and plans that count, but the actual hands-on initiatives and activities of the people themselves. The alternative is the death of a culture at the hands of blind commercialism and/or stifling bureaucratic regulations.

But then, how would one define the term *public* in the phrase "public digital culture?" This public does not necessarily form the same constituency as that of the traditional media, the occupants of the public domain in real space, or the electorate in general. Even if some of the basic tenets of the public domain (especially its ethics) can be transferred to cyberspace, their mode of implementation has, for the most part, yet to be invented, agreed on, and then put into practice. Contrary to a certain prevailing ideology about the networked society, our experience in Amsterdam has shown that the barrier of computer literacy is still operative, and that this barrier shapes both the actors involved and their actions. The digital culture of the late 1990s remained to a great extent the preserve of geeks/hackers, students, media professionals, and a smattering of people who had gone to the trouble of becoming conversant with computer systems. Hundreds of thousands of new users may have entered the scene over the past few years, but they do not necessarily aspire to be part of an online culture or a public sphere as such. Their computer use is limited to just a few applications (usually provided in a Microsoft environment), and they perceive the Internet as a mere component—and probably not the most important one—of the increasingly gadget-filled telecommunications sphere.[7] This, by the way, is not meant as a moral judgment. But the creation of online communities requires skills and practices that go beyond the mere possession of a device. Internet use and new-media literacy are not the same.

The next issue is that of the extent to which a digital public realm is desirable or feasible. To a great extent, this is the same discussion as with the subject of the urban public domain, and sometimes the same actors show up. The answer has now become clear, at least from our standpoint, and it is a negative one. In almost the whole of Europe—France being the usual exception—the state has declined to administer or design, let alone finance, the public part of cyberspace (with a few exceptions such as Bayern Online, Bologna's "Iperbole," and some others). Rather, we now have a narrowly, but from the political point of view, comfortable, economic approach to the opportunities offered by the information age. Meanwhile, at the street level, we are witnessing a proliferation of Internet cafés catering to the need for connectivity that public utilities decline to provide. In fact, and completely in tune with the prevalent ideology of market conformism, even universal access is not seen as something for the authorities to intervene in, as one can infer from the very limited, usually fruitless, efforts to make public-access terminals generally available.

Returning now to the Dutch new-media cultural scene, the *Polder model* ("the society of dialogue and consensus") has engendered its own digital clone, going under the name of the *Virtual Platform*. This partnership of sorts between various new-media-related cultural institutions was established in 1997, with the aim of creating and maintaining a working consensus among its members, thereby avoiding harmful competition. By enforcing a modicum of corporatist discipline—brought about the Dutch way, by endless rounds of meetings—it ensures that the fledgling institutions do not go at each other's throat over such (financial) support as is provided in homeopathic doses by the largely indifferent national and European government bodies.

The practical outcome of this model is that a limited number of organizations (V2, De Balie, Society for Old and New Media, Steim, Paradiso, Montevideo, and a few others) have shed their start-up/experimental/ anarchistic avant-garde status and have consolidated themselves into new mainstream institutions without being forced to merge or to disappear. The shadow side is that since the Virtual Platform is not a truly open body, its very existence substantially raises the threshold for those newcomers who, for whatever reasons, are not yet members. This then begs the question whether a limited number of not necessarily representative organizations can claim to embody the public digital realm. In the meantime, as could have been predicted, the Virtual Platform has mainly turned into a convenient vehicle by which the Ministry of Culture can outsource its administrative chores and its policymaking headaches and thus retain patronage without responsibility. For better or worse, this concept has proven a successful formula, and its format, already adopted and adapted by, for example, Belgium and (pre-Haider) Austria, is poised for further export.

These state policies and attitudes have had yet another surprising outcome: as creative spirits left the confining spaces of the not-for-profit cultural sphere, they moved on to create their own (ad)ventures on the commercial front. These days, doing business is being experienced as challenging, rewarding, and fun. But it should not hide the fact that the current enthusiasm for entrepreneurial drive was basically the only available option under the circumstances. The Digital City remains, of course, the prime example of this flight into capital—as a belief system. But it is far from being the only one, and having now all but floundered, far from being the most successful.

The commercial analog of the Virtual Platform has also come into existence under the acronym ANMA, the Amsterdam New Media Association, modeled after the New York original. It has something of the "First Tuesday" format, with less emphasis on the business-angels or venture-capital approach, concerning itself more with social networking, debating, and even policymaking. Oddly enough, the municipality's economics department has awoken to this development and has turned out to be an enthusiastic supporter, maybe too much so.

With this we have come full circle. The allegedly recalcitrant state turns out to be very much present after all and manages to participate without applying governance. Under this new dispensation, a ubiquitous yet absentee state likes to portray itself as just another business partner. Within this depoliticized framework, representation and accountability have been instrumentalized away in favor of convoluted yet subtle networked procedures, responding to "benevolent" markets. French thinker Alain Minc has said it all before: "Democracy is not the natural state of society—but the market is."

Codirector Joost Flint and his business partner (and the other DDS director) Chris Gödel devoted most of their energy hatching and negotiating their corporatization plans and management buyout scheme. These efforts were finalized on March 1, 2000, when the Digital City was formally incorporated as a limited company. DDS as a whole was vested in a holding company (DDS Holding BV) and its operations split among four limited companies: DDS Ventures for research, DDS Services for hosting, DDS Projects for web design, with the community part transferred to DDS City. This setup merely formalized the practices that had developed over the years. However, in a commercial environment, it reinforced the differences between the "earning" and "spending" departments, this time to the detriment of the latter.

In the original business plan, the community was seen as a potential breeding ground for all sorts of value-adding activities, which, though they need not be commercial in themselves, would reflect positively on the balance sheet of the other DDS companies. Unfortunately, the dot-com craze was going belly up at the time, and the community began to be seen as a drag on resources. Hence, in November 2000 the DDS content staff got the sack and the news on the opening pages of the portal was discontinued. Meanwhile, Internet College, a high school students' portal site, which was the sole component of DDS Ventures, had been sold to an educational publisher, promptly followed by the sale of the hosting company, DDS Services, which was bought by the English Electricity Utility Energis. This left DDS Projects, the web-design bureau, as the sole revenue-earning company among the holdings, further undermining the community's financial base. At this stage Flint and his partner let it be known that they were seriously considering pulling the plug from the Digital City as we knew it.

In January 2001 a group of Digital City "inhabitants" (users) decided to forestall, if possible, the likely demise of the public-domain section of DDS. An initiative launched by Reinder Rustema in the columns of the online magazine Smallzine attracted a lot of enthusiasm. Before long over 400 people had joined the ranks of a Save the Digital City association, now registered as the Open Domain Association (http://www.opendomein.nl) (this because of a conflict with the holding company about the "protected brand name DDS"). The association's goal was to take over as much of the old DDS as possible—that is, the networked-community part—with the aim of preserving the spirit of a public domain in cyberspace.

The association initiated talks with the current owners of the DDS, but finding a common ground appeared to be an uphill task. Apart from the fairly deep distrust both parties harbor about each other's agenda and actions, there was a virtually insurmountable conflict of interest with regard to the domain name (dds.nl), and with respect to the value of the individual, private accounts (now believed to number 70,000 at most, half of them active). This was an important issue because the mere creation of the association has suddenly revived the market's valuation of the DDS, while its subsequent activities even gave credence to the feasibility of transforming dds.nl into a fee-earning ISP.

According to Manuel Castells (2001, 151), it was competition that killed DDS. Another reason Castells mentions, based on Van den Besselaar's research, is the steady decrease of activity in political forums. The commercial success of DDS and of the Internet in general "created major contradictions among the idealistic activists at the origin of the network and the managers of the foundation" (p. 151). Responding to Castells, Patrice Riemens observes that "the fact that the telephone system is the property of the people does not entitle them to occupy the telephone exchange" (p. 152). Castells seems to disagree with Van den Besselaar's conclusion that the experiment of DDS has failed.[8] "As usual," Castells says, "the process by which historical change muddles through is far more complex. Instead of emphasizing failure and decline, the networked community scene appears to 'forshadow a new, global civil society'" (p. 154). He even talks about a "new, meaningful layer of social organization" (p. 154).

Again and again Castells proposes close links between community networks and the local state, counterbalancing the merger between the nation-state and global capitalism. Yet the DDS example points in another direction. A lively civil-society network may as well be seen as a potential competitor to the interests of local politicians who do not see why they should fund media initiatives that are not under their direct control. For good reasons, community networks are reluctant to create a long-term dependency on local government. Often, community networks with close ties to local politics look dull and dead, offering few resources for users. Instead of calling for more (local) funding, it may be better to diversify income sources through membership fees, micropayments, content syndication, web banners, sponsorship, donations from private foundations, consultancy work, online services, and reselling of Internet capabilities.

The DDS story calls for Internet-specific forms of democracy and for the development of legal structures to prevent a small group from highjacking/ privatizing the digital public domain. The lesson of the Amsterdam Digital City, now an ordinary commercial provider offering DSL broadband services, is an economic and legal one. It deals with the fine art of staying independent in an increasingly commercial environment, no longer relying (solely) on government support.

Notes

1. This distinction between three types of digital cities is taken from van den Besselaar, Tanabe, and Ishida 2002.

2. The TV pirates were thus eliminated, but the radio freebooters stayed on. Three nonprofit "cultural-pirate" radio stations are still tolerated today.

3. Adilkno, the "foundation for the dissemination of illegal knowledge," an intellectual collective originally based in Amsterdam, described the process in these terms: "Sovereign media insulate themselves against hyper-culture. They seek no connection; they disconnect. . . . Once sovereign, media are not longer attacked, but tolerated and, of course, ignored" (Adilkno, 1998, 12–15).

4. Hacktic Network, renamed XS4ALL ("Access for All") for obvious marketing reasons, became a profitable, albeit always very tricky, business venture. After protracted negotiations, which ensured complete policy independence for a period of three years, it was sold to KPN Telecom, the former state monopolist, for an undisclosed but large amount of money. Both its six owners (key members of the original Hacktic group as well as some associates) and permanent staffers can look at the process with satisfaction. Parts of the proceeds of the sale have also benefited worthy causes, such as the Dutch Branch of the EFF, the digital liberties watchdog Bytes of Freedom (www.bof.nl), and the political-content provider contrast.org.

5. It has turned out that this option was deliberately turned down by the management, which wanted to make it available to a number of selected—and paying—customers only.

6. Over the years, University of Amsterdam researcher Peter van den Besselaar conducted comprehensive research on DDS in general and on its users' profile in

particular. In the beginning, these quantitative inquiries happened with the permission of and in collaboration with the DDS's management. Such assent was withdrawn, however, when the DDS's privatization drive transformed these data into commercially sensitive information. See 2001; Van den Besselaar, Melis, and Beckers 2000; Van den Besselaar and Beckers 1998; Van den Besselaar and Beckers 1997.

7. There are in fact ominous signs that mobile telephones are going to constitute the main immersive communication environment for the masses, and that, for the moment at least, Internet applications will be a mere, and probably klunky, add-on—Japan seeming to be the exception.

8. Van den Besselaar writes: "We may have to rethink the role of the public sector for guaranteeing and regulating the electronic public domain. As with the physical public space, virtual public space requires care and maintainance, and resources to do so. The main question is whether there is room left for non-commercial Internet culture and social interaction" (quoted in Castells 2001, 153). I am not sure about the usefulness of such nostalgic calls for a return of the welfare state. Rather, activists should prepare for a further withdrawal of the state and a lessening of its obligation to care for and innovate national infrastructure.

7 Community Networks Go Virtual: Tracing the Evolution of ICT in Buenos Aires and Montevideo

Susana Finquelievich

This chapter draws on the results of research carried out by a binational team (the Research Institute Gino Germani, Faculty of Social Sciences, University of Buenos Aires, and the Department of Sociology, Universidad de la República, Montevideo) in order to evaluate the social impact of ICT uses in the practices of civic networks and their potential for increasing citizen participation in public matters. This research involved an investigation of the operational incorporation of ICTs by community organizations in the cities of Buenos Aires and Montevideo, and their initial impact. Primary and secondary data were used, including electronic surveys, face-to-face and electronic interviews, and project analysis, in both municipalities, of ICT incorporation and current implementation.

Data from both studies will be presented in this chapter and a comparison of commonalities and differences made. This will inform a discussion of how the Internet is impacting civil society, the public sphere, and democracy in general in South America. The chapter concludes with a consideration of some of the most salient points raised and how these might affect the future.

The fact that a large MERCOSUR[1] country such as Brazil is investing strongly in e-government systems and related software[2], as well as creating a nationwide network of 30,000 public computer terminals, will undoubtedly affect Argentina and Uruguay.

Community Networks in South America: Building the Information Society on Both Sides of the Río de la Plata

The practice of citizen networks utilizing ICTs is not a new social phenomenon, but their numbers have multiplied quite dramatically since the late 1990s. Artopoulos (1998, 53) writes, "These experiences are the outcome of a political–technological movement's activities, as opposed to the centralized informatics systems of the North-American military-industrial complex. . . . Deviating from the postmodernist thesis, alternative uses of information technologies not only express cyberpunk rebellion but also the utopian views of citizen participation in the center of the community territorial space—the city."

Community networks (CNs), also called electronic citizens' networks (ECNs), provide an additional access platform for multiple sources of information for the community. In addition to providing local information, many ECNs offer connections between people and ideas. Many organize weekly newspapers or electronic bulletins, provide connections to national and international networks, and offer community access to cable television. Focusing on interactive communication, many ECNs perform as catalysts and conduits for broader community projects.

ICT Adoption and Use in Buenos Aires Civil Society

In focusing attention on the development of civic networks in cities such as Buenos Aires and Montevideo, it should be understood that the size and scale of a city have a tendency to influence forms of civic participation. Indeed, it has been noted that the bonds between the state and civil society in rural municipalities, towns, intermediate-sized cities, and metropolitan areas differ quite markedly (Arroyo and Filmus 1997). Using a categorization scheme developed by these authors, it can be seen that Buenos Aires civil society is a complex structure, comprising base organizations[3], intermediate entities,[4] and support organizations.[5] This heterogeneous—and dense—associative nature of Buenos Aires is reflected in the fact that the city registers the biggest concentration of NGOs of the country (46% of the total number).

Centro Nacional de Organizaciones Comunitarias (CENOC)[6], a national institution with an extensive database of community organizations, identified 483 such organizations in Buenos Aires City, mostly civil associations and foundations. The most frequent thematic areas are social development, health, and education, and the most common form of social intervention includes the provision of training, basic care, and consulting services. Half of all community organizations participate in networks and most carry out activities of wide territorial reach (44% of them work at national level).

Using a 3-element selection system, the study focused on nonprofit civil-society organizations that (1) were institutionally independent of both state and private enterprise, (2) promote innovative forms of collective action, and (3) use ICTs and the Internet (either through their own websites or e-mail). Traditional organizations such as unions, neighborhood clubs, churches, school cooperatives, political parties, and senior citizens' centers were excluded. Also excluded were organizations providing information for directive areas—for example, consultants, political foundations, private universities, and private academic centers. This work facilitated the gathering of statistics on ICT use and the implications for strategic aspects of the production and use of information, communication, and generation of new services.

The most evident result was the increase, both in quality (based on indicators such as the quality of informatics equipment, Internet connections, cable connections, and dial-up access) and quantity (the amount of the ICT infrastructure installed in NGOs). Support organizations in Buenos Aires have on average five computers per organization; an average of four computers are connected to the Internet. One-third of organizations are connected to the Internet[7]. The equipment is usually acquired for an organization's exclusive use, although they may also use computers in the homes of members.

The issue of ICT training is an area that provides some interesting insights into the disparities existing among Buenos Aires community organizations. Well over 33 percent have no funds available for ICT training. However, among those in a position to allocate a budget for ICTs (services supplier, phone expenses, website hosting and maintenance, software, and so on), twenty-three made up to 5 percent of this available for training, while in sixteen cases the figure was as high as 11 percent. Despite these figures, 51.2 percent of all organization members taught themselves to use ICTs, with only 16.3 percent learning inside their organizations. However, there are indicators that NGOs are beginning to invest both in technology and in technological training for their members.

Most organizations (fifty cases) have been using the Internet for three years or more and another fifteen for at least two years. The Internet services most widely used by organizations are e-mail and the World Wide Web (42.8% and 25% respectively). Discussion forums are also used quite extensively, at 18.9 percent. A similar story can be told about organization members. Almost half the members surveyed have access to electronic mail (47%), but only a third have access to the web.

Most of the organizations (sixty cases) report using the Internet to disseminate information through their websites. Basic information is provided by only 36.3 percent of NGO websites. Another 20 percent provide access to an electronic newsletter, while 15.6 percent and 11.9 percent respectively have databases and discussion lists on their websites as well. Half the organizations update their website contents monthly, while the other half update two or three times per year. Only 20 percent of the NGOs claimed that the main benefit of using the Internet was improved access to information and dissemination of activities. Another 19.3 percent mentioned that communications with other organizations had improved, while 15.1 percent claimed that administrative tasks had additionally been simplified. These figures confirm what preliminary interviews with key informants had already suggested: at the time of data collection, many organizations in Buenos Aires were still ambivalent about the Internet. Some saw its concrete benefits, but nevertheless, there was a clear cultural resistance to using the Internet to its full potential.

However, the evolution of the process of ICT dissemination among NGOs gained momentum. Community and voluntary-sector groups discovered that by utilizing ICTs as developmental tools, they could contribute more effectively to community networking in Buenos Aires, and in Argentina. One of the most outstanding aspects was the Internet's potential for networking, both among NGOs, and between NGOs and the local government. Most of the organizations integrate networks (sixty-four cases). These networks are integrated by national organizations (38.7%), foreign organizations (36.3%), and local organizations (25%). Evidently, organizations that have their own websites interact more with other organizations at national and international levels than do NGOs that have not yet built their own websites, not only because they have better means of disseminating their missions and actions, but because they already reflected a "networking-prone" attitude.

When asked about their relationship with City Hall, 19.7 percent of the organizations said they participated in some City Hall activities, such as attending meetings. Another 17.9 percent received some form of financial support for their activities, while another 14.5 percent accessed municipal information through the Internet. However, it should be noted that a significant proportion of NGOs (27.4%) have no relationship with City Hall whatsoever. These figures suggest that, in spite of an increase in ICT use among NGOs, there is still a ways to go before ICTs become an active means of interaction between civil society and local government. This may be due to the fact that the Buenos Aires government has traditionally overlooked dialogue with citizens. Hence, this cultural inertia is transferred to the Internet era: ICTs are mainly used by local government for internal management issues, rather than as an instrument of communication with city residents.

Those organizations currently using the Internet are beginning to understand its potential for improving access to information through the use of online databases and participating in virtual communities. However, this is not the only change emerging in the behavioral and activity patterns of community organizations in Buenos Aires. In their role as information providers, organizations are increasingly moving beyond the use of websites as "message boards." Community organizations are beginning to visualize the potential of the web to access resources and generate new services. In most of the websites analyzed, we found the creation of innovative tools that improve access to scarce resources, facilitate donations, raise money, solicit volunteers, and provide virtual training. Many of these new ICT-supported services are used to disseminate demands from and strategy ideas to the neighborhood assembly, provide advice on community issues and access to training, and organize campaigns via e-mail, as well as enabling access to community information through portals.

Increasingly, Buenos Aires community organizations are actively engaging in the global communications system. Many are beginning to develop strategic uses of the Internet, linking it to their specific goals, projects, and missions such as public safety, community health, or human rights. The next section provides insight into events that were the catalyst for this change in NGO use of ICTs.

The Boom in ICT-Supported Citizen Networks

So far this chapter has focused on the behavior of medium and large NGOs as being reflective of Argentine civil-society ICT usage. However, the December 2001 financial crisis not only generated a powerful social explosion leading to the demise of two presidents; it also created a new citizens' information outburst. Hundreds of antigovernment e-mail chains emerged among the 3.6 million Argentine Internet users. On December 19, the first of many public citizens' protests occurred when thousands of indignant citizens took to the streets clattering their pots and pans, in one of the first "cacerolazos,"[8] to protest against the Etat de Siege.

Groups of citizens from different neighborhoods in Buenos Aires and other large Argentine cities began to meet and organize on street corners or in cafés after hours to discuss "proposals for a new Argentina." Within days, similar demonstrations were being organized as these grassroots networks started to utilize ICTs and the Internet to support the activities of the emergent citizen movements. Electronic forums emerged to continue debates online and to inform neighbors who could not get to meetings. Many websites were also designed to spread their actions and proposals.

Gradually, the different neighborhood assemblies—there are currently more than fifty of them in Buenos Aires—began to communicate with each other through e-mail and via their websites. Within two weeks interneighborhood meetings had been organized for every Sunday, where issues were discussed and proposals for action debated. Results of these meetings were, and still are, disseminated through websites and electronic and hardcopy newsletters.

ICT-Supported Social Movements: A New Form of Democracy?

The spontaneity of the street protests seen in the early days of the crisis gave way to a more planned form of campaigning as the neighborhood groups started to organize and lead the demonstrations. The Assembly's discussions were uploaded to web pages, and electronic lists of information and proposals for action became commonplace. One such example is Cacerolazo.com, a portal of international civil protest, where people can leave messages and participate in a protest forum. The site claims that "we don't put the saucepans away, we have to have them visible, don't let them manage us" and urges action: "let's all march to claim May Square" (Cacerolazo.com, 2002). Neighbors are invited to become active contributors and upload information about the events planned by their local assemblies. Another site—http://www.rebelion.org—is an electronic newspaper that covers the diverse demonstration agendas.

Among the best designed of the action network sites is the Indymedia Argentina web page (http://argentina.indymedia.org). Indymedia Argentina is an international organization providing information about protests in over 130 cities around the world. Another site featuring analysis of national events and presenting a "cacerolazos" agenda is El Atico (http:// elatico.com). Vaciamiento.com (www.vaciamiento.com), born from the Aerolineas Argentinas conflict,[9] today analyzes national politics. In addition to these efforts, many tentative online attempts to generate civic awareness about the importance of fighting together can be found in the "Politics and Government" and "People's Opinion" sections of Yahoo! Groups (http://ar. groups.yahoo.com).

All these sites provided agendas for the demonstrations planned, not only in Buenos Aires, but in different cities throughout the country. On many websites, updated news on the evolution of the social conflict appeared once or twice a day. Electronic forums and chats complemented and continued the face-to-face discussions in neighborhood assemblies. Articles written by well-known journalists and political analysts, as well as by the neighbors, contributed to building public opinion. Actions taken by other assemblies were disseminated, and citizens could be informed about the current debates between different factions in the neighborhoods. Many neighbors that had been skeptical until then about the Internet's potential, received crash courses in ICT use from friends or children and became frequent users. Low-income citizens who did not have computers at home used the free community technology centers (CTCs; there are 1,300 of them distributed throughout Argentina), cybercafés, or low-cost commercial Internet kiosks.

To summarize, prior to the momentous events of December 2001, access to the Internet tended to be the domain of the middle classes, but since the protests that emerged from the streets it is no longer limited to the middle-income groups. Civic use of the Internet has become broader and more inclusive, as social movements have adopted it as a communications tool. An example of this can be seen in the convocation of the Federation of the Earth, and Housing and Habitat of the Workers' Power—an organization of blue-collar workers who became unemployed as a result of the recent deindustralization of the country. The unemployed workers were invited, via e-mail, by the Neighborhood Assembly movement to engage in dialogue with the victims of the financial *corralito*.[10] The intention was for the saucepans and picketers to meet for the first time in May Square, as a symbol of a new alliance between the workers, the unemployed, and the middle classes. Although the alliance was brief, the portent of things to come set off alarm bells for the politicians in power.

While this chapter is being written, in August 2002, this social process is showing signs of tiredness. Fewer neighbors attend the weekly assemblies, although those who still do civic work are better trained than ever. Some websites have closed, mainly for lack of financial resources to keep them online, but they have kept the electronic forums and chat rooms going. Neighborhood assemblies have had modest successes: helping elder care centers, providing food and shelter for street children, collecting medicines for public hospitals, or organizing public control of municipal-run public hospitals. They have also succeeded in alerting citizens to the current economic and political problems. However, they could not—until now—accomplish one of their main goals: to generate an alternative project for the "New Argentina," including innovative, young, uncorrupted social leaders.

Whatever the future, leaders and members of the new Neighborhood Assembly movement agree that this massive organization could not be implemented without the Internet. As events unfold in Argentina, the Internet will continue to be utilized as a communications tool by civil society in its attempts to campaign for the establishment of a popular Assembly-based government.

Electronic Community Networks in Uruguay: The Pioneers

Civil-society organizations (also called Third Sector organizations, to differentiate them from government and private-sector organizations) have played a fundamental role in the process of Internet dissemination in Uruguay. At the end of 1985, after the military dictatorship, and during the first years of democratic restoration, the world of the NGOs was revitalized in a new liberal context. Cooperatives and community organizations, including the research centers that provided them with information to resist the dictatorship, were strengthened and reinforced by repatriated exiles. These young people returned to the country bearing new knowledge from abroad (Europe, United States, Canada) and were eager to put into practice the innovative public-participation strategies they had experienced or learned about.

One consequence was a developing interaction between the main community organizations and the University of the Republic. As researchers and professors returned to the country and joined those who had taken refuge in private centers during the dictatorship, it became necessary to maintain and consolidate the social and academic networks and maintain the international contacts the exiles and NGOs had developed. ICTs were utilized by the NGOs working on economic and social research to network the social and technological scientists collaborating with them. For example, in 1986 the Institute of the Third World (ITeM, headquartered in Montevideo; http://www.item.org.uy/) was already using ICTs to communicate with a vast network of correspondents. This provided low-cost access to databases all over the world.

News of this technology spread rapidly across the country and ITeM began providing communication services to Uruguayan NGOs, especially human rights organizations, private centers of social research, and feminist NGOs. In 1989 ITeM, together with a dozen NGOs, obtained a $10,000 donation from the Dutch Organization of Cooperation for Development (Novib) to start the first connection server for civic use in Uruguay. Named after ancient aboriginal messengers, Chasque was housed at the BBS of GeoNet in England and requests for e-mail accounts began pouring in from NGOs.

Imbued by the democratic and participative spirit of telematic communication pioneers, the group of enthusiastic engineers, students, and computer specialists that sustained this first Electronic Community Network established links with institutions in Nairobi (EconewsAfrica) and Penang (Third World Network). They also created NGONET, a network dedicated to promoting civic participation in the processes of international negotiation.

Chasque was fundamental to the process of extraacademic dissemination of the Internet, even though it was based in the academic world, and it maintained strong bonds with the SECIU (University Central Service of Computer Science). In 1994 a direct line between SECIU and Chasque was laid and in August 1995, Chasque began providing Internet access to the general Uruguayan community. Uruguayans began to surf the World Wide Web, uploading their own web pages without the need for registration or affiliation, while being billed directly to their phone accounts.

However, from that date on the sociotechnical panorama began to change in Uruguay. The role of NGOs as promoters of Internet dissemination passed to the state and private enterprise. Chasque fell into the vortex this situation created. Today, some people, pointing to its corporate approach to service provision, question its tax-exempt NGO status. This is an especially sensitive issue, because Chasque no longer offers special connectivity or web hosting to NGOs and does not differentiate their content from a classic commercial portal.

The process of massive Internet dissemination caused a change in the profiles of both users and providers of services and contents. Twenty-six percent of the population has a PC at home and another 13 percent at work. Twenty percent of the urban population claim to be frequent users of IT and 10 percent are connected to the Internet, the highest percentage in Latin America.[11] The web users' growth rate is 40 percent yearly. ICT-supported services are also increasing. In 2001 there were 54,065 hosts with a ".uy" (for Uruguay) extension.

However, the distribution of ICT access (through PC-ownership indicators, according to socioeconomic level) reveals a digital divide in Uruguay. In high-income groups, 58 percent have a PC at home, and 25 percent have another at work, against 22 percent and 14 percent in middle-income groups, and 2 percent and 8 percent in low-income groups. Ten percent of the population as a whole has access to the Internet. Within this 10 percent, there is a generation gap, because 62 percent of Internet users are younger than thirty and 19 percent are between thirty and forty. These proportions diminish to 11 percent for those forty to fifty and decrease to 8 percent among those older than fifty.[12]

One of the most striking differences between the situations of Argentina and Uruguay is that unlike the Argentina case, the Uruguayan population's interest in ICT is reflected in the corporate world. Both the national government and the most innovative enterprises consider ICT an economically viable solution. The paramount sector of the information society in Uruguay is the software industry. Uruguay's software industry is consolidated now as relevant in Latin America in the development of information systems for companies, an area in which world-class competitive capacity has been reached. According to the Competitiveness Agenda's results (1999) for the main entrepreneurs of the sector in the Ministry of Industries, the informatics sector is integrated by twenty large companies and fifty medium-sized firms, which export software for around U.S. $60 million per year.[13] The positive attitudes toward technological innovation in the corporate and government spheres are reflected in the civil society. Unlike the situation in Argentina, proactive national policies that promote ICT contribute to a wider dissemination and use of these technologies in Uruguay.

A View of ICT in the Organizations of the Uruguayan Civil Society
Active citizens' networks have increased in number in Uruguay in the last few years. Some examples are:

• A group of pioneer Organizations of Civic Electronic Networks, integrated by ITeM and Chasque, has been set up to fight poverty and its causes, and campaign on human rights issues.

• Solidarity Uruguay—Uruguay Solidario—is a portal that promotes and interconnects community NGOs. It is an initiative of the Fundación ACAC, belonging to a cooperative bank. Its website features a national directory of NGOs.

• VECINET (Neighbors Net) focuses on the electronic publication *Local Self-Management*, which disseminates local news via e-mail. The website publishes documents of community interest and on urban management, budget matters, human rights, housing and productive cooperatives, and self-management.

The Uruguayan cooperative movement has a strong tradition and solid organizations. Although they cannot be considered NGOs, they have played and continue to play an extremely important role in supporting, promoting, and collaborating with the Uruguayan social organizations. Recently, the Programa Neticoop has been developed and maintained by the Uruguayan Confederation of Cooperative Entities (CUDECOOP), a representative organization of the Uruguayan cooperative movement. Their purpose is to promote the use of available ICT, in particular the Internet, among the Uruguayan cooperative organizations and their partners.

Citizens' Organizations and Community Telecenters
Centralized national policies in Uruguay put the accent on private, home-based, and corporate Internet connectivity, and little consideration was given to alternative community-access ICT-based civic socialization. Indeed, until as recently as mid-2000, Uruguay had no telecenters or (even) cybercafés, even though citizens' organizations were championing the popular and social appropriation of ICT in the form of telecenters. It fell to an NGO specializing in poverty and marginality, and the leftist City Hall in Montevideo, to generate an outstanding innovation in the national connectivity strategy with a system of telecenters distributed in the capital—the Billiard Project.[14]

This innovation was born from an agreement between the Franciscan Research and Ecological Promotion Center (CIPFE), the Intendencia Municipal de Montevideo (IMM), and the Montevideo City Hall. The City Hall provided twenty Zonal Communal Libraries, which are distributed across the city, while the NGO installed four computers in each and provided an informatics teacher and Internet tutor. The project started in 1998 with the goal of implementing a telecenter providing technological training and connectivity at low cost—students pay U.S. $23 per month—in each library. This money finances the teachers' and tutors' salaries. The telecenters provide four hours of free Internet access daily. In return for the use of library facilities, the databases and administration of each Zonal Library are being computerized.

To date these telecenters have infotrained 1,700 students, and 800 more are currently studying. User profiles range from children and teenagers, to men of up to eighty-five years, housewives, youths in search of jobs, and workers searching to improve job prospects. The economic profiles vary according to urban areas but the project prioritizes low-income areas.

The Star Media Foundation, together with the National Youth Institute, has implemented another outstanding project, called Escuelas de Informática y Ciudadanía (Schools for Informatics and Citizenship). The project is managed by the Committee for Computer Science Democratization in Uruguay (CDI Uruguay)—an NGO branch of the American CDI. This organization intends to create self-sustaining computer science schools throughout the country. They have already implemented the first school and center to train future educators, and three more schools are planned in the near future. The model aims to compensate for the uneven progress existing in the public informationalization process in primary and secondary education.

In 2002, more than 5,000 youngsters in the poorest neighborhoods of Montevideo received free courses on informatics, in a specially equipped bus, called "La P.C.Ra," a word game between PC and "the fishbowl." The "La P.C.Ra" project is an outgrowth of a general policy designed to have a high social impact—a policy carried out by the Montevideo City Hall, Microsoft Uruguay, and the transportation enterprise Cutcsa. The project emphasizes democratic access to technology, and facilitates the entry of poor young people into the labor market.

Montevideo NGOs: A Survey of ICT Use

How do Uruguayan NGOs use ICT? To obtain comparative data, a questionnaire similar to the one used in Buenos Aires was distributed to a representative sample of eighty NGOs. Complete information on ICT use was received for sixty NGOs. Twenty-five percent of the NGOs were created before the 1976 military coup d'état and another 25 percent during the dictatorship; the third 25 percent were established between 1985 and 1992, and the last quarter emerged after 1992. Three-quarters of the NGOs have paid staff. A quarter of these are small organizations of between one and five paid employees. Another 25 percent have between five and thirty employees, while the remaining 50 percent have more than thirty employees.

The data provides some interesting insights into ICT ownership among NGOs, which appears to be quite high in Montevideo. Some 87 percent own at least a basic PC, while 55 percent possess multimedia equipment. Seventy-eight percent have a printer of some type. Forty percent own a scanner and 20 percent have a CD copier. Internet use is also relatively high, with 60 percent of NGOs possessing Internet connectivity. Seventy percent of these organizations have an exclusive mailbox but only 25 percent have their own web page. Interestingly, almost 18 percent of these organizations were already using ICTs before 1994. Twenty-one percent of organizations report having their own intranet system. This group of more technologized NGOs is also the most active in its interaction with local government. At the other end of the scale, 10 percent of organizations indicated that they share equipment with other NGOs, while another 11 percent used ICTs in a member's house.

Despite this relatively high rate of ICT use among NGOs, it is the more traditional technologies that remain the most broadly used for communications purposes—the telephone (93%), fax (68%), and traditional postal mail (73%). Fourteen percent of NGOs have more than five phone lines, while 38 percent have only one phone line.

Although Uruguayan NGOs have incorporated ICTs quite intensively into their operations, a multimedia mix of modern and traditional communications technologies underpins their communications policies and strategies, which tend to be coordinated and integrate citizens' organizations into communicative social networks.

However, as in Argentina, intensive use of the Internet does not ensure a fluid dialogue with the local authorities. The Montevideo City Hall does not, in its practices, foster public participation through electronic networks. There are also other limitations in the use of the ICT to interact with NGOs, besides problems affecting e-mail communication between NGO members and civil servants. For example, the distribution of municipal information by e-mail to the NGOs and to the citizens is not conducted by City Hall itself, but by NGO VECINET, using press releases distributed by City Hall.

The Uruguayan social sector has a proactive attitude toward ICT: it has made significant progress in encouraging the national government to promote Uruguay's integration into the information society. However, so far, social organizations have not had an opportunity to monitor the progress of government efforts to increase citizen participation in the information society. Nevertheless, this possibility is regularly proclaimed in official speeches.

ICT and Civil Society on Both Sides of the Río de la Plata: Commonalities and Differences

If Argentina and Uruguay are similar in their use of ICT for local governance, they differ dramatically with respect to ICT use in community networks. Both countries have a long history of involvement in social movements and community organizations. Both were strongly influenced by European immigration in the nineteenth and twentieth centuries. In relation to the social use of ICT, however, the NGOs in each country travel divergent paths. One of the main characteristics of Argentine NGOs is their relatively late participation in the world of information technology, especially medium and small organizations. Even recently, with millions of people in universities, commercial enterprises, mass media, and government organizations using the Internet, NGOs still lagged way behind.

In Uruguay, however, the reverse was true. NGOs championed Internet use and played a significant role in its diffusion and adoption throughout the country. They used the Internet to transmit the values of a relatively well-organized civil society and strong union and cooperative movements, starting in integrated global networks and later communicating with local and national organizations. Whereas Uruguayan NGOs have a tradition of collaboration and working collectively, Argentine NGOs had a tendency to act individualistically. Until the emergence of the street protests, they rarely fashioned any form of civic networks, and it is only recently that they have begun to exchange information and resources. The lack of a national federation of NGOs has not helped in this regard, and individualism was reflected in the NGOs' use of ICT. Networks took the form of internal organizational mechanisms rather than externalized interorganizational networks. However, the emergence of the Neighborhood Assemblies movement indicates the potential for a more collaborative form of civic networking in Argentina.

The relationships between community organizations and the state show similarities between Argentina and Uruguay, with little evidence of cross-sectoral strategic ICT partnerships existing. Argentinean NGOs contend that the state must take responsibility for the dissemination and facilitation of public ICT access. The state does determine civil society's ICT needs, but there are no common actions, policies, or programs implemented to address these needs. A similar situation exists in Uruguay. However, the emergent system of free-access municipal telecenters in the Montevideo Zonal Communal Centers indicates that collaboration between government and civil society may be possible in the future.

Despite a lack of coordination between social actors in Uruguay, there is some evidence that civil-society organizations, the state, and commercial enterprises appear to be set on steering the country into the network society. This tendency is particularly noticeable in terms of the NGOs. In Argentina, the three main social actors (NGOs, government, and commercial enterprises) deliver pronouncements about the necessity of integrating the country into the network society, but there is little coordination of effort between the different actors, or inside each actor's environment. Consequently, Argentina displays a slower integration of civil-society organizations into the network society, at least in the short and medium term.

Despite the differences of approach in Argentina and Uruguay, it is important to understand the wide range of economic and political contexts in which ICT experiences have evolved in both countries. These include conflicting demands for regional and international competitiveness, the economic crisis, national interests, local objectives, disagreements between the groups in power, cross-sectoral tensions, and the need for a reconstruction of democracy. All of these factors have greatly influenced the projects and processes involved in the development of the network society in both countries and go some way toward explaining present circumstances.

Democracy, the Internet, and the Public Sphere

Can the events in Argentina and Uruguay be described as an example of the construction of an innovative public sphere? Drawing on the Habermasian concept of the public sphere, Rheingold (1993, 13) provides thought-provoking insight:

The idea of modern representative democracy as it was first conceived by Enlightenment philosophers included a recognition of a living web of citizen-to-citizen communications known as civil society or the public sphere. Although elections are the most visible fundamental characteristics of democratic societies, those elections are assumed to be supported by discussions among citizens at all levels of society about issues of importance to the nation.

The origins of the idea of the public sphere and its central role in democracy can be traced to ancient Greece, and even today Western democratic ideals often incorporate similar notions. This in turn strongly influences our understanding of what the public sphere should be.

Habermas (1989) extends this notion through the development of a normative understanding of the public sphere as a part of social life, in which citizens can contribute to public opinion through the exchange of viewpoints on important issues for the common good. This public sphere exists when individuals meet to discuss political issues. Of course, Habermas's work is based on the description of historical moments during the seventeenth and eighteenth centuries, in which cafés, salons, and other meeting places had become debate centers. However, he extends these concepts to an ideal of participation for the current discourse on the public sphere. That is, he suggests that the discussion process should adopt the form of a critical and rational debate, in which participants have a common interest—truth.

Habermas stresses the fact that a citizen's individual opinions, when given as an answer to a specific demand (e.g., a public opinion survey), do not constitute the public sphere, because they are not inscribed in a process through which public opinion is constructed. Arguing against the "envy of

Athens," he states that if "democracy is implemented in the present huge, complex societies, the idea of a physical collective of consenting members should be overcome" (Habermas, in Porter 1996). Developing this point, Habermas proposes that citizens who are not necessarily present can develop other nonphysical forms of communication.

Far from the Athenian model of democracy, the Internet holds the potential to build public opinion, according to Habermasian ideals. Since the public sphere depends on free discussion and the communication of ideas, Rheingold (1993, 282) argues that "as soon as a political entity grows larger than the number of citizens that can get into the meeting room of a modest City Hall, this 'marketplace,' vital for the generation and discussion of political ideas, can be powerfully influenced by changes in communication technologies." Virtual communities may help citizens revitalize democracy, by enabling massive participation in the political process, or they may cheat them into buying attractively packaged substitutes for democratic discourse.

It is not yet clear whether the Argentinean population will continue to use the Internet for social organization, or whether the Uruguayan people will continue on the collaborative path they set out on. What is certain is that in late 2001, a remarkable increase in the use of home banking, cybercafés, Internet booths, and community technology centers or CTCs (free public-access places to connect to the Internet) occurred in Argentina. Despite Uruguay's embracing of monetarist economic policies, civil society has continued to be a driving force behind ICT communications diffusion and adoption in that country as well. Whether ICT and Internet use will continue to grow in Argentina, where the middle class has become impoverished through unemployment, a shortage of new revenue sources, and lack of access to their savings, remains to be seen. A recent study suggests that one million telephone users have canceled their telephone service, while many others have cut their Internet connections and drastically reduced their telephone expenses since February 2002 (Prince and Cooke 2002).

At the same time, bandwidth availability has decreased, because many ISPs found it difficult to pay for it, and international carriers have reduced the bandwidth of international connections. Under such extreme conditions, Argentina runs the risk of becoming a giant intranet, without links to the external cyberworld.

Another risk is the rapid increase in the cost of informatics goods and services, which are imported and valued in U.S. dollars. The Chamber of Computer Services Companies (CESSI) has already warned of the danger of informatics and telecommunications supplies drying up as a result of current economic policies.

It is not certain whether the current socioeconomic situation will reduce the appropriation and spread of ICT. Clearly domestic connections to the Internet could be replaced by CTCs. At present, of the original 1,300 CTCs, 900 still survive, coordinated by the National Communications Secretariat (SECOM). CTCs would be an excellent solution for citizens' networks, but even this is a complex situation. CTCs have become a hot political issue recently. The Communications Secretary resigned, and SECOM remained without its highest officials for almost four months. CTCs have also become desirable prey for the politicians and local leaders who favor the patronage system, with CTC resources being granted only to specific neighborhood leaders who belong to their political parties.

ICT, Democracy, and Social Capital

The "Information Society should be mainly about people. We should put people in charge of the information,instead of using this to control them" (Tsagariousianou, Tambini, and Bryan 1998, 204). However, harmonizing social, administrative, and technological policies can be problematic, and in many countries in which "electronic democracy" is being implemented, the results have not been faithful to these concepts. Several reasons exist for this situation:

1. *The decision-making area in the field of science and technology has been histor-ically, and is still, less democratic than other types of policy decisions (Sclove 1995).* The very technical nature of policy formulation in this area excludes non-experts and prevents their involvement in decision making. On the other hand, areas such as transportation, economics, environment, health, security, and education are often subject to intervention from social groups or com-munity organizations that may influence decisions. Similar intervention with scientific and technological issues has not been possible until recently.

2. *In general terms, government initiatives that use the language of democ-racy are not based on a corpus of academic research from which theories on democracy in the network society can emerge and develop.* The shortage of

intellectual criticism of the supposed democratic qualities of ICT stems partly from the lack of empirical research from which critical debate can arise. This is reflected in the resistance, by much of the academic community, to the notion that the social impact of ICT is a topic deserving sustained attention. However, it should be noted that this resistance by academics is largely the result of a refusal by government officials to support and consult academics working in these areas.

3. *Technological innovations are taking place in a changing political atmosphere, in which rigid government control of the organizations and institutions that implement and disseminate these technologies is no longer accepted as a structure of political control.* The necessary investment to keep up to date in technological development is beyond the reach of many government budgets, especially at the local level. The monetarist philosophy currently in vogue, with its emphasis on control and cuts in public expenditures, makes the financing of technological development by private capital inevitable (Tsagariousianou, Tambini, and Bryan 1998, 310).

The emergence of different types of ICT-supported social movements, at both the local and global levels, suggests an urgent need to develop more and better research on the empirical base of electronic government and electronic democracy.

Our research reveals that electronic government in Argentina and Uruguay will not develop fully if government policies are not informed by a deep-rooted understanding of citizens communication needs and their need to participate in the network society. Other prerequisites to the successful development of the electronic government include the transformation of institutional cultures and the intervention of civic organizations and the academic sector in social and technological policies. On the other hand, many of the objectives pursued by civic organizations will not be reached without a fundamental transformation of the regulation of telecommunications technology.

Technological tools accelerate a network-structuring process that depends largely (but not exclusively) on shared values, a participatory culture, the capacity to act synergistically, and the ability to regenerate networks, invigorate horizontal communication, build partnerships between different social actors in the pursuit of common goals, and forge agreements successfully. ICT-supported social networks do not necessarily ensure effective communication or create communities where they do not exist. They do, however, facilitate the contacts and the necessary knowledge to strengthen the integration of organizations and the promotion of new social spaces.

ICT-supported social networks possess the potential to protect, maintain, and promote social capital in our societies. In general terms, *social capital* refers to the social organization as a system of networks, norms, and trust, which facilitates coordination and cooperation for mutual benefit. As has been seen with the emergence of Neighborhood Assemblies in Buenos Aires, electronic networks can favor the invigoration of local organizational cultures sustained by models of horizontal communication associated with the global organizational culture. They can also accelerate learning processes configured around a networking culture in organizations that generates and reinforces links between institutions and facilitates participatory mechanisms:

The importance that innovations introduced by information and communication technologies have for citizenship is most relevant. The public and private spheres are alternatively intertwined and redefined. To inhabit freely the physical city and the political city demands that, in diverse places and moments, one can enjoy the conditions of "invisibility," reserved before only at the moment of voting. Control about our own information, access to relevant social data and the possibility of uninterrupted communication, become necessary conditions for the preservation of individuality, and for collective action. The possession of the technological dimension is born from literacy and it finishes in the reconstruction of the democratic procedures. (Rodotá 2000, 137)

Issues to Debate

Based on the research I have conducted and coordinated, as well as on other findings, I believe that these social movements are representative of major trends in society today. As Litz Vieira (2001, 12) states, "The democratization process has stopped being fleeting and functional and become a permanent form. It is a process of adjustment between legality and genuineness, between morals and law. This new interpretation opens a space for the social movements and civil society organizations, while it incorporates new concepts, including a revision of the public sphere, in the democratization process." He adds: "The processes of reproduction of cultural patterns become political forms in the public space." This is space that, as the antiglobalization movements have shown, belongs as much in the physical space of streets and cities, as in the space flowing around the web.

These social organizations are extending the concept of public space beyond the limits of political parties. They are adding new topics to political agendas and playing a fundamental part in the construction of a new public sphere supported by electronic networks. In this sense, they are movements that are neither radical nor conservative but socially innovative. They have been successful in generating social and cultural changes in their target populations and in society in general. In a wider sense they are contributing to the creation of a new concept of democratization, identified with the practice of citizenship. This concept highlights the limitations of both state and market and allows for the concept of democracy as a social practice in which citizens are direct actors.

One of the most direct cultural impacts—a process and a tool—is the social appropriation and dissemination of the tools of the network society. No longer are these tools available only to an elite class. Another result is the construction of a social, public subjectivity. The emerging values and actions in civil society are opposed to the characteristic values of state and market, and are generating new forms of sociability, reciprocal changes in social practice, and the production of subjectivity. Another development is the practice of operational solidarity, through which the "Neighbors" have provided help to retirement homes and nursing homes, street children, unemployed parents, and other groups in social need. At the economic level, however, little impact has been registered so far.

The technological and social changes have left less of a mark in the formal political sphere, and a word of warning is appropriate. As Vieira explains, the plural occupation of public space can entail an imbalance in the relationship between actors. The hegemony of political society is sometimes maintained by the insertion or participation of civil associations in the state, so that they acquire semipublic status (Vieira 2001). Despite this risk that undemocratic and outdated regimes will be legitimized, one thing is certain. At least some of the political and social claims promoted by civil society will find an enduring place in the political agendas of national and international organizations in the years ahead.

Notes

The data for this chapter was collected and analyzed by Pablo Baumann, Alejandra Jara, Silvia Lago Martínez, Alén Pérez Casas, Raquel Turrubiates, and Martín Zamalvide.

1. MERCOSUR, the Common Market of the South, is an economic alliance of Brazil, Argentina, Paraguay, and Uruguay. Chile and Bolivia recently have become associate members.

2. Petropolos-Tecnopolis, a technopole located sixty-nine miles from Rio de Janeiro, is currently the first Latin American technopole specializing in software and hardware for e-government.

3. A "base" organization is defined as an association of people working for their own local interests as a group, such as community improvement. Their scope and target population are generally local. Base associations emerge from the community, to solve local problems.

4. Intermediate entities are organizations—research centers, consultants, and so on—that offer information and advice on technical and organizational issues, to base and support organizations.

5. Support organizations are defined as associations of people working to help base organizations, as well as the community, in a larger sense. Their target population is generally large and their scope usually national or international. Support associations emerge from universities, international organizations, and research centers, and are dedicated to supporting community organizations.

6. National Center of Community Organizations.

7. This data pertains to the year 2001.

8. *Cacerolazo*: slang for a citizens' demonstration, clattering their pots and pans, either from their windows and doorsteps, or marching in the streets.

9. Aerolineas Argentinas (Argentine Airlines, formerly an Argentine firm) was privatized in 1997, and acquired by Spanish capital. In 2001, the enterprise declared bankruptcy and fired most of the employees. The employees protested vehemently. Finally, Aerolíneas reopened, financed by Spanish and Argentine capital.

10. Corralito (little corral) is the popular name given to the system implemented by the government to inhibit financial outflow from the banks, on December 21, 2001. The system freezes the bank accounts, so that account holders cannot touch their own savings.

11. These statistics are from the year 2001.

12. Source: Association for Progress in Communications, (APC), http://www.apc.org/espanol/index.shtml.

13. http://www.cusoft.org.uy/docs97/agenda.zip.

14. Source: interviews with key informants.

8 Civil Networking in a Hostile Environment: Experiences in the Former Yugoslavia

Veran Matic

[This chapter tells the fascinating—and inspirational—story of how media systems can be threatened, and of how they can be resourceful and resilient in the face of threats. This chapter is constructed using selections written over a two-and-a-half-year period and begins with a BBC Online news story. —Editors]

"Press Freedom Hero" Award

BOSTON, May 3, 2000—In Boston today, on the 50th anniversary of the Vienna-based International Press Institute, IPI, an elite organisation of directors and editors-in-chief of world media, World Press Freedom Hero awards have been awarded for each of the last 50 years. Alongside Veran Matic, other award recipients were Adam Michnik, Jiri Dienstbier, Catherine Graham and more. At the press conference, Matic launched an international campaign to help the media in Yugoslavia. To illustrate the plight of the media, he spoke about media repression in the former Yugoslavia over the past few years: 26 employees of the media have been killed or died in accidents, none of which has ever been fully investigated; fifteen journalists have been arrested and at least 6 of them have been given sentences ranging from 10 days to one year imprisonment; at least seven journalists have been beaten up and physically injured; 178 public requests for radio station licences have been refused.

Yugoslavia began falling apart following the death of "the immortal son" of the Yugoslav people—Josip Broz Tito, on May 4, 1980. Undoubtedly, Slobodan Milosevic provided crucial momentum in the disintegration process after his accession to power in 1988. The following year, at the celebration of the 600th anniversary of the Battle of Kosovo near the province's capital of Pristina, Milosevic first announced that the Serbs might have to wage a new battle for their freedom. In 1991 the final stage of the Yugoslav disintegration began to unfold—first skirmishes and short-lived armed conflict in Slovenia, the northernmost Yugoslav republic, then war in Croatia, and finally, in 1992, war in Bosnia-Herzegovina as well.

Macedonia managed to escape unscathed from Yugoslavia and declared independence. The signing of the 1995 Dayton Peace Accord put a stop to bloodshed in Bosnia-Herzegovina. From 1998 onward, another armed conflict escalated in the predominantly Albanian-populated southern Serbian province of Kosovo. After the failure of the peace negotiations in Rambouillet, France, NATO launched a sustained air-strike campaign against Yugoslavia. Yugoslav armed forces subsequently expelled about 800,000 ethnic Albanians from the province.

This is the shortest possible summary of the tragic events spanning the last decade of the twentieth century in the former Yugoslavia. Of course, Serbia is the focal point. Complex political conflicts were taking place as a consequence of a "discovery" of national sentiment and erosion of communist ideology, but the clash between traditional and modern values also played a role. The first multiparty elections in 1990 were marked by a gloomy atmosphere imbued with a sense of impending doom, fear, and alleged threats to national identity as perceived by the general public.

In March 1991 mass protests against the regime took place in Belgrade. These demonstrations were the first sign of citizens' deep-seated discontent. After the failure of the first demonstrations, civil protests recurred almost each year. However, this did not seriously threaten Milosevic's regime, which was relying on several pillars of power: total control of economy, judiciary, police, and army as well as a monopoly of the media—television and radio broadcasters in particular. The first real political challenge to the regime were the 1996–1997 mass civil protests sparked by Milosevic's brazen attempt to rig the local elections. Milosevic ultimately lost power in about forty major cities and towns in Serbia. Thus, the momentum of resistance was transferred to the grassroots level. Independent media were becoming increasingly more important in this process in comparison with democratic political parties. Radio B92 expanded its network to additional thirty local radio broadcasters throughout the country. Local print media also formed their own professional association.

Radio B92 was founded in 1989 as a small, urban youth radio station. In a short period of time, this local urban broadcaster—cherishing a specific style and taste in its approach and manner of communication with its listeners—developed into a radio station featuring the best, the most credible, and the most objective current affairs and news program. While its popularity skyrocketed, B92 was also launching public campaigns against war, hatred, poverty, and politicians' manipulation of ordinary people.

Radio B92 quickly expanded its activities to encompass publishing, cultural affairs, music and film production, and the Internet. With each new field of activity, we were not only attracting larger audiences but expanding our potential impact on society.

Repression against the independent media was particularly conspicuous in times of severe political crises. The independent media were never a mouthpiece for disunited and fragmented political opposition but an authentic, genuine voice of the entire civil sector. They were constantly targeted by the regime by way of police force and abuse of legal powers. In November 1998, the Serbian parliament adopted the notorious Public Information Act intended to suppress any critical voice in the country. This was a part of the preparations for the war in Kosovo. On March 24, 1999, the state introduced censorship, Radio B92 was banned, and persecution of journalists and editors began. In April 1999, Slavko Curuvija, proprietor and editor-in-chief of newsmagazine *Evropljanin*, was murdered. The perpetrators of this crime have never been found.

When the war in Kosovo came to an end, B92 had to start from scratch—searching for new premises, new transmitters, even a "temporary" new name—B2-92. The media once again gave crucial impetus and energy to the discouraged opposition to the political elite.

Statement Delivered in Seattle

[The raid and closure of Studio B and Radio B92 prevented Veran Matic from attending the "Shaping the Network Society" symposium in Seattle on May 20, 2000. Douglas Schuler read the statement that Matic had sent via e-mail. Matic's chair was left vacant and his name card was left on the table as a visible reminder of his absence.]

This is the speech that was delivered in Seattle in my absence:

When I began preparing for this trip to Seattle I had planned to discuss the experiences of our radio and our media association with new technologies in resisting repression in Yugoslavia. We were also to discuss the role of new technologies in the promotion of human rights, freedom of expression, and all other freedoms. For me, the most important part had to do with our development. We expected the repression to increase and we expected to be in a situation where we would have to be very creative in order to survive and continue operating under a dictatorship.

We hoped to complete these important preparations and to be ready for a steamy autumn when the first elections are due. I had wanted, here in Seattle, to present the projects we hoped would help us operate much more efficiently. These include new networking technology and new means of distributing information, research, training, and other projects.

In the meantime, unfortunately, we have been banned for the fourth time in our history. Several other media outlets went down with us. We have had to resort to every possible alternative form of broadcasting. In situations such as this, it is extremely important that the lines of communication are maintained. During the ban of 1996, we fought back alone with the help of the Internet and satellite. Radio programs were sent via Internet to Amsterdam (and later London) and them beamed back to local radio stations and individual listeners via satellite (Pantic 1999). Our position is now much easier because we have a network of more than fifty radio and television stations that continuously receive our programs, produced by journalists in various locations.

Within hours of the police occupation of our studios we were able to resume production of news programs. These are relayed to local stations around the country via satellite. Net-Radio has been launched and we are preparing for 24-hour-a-day satellite broadcasts. We also deliver packages of our television program to local stations. Where necessary these are distributed on ordinary VHS cassettes, which are then screened in town squares, clubs, and cafés. Our text news bulletin is printed out from our website and distributed by hand in Belgrade and in towns in the heartland of Serbia. We hope to be able to secure FM coverage of Belgrade within a couple of days, effectively overcoming the ban.

Each of these moves, of course, increases the danger to us. The regime can no longer back down. It has accused us of terrorism and all that that entails. This is a clear signal that we have entered the final stage of the struggle for democracy and that the regime has entered the final stage of its struggle against everyone who wants to see democracy in Yugoslavia today.

If the opposition fails to achieve greater unity we will reach a situation in which we will be isolated, even from one another.

Every broadcaster today needs help so that everyone could put up resistance to bans and restrictions imposed on their work as successfully as possible.

Large-capacity, higher internet bandwidth as well as the means for electronic communications are essential prerequisites.

Each new attack can be expected to be more brutal than the last. In order to be able to respond rapidly and decisively we need the best possible communication technology.

Just yesterday Deputy Serbian Prime Minister Vojislav Seselj announced that he would never again allow B2-92 back on the air and that the Association of Independent Electronic Media, of which B2-92 is the founder, would also be banned. He went on to say that we would be reduced to satellite broadcasts.

I don't suffer from the delusion that Serbia will be a paradise after the change of government. It is going to be very difficult after that change, and the experience and knowledge we have and will acquire will be very important in the promotion of human rights and freedoms in the period of transition. This will be a time when we will have to struggle against the dangers of modern totalitarianism, commercialism, the drive for profit, soft democracy, and pseudofreedom. What we are able to acquire now as assistance in a technological sense will enable us make up for the years we now lag behind in comparison to developments in the rest of the world.

Methods of Media Resistance—the Example of Radio B2-92

[Originally dated 10/22/2000]
Even though a certain amount of coordination and joint planning between the independent media and the representatives of the Democratic Opposition of Serbia (DOS) was in place, the lion's share of the job was done by the independent media themselves. Support provided by international organizations and donors was certainly important but not crucial. All the planning, organizational structure, and methods of struggle of the independent media against Milosevic's regime were the result of their own creativity, ingenuity, and effective strategizing. The example of Radio B92 and the Association of Independent Electronic Media (ANEM) clearly shows how our own experiences, technological innovations, and creativity in our programming contributed to the creation of a parallel and powerful information system. Despite the repression, this system ultimately developed into a source not only of unbiased and balanced news and information, but of new social values as well.

Even before it became clear that DOS achieved a historical victory in the federal and presidential elections on September 29, 2000, the regime's preparations for the final showdown were already underway. Everyone knew that Milosevic would not accept defeat and hand over the reins of power peacefully. This was why illegally mounted links and powerful radio and TV transmitters, above all in Belgrade, were activated precisely on October 5. The first images of dramatic events in Belgrade on October 5 were broadcast from one of these RTV B92 transmitters in downtown Belgrade. This was the footage rebroadcast by CNN that the whole world could see. At the same time, this was the official launch of TV B92. Another radio transmitter was set up by Radio Pancevo in Zemun as part of our contingency plan—in case the police shut down our own radio transmitter. The circulation of the independent press almost doubled during the period from September 29 until October 5. Undoubtedly, this translated into enormous political pressure on the regime.

As chair of ANEM in the former Yugoslavia, and former chief editor of Belgrade's leading independent radio station, Radio B92, I have often heard questions such as the following: "How have you managed to survive and develop the independent media in spite of the oppression Milosevic's regime has imposed for the last thirteen years?" Besides displaying curiosity, the question often reveals reservations about the authenticity of the local media scene. The answer is simple: our actions have been inspired by a devotion to the original principles of human rights, by the principles derived from the best tradition of journalism, and by a readiness to make changes regardless of the level of oppression. Nevertheless, I have to emphasize that without the use of new technologies, continuous experiments, and endless efforts to connect the media and the entire network of independent organizations, mostly by creating new media, it would never have been possible to develop media networking and keep it alive. A number of situations have demonstrated the crucial role of the Internet in overcoming censorship and other problems, as well as in strengthening and intensifying the democratization process within the media, because now almost everyone can have their own electronic media thanks to the Internet. However, the Internet is not capable of providing solutions on its own. On almost every occasion, it is necessary to merge the latest technologies with traditional media techniques.

At present, we are trying to begin at the beginning. The Pact for Stability in Southeast Europe has presented a usable model. The Stability Pact was founded for the purpose of supporting democratic processes, peace, and stability in this part of Europe. The underlying concept is reminiscent of the Marshall Plan, which helped spur economic recovery and restore democratic values in Western Europe after World War II. An increase in local cooperation among media could lead to the development of structures that would help to eliminate border barriers in distributing free information when free speech is radically choked.

The interconnection of regional media is necessary to resolve the censorship problem and combat other forms of oppression. The connection between political and economic events within the region is extremely high, and the fallout from radical political events leads to substantial interference. The attempt to clog the "infected" space from the outside has not produced the expected results, while it has produced even bigger problems, spreading them from the "contagion" epicenter. As a result, an inverted "therapy" has to be applied—a broad opening. This can be achieved, above all, by increasing the range of broadcast information. Having access to a broad range of information, with in-depth quality, is extremely important for any society that has experienced serious trauma stemming from war and totalitarianism. Information resources of this type must originate locally, since ordinary citizens are still very suspicious of anything coming from abroad. At the same time, news and information from local sources help suppress and root out the xenophobic frame of mind developed under the former regime. Nationalist and neofascist political forces are constantly endeavoring to present the "outer" world as hostile, alien environment and recent history as a complex story of conspiracies and vicious schemes. Radio B92 particularly sought to create programs aimed at protecting minority groups and at reinforcing the concept of diversity, emphasizing that a diverse heritage is an advantage for the country we live in. Often, such an approach was quite risky, but in time this became a trademark of the projects Radio B92 was working on.

After the information epicenter of Radio B92 had been banned four times, along with a number of stations within ANEM (there are more than fifty of them), we were forced to resort to distribution using a combination of many methods. It is of prime importance that the editorial staff remain in Belgrade despite the daily menace. At present we have three dominant ways of broadcasting—radio, television, and the Internet—and we combine them all.

The radio is broadcast on the Internet in RealAudio and MP3 formats. Text-based news is distributed on the Internet in Serbian, Albanian, Hungarian, and English. These announcements are designed in such a way that they can immediately be printed and distributed as bulletins in areas where there is no access to the Internet (which has been done in a number of cases).

Apart from providing the news, the site offers analyses and daily discussions of several topical issues.

Radio B2-92 is downloaded from the Internet and distributed via satellite as an analog broadcast from the BBC satellite, and digitally using commercially leased satellite time. In this way the satellite and Internet perform two simultaneous functions. First, they broadcast information directly, and second, they act as a "prosthesis" enabling simple rebroadcasting. As a result, thirty radio stations in the country and ten or so within the region are rebroadcasting the radio program, which is important because for most citizens this is the only way of accessing B2-92. The stations cover parts of Serbia, including Belgrade, and in this way they compensate for the lack of free electronic media in Serbia. The idea of free regional program transmission has practically been accomplished, and this transmission is important for freedom of speech, for democracy, for resistance to war and terror, and so on. The entire distribution is administered by media structures within the country, in cooperation with partners in the region. This increases independence, the best strategies are used, and the imposition of other strategies and distribution systems is avoided.

Apart from receiving the signal through ground transmitters, there are numerous alternative ways of distributing the signal. A great many independent television stations broadcast the B2-92 current affairs programs covered as teletext from the website at <http://www.freeb92.net>. A huge number of nongovernmental organizations arrange public access to the program by receiving the signal from the Internet and rebroadcasting it through public address systems in city squares, coffee shops, and clubs.

This has been the radio's destiny for the past five years—an ongoing combination of both supersophisticated and primitive means of transmission. Such a range offers myriad combinations depending on local possibilities and on one's imagination. The production centers have been organized flexibly. If the police storm the offices again, the program can be immediately produced from different locations connected with ISDN and from sites where journalists trained in editing and live distribution can send material to the main server. The server is controlled remotely and located in a place where no staff are located. In case Internet traffic is disrupted or the telephone lines are disconnected, the most important locations have wireless connections (this has already been established as a parallel network) and the broadcast will be resumed within ten minutes.

Television broadcasts can be arranged in various ways. Since the technology is complex, it is difficult to conceive of simple strategies and to protect the production center. For the time being, production is based in various minicenters. As for the main news, each center, branch office, and local transmitter has equipment that enables it to broadcast material through ISDN to the coordination center, where it is packaged into the integrated current affairs programs. At the same time, a PC dish allows the downloading of reports from other television stations. The center sends the packaged news program via the Internet through a rented tunnel to the center abroad. From there it is forwarded via satellite to local stations. These later transmit the program via ground transmitters. In the same way, the program reaches stations within the region from which it has been rebroadcast, so that it can be watched in Serbia, including Belgrade. In this case too, we are forced to combine the sophisticated and the primitive, so the program is sent, often by car, to a center for satellite distribution because of possible interference and frequent telephone traffic cutoffs.

In addition to the ground rebroadcast, the program is screened on video projectors in squares, coffee shops, and clubs or at specialized video projections in cinemas. Some private cable systems also rebroadcast the program. The television program uses the site <http://www.freeb92.net> and its news services and converts it into teletext format. The content of other sites is also presented, which enables users to obtain very full information. This is extremely important, because few people can afford to buy newspapers, while independent newspapers are suffering newsprint shortages that limit their circulation. In some cities, with no local television stations, rebroadcast via video senders is being used. The program is received via satellite dish and recorded onto a VHS tape. Later, by means of a video sender it is broadcast throughout the entire neighborhood at a scheduled time published on leaflets and distributed as part of the scheme.

In this way, it is possible to cover entire towns with the program, depending on the topography.

An additional level of communication and information provision is a regular information service distribution through mobile-telephone short message services (SMS). SMS is free of charge in Yugoslavia, and the most important news from the site is packed into appropriate packages and sent to interested mobile-phone owners. SMS is also used as means of communication in extraordinary circumstances, during protests, periods of violence, and so on. In addition, a lot more citizens in Yugoslavia own mobile phones than computers. Thus this form of information infrastructure is of major importance, and can be averted only by preventing all SMS distributors from accessing the local mobile-telephone system. In this case the website is a central news checkpoint, which, beside being a regular website, provides information to the classical distribution systems: radio, television, satellite, microtransmitters, SMS, print, public-address systems, cinemas, and so on.

Since the regime has threatened to take over control of the Internet or to supervise Internet communication more rigorously, developing secure web mail with the help of XS4ALL and MDLF is in progress. All appropriate organizations and individuals will be able to use the <freeb92.net> domain services, and traffic among those supplied with an address will be absolutely safe, which is of great importance in Serbia nowadays. The only requirement is Internet access through any provider. A possibility for alternative access is being prepared in case the state blocks the classic Internet access (though this is hard to carry out, it is always necessary to have couple of alternative options in order to prevent panic and to provide security).

The existing exchange of materials and programs, which has been done in a traditional way via satellite, is moving to the Internet as well. Correspondents from the province have been provided with laptop computers and have been trained in editing and posting material prepared for broadcasting. Like the central studio, all individual stations will be able to use the material. To ensure security, servers outside the country will be used. This will increase communications opportunities. Because of similar projects developed by One World and the Baltic Media Center, this form of communication will cover the entire region, which will also increase the transfer of free information and will advance the spread of media communications.

Sets of DV cameras and editing equipment have been provided to branch offices and material distribution is carried out as if it were radio: the material is sent directly to the central studio, but also posted onto servers so that the stations within the network may use them and download them by means of PC dishes. It is possible to combine DV cameras, laptops, and satellite phones in cases where communication is unusually restricted.

Ongoing education is of major importance. Training journalists in using the Internet, computers and software, digital recorders, and DV cameras creates an integrated system in which a journalist turns out to be a powerful medium for news production and distribution. Another aspect of education is connected with training representatives of NGOs and similar organizations in the use of the Internet as a tool for the creation of their own media that can fit into broader information systems. At the same time they would take responsibility for the information posted. Media decentralization like this creates systems that can lessen the force and influence of monopolies and processes that marginalize minorities and marginal groups. Coordinating the central program with local programs by supplementing and synchronizing the information content renders the artificial issue of viability of local media pointless. A networked local media loses its mark of locality—at the same time it is both national and regional, minority and urban.

The possibility of carrying out these developing projects leads us to the conclusion that it is necessary to create a new kind of journalist who, apart from having elementary journalism skills, possesses a high level of responsibility and knowledge of how all the media function. Such multiformat skills are essential for a media system such as B2-92. It is in practice necessary to introduce the concept of a universal journalist, not an encyclopedic polymath familiar with a broad range of fields, but a professional familiar with print journalism, radio and television, online journalism, and information-distribution mechanisms (of his or her personal product). This should be someone who knows how to take advantage of the technological capabilities of the equipment and how to use the information available in the most efficient way.

These new abilities are not all that is required, because the need for legal protection increases with increased information transfer. Legal interpretation of the consequences of providing certain information is also needed, as is information on legal regulations, on the results of expanding the limits of intellectual freedom, and so on. For this reason, a virtual network of lawyers and legal media experts is being created to enable faster protection of journalists through the existing and real ANEM lawyers' network. By regionalizing the project, a more efficient network for monitoring the threats to media and to freedom of speech is being developed.

Radio networks, television networks, print-media networks, and the Internet media can only come together as an integrated media system if they are connected with the Internet.

The controlling element that prevents this network of networks from turning into a dangerous media monopoly is the network of nongovernmental organizations and movements. This is especially true of the cultural and subculture institutions, which promote numerous progressive causes but are neglected and marginalized in the main media arena as media outsiders. This kind of networking is the only way to establish a balance with the monopolized media controlled by a few people. If we manage to preserve the media as communications channels independent of business and government, the interests of diverse social groups can be represented.

This is extremely difficult to achieve among public, state-owned facilities and where other private or ideological monopolies exist—but in some periods, Radio B2-92 managed to function as a commercially successful medium without losing its basic characteristics: political and financial independence. The ANEM network also demonstrates that it is possible to establish dynamic communication between public and private media within the same network with the aim of cooperating in support of the universal principles of human rights and of good journalism. Interaction with other media networks and media from other countries is becoming necessary for media functioning, which makes media isolation on the part of a society quite impossible.

We are aware of the difficulties this kind of utopian project will face in order to survive the period of transition and the conflicts that will emerge from the free market once the authoritarian state and the walled-off society are a thing of the past. We will do our best to preserve these models in spite of all the misfortunes the transition period brings. To do this we will rely on the same subversive use of new media and new technologies that we now employ in pursuit of freedom in a hostile environment.

B92 Today, between the Past and the Future

[Written in July 2000; supplemented in 2002]
In July 2000, the social and political climate in Serbia was rather paradoxical. The entire civil sector and independent media radiated positive energy and optimism that a historical breakthrough would take place in the elections on September 29, but at the same time, the representatives of the Democratic Opposition of Serbia (DOS) were much more restrained. However, this picture slowly began to change for the better. It looked like the independent media and the civil sector managed in time to transfer their energy and optimism to opposition politicians. One of the key elements in the crucial turning point was the regime's brutal repression of the members of the People's Movement "Otpor" (Resistance). Torture, harassment, and beating of young Otpor activists by the police and ruthless mercenary thugs sparked popular revolt against the regime.

The media served as a particularly important fulcrum for the rebellion. They were not only reporting on all the incidents, but also published information and analyses of the ongoing changes in public opinion. Thus, hopelessness and despair were replaced by optimism and determination to bring about necessary changes.

To be able to speak a little longer on the subject of "B92 Today, between the Past and the Future," I will present a brief overview of B92 and its most important projects.

B92 today consists of a diverse range of civic communications activities. Radio B92 is the most successful radio station in Serbia, with the highest ratings in the region it covers. Through the ANEM network, the program is rebroadcast by up to seventy other radio stations in Serbia, Montenegro, Kosovo, Bosnia-Herzegovina, and the entire world, via the Internet in MP3 and RealAudio format.

Television B92 has been the most interesting media product in Belgrade in the last few years. It has one of the highest ratings in its viewing area, with credible news programs, debate on formerly taboo issues, quality popular science programs, cartoons, and live coverage of war-crimes trials from The Hague. In terms of content, TV B92 may be seen as a public service that has tried to develop a model through which it pays for itself.

Another key component is <B92.net>, a website serving as the shop front for all B92's projects. This site has the heaviest traffic of any site in the former Yugoslavia and is the only medium carrying news in Albanian, Hungarian, Serbo-Croatian and of course English. Its forum opens daily debates among people of different nations and points of view and of various political, social, and sexual orientations.

B92 publishing brings out more than forty books a year and two magazines.

More than ten new CDs of the most popular local rock bands are released each year under the B92 music label. The best known B92 DJs are Boza Podunavac, Gordan Paunovic, and Vlada Janjic.

B92.Rex is a cultural center, with the international Ring-Ring festival of world music, alternative theater, political debates, and provocative presentations.

B92.wars 91–99 is a documentation center dealing with activities such as the archiving of documents, books, studies, films, and oral histories of the wars of the last decade. This program is designed to launch news as well as educational and science projects in order to provide the public with extensive information about events buried by state propaganda.

The B92.concert agency now hosts a series of concerts by the big names in Roma music from around the region, as well as celebrated musicians and DJs from all over the world—acts like Giles Peterson and Manu Chao.

B92 also organized two large concert tours. The "Silence Won't Do" rock tour was conceived as a protest tour with the three best young Serbian bands at the time, to mark the first anniversary of the draconian 1998 Public Information Act intended to choke the independent media in the country. The bands of the moment were Sunshine, Darkwood Dub, and Kanda, Kodza, and Nebojsa, and they toured twelve Serbian cities and towns in November and December 1999, with the extensive logistical support of the ANEM network. Rock shows throughout Serbia represented miracles in themselves, after years of steady economic collapse that rendered any efforts of local promoters to organize such events infeasible. It was obvious that such spectacles would attract large audiences of young people, and we took advantage of the momentum to organize parallel roundtable discussions focusing on the state of the Serbian media in order to stir up a nationwide public discussion on the issue.

Our "Rock for Vote" tour was even more ambitious, and the B92/ANEM team pulled off another miracle—the biggest rock tour in the history of pop music in Serbia, a traveling festival with six to eight bands playing in twenty-five cities and towns throughout the country. All of this was organized despite enormous political pressure on the part of the regime while Otpor activists (providing essential logistical support in the field) were being molested, harassed, and detained by the police on a daily basis. We managed to capture the attention of 150,000 young Serbian citizens, and the final outcome of the 2000 parliamentary and presidential elections proved that the main objective was achieved—80 percent of first-time voters did go to the polls after all . . . casting their ballots to bring about fundamental change in the country.

A rock tour, part of Save the Children and RTV B92's "I Have a Say, Too" campaign, was organized in June and July 2001. The tour of local bands included cities with children's centers. The campaign was aimed at educating the public on the issue of children's rights. All profits went to orphans and other children in need.

B92.communications is responsible for Internet provision and satellite links. This involves technical support for our other activities as well as commercial Internet provision. Increased communications capacity is crucial for professional journalism, democratic processes, social reform, NGO operations, the process of facing the past, links to other media, and the exchange and dissemination of information.

B92's idea to launch the truth and reconciliation process began to take shape during Milosevic's rule. In addition to producing the radio shows "The Hourglass" and "Catharsis," B92 published a whole series of books about the wars and the disintegration of the former Yugoslavia. Thus, a translation of the book on the Srebrenica crimes was first published in Belgrade, and only later in Bosnia-Herzegovina. In early 2000 the first international conference, titled "In Search of Truth and Reconciliation," was organized. Journalists, intellectuals, and representatives of NGOs from all the former Yugoslav republics took part. In May 2001 another international conference, "Truth, Responsibility, and Reconciliation," took place in Belgrade. It featured the experiences of other countries going through similar processes, particularly the experiences of the South African Truth and Reconciliation Commission. Radio B92 set up a special documentation archive on the wars from 1991 to 1999, collecting testimony, documentaries, video footage, books, and various documents related to this tragic period. At the same time, exhibitions, screenings of documentaries, and public discussions on these topics were being organized throughout Serbia.

At this time, B92 is broadcasting the following programs:

Radio on

- One FM frequency, certain segments of which are rebroadcast on more than seventy radio stations that are members of ANEM
- One satellite channel for the whole region, certain segments of which are broadcast on more than thirty television stations belonging to ANEM
- The Internet in MP3 and RealAudio format

Television via

- Four television channels, with another twelve in the pipeline
- Satellite
- Another satellite for live coverage from The Hague
- A third satellite is to be activated soon for the regional daily exchange of news packages intended for a central news program with CCN in Croatia and Mreza Plus in Bosnia-Herzegovina.

B92 Montenegro and B92 Kosovo are both in the pipeline.

The media group must be organized in this way in order to be able to present its programming as efficiently and successfully as possible, so that the content may have the broadest influence possible. If the distribution goes awry, the quality programming could go unnoticed, which immediately means the entire project is unsuccessful. This often results in more than just one unsuccessful project: it usually involves compromising the goals that should have been achieved.

Basic Features of the B92 Program Concept

Some of B92's activities in the past have functioned as an informal truth-and-responsibility commission.

B92 Radio

B92 radio has for years broadcast a weekly program called "Catharsis." This uses investigative reporting and professional radio reports to reveal war crimes committed in the former Yugoslavia. The idea behind this is to "put your own house in order first." But it does not balk—usually in coproductions—at discussing crimes committed by other nations.

B92, for example, works with the media outlets and production houses from Croatia, Bosnia, and Kosovo. It has just finished a documentary on the crimes committed in the territory of Kosovo, in Suva Reka (in coproduction with Kohavision, Albanian TV station from Kosovo) and on the crimes committed in Western Slavonia (in coproduction with the Croatian independent newspaper *Feral Tribune*).

The weekly program "The Hourglass" has won a large number of awards for the two journalists who produce it. The program has tackled a series of taboos, critically and without compromise, generating an ongoing polemic on topics such as crimes, both actual and spiritual, as well as the issue of lustration. By "lustration" we mean preventing those who breached the laws and caused great tragedies in the region from continuing to work in state and public institutions. For example, journalists who were actively involved in the Milosevic propaganda machine are still working in state television and receiving salaries from the state budget. They should be allowed to work in private media outlets, but they should be forbidden by the act of lustration to work in the media that should serve as a public service and that are being financed by the taxes of the citizens.

Such topics are also a priority in our regular news programs.

B92 Television

One of our highest-rated programs is the series "Truth, Responsibility, and Reconciliation." This presents the most significant films on war crimes, and films that present an analytic and documented view of the fall of Yugoslavia. The films are followed by live debate among witnesses, victims, and perpetrators of the events with experts, historians, and the like.

We produce television documentaries as research on individual cases. These have included films about crimes in the Croatian region of Slavonia and films about the role of state television in inciting crimes. A film investigation of crimes against Muslims in Strpci and Sjeverin has been completed. In that investigation the crime against sixteen Muslims is reconstructed and the murderers are discovered. After the film was released, charges were brought against them; two of the men were arrested and are currently facing court trial in Belgrade. This is a very good example of how investigative journalism can initiate change within a society. Through this film, the Muslims in this region can witness how the Serbs exposed the crimes and found the murderers, thus creating the mechanism for their later trial. By this gesture, although it is painful for them to go through this horror again, they still have a feeling that the matter is over; no matter how hard it is for them, they also feel that justice can be satisfied. This may be the best example what we want to accomplish through such initiatives.

These projects frequently rely on coproductions. We are currently collaborating with Pristina's Kohavision TV on a major documentary about crimes against forty-eight Albanian civilians in Suva Reka in Kosovo.

Through our coproductions we are building professionalism and emphasizing the dynamics of collaboration. This is often necessary—for instance, B92 does not have access to material on crimes committed in Kosovo, while Kohavision cannot work on the story of mass graves around Belgrade without serious risk.

Direct live coverage of the trials in The Hague as a joint project with IREX is one of our largest undertakings. This is not only because of the technical requirements of covering the trial itself, but also because we are able to produce a whole raft of supplementary material. This includes live reports from our correspondents as well as programs about the way the court works and about the prosecution and detention center. This serves as an educational program for the entire society on the way justice works in the West. It is a chance to see a court that has integrity and to understand how that integrity is achieved. This project also includes programs about the crimes, interviews with experts on the trial, and coverage of past trials in which sentences have already been handed down. We have also produced programs about the media corruption of the past under the title "Lest We Forget."

B92 Documentation Center

The B92 Documentation Center organizes public debates that are filmed and then broadcast on television. Debates are organized throughout Serbia via our website. Thus, for example, several debates on the topics featured in the book *How Did I End Up in a War?*, published in Croatia, were organized. Participants from all sides in the wars in the former Yugoslavia took part in these panel discussions. The exhibition of photographs by Ron Haviv also caused a tumultuous response on the part of some members of the public, which, in turn, was the occasion for organizing several debates on this issue. These are only some of the issues raised by RTV B92.

B92 Publishing

B92 Publishing produces books on war crimes and the experiences of other nations in the process of confronting the past.

B92 also organizes conferences on truth, responsibility, and reconciliation. In terms of sheer volume we have done much more than the state in this area to date. This kind of engagement is based on the belief that

- If we do not grasp our recent past, we will build our present and our future on false assumptions, beliefs, and stereotypes.

- If we do not face the errors of our past, we will again seek excuses for our present in the same place Milosevic sought them—in the guilt of others, global conspiracy, and so on—rather than in the weaknesses of the society. These weaknesses must be faced in order to understand reality.

- If we do not fully comprehend our reality, reform programs will be based on false premises.

- The problems of the repressed past will boomerang, like the permanent problem of lack of cooperation with the tribunal in The Hague, or the problem of Mafia and police links, or problems with the business elite who amassed their wealth through privileges granted by Milosevic.

- Without a radical break with the past there will be no change in the cultural model under Milosevic, which has overwhelmed the entire society, from culture, through education, to the media.

- Unless we face the past, we will never know what is good for us and what is bad for us.

- By not facing the past, we neglect our duty to the future, leaving new generations to pay our debts, just as our generations have paid for the repression of World War II in our country. This gave rise to new vengeance forty years later.

- And, finally, without engagement we will be unable to demonstrate authentic belief and strong will to institute changes that should benefit every single individual.

This is a very difficult project. People are finding it very difficult to face the past. The wounds are still open and people's reactions are often highly emotional. Pressure from the right is disrupting some events, such as the exhibition of photographs by Ron Haviv and certain debates. But some very noble human characteristics have also emerged from these debates. This is a promising sign, indicating that it is possible to undertake a program of cleansing and healing, both of the society and of the individual.

The Present

For the past year and a half, B92 has been trying to obtain licenses for national coverage of the whole of Serbia. After a series of skirmishes and our refusal to compromise, some progress has been achieved and we have received temporary licenses. We are now working on implementing our project for national coverage that will enable us to be competitive in the market. We ignored the prime minister's refusal to extend our coverage, when he said "We'll give them medals, but not frequencies."

We have leased a building in which we will bring together all our operations, which at present are scattered throughout six locations around the city. This will increase our efficiency and cut costs and, by interaction among the different media, will result in a stronger influence on the audience.

We have recently finished the privatization of the part of government owned capital, and MDLF (Media Development Loan Fund) became one of the owners. B92 employees now own 70 percent of the capital, and MDLF owns the remaining 30 percent. (MDLF is known for supporting ideas and initiatives in the media sector worldwide). In this way, we will succeed in keeping an independent editorial and business policy as well as shield ourselves from media moguls and the media monopoly.

Our progressive and critical concept of the media as a watchdog fighting for the public interest remains unchanged.

B92 has managed to keep its balance in a position where it has had to participate in the changes taking place in society, to expedite reforms and other aspects of the transition, and to educate the public about the inevitable hardships they are living through—in other words to support the establishment of a legal, efficient, democratic state. At the same time it must act as a watchdog and be uncompromising in its criticism of the shortcomings of the authorities, along with any irregularities, injustices, and abuses that may occur.

We are now hard at work transforming our management, bringing in new people who are not burdened by the legacy of the past and by a guerrilla mentality. Intensive training and exposure to new experiences are assisting us in formulating new strategies and structures, which is all part of our day-to-day job. The constant attention of experts brought in by IREX (the International Research & Exchanges Board is the premier U.S. nonprofit organization specializing in higher education, independent media, Internet development, and civil-society programs in the United States, Europe, Eurasia, the Near East, and Asia) and of those who have been connected to the B92 project for a long time gives us an opportunity to evaluate these changes ourselves.

The Future

A series of public-service-style programs on B92 radio and television are being planned on the following topics.

- On privatization, in cooperation with Ministry of Privatization
- On savings, with the Yugoslav national bank
- On the rational consumption of electricity, with the Ministry for Energy
- On the badly needed new cultural model
- On the development of local-government democracy, which is impossible without professional local media
- On the fight against corruption, which is impossible without constant public questions, investigations, and checks and balances
- On the freedom of speech and the need to monitor the repression of journalists and the media
- On young people and the challenges they face
- On the transition, as a public educational service
- On nonviolent conflict resolution
- On violence and terrorism, and on the radical right and their ideas and development
- On new technologies and opportunities to catch up with the rest of the world

To a large extent the independent media have retained the credibility and confidence of the public. This is why they are the simplest tool for the democratization of society and for the establishment of peace and stability.

By opening up the region, B92 is attempting to create channels of communication for all the processes involved in stabilizing the region.

Without the flow of information from credible institutions, of which the region has precious few, there will be no open communication on other levels.

It is most important that B92 cooperate with nongovernmental organizations, as well as with government and state bodies, cultural institutions, and international organizations, in a series of programs and projects that demonstrate the people's resolve for uncompromising reform and change.

This has been a very brief glance at a complex project that has been built up over thirteen years. It will continue to develop, as a genuine project that encourages a range of initiatives and that supports individuals and groups in any country, in any part of the world under the yoke of dictatorships and tyranny, any place where there are problems with political and social transition and with the vision of the future.

Confronting the Past, Facing the Future

This chapter was written several months before (July 2000) the peaceful revolution in Serbia on October 5, 2000, which toppled Slobodan Milosevic and his regime.

What is the real contribution of Radio B92 to the development and strengthening of civil society in Yugoslavia? It would be very difficult to assess the contribution of various participants in this lengthy, painful, and, quite often, extremely risky process. However, it is possible to present an outline of Radio B92's impact. The process of social transformation—from extreme nationalism, xenophobia, and widespread fear to democratization, tolerance, and optimism—is still an almost alchemical mystery. But these are the challenges that every serious analyst of social and political processes and of the traumas of the past has to confront. During the Milosevic regime, Radio B92 was something of a shelter for all minority groups—antiwar activists, opponents of nationalism and war, members of ethnic minorities, young draft dodgers, refugees who found themselves in Serbia after suffering the horrors of war, and NGOs fighting for basic human rights. The voice of truth and reason in such times involves not only encouragement but also a call for action. This was why Radio B92 was under constant pressure from the regime. Thousands of well-educated and creative people have been a part of B92 for the past decade. Their creativity, as exemplified in the programming of Radio B92, was a precious experience and the best antidote to hopelessness and despair. Harboring hope and keeping it alive was the most essential task of Radio B92, which helped interconnect and develop citizens' consciousness and social progress in Serbia and Yugoslavia.

Radio B92 was founded in 1989 and banned four times—in March 1991, then in 1996, in 1999, and the last time in 2000.

After B92 was taken over by the apparatchiks of the Milosevic regime in the midst of the NATO air strikes against Yugoslavia, an international campaign under the name of Help B92 was launched. The epicenter of this campaign was in Amsterdam, with the support of the Dutch ISP XS4ALL, with which OpenNet (B92's Internet department) had been cooperating since 1995, and with help from the cultural center De Balie. The ultimate objective of this campaign was, above all, to attract the attention of the international public, which was at the time riveted to the refugee crisis in Kosovo and to the NATO bombing, to the fate of B92 and its staff. Help B92 was also intended to show to the B92 staff that despite the war, they had not been forgotten and still enjoyed the support of international media activists.

One of the actions organized by Help B92 was NetAid, a twenty-four-hour nonstop program on the Internet (netcast) consisting of messages of support and music dedicated to B92. The well-known musicians and DJs who gave their support included REM, Neil Tennant (Pet Shop Boys), Sonic Youth, Mike Watt (Minutemen/Firehose), Kruder & Dorfmeister, Sofa Surfers, John Acquaviva, and many others. Radio B92 celebrated its tenth birthday in exile with its first NetAid organized on May 15, 1999. NetAid events were held five times in all; the last ban was on May 17, 2000, several days before I was due to appear as a guest in Seattle at Computer Professionals for Social Responsibility's (CPSR) "Shaping the Network Society" symposium. During the following five months we managed to implement a strategy that was instrumental in the way the dictator was overthrown.

At that time B92 was known as B2-92 because the regime, during the previous banning, had hijacked our premises, our name, our equipment, and everything we had. Within hours of that banning we had resumed transmission from an illegal location (where our studio is still located) via an Internet connection to an uplink outside the country. This distributed our signal to about thirty local stations inside Serbia. Interest in our news program was growing daily. We rapidly created a situation in which, for the first time, the rest of the country was receiving better information than the capital. This was the beginning of the end for Milosevic, because this is when we began creating the concept of the march on Belgrade, which happened on October 5. We knew we had to cover as much territory as possible and so began creating the Pebbles project, a ring of transmitters outside Serbia's borders that would supplement the broadcasts from local stations in Serbia. We also launched a television program from an illegal location in Belgrade.

We established:

• Several illegal studios in Belgrade for the preparation and broadcast of radio and television programs and web content.

• A studio in Bosnia that enabled the repackaging of programs and transmission to the satellite; we combined distribution of television programs on cassette with distribution via the Internet; the radio station was operated remotely via the Internet from Belgrade.

• A satellite uplink in Bosnia-Herzegovina from which the radio and television programs were distributed to the transmitters of local stations and to NGOs in places where there were no independent stations.

• We installed a powerful radio and television transmitter directed to Belgrade and Vojvodina on a mountain in Bosnia (this was blown up, probably by supporters of Milosevic or Karadzic and Mladic on the first day of transmission; however, we quickly restored the system and set up new transmitters).

• We established a news system on a high mountain in Romania that covered the territory of Serbia.

• We established an illegal television transmitter in central Belgrade in a municipal building housing many opposition representatives who could mount a defense of the transmitter, which began broadcasting on October 5 in agreement with opposition leaders.

We acquired mobile equipment that did not weigh journalists down too heavily. We also insisted on several sets of communication equipment to connect journalists, which was extremely important for the safety of each journalist and editor. We leased a number of illegal apartments in which journalists and editors could hide from possible danger.

When the march on Belgrade began, we had organized total coverage in order to create a winning atmosphere, to show the resolve of the demonstrators to see it through to the end, and to present every incident involving the police, so that the world would be aware of what was happening moment by moment. By that time the ANEM network covered almost all of Serbia. On October 5 we managed to reclaim our premises that had been seized by the regime eighteen months earlier.

That day marked a new period in the development of B92 (we are using our original name again).

We resumed operations as a multimedia platform, the highest-rated radio station in Belgrade, the emerging television channel, and the most-visited website in Serbia. All of these operate as separate media, but with a high degree of interaction, in order for each of them to become more efficient and stronger together.

The new democratic authorities have not realized the importance of the independent media in the transition period; they have not grasped the fact that these media can become a dynamo for reform and change. Instead of redressing the injustices done to the independent media by the Milosevic regime, the government decided to freeze the situation. This left the independent media in a disadvantaged situation, because most of them still do not have the licenses they were denied, for political reasons, by the Milosevic regime. Meantime, those broadcasters who had acquired privileges under the Milosevic regime continued to enjoy these privileges under the new authorities in exchange for their loyalty and their propaganda services. Subservience was regarded as of higher value than professionalism and unbiased reporting. The independents continued to struggle.

Today, a year and a half later, new broadcasting legislation is being adopted. Under this legislation the government will again have a predominant influence on the allocation of frequencies. There is a measure of disappointment among the media, but also great maneuvering space for new battles for unbiased journalism.

B92 has not changed its concept: it still plays the role of watchdog of democracy as well as actively assisting and supporting reform processes. We are trying to present B92 as a regional project because it is the only media company that has positioned itself in a balanced way between the past, the present, and the future. Only B92 has provided comprehensive, live coverage of the Milosevic trial in The Hague, through our own satellite system with a crew covering all the events from The Hague.

Without properly facing the crimes of the past, without acquainting all citizens with what was done in their name, it is impossible to create a concept of a better future. A repressed past will always return.

9   Rethinking Telecenters: Microbanks and Remittance Flows—Reflections from Mexico

Scott S. Robinson

The community telecenter movement is barely underway in Latin America (see www.tele-centros.org). Telecenters share many different labels (e.g., Centros Tecnológicos Comunitarios in Argentina, Infocentros in El Salvador, Cabinas Públicas in Peru, Centros Comunitarios in Mexico). But in essence, they are public places where for a reasonable fee users have access to the digital resources of the Internet, some information technology (IT) training, and local content development. Telecenters can be interpreted as cybercafés with a social conscience, and may be perceived to be in competition with each other. Both offer Internet access, but telecenters are grounded in community protests and organizations while cybercafés are strictly commercial. While the first phase of pilot telecenter projects (1997–2001) is now over, or should be, many of the lessons learned have yet to be assimilated by policymakers and funding agencies, domestic and international, allegedly concerned about digital inclusion (or the conventional misnomer, "divide").

Meanwhile, public schools and libraries languish without connectivity, and in the name of privatization and structural adjustment throughout the region social services have been curtailed across the board. At the same time, the let's-get-everybody-connected slogans, such as those that appeared in an April 2000 *Time* Latin American edition, confuse public opinion. Moreover, costly, hardware-based, high-profile, difficult-to-replicate pilot programs may be polarizing the development business (or is it the business of development?).

The World Bank is galvanizing a Global Development Portal, www.worldbank.org/gateway, which is encountering significant opposition among nongovernmental organizations. Current funding sources and independent websites may be displaced by the institutional megainertia of one of the world's foremost development agencies, whose actions (and inactions) influence many agendas everywhere. The major players, both in the IT industry and in the public sector, are trying to position themselves to benefit from rolling out connectivity to the digital have-nots throughout the region. And all of this is taking place in a context of countries with limited if not null economic growth.

Few are lobbying for public policies that employ the public sphere to catalyze social development with Internet-based financial institutions linked to local organizations. These organizations would provide the connectivity allowing diaspora groups from many lands to finance projects they design and control (there are precedents far away: www.communitybank.com.au). And it may turn out that without these policies, fewer than expected can play in the "new economy," because the entrance fee is exorbitant for the majority who today and tomorrow will have no telephone, no personal computer at home, and no credit to acquire the basic components of knowledge-society participants.

The argument here is simple: community telecenters represent a cost-effective strategy for offering digital services (especially nowadays, when bidirectional Internet by satellite access is becoming an affordable reality in the region). When paired with microbanks, telecenters can be paid for in large part by migrant organizations, which may invest in this mechanism to lower their communication costs with kin at home while dramatically lowering their remittance-transfer costs as well.

In today's world where borders are porous, just lines on maps, the savings on costly telephone calls and the usurious transfer tax currently being paid to Western Union, Money Gram, and fellow competitors could more than pay for the dual telecenter networks. This strategy would work among the transnational migrant neighborhoods in the North and in the villages, towns, and urban slums in the New South (Mexico, Guatemala, El Salvador, Honduras, Nicaragua, Dominican Republic, Haiti, parts of Colombia and Ecuador, to cite Latin American examples). To be fair, there are analogous networks of migrants inside and ringing São Paolo, Buenos Aires, and Santiago, all centers for low-skill jobs in the southern cone of the Western Hemisphere, drawing migrants from Bolivia, Paraguay, Peru, and beyond. The impediments to this proposal are regulatory—that is, political—no longer technological.

If the Second (socialist) World disappeared after the fall of the Berlin Wall, perhaps that label may now be transferred to those migrant populations beyond another wall—one that separates those with connectivity from those without. Certainly, the millions of foreign migrants working in flourishing industrial and service economies in the North (including the Gulf states) and far South (e.g., Johannesburg, Capetown, Singapore, and Sydney) represent the perverse, new Second World created by the surging capitalist economy and today's consolidated global labor-migration patterns. However, these minorities are today spread throughout many lands, and live on the fringes, often sharing an illegal status. They are relatively unconnected to digital services, are increasingly organized in hometown associations (HTAs), and share a purchasing power not found at home, in everybody's Third World.

Meanwhile, the connectivity rate, or digital density, is growing for the inhabitants of the First World and their cultural cousins among the elites throughout the class-and-ethnically-polarized Third World, whose masses are obliged to migrate so that families may survive. A strong argument could be made that we are witnessing a return to the colonial dual economies of yore. The metropolitan capitals and ports generate wealth and work, feeding their own while exporting value abroad, while in the traditional industrial and new technological cores, a Second World provides cheap labor for the First.

Remittance economies now drive families' subsistence strategies at home in the South while fueling labor-intensive service and assembly industries in the North (and far South). These economies exploit the migrants' illegal status and adaptability to harsh conditions as a result of their cultural and kinship networking (an asset the economists label as social capital). In fact, the migrant networks are a de facto employment agency subsidizing many companies and regional economies.

In Latin America to date, digital inclusion is not a priority (some critics even question the elites' commitment to this process). For example, mediocre public school systems and their dropouts are not being equipped with, nor are their teachers and students being trained to use, today's digital tools. While some vanguard cities in the North offer free wireless connectivity (WiFi, 802.11b), most of rural Latin America is only watching television. Or, if they are fortunate, they are chatting and superficially surfing the Net from strictly commercial (and expensive from the perspective of local purchasing power) cybercafés, where the available digital resources are vastly underutilized.

Similarly, public libraries, abounding in the North, are either nonexistent or subsist with few books and services in the South. Nurses, always on the underequipped, underpaid, and gender-sensitive front line of public health services, staff rustic clinics in which medicines are scarce, work demands are overwhelming, epidemics are underreported, and continuing education courses are often unknown. Some migrants' hometown associations are supporting improvements to health services back home.

A few privileged public universities offer online extension courses, but duplication of expensive efforts is rampant and planning for economies of scale often nonexistent (even among U.N. agencies). Providing public-domain information and training in its production and use is not a priority for policymakers in Latin America today, with the exception of the unique INFOCENTROS project in El Salvador at www.infocentros.org.sv and perhaps the www.telecentro.cl project in Chile. Argentina is retooling the destiny of its incipient national network of community technology centers (www.ctc.net.ar). Before the October 2002 federal election, Brazil failed to open a transparent funding spigot with the vast resources available in its FUST program (Fondo Universal Servicios de Telecomunicacoes). Colombia is launching Compartel with Telefónica de España at the helm (experiencing technical and financial problems with its partner, GILAT). Mexico has announced an ambitious e-Mexico program (www.emexico.gob.mx)that may become a gold mine for hardware and software providers, in accord with a top-down plan, dumping computers into local-government installations without trained staff and without some degree of consensus around the central query: What can the Internet do for us and our community?

Thus, it should come as no surprise that universal access, microbanking, and community telecenter services, as well as content creation attuned to public, local needs, are either absent or are low priorities among public telecommunications agendas throughout the region. Meanwhile, commercial television generates demands for the delivery of knowledge and skills that few countries in the South are committed to providing, much less equipped to supply in the short term. This frustrated, pent-up demand for access to the jobs, resources, infotainment, and opportunities implicit in the new information economy may be one of the elements subtly fueling widespread rural and urban discontent, understood to be more than the everyday indignity of widespread poverty.

The reality of capital (profits and loan repayments) and migrant-exporting economies in the South conflicts with the rhetoric of expensive-to-maintain Dot Forces, Digital Dividends, U.N. task forces (and documents) calling for more attention to digital inclusion and exhortations preaching market-driven development from the North. Increasing globalization appears to translate into more food insecurity and environmental degradation, as traditional farmers get forced off the best lands so that these can be used for profitable export crops. In Mexico, for example, half the population lives from and in the informal economy, and over half the population is by official reckoning poor.

It should come as no surprise, then, that vast regions in many countries now live from remittances from émigré family members obliged by conditions at home to move abroad, with papers or without. These resources now account for the majority of aggregate incomes in many small towns and villages throughout the region (www.worldbank.org/wdr/2000).

This chapter proposes a novel use of ICT, linking the First and Third Worlds via the transnational Second World of extensive migrant populations who already bridge the poles. As noted above, the idea is straightforward: expand the extant, fledgling network of community telecenters using either satellite or local Internet service provider (ISP) Internet connections linked with local and regional microbanks. These facilities can provide digital remittance services while offering a set of generic financial, communication, education, informational, insurance, and even e-commerce resources. For more information on telecenters, see (www.idrc.ca/pan/telecentres.html.)

To begin, we need to ask who would use a rural or community telecenter, especially if the best and the brightest have already left the village. Observing the pattern of telephone usage in rural, migrant-exporting regions, we can see that significant resources are invested in communicating with kin abroad. Many of these communication exchanges, we assume, fall into the category of "when-are-you-sending-money-home?" conversations. In Mexico reliable estimates peg the total transfer costs of remittances at an average of 18 percent of the more than U.S. $10 billion sent home every year by the more than 18 million *Mexicanos* who are living north of border, 10 million of whom are relatively recent (<25 years) migrants. This is now the second source of foreign exchange for the Mexican economy, ahead of income from the tourism industry in the national accounts.

In addition to having to deal with a poor exchange rate—one usually below the going market of currency conversion—migrants pay a service charge on both ends of the transaction. Together the transfer and communication costs represent a significant chunk of capital that could be redirected to create a rural microfinance system currently absent in most regions of the Third World. The operational premise here is that practical people will use the system if it represents a significant savings over current practices and if it is secure, user friendly, linked to hometown associations, and available close to home on both ends (see www.cap.org for a profile of microfinance institutions).

The microbanks required to handle digital remittance transfers can assist their clientele in exploiting certain benefits of electronic commerce and can operate back to back with telecenters offering ICT training and skills, which are useful in the migrant job markets. In addition, local people may be trained to create and maintain a public domain of local information and decision support systems, which are yet unavailable in Mexico and other migrant-exporting countries, for example. The telecenter, on the back side of the microbank, may also offer voice over the Internet protocols (VoIP), distance-education services (www.icde.org), and access to basic medical insurance for those who today have nothing. Simply put, this initiative could represent a win-win scenario for migrant communities North and South.

What is required to jump-start this telecenters-cum-microbanks proposal? Because migration networks are community based, each microregion is the hub for its respective network of citizens who have left to work elsewhere. Therefore, research needs to detail each migrant-exporting hub (regions tend to share an overlap in destinations and patterns) as well as the location of migrant clusters and the credibility of hometown associations. Information would also be needed on the existence and location of credible institutions open to negotiating low-cost digital alternatives for sending money home with state-of-the art tools (credit unions in California, for example), as well as on the community's commitment to collaborating with the proposal.

The goal is to develop a managed and secure system that drops the transfer cost to a minimum, estimated to be about 2.5 percent of amounts sent, while providing a series of Internet technology–based benefits and services as well as an introduction to the culture of information, as asset by itself.

In effect, the marginal condition of domestic and international migrant communities, the Second World, remains a social liability. However, their increasing political clout can be transformed into an asset—the motor for local and regional development at home—by a judicious application of ICT in conjunction with community will and local organizations. The Mexican government for one now seems to understand the strategic value of working closely with migrants and their organizations inside the United States.

The issue of connectivity is being resolved by what promises to be a competitive market in Internet-by-satellite services recently announced for Latin America (see, for example, www.panamsat.com, www.gilat.com, and www.newskies.com).

Whether connectivity is achieved by satellite or by dedicated lines (which the Red Científica Peruana first demonstrated to be feasible in Peru around 1995 and with joint ventures elsewhere), this proposal is no utopian fancy. Instead it is a function of local infrastructure, the portal players and their carriers, and, oftentimes, regulatory caprice.

A complicating issue is the lack of a clear and public commitment on the part of Latin American national telecommunications regulatory bodies, whereby universal access and competitive markets and pricing may be induced by the rules of engagement and politics in each domestic market. It is almost redundant to remind ourselves that the public sphere requires such commitment from the appropriate agency of the state charged with advancing and protecting the universal-access policy goal. Nor should we forget the historical impotencey of civil society and/or nongovernmental organizations' (NGOs') policy proposals in the increasingly lucrative and oligopolistic Latin American telecommunications scenarios. This is cause for major concern and debate. In addition, the latent complicity of the regional development banks (for example, the Inter American Development Bank) should call our attention to their lack of any systematic proactive policy regarding the regional telecom services' regulatory environment.

It may not be farfetched to suggest this waffling on such a key issue is deliberate, employing the handy argument that we cannot violate "national sovereignty" in this age of blatant globalization of capital flows and market access. Without this pressure from the multilateral financial institutions, local accountability, and citizen input, national regulatory commissions are beholden to their clients: ruling elites, the small group of international carriers and their associated portal players. This does not bode well for the future public sphere and innovative proposals therein. One option to counteract the closed-shop script now in play involves using existing international organizations, such as the Internet Society, together with coalitions of activist NGOs and progressive international funding agencies (for example, the Canadian IDRC; see www.idrc.ca). These groups could create countervailing pressures and credible policy proposals difficult to ignore by all of the institutional and corporate actors involved.

The issue of the appropriate software for secure remittance transfers and other banking and commercial functions is central to a project of this nature. It requires an effective public key infrastructure (PKI) (www. pkiforum.org), which consists of three components: a certificate authority (CA), preferably to be installed in each country where operative; a registry authority (RA) for each institutional and individual actor in the network; and a repository of all certificates. Such a system also implies using a personal digital ID card (readable with a biometric device, for example) to be installed at both ends of the system. This is no small challenge, and there are currently efforts to resolve the formidable cross-certification issues (CA-to-CA operations, issues also linked to permissible encryption software exports). Making secure remittance transfers possible on a large scale requires resolution of the problems inherent in designing a PKI with CA cross-certification (Moskowitz 2000).

Low-cost digital remittance transfers permit the creation of microbanks on a broad scale in home towns, villages, and periurban neighborhoods. In effect, each migrant could administer a personal account at a terminal with an IP connection, from anywhere. To be sure, the established commercial banking community in migrant-exporting countries such as Mexico and others understandably do not embrace this financial innovation with enthusiasm (although some innovations have been announced as the competition increases). It is a situation analogous to the legacy technology telephone (POTS) companies, pressing regulators to outlaw (as long as they dare) VoIP or Internet telephony. There may not yet be a generic microbanking model with the requisite off-the-shelf accounting and operational software, but the present convergence of interests and proposals is today historically unique (see www.soc.titech.ac.jp/icm/icm.html). Again, the points of resistance are regulatory, hence political—not a function of the available technology.

International NGOs and some of the major foundations assume microcredit and banking to be a central issue on today's agenda (see, e.g., www.gsips.miis.edu/ips1/ips1d7_IS581.html). In sum, digital remittance transfers can capitalize local and regional microbanks in migrant-exporting communities and countries. These microbanks and their associated money transfer operations, once approved by national financial regulatory agencies in each country, may be an appendix to established credit unions or local savings and loan institutions. Each branch requires the requisite PC with a reliable connection to the Internet and the PKI CA and RA software, as well as the means for dispensing cash to clients. This latter function can be the most problematic component of the proposed system, because the cost of secure armored-car service to remote regions in Latin America is almost prohibitive and logistically complex.

Until key local merchants are willing to accept debit cards issued by microbanks, for example, the cash-dispensing function will remain an obstacle for bank clients in the villages and small towns without regular bank branches and orthodox automated teller machines. (In Mexico, two-thirds of the nation's 2,443 municipalities do not have a branch bank.) The development of a low-cost, third-generation ATM for microbanks in Latin America is an innovation waiting to happen.

The issue of "community currency" is relevant here. The concept of "open money," analogous to "free software" and hinged on trusting social networks, may become an operational fulcrum of future microbanks offering many services in the "virtual capitalism" predicted by today's visionaries (see www.openmoney.org.) While such speculation is far removed from today's context, it should remind us that money is a symbolic system, and the rather closed circuits of migrant organizations from the same set of villages and small towns offer a potentially fertile ground for experiments relating to community currencies (Hart 2000).

On the back side of each village microbank there will be a telecenter—a public, low-cost access point for the Internet and IP services, including telephony. The voice over the Internet protocol service together with web-cams alone will pay for the operation of the fully equipped telecenter. Each telecenter may have five or six PCs in a LAN connected to the Net—some by satellite and dedicated lines where available—and others may be obliged to use dial-up services to regional ISPs in the meantime. Regional fixed wireless options are also becoming viable, whereby microregions share a single medium-speed Net connection while linking themselves with unlicensed 2.4-GHz fixed wireless modems and antennas. Telecenter users may not only communicate and see their relatives for less cost than long-distance POTS calls involve, but also may have the wealth of Internet-supplied information and content services at their disposal.

It is, however, important to distinguish a telecenter from a cybercafé. A telecenter offers IT training and generates reliable local and regional information, placing it on a website for public consumption. Cybercafés offer Net access, but they have no or a very limited role in local institutions and training programs. A telecenter may become a key auxiliary to schools and clinics, offering continuing education for local teachers, nurses, and doctors, if any. As noted above, a telecenter is a cybercafé with a local heart, user training programs, and commitments to social programs.

The issue of who will create and maintain the continuing education courses as well as lobby for their certification on the part of national education and health authorities is central to the microbank-cum-telecenter strategy. The issue cuts to the heart of the potential transnationalization of public services, a process certain to raise the hackles of legacy bureaucracies. Basic and intermediate IT training packages plus decision support systems—in addition to elementary PC software usage plus Internet browsing—can be another component of each telecenter's menu of content services. For example, a three-telecenter project in Morelos state, Mexico (www.telecentros.org.mx), demonstrated a pressing need for decision support systems for small farmers, high school students considering university study options, and municipal employees navigating state and federal rules and resources.

Given the current rates of out-migration, the growing strength of home-town associations, the improbability of major changes in the current skewed global development model, plus the impossibility of attenuating the observable and widespread ecological impoverishment in the diverse regions, it makes sense to offer job skills that will be useful in the future workplaces in the North (yes, online training for migration!). This is a need that younger returning migrants have expressed to me in a number of different locations within Mexico.

Viewed in this fashion, local telecenters complement microbanks by offering communication services, IT and other skills training, and continuing education for local professionals who staff local institutions. (See www. telecentros.org for information regarding Latin America–wide efforts to create telecenters, and www.telecentros.org.mx for access to a pilot microregional community telecenter project in Morelos state, Mexico.) It remains to be seen if cybercafé owners and operators are keen to collaborate with the more socially oriented community telecenters, but if they do the resulting network offers ample connectivity today for Mexican migrants. Paradoxically, the obstacle is the lack of points of amicable access inside the United States, where the hometown associations have been slow to innovate with Internet connectivity services for their respective constituencies. Public libraries tend to not be user friendly points of Internet access for Latino migrants.

On balance, microbanks capitalized by digital transfers from Second World migrants in the North sharing Internet connectivity with telecenters in small towns and villages in the South translates into another level of consolidation of today's parallel migration-fed remittance economies. This regional dual economy wherein migrants are feeding their extended families at home and subsidizing small and medium-size manufacturers with their cheap labor in the North is now a vast, regional if not global phenomenon. The geography is impressive, as noted; it extends from the U.S.-Mexico border, around the Caribbean, and down the Central America isthmus, in pockets throughout Colombia and Ecuador, and as far south as Peru. And the Africa-Europe and South Asia–Middle East Gulf States' energy economy–based networks are analogous.

Today this is a U.S. $100-billion-plus volume of transfers, larger than foreign aid and development loans combined. In order for the novel public-sphere initiative proposed here to move forward, considerable research is necessary to investigate these "markets," and to create the series of reliable databases for each community-based overlapping social network in each national migrant stream. The Inter American Development Bank has begun this task, via its Multilateral Investment Fund. In fact, this research has established that the migrant-exporting Latin American and Caribbean countries received U.S. $23 billion in 2001, an amount surpassing all the bilateral and multilateral aid budgets for the region (Fernández-Vega 2002).

Today, that research is neither uniform in its coverage and detail, nor available for many countries' migrants. Research in Mexico has produced an enormous body of materials (see www.embassyofmexico.org/english/4/3/migration3.htm, as well as www.thedialogue.org/publications/lowell.pdf). This information is often updated, because the government has finally publicly recognized the importance in the national income accounts of the more than U.S. $10 billion that Mexican migrants send home every year. (This sum includes over $8 billion via commercial courier services, registered by the banking system, and an estimated $2 billion by personal messengers; accurate figures do not exist.) While the statistics are uneven, nevertheless there are a few overview reports in the public domain offering current data and profiles of migrant networks, remittance-sending patterns, and resource use in home villages (see www.pop.upenn.edu/mexmig/, www. globalexchange.org/economy/alternatives/americas/Immigration.html, as well as www.thedialogue.org/publications).

For example, El Salvador is now considered a full-blown remittance economy, receiving approximately $1.5 billion a year from its transnational community abroad (www.jhu.edu/~soc/pcid/papers/18.htm). Guatemala, Honduras, and Nicaragua rank in the same category, although their respective national financial elites refuse to disclose accurate national-accounts figures. For example, available El Salvadoran online data and analysis contrast dramatically with those of its neighbor, Guatemala, where few credible contemporary studies of the pattern of native Mayan out-migration and remittance transfers appear at www.gtz.de/orboden/thiesenh/thi4_b.htm and di.uca.edu.sv/publica/proceso/proc755.html. The same statement applies to the rest of the Central American countries, with the exception of Costa Rica, which receives many migrants (rough estimates peg it at 800,000 people) from neighboring Nicaragua. Not too many of the million-plus Panamanians leave home.

In sum, a substantive public sphere attuned to the needs of the extensive migrant communities has yet to appear in most of the nations with remittance-driven economies in the South. Given the current cyber–gold rush underway whereby carriers, megaportals, cable companies, satellite service providers, franchise ISPs, and all of the major IT players enjoy a feeding frenzy in high-carat markets, many loosely regulated at best, it is unlikely much priority will be assigned to the public sphere and the priorities of underrepresented diaspora Latino migrant communities spread around the United States, Canada, and Europe (often ignored or discriminated against by their respective consular officers).

It may be that the extensive migrant communities and organizations, today's Second World, will create and pay for a network of microbanks and telecenters to serve their own needs while simultaneously crafting a new digital public sphere in their home countries. This is not as far-fetched as it sounds. Each telecenter would generate a menu of local and regional information that municipal and provincial governments do not offer in the public domain at this time. In effect, the telecenters would substitute for certain functions of local government as well as educational and health institutions (see som.csudh.edu/fac/lpress/articles/villages.htm).

Again, it is paradoxical that those with the least may creatively gain the most while generating a public sphere of information and accessible online opportunities that national elites today are reluctant to offer, much less support, with investments of the public resources they control. The Second World may hold the key to an effective multiplier effect for their kin at home, as well as for the balance of their respective national populations. In addition, remittances today assure balance of payments' stability. The irony of this linchpin effect, linking the First and Third Worlds, should not go unnoticed.

If the migrant organizations catalyze the telecenter and microbank rollout in their countries, this would constitute a globalization irony bar none. This scenario may soon turn into a reality in key Latin American regions, given the following prerequisites: the convergence of IT-conscious transnational migrant organizations, the growing rural microcredit movement, a few pilot telecenter projects, an extensive network of cybercafés throughout the region, some enlightened regulatory agencies on both ends, available connectivity and open-source shareware, plus increased innovation by IT-savvy local entrepreneurs. I trust it will happen soon. How can you participate?

Notes

An earlier version of this chapter appeared in *OnTheInternet* magazine, 6(2) (fall/winter 2000): 20–24.

10 The Role of Community Networks in Shaping the Network Society: Enabling People to Develop Their Own Projects

Fiorella de Cindio

Many attempts have been made to provide a definition for "community network" (see, e.g., Center for Civic Networking, 1993; Schuler 1994; Beamish 1995) or related initiatives, such as "free nets" and "civic nets." Furthermore, over the years, community networks (CNs) have addressed a variety of goals and evolved along several paths. The original idea, the subsequent initiatives and their evolution, their successes, and their failures, lead to a concept of CN that includes:

- Initiatives that guarantee everybody Net access, thus granting everybody citizenship in the networked society (Gurstein 2000)

- A free online environment designed to promote and favor communication, cooperation, and the exchange of services among citizens and all the public and private members of a local community (nonprofit organizations, government institutions, and companies), while simultaneously opening the local community to online communication with other parts of the world (De Cindio, Sonnante, and Cannada 1997); from this perspective, the expression "community portal" has been applied

- Virtual cities, interwoven with the real city, that support communication and work, thus extending the city into a new dimension where time and space constraints are reduced (De Kerchkove 1998)

- Intelligence systems for local communities (Civille 2000; Schuler 2001).

All these characterizations are accurate, in the sense that they focus on different aspects of CNs. However, probably the most adequate and powerful way of representing CNs is as enabling environments that promote "citizen participation in community affairs" (Schuler 2000). Going a bit further, we could say that they incite citizens to conceive and implement projects of their own that are relevant to civic life through the interplay of four elements:

• The net—typically through thematic forums—brings people with related interests together and encourages them to collaborate.

• Civic/community networks focus on a specific geographic area, and this, in turn, implies that online encounters of those who share an interest are easily translated into face-to-face meetings.

• The attention paid by civic/community networks to promoting "citizen participation in community affairs" increases the likelihood that virtual and real relationships will generate ideas for action and projects designed to improve the quality of life for all the members of the local community, a feature that does not rule out the possible business nature of the projects, which may have an impact on people's professional life in any event.

• The community network provides a technological, organizational, and possibly institutional context—that is, a computer-based cooperative environment—that fosters the accomplishment of projects.

Briefly stated, CNs can be seen as the appropriate sociotechnical environment for enabling citizens to develop their own projects that shape the network society. I will try to give evidence for this on the basis of the nine years of activity of the Milan Community Network (Rete Civica di Milano, or RCM for short).

I first present RCM's initial goals and design principles. Then, after a short summary of RCM's state of development, I describe several projects that have been carried out over the years on RCM. These projects concern government institutions as well as schools and nonprofit associations, but they are presented through their promoters' stories and words. Finally, I summarize the outcome of these projects and discuss whether and how they can be seen as ways to shape the network society.

Declared Goals and Design Genes of RCM

When we started RCM, in September 1994, our "declaration of inspirational principles," designed as the network's online presentation, stated that

RCM intends to make available to citizens an online and free environment designed to promote and favor communication, cooperation, and the exchange of services among various components of the local community: citizens, their groups and associations, public-sector organizations and companies, enterprises that operate in various sectors of the market, and information providers; thus helping guarantee the de facto right of online citizenship to all, while opening the local community to online communication with the rest of the world.

The above sentence includes the three basic goals we declared for RCM:

- To provide citizens with access to the Net: a free and easy-to-use environment offering everybody *hands-on* learning in information and communication technology

- To offer the various elements of the local community, especially its citizens, a shared field for mutual cooperation

- To affirm, two centuries after the French Revolution, the right of citizenship in the global networked society

These three goals are largely shared, with different focus, by nearly all the experiments in community networking. If we wish to extrapolate the peculiarities of the Milan experience that make it significantly different from other similar experiences, especially in Italy and elsewhere in Europe,[1] it is probably most important to describe a set of features that are, to some extent, all mutually related. I will call them the *genes* to stress that they come from the origins of RCM and played a fundamental role in its development. It is no accident that several authors, including Winograd and Flores (1986) and Rheingold (1993), point out that the images and conceptual apparatus of biology are well suited to a description and study of the evolution of the Net. We realized "ex post" the fundamental role of these genes in explaining the strengths and weaknesses, and successes and failures, of our initiative.

The University Gene

RCM was launched as an initiative of a university laboratory, within the Information and Computer Science Department, rather than being promoted by a local governmental institution (municipality or province, roughly equivalent to a county) as was the case with the vast majority of CNs in Italy and other European countries.

Like schools and libraries, universities are public bodies, but unlike local governmental institutions, they are *free from* the direct influence of *politics*. Especially in Italy, where every action, project, and idea is immediately labeled either as "on the left" or "on the right," this independence from politics has been a fundamental feature. As part of its university heritage, RCM adopted the institutional and "universal" approach. It believes it has a duty to relate to all, starting with the local governments democratically elected by the citizenry, and is committed to avoiding discrimination or favoritism and instead to offering opportunities to everyone. RCM is financially poorer than other Italian CNs directly supported by their municipalities but is richer in terms of freedom (since the financial support the other CNs receive comes at a price: they are ultimately controlled by politically oriented local government). We believe that in the medium to long term, RCM is healthier because of this freedom. Often, as new local administrations have been elected, those coming to power have viewed the local CN as a project of their predecessors that was not likely to reward the new administration, and they have thus neglected the general interest and left their town's CN to its own devices. Where such CNs had not developed an independent identity of their own and become self-supporting, they had to reconfigure themselves along new guidelines (usually turning into the institutional website of the municipality (Miani 2000), or they withered or closed down (Luisi 2001).

Universities—like schools and libraries—have education and the spread of knowledge and culture to everybody as their major goals and activity. Moreover, the university, especially a computer science department, promotes research and innovation. Unfortunately, research often is merely academic and does not relate to the local community. The Department of Information and Computer Science (DSI) of the University of Milan has a long tradition of research and experience in networking technologies, in the culture of computer-mediated communication, in security, and in the computer-supported cooperative work (CSCW) that has been the cradle of development for the prototypes of many of today's most widespread network applications. The ability to distill the best of the many ideas and products offered by the world of information technology (IT) and, later, of information and communication technology (ICT), is not the exclusive property of the university context, nor is it guaranteed by it. However, if things work as they should, the university provides greater opportunities not only to stay abreast of the rapid pace of innovation but also to keep a pulse on the situation in order to understand which ideas have a future and which do not. This ability to understand and evaluate innovation arises only if and when good and reliable communication channels exist among teaching faculty and researchers (who have developed an ability to think in abstract terms), students (who have the energy and enthusiasm for the new that the former may tend to lose over time), and the outside world of enterprise, professionals, and alumni who compel the university to develop new projects. Students and graduates in computer science and other degree programs working as interns at the Laboratory of Civic Informatics (LIC) have always been the resource that enables RCM to tap new talent and new ideas,[2] allowing for what might be termed an "amortized" and enriched turnover. And, because managing a CN (like, more generally, any virtual community) usually is extremely stressful and leads even the most resilient to burn out, this factor may be the key to avoiding death by fatigue and abandonment.

The CSCW Gene

RCM began in a university laboratory that inherited know-how and perspective from CSCW with a twofold focus. On the one hand, Winograd and Flores (1986) and others (De Cindio et al. 1986) focus on conversations, semistructured patterns of speech acts, through which people make commitments and shape the social relationships of the group. On the other hand, C. A. Petri (1977) and others (De Cindio, De Michelis, and Simone 1992) emphasize the pragmatics of communication, through communication disciplines that must be considered in order to understand communication problems within social contexts. From these backgrounds RCM inherits its continuous, dogged insistence on not wanting to reduce the Net to a new broadcasting medium. Instead, the Net is seen as a communication, cooperative, and knowledge-sharing environment. In turn, RCM's experience, according to Schuler 1997a, contributes to extending CSCW concepts and technologies from their original emphasis on work to a broader focus on all facets of human activity.

The Participatory-Design Gene

The second fundamental background element that the RCM laboratory inherits from its "parent" laboratory is participatory design. Computer scientists and professionals learned at their own expense that computer-based (CB) systems have to be designed not only *for* the users (as trivially understood by any systems designer and software developer who wants her or his application used by those who need it), or *with* the users (as promoted by the sociotechnical design tradition). The development of such systems, to be successful, requires the direct and *active* involvement of users—that is, CB systems must also be designed *by* their users (Briefs, Ciborra, and Schneider

1983). Participatory design has evolved over the years (Schuler and Namioka 1993; Blomberg and Kensing 1998). As with CSCW, the need—imposed by the emergence of the network as the common platform for any computer-based application—is to extend the process from its original emphasis on work to all facets of human activity. The slogan that has always been on the RCM desktop and home page— "La rete siete voi" ("You are the network")—springs from this tradition and aims to inspire everyone logging onto the network to be an active member and promoter.

The choice of developing RCM from the bottom up, according to people's interests and needs, was further stressed at RCM's launch. In September 1994, RCM consisted of only a couple of forums filled with a certain amount of content by about fifty beta members. But it also included an empty folder called "RCM che vorremmo" ("The RCM We'd Like to Have") with subfo-rums such as "The City of Women," "The City of Kids," "The City of Cinema," or "Palazzo Marino" (the name of the building that serves as Milan's city hall) to declare the possibility of opening these areas under the condition that one of the community members was interested in moderating and promoting them. Adopting Winograd and Flores's terminology (Winograd and Flores 1986), we presented RCM as "a declaration of possibility," which was another way to stress the participatory-design approach. It is interesting to note that even today "RCM che vorremmo" is a lively RCM forum where the community's most active members discuss RCM's future. If the broad categories classifying groups of forums that appear on RCM's home page today (www.retecivica.milano.it) are substantially the same as those of all the major portals, they do not arise, as do those of the portals, from an a priori definition of possible areas of interest or discussion. Instead they are the fruit of a process of *budding* and *dividing* akin to what took place among Internet newsgroups, with the important distinction that moderation—applied from the outset—has guaranteed that discussion is kept relevant.

As a final consequence of the participatory-design gene, the RCM staff has always conceived of and presented itself to the community as enablers of the social actors, dedicated to:

- Guaranteeing that the network stays up
- Monitoring the dynamic articulation of the network in sections and subsections and providing maintenance such as reorganization and the replacement of moderators who are no longer active

- Keeping the relational dynamics of the network under control[3]
- Supporting the realization of the projects that are proposed from time to time by both individuals and groups, needing "only" (but what a hard thing to do!) to assign priorities in allocating constantly insufficient resources

The Civic-Engagement Gene

The three genes above would not entirely explain RCM's origins. There is a fourth gene, the civic engagement of its promoters. My own civic engagement dates from the time of my master's thesis, which discussed what was then the initial impact of computerization on the public sector. In the early 1980s I collaborated with Italian trade unions in enabling workers to participate in redesigning work that was changing due to the effects of IT (De Cindio et al. 1983). The project paid special attention to the particular problems and opportunities that such changes presented for women (De Cindio and Simone 1985).

In Italy, the initial spread of the network outside the enclave of research coincided with the most significant moment of political change since the Second World War. In 1992 and 1993 a group of public prosecutors from the Milan court (known as the "Clean Hands" Pool) revealed the corruption that had characterized Italian democracy. The political class was thus forced into radical change, while civil society—known in those days as the "fax people" because its voice was heard through the faxes people sent to the newspapers—asked to play a greater role. These events transported the country from the First to the Second Italian Republic.

The social and political climate of those years made it imperative to understand whether and how ICT might foster this process of change in Italian politics. The technology not only looked as though it might give a voice to those who had had none so far but also appeared likely to play a role in freeing politics from the overweening influence of large parties. It seemed poised to increase direct communication between people who, despite differing views, wished to exchange opinions outside the confines of ideological prejudice.

Milan was the ideal setting for an experiment of this type: the "Clean Hands" movement was rooted in Milan, which had—and still has—the greatest penetration of ICT of any city or town in Italy, both in offices and in private homes.

The initial RCM staff consisted of the writer and two young people, one who had already chalked up ten years' experience in the world of free BBSs and one who had just finished his master's thesis in the field of CSCW. We were joined by a newspaper reporter well known in the ICT environment in Milan, who provided us with the first contacts with ICT companies through which we were able to obtain hardware and software donations. All of us, and many of RCM's early members, wanted to verify *in action* whether the network could improve civic communication in our city (among citizens and between citizens and local government), bring together people with shared interests and projects, and thus increase the quality of life in Milan and the Milan area.

RCM's Evolution

Declared (explicit) goals and (implicit) genes have driven our activity from September 1994 to the present. The evolution of RCM can be described:

- In *quantitative* terms, through statistics
- In *qualitative* terms: first, by describing the relevant organizational change that occurred in December 1998; second, by presenting the most relevant projects carried out over the years

This latter point is the most relevant one, and most of the rest of the chapter is devoted to it. Before that the two following paragraphs cover the former points.

An overview of RCM's development can be gleaned from a few numbers, as of the summer of 2003—that is, after nearly nine years of operation:

1. RCM now has nearly 15,000 registered members[4] among the approximately 1.3 million citizens resident in Milan, so that the ratio of RCM members to the larger population is 1 to 87.[5]

2. The growth curve has been essentially constant at a rate of about 200 citizens per month (for 11 months per year).

3. The number of different accounts logging onto the RCM server provides an estimate of how many of these registered members are active today:

- From September 2001 to June 2002 (10 months), 6,397 different accounts logged on.

- From April 2002 to June 2002 (3 months), 3,677 different accounts logged on.
- During May 2002 (1 month), 2,784 different accounts logged on.

4. The RCM server handles messages organized in moderated forums with different access rights: a forum is *public* if all registered users can read and send messages to it, and *semipublic* if this right is reserved for specific groups of users and generic registered members can only read the messages. The semipublic forums allow nonprofit, public, or business organizations to publish information and to inform people about their activities. In RCM there are about[6]

- 187 public forums directly managed by community members
- 348 informational forums managed by nonprofit, public, or business organizations
- 179 discussion forums managed by nonprofit, public, or business organizations for communicating publicly and transparently with citizens: we call these "direct lines"[7]

5. The core RCM staff now consists of three full-time people (although under different contracts, which is outside the scope of this discussion) and a secretary:

- A community manager, who follows online discussions, manages the discussion forums, intervenes in case of flames, and tries to keep the discussion as fair and polite as possible
- A webmaster
- A system administrator who maintains all the RCM computers
- A half-time secretary

In addition, RCM relies on several outside paid consultants dedicated to specific issues or projects. It is worth mentioning that one of these consultants is RCM's lawyer, who plays a significant role in supporting the community manager in keeping the dialogue fair. (On this crucial issue, see De Cindio et al., 2003.)

The RCM Participatory Foundation

Since December 1998, RCM has no longer been just an initiative of a university laboratory, because it acquired independent legal status as a participatory foundation.

The idea of a foundation was taken from Amsterdam's Digital City, which also became a foundation, in 1998. It was our good fortune to come into contact with Enrico Bellezza and Francesco Florian, who were bringing to the Italian legislative framework the participatory foundation, which is more widespread in the United Kingdom (Bellezza and Florian, 2001). A participatory foundation is a cross between a traditional foundation—usually set up by public and/or private bodies to manage investment income to be used for social purposes—and an association of people who share some interest or goal and desire a legal framework to pursue it. Bellezza and Florian propose participatory foundations as an appropriate institutional form to lend stability to various cultural initiatives: local government bodies put in the capital that makes up the participatory foundation's endowment, while citizens contribute through membership dues and/or voluntary work. Other examples of participatory foundations include one whose mission is maintaining a theater in Milan, one that conserves historical documents, and so forth (more about participatory foundations and other examples can be found at http://www.studiobellezza.it/servizi/fondazioni.htm).

The RCM Participatory Foundation (FRCM) was set up to "(a) sustain, also economically, and manage the Milan Community Network (RCM) . . . ; (b) promote the network, spreading its use among citizens, public and private bodies through initiatives which encourage its use by those people who have less opportunities because of age or social condition; (c) become a center of technological, cultural and social innovation" (quoted from article 2 of the FRCM Statute). Local government organizations (the region, the province, and the Chamber of Commerce—while we continue to await the municipality) and the University of Milan, where RCM maintains its operational headquarters, are charter members: each of them has a representative on the FRCM board. Private enterprises are supporting members, contribute a fee equivalent to roughly U.S. $5,000, and elect a representative to the board. By becoming participants (simple members) of the foundation, citizens (who pay dues of about $25), nonprofit associations and school (dues are about $100), as well as small and medium-size private companies (for dues of about $500) acquire the right to participate in managing the foundation by electing a representative to the foundation board. We believe that this structure is entirely consistent with the foundation's overall project, as well as with RCM's goal of favoring communication and cooperation among the various components of the local community. The foundation that manages RCM is based on the participation, in different roles, of the various bodies and of citizens.

So far, in addition to the charter members mentioned above, RCM has 3 supporting members and 111 participants (99 individuals, 8 associations and schools, 4 small and medium-size enterprises). We believe that this percentage, which is low compared both to the total number of registered RCM members and to the number of its active members, can be attributed partly to the fact that the context of the "free Internet" leads people to view the network as a free service, save for the one inevitable toll of local phone-connection charges. The low percentage may also be due partly to the fact that the staff has not yet dedicated the necessary attention and resources to the foundation's membership drive.

People's Projects through People's Words

When I find myself, in a broad variety of contexts, having to give a public presentation on RCM's activities, I repeatedly end up realizing that behind those operations, which often take on institutional importance, there was originally a person who came across RCM, devised a project, and carried it out with varying degrees of involvement on the part of the staff. It is as though, by opening and running RCM according to the principles outlined above, we had randomly sown the seeds and then, over time, put our energies into cultivating those that had sprouted on their own initiative. As a result, we would essentially be in a position to present the projects conceived of and led by some of the most active members of the community without directly involving the RCM members who had thought them up and brought them about (usually the most active volunteer moderators who have used the CN as a platform for projects with implications beyond RCM itself).

However, in the spirit of this work, I decided to ask—once more—for their collaboration. I sent a questionnaire consisting of seven questions with multiple-choice and open-ended answers to a selected sample (eleven people) of community leaders engaged in different sectors of activity. I received eight answers, and all of them authorized me to publish their comments and names. Because of space limitations, I have had to omit one of the answers.

Voluntary-Sector Projects

Maurizio is one of the preeminent figures in RCM. He works full time running a volunteer association that aids drug addicts and immigrants located near the central railway station. His organization, SOS Droga Milano (SOS Drugs Milan), is one of the most active such groups in Milan. Maurizio came across RCM at the outset of the CN, after SOS Droga Milano charged him with developing its online presence. Maurizio writes:

In RCM I have developed several social-awareness and communication projects:

• The SOS Droga Milano initiative is aimed at informing people and preventing substance abuse. This initiative is currently on the Internet as the Osservatorio Nazionale sulle Tossicodipendenze (Italian National Observatory on Drug Addiction) and has a forum, which was originally started on RCM itself as the hotline of the SOS conference.

• In 1996 we also started a project named Solidarietà, whose objective was to group the various Milanese associations and volunteer organizations that were sensitive to the issues of social solidarity. This project gradually grew to focus especially on disabilities, immigration, and societal exclusion.

• At the end of 2000 we opened a new online forum known as "Ricerca Sociale e Storica" ("Historical and Social Research"), whose purpose is to gather material and documentation in areas of specific interest that do not receive the attention they deserve. This forum has also made it possible to develop an in-depth discussion of themes such as immigration, undocumented work, and the relationship between politics and violence.

"Some of these projects," continues Maurizio, "have been redesigned and reworked over time. For example, the project that was originally known as Droga Milano SOS has now become the forum of the Osservatorio Nazionale, while the second project, the Solidarietà space, was fairly successful in obtaining the cooperation of various associations. But the awareness-building and facilitator-communication initiative on social solidarity never really took off."

Maurizio makes an interesting observation about the role of a CN in building activities and socially significant campaigns compared with that played by other media: "I am more often recognized by everyone for my activities on RCM than for my activities on the Internet, in newspapers (and there are many of these), or on television (likewise)." According to Maurizio, one of the reasons is that "countless projects designed to build awareness and social communication are off limits in other media, where they simply cannot overcome the filtering imposed by communication through the mass media, newspaper editorial boards, and TV content managers."

The results are not earth-shattering "though we need not be discouraged because this tool often helps raise the awareness needed to get other media with larger audiences and more users involved. I could cite many cases: the campaign to stop the Province of Milan from closing the Centro Idroscalo Sud,[8] when pressure was originally brought to bear through RCM, and several other cases in which RCM was the means of communication that created the basis for discussion and attention that was then taken up and amplified by other media."

Maurizio finds that RCM plays a fundamental role by making the network platform available and because it provides the projects with a laboratory or experimental context, although the flames that tend to flare on the community network can be harmful. In personal terms, he says that the RCM projects he has worked on have been "positive because they have enabled me—in spite of many obstacles (indifference, small audience, lack of concern for social problems)—to maintain a thread of continuity with the commitment I had made, and negative, as was to be expected in a communicative gamble of this sort, because this confirms how little attention people pay to these social problems."

Mauruzio's work has gained recognition at the national level. The Italian National Drug Addiction Observatory is now linked on the websites of the Health Ministry and of the Welfare Ministry, and access statistics show that it has become a common reference point for people in this field.

Projects in Education

Not even at the time of start-up in 1994, long before the era of the "free Internet," did RCM think of itself solely as a provider: even the free distribution of e-mail addresses was only the first step in a series of opportunities for the guided use of the network in an easy-to-use environment. We used a metaphor rooted in Italian tradition but one that many may recall thanks to the 1953 movie *Roman Holiday*, in which Gregory Peck drives Audrey Hepburn around Rome on a motor scooter. In the postwar period, the growth of Italian private motorized transportation was fostered by the use of motor scooters, inexpensive and easy to use. In the Internet era, we offered RCM as the scooter that makes it possible to learn to drive in the city. After people gain confidence and mastery of the vehicle, they can venture onto the Internet information highway. The driving instructors were the RCM staff members and the "helpers"—the participants in the community with greater expertise in ICT and willing to offer assistance to others.

Things are substantially unchanged in the era of the (seemingly[9]) free
Internet: Clement and Shade (2000) claim that the access problem is not
totally solved because access must be secured at several levels. Mere connectivity does not suffice; people need primary and continuing education
in an appropriate sociotechnical, virtual, and real environment. We
believe that CNs in general, and RCM in particular, provide such an educational environment in which people approach the Net and find—not
once and for all, but over time—ways of understanding how the Net can
support individual interests or personal and professional needs. That is to
say that CNs can be seen as a learning community in which to gain confidence with the communicative opportunities offered by ICT and to stay
abreast of their evolution in a context that provides room for judgment
and evaluation free from conditioning.

This original emphasis on education explains the vast number of educational projects started within RCM. Loredana, Cesare, Laura, Attilio, and
Philip have promoted educational projects in three different segments:
compulsory education (Loredana, Cesare, and Laura); adult learning
(Attilio); and Philip's original project of "online assistance in using English
as a foreign language."

Loredana, Cesare, and Laura can certainly claim the greatest "objective"
success for "their" project, Scopri il Tesoro (Discover the Treasure).[10]

They explain that thanks to the experience accumulated over the years in RCM and
to the concrete cooperation developed among a group of teachers and schools, during the 1998–99 school year a project named 'Scopri il Tesoro') was launched as a
free, practical learning space. This took the form of an online treasure hunt designed
to increase awareness and encourage students, teachers, and parents to gain practical experience in the use of ICT for study and research activities. Alongside the warm
and family-oriented environment of the RCM conferences, we set up a website,
www.retecivica.mi.it/tesoro. This site was designed according to current standards
for access and usability, as a working tool for all—children and adults, computer
whizzes and pupils with disabilities—that develops both the use of new media or
online communication and skills in editing texts, images, and sounds. This represented a natural outgrowth of teaching plans usually applied in the classroom and
the abilities needed to do "homework."

The project makes available to schools a complete and flexible teaching plan that
covers all subjects through online quizzes and logic games. Teachers and parents can
attend distance-training courses to learn how to build multimedia sites, with the
support of tutors, and publish their creations.

"The results," according to Loredana, Cesare, and Laura—who make up the Scopri il Tesoro team—"are more than satisfactory and of higher quality than expected. In the three years the project has been underway, the level of participation of students and classes has been extremely high; more than 600 groups and 6,000 pupils from 350 schools in Italy and abroad have taken part. In addition to Italy, the countries represented include Switzerland, Germany, Uruguay, Belgium, France, the United Kingdom, and Costa Rica." About the role of RCM, the team points out that the CN offers "a protected family environment that appeals to children, to schools, and to families." Yet the Scopri il Tesoro team bemoans the "meager attention of scholastic institutions," which affects their strictly personal evaluation: "This has been a positive experience because it has made it possible to build a community of cooperative teaching that becomes a concrete stimulus for sharing experiences, drawing schools, classes, and teachers to interactive online communication." They add that "it has been an incentive for our group of teachers and specialists to seek additional professional training and has multiplied the relationships with schools, training centers, and sponsoring companies." However, the support in the form of lip service from "the educational authorities that have underwritten the project" led to "an unfortunately excessive financial commitment for the self-supporting project and too great a burden on the educators (because the project is too large to be developed during our free time and the organizations that ought to have undertaken its development failed to assign the necessary human resources)."

Attilio also reports on a project "that sprang from my imagination and was then put together with a group of teachers"—a project that has constantly grown "while nevertheless remaining small," as he modestly phrases it. The idea, simple in and of itself, is to provide adults who reenter training programs and continuing education the ICT skills necessary to guide them in acquiring a knowledge of RCM and then the rest of the Internet. The project stresses the aspects of two-way communication, involvement, and participation. But, as Attilio specifies, it also teaches "civic informatics as a social science that trains people to educate themselves as well as to do remote collaborative work." Attilio emphasizes that RCM lends the project an experimental and laboratory framework and points out that "the success and acclaim of the initiatives proposed have far outstripped my own expectations. The objective has now shifted to other colleagues of mine who may be interested in working on this independently. They need training and the limiting factor is the resources, the time needed to coach them and make them independent." Attilio expresses a decided optimism about the chances for putting this into practice: it is a viable route "that can be taken with *more than* satisfactory results."

Philip has "launched several projects on RCM and nearly all have enjoyed modest success." However, this evaluation perhaps needs to be calibrated against an extremely ambitions original objective: "My original mission statement—making global culture seem less foreign by feeling ourselves a part of it—has been adopted by others both inside and outside the scope of my original project for online assistance in using English as a foreign language." Furthermore, the context in which Philip's project was originally launched has not helped. The city-run schools, directly managed by the municipality, were in danger of closing in precisely those years. They were not in fact shut down, but the education department was certainly not a priority of the municipal administration, to the point that, when city offices were wired, city schools were not included, leaving them with modem connections to RCM as their only access to the Net. Indeed, Philip writes that "city government has been reluctant to allow the adoption of new technologies to influence organizational structure. This reluctance has largely been the product of two fears, a nondescript fear of innovation and a hierarchical fear of individual empowerment. Nevertheless, RCM has certainly improved the quality of city-run schools, especially continuing education, because it has reduced isolation." The idea of reduced isolation crops up again in his personal evaluation: "The project offered me career growth because networked communication has altered the landscape from one of impoverished resources where the educator was a lone combatant in the wilderness to one of exploitable resources in which effort partly is distributed." And I would add that the project promoted through RCM in the city-run schools was a qualification on his résumé in his appointment as a temporary professor teaching technical English in the digital communication degree program at the University of Milan.

Projects in Public Communication
Philip's observations on the reluctance of the city government, echoing the remark by the Scopri il Tesoro team on the lack of attention from the school boards, lead us to key questions for CNs, especially in countries,

like many in Europe, in which the role of the state is greater than in English-speaking countries.

At the outset RCM had no formal relations with local governments. This was no accident: we wished to start up independently both economically and in terms of content. The sections of the network potentially reserved for local government were part of our "declaration of possibilities," but our intention was to seek a relationship with government organizations predicated on our independent existence. We invited the municipality to speak at the RCM inaugural press conference, but at the last minute no one showed up. Thence a long story of basically troubled relations with the City of Milan administration ensued, although RCM has always had much better relations with a large number of city employees. We met with leading figures from the other local government bodies, the province, the region, and the Chamber of Commerce, shortly after RCM was launched. All these organizations are now among the founding members of the RCM Foundation (though we are still waiting for the city), but the CN's relationship with each of them is constantly evolving. Periods of significant collaboration alternate with long silences. Even in cases where the relationship seems consolidated, trifles are often enough to strain it.

All this does not come as a surprise: anyone who has had to deal with government bodies in Italy is used to the ups and downs that often depend on behind-the-scenes politics. Thus we can truly claim that what good RCM has done in the field of *comunicazione pubblica*[11] is thanks to the work of functionaries and officials of the given government body—at any given moment—who viewed RCM as their *own* tool and resource for accomplishing innovative projects and initiatives. If kept within the framework of the government organization, these projects and initiatives would have required much longer to develop and would not have allowed individual officials to take such a leading role. Nevertheless, the "tool" remained part of the public sector, given its position inside the university, and, moreover, part of a public institution that was unbiased because it was shielded from the dictates of politics.

Likewise, difficulties cropped up when these key officials began to show signs of the inevitable weariness that comes with the effort to overcome the "reluctance" noted by Philip. Especially problematic were attempts to use the network not merely for publishing existing information online or supplying electronically services that already exist but also to increase accountability in the relationships between government bodies and citizens. The weariness just mentioned is due to a variety of factors: the inevitable comparison with the glittering portals of the Net economy, where hits are counted in the millions rather than the thousands of community members who send a limited number of questions; the effort required to manage dialogue with the citizenry in a public forum where not all messages are complimentary; and the resistance encountered from politicians, who are still vastly more inclined to pay lip service to the importance of the Internet than to make it truly part of the infrastructure for communicating with citizens. The bottom line is that a press release or a press conference or a short interview with local television, given the filtering provided by reporters and editors, enables politicians to expose less of themselves and to tell only their own version of the truth.

Despite these difficulties, RCM can claim remarkable results in public communication. We have already presented (in Casapulla et al. 1998) the positive results of the projects carried out in cooperation with officials and functionaries of the City of Milan and of the Region of Lombardy. Elda was the key player in the collaboration between City Hall and RCM: "I was a complete newcomer to networking and the ease of using RCM opened the online world to me, thanks to the support of its system administrators. That enabled me to have significant experience under my belt when it came time for my administration to open its Internet site." That experience was truly very significant, given that Elda, who had no prior online experience, is now the de facto content manager of the City of Milan website. And indeed she doesn't hesitate to consider the experience decidedly satisfactory "as long as the organization I work for carried through with its project." The collaboration with RCM is actually not completely terminated because RCM continues to host the still-active "direct line" between the citizens and the city council chair www.retecivica.milano.it/ vicesindaco-ld. However, this is not linked on the city's website—certainly not by Elda's choice. In June 2001, a new direct line was opened with the city council chair (www.retecivica.milano.it/presidenteMarra-ld).

These direct lines are a characteristic feature of RCM's collaboration with local government bodies. A direct line is nothing other than a public forum for discussion and dialogue between citizens registered on RCM—or, at any rate, citizens using an Internet account who have accepted the RCM netiquette known as "Galateo"[12]—and government offices, administrators, public officials, or experts in a certain field (such as tax consultants, lawyers, or labor arbitrators). For those familiar with the network, but not for most people, there is an obvious difference between opening a direct line and simply publishing an e-mail address, as happens on nearly all Italian public-sector websites that provide the e-mail addresses of the mayor, the city-council committee chairpersons, and some or all City Hall employees. Sending a private e-mail is rather like sending a private letter or a fax: it may fall into a black hole and no one will be the wiser.

The dialogue that a direct line makes possible, on the other hand, is precisely that of a newsgroup: here we find the "game of shared gain," the sense of community (I spend time replying to your posting because a query or reply of yours may be helpful to me in discovering and understanding what citizens think) that is the "mother lode of the Internet." It is true that an effectively designed public-service website is an advantage for Italian citizens, who are often forced to waste time asking for certificates and filling in forms, and generally following the complex course of bureaucratic procedures that are required for the most mundane tasks. But what is needed in a country with an intrusive state apparatus like Italy's is the utmost exploitation of the opportunities inherent in ICT for putting institutions in immediate touch with their partners in the social pact:[13] citizens, nonprofit organizations that contribute to the general welfare, professionals, and small, medium, and large enterprises.

The Province of Milan is the local government body least familiar to citizens. The group of officials in charge of communication saw the network as an ideal tool to increase citizens' awareness of the province's activities and initiatives. It sought to use the website to spread information, especially the more static information, while using RCM's direct lines for a more direct and immediate dialogue with citizens, especially the opinion leaders that spontaneously emerge. The success of the direct lines with the province (run by the officials in the communication department) and of direct lines with many other offices led to the opening of a direct line with the president of the province, as far as we know the highest public office on any Italian website committed to publicly answering citizens' questions (www.retecivica.milano.it/PresidenteColli-ld).

The direct line with Province President Ombretta Colli is managed by members of her staff who read citizens' messages and help the president reply. The replies are at times signed by the president (i.e., posted from her e-mail account) and at times posted by her online alter egos, who, as is clear to all, provide official replies in any event. The direct line with provincial President Colli has been the locus of animated discussions about measures adopted by the provincial administration (e.g., the campaign against closing the Centro Idroscalo Sud that Maurizio mentioned above). One thing that clearly emerged from that episode is that the participation of a politician or public official in an online forum is no simple matter, requires the politician's time, and must be desired and enacted with a series of steps that make it real and not merely for appearance's sake. With the help of Daniela, the RCM Foundation lawyer as well as an active member of the community, and of Chiara, who is the officer of the province coordinating the direct lines, we drafted a clause for the Galateo that serves to orient citizens in their use of the direct lines with government bodies. If we want the network to truly bring together administrators and "administrees," citizens and politicians, to become an instrument of democracy, we need to understand that those who reply in an institutional role cannot answer immediately or in the informal terms that have traditionally characterized online discourse, even while we are watchful not to give rise to online gobbledygook or fall back into the geological time frames typical of communication with government authorities.

Another interesting example of the fruitful cooperation between the Province of Milan and RCM can be seen in a service that went online in June 2000 and is now being extended to the entire Region of Lombardy. "@ppuntamenti Metropolitani" (Metropolitan Events, www.retecivica. milano.it/appuntamenti) provides information about what is going on in and around Milan on the web and via SMS (short messages). What is relevant for our purposes here is that the province itself took up a service that had been a characteristic of RCM from its outset and was subsequently long managed in collaboration with municipal officials under Elda's direction. The service consists of enabling announcements of events to be posted not only by institutional officials but also by individual citizens or organizations. This makes it possible to obtain information not only about major happenings but also about minor events, which, though worthwhile, often end up being ignored, totally or nearly, by other media. This achieves the goal that, thanks to an appropriate use of the network, anyone may not only be informed but may also provide information.

The value of these direct lines and the efforts to use the network in order truly to bring government bodies and citizens together gained recognition for the province in the form of an award at a major national exhibition on ICT in the public sector. However, it must also be noted that the opportunities offered—dialogue with major public officials, the chance to contribute to the "@ppuntamenti Metropolitani" service with one's own postings—have so far met with a cooler reception from citizens than might have been expected. Chiara notes that "when measured against the effort required to convince administrators and offices to open a direct line, receiving only a few public questions compared to the avalanche of private e-mail pouring into the president's mailbox is not very fulfilling. There are still not many citizens who appreciate the difference between a direct line and e-mail. This is partly due to the fact that other local government organizations—that is, the municipalities and the region—may not be using direct lines."[14]

This situation brings us back to the issue of mass education about online communication opportunities. It is hard to overcome the habit of using media passively, not only for politicians but also for citizens in whom the preference for private dialogue with their leaders is now ingrained. Moreover, citizens so inured tend to view being informed as a service that is owed them rather than an asset to develop and to which they can contribute. This issue, however, led those of us who manage RCM to recognize the need to promote the services we develop directly. For a long time we subscribed to and put into practice Rheingold's (1993) statement that virtual communities make themselves known through word of mouth. But if CNs really expect to play a significant role on the local level, this approach, as Philip rightly points out, "pales beside the influence of the overweening trailblazing accomplished by the profit-driven rush of enterprise along the toll-free information highway." It also mandates that word of mouth be bolstered by clear—albeit as inexpensive as possible—marketing initiatives.

Community Networks for Shaping the Network Society

In the 1960s and 1970s, the introduction of information technologies in manufacturing and offices gave occasion for a radical redesign of work. Participatory design arose, along the lines pioneered by Enid Mumford's sociotechnical approach, to avoid the failures to which the redesign of work is condemned if it is driven by top management without involving and listening to those who are experts in the work: the workers and employees. However, years of experience have shown that collecting workers' knowledge and exploiting it to innovate work practices in a computer-supported environment is not an individual process. Success comes from knowledge *sharing*, in project teams, in quality circles, and so forth. This social context also supports the negotiation of inevitably different, possibly conflicting opinions and suggestions, and offers a way to arrive at agreed-on solutions (De Cindio et al. 1983).

Today, ICT is not only continuously redesigning work, but is shaping life and society, while humankind is called on to address a multitude of problems, both minor (however relevant at the local level) and major (typically, the environment and globalization). These points are made in the so-called Seattle Statement (Seattle Statement, 2000) developed at Computer Professionals for Social Responsibilitiy's (CPSR) 2000 "Direction and Implications of Advanced Computing" symposium.

A redesign of social institutions and processes that emphasizes top-down planning, based on directives from the decision makers (politicians, influential businesspeople from multinational corporations, opinion leaders in the broadcast media, even a few representatives and spokespersons from civil society) is condemned to failure. To succeed, it must involve and employ the skills and suggestions of the true experts in living, the women and men who are the citizens of the world, whether they live in the First, Second, or Third World.

Nevertheless, gathering and putting to use the experiences and abilities of the citizens of the world and creating the right conditions so that the inevitable contradictions and conflicts can find a means of expression, comparison, and consensus are extremely complex tasks. Redesigning work, in contrast, essentially takes place on a local level, in one factory, office, or company.

In other words, this goal of inclusiveness involves finding the equivalent of project teams and quality circles. It is not even imaginable to implement the sharing of their knowledge and experience without relying on communication technologies that make it possible to reduce barriers of space and time and enable knowledge sharing so as to effectively exploit the complex content made available to a multitude of content providers.

I believe that the experiences I presented in this chapter—and others left out for reasons of space—show that CNs can provide a platform that should be seriously considered from this point of view. By conceiving of citizens as neither "subjects" (as occurred in the past) nor "clients" (the role they play as visitors to and consumers of online public or private services at glittering websites) but as independent actors, owners of a sovereignty and therefore entitled to play a key role in shaping the network society, CNs actually make it possible, on a local level, to:

• Conceive of experiences of social innovation that collect and utilize the experiences and abilities of the citizens of the world, starting locally, where they have greater planning capacity and a greater opportunity to make a difference

• Lead people to the discovery of the potential of ICT, in the broad sense, but with special emphasis on technologies for communication, cooperation, and knowledge management

• Share projects and experiences, extending involvement to individuals and groups beyond the initial promoters, which also guarantees continuity in the face of burnout or other obstacles

• Draw inspiration from others' projects in imagining one's own

We believe that it can reasonably be claimed that these are projects for shaping the network society from the bottom up, by utilizing people's "creativity, compassion, intelligence, and dedication, which can help address the multitude of major problems the human race is faced with" (Seattle Statement, 2000). In this sense, we agree with Schuler (2000) that CNs support "smaller communities within the larger community": the point is that these smaller communities act as a kind of sociotechnical laboratory. It matters little that they may not involve the whole or even a majority of the population of a given area; what matters is that the members of the CN be active promoters of projects that are relevant to all.

Community Networks as New Social Enterprises

Conceiving CNs as sociotechnical environments for supporting the citizens of the world in shaping the network society is an ambitious and demanding goal. Comments from project leaders again shed light on this process. Davide's project in RCM is the "Progetto Associazioni: laying the foundations for the birth and development of a 'portal of the associations,' through which hosting, tools, and services are to be offered to nonprofit organizations in the Province of Milan. The project grew out of the union of my personal interest in the nonprofit sector with the Rete Civica's desire to increase and reevaluate the support given to nonprofit organizations on the Net." In responding to the survey, Davide looks to the future of the project and raises a delicate point:

Community networks are a unique area in which to germinate projects and initiatives that would be hard to accomplish otherwise. In a few cases, however, CNs risk stunting growth, as projects that originate in this context outgrow it. Such projects may need a more stable web presence and find that bringing more resources into play requires a qualitative leap. In my opinion, this is the most delicate point. At the outset, the resources and the assistance given by the Rete Civica are viewed as heavensent. They become the basic soil on which to nurture a tender sapling. As the plant grows, it needs a larger pot where it can grow stronger roots to become a tree that is recognized and respected throughout the forest. In the Rete Civica pot, the loam is of better quality, rich in stimuli, and extremely fertile. But in order to grow as fast as required a project may require greater resources (not just economic resources but human resources as well). In this sense, I am a bit worried about the future of the Progetto Associazioni. I hope that a way will be found to give it the economic and human resources to develop and to serve as a guide in the long run, guarding against the risk, which always lies in wait on the Net, of stalling prematurely.

Just as the creative capacity for redesigning work was often undervalued or even opposed by shortsighted managers, so today's citizens' expertise is often not utilized. Even projects that can claim undeniable success struggle to find—and often do not find at all—the support needed to grow beyond the experimental stage and consolidate. The Scopri il Tesoro team, Philip, Elda, and Davide, say so openly, and many others would agree. Because of this—Davide concludes—"after having used RCM to take off, there is a tendency on the part of those who have launched a project to want to break away, diving into the commercial world to propose the idea again and seek possible routes for independent development." However, this rarely occurs with any success. The world of the so-called Net economy has so far been a gravel crusher for people and ideas. The crisis in this model of exploiting the network has caused many of those who had left to come back to the "fertile ground" of the CNs.

That does not make it any less important, but actually makes it more urgent, to find strategies to enable the public and private organizations that claim to be interested in the development of the network society to provide, through community networks, decisive and not marginal support to the projects that develop there and that would have trouble finding the conditions to take root elsewhere. Public institutions and private enterprise, including the broadcast media, need to be made aware that the resources they would have to invest would still be far less than what they spend year after year for generic promotion on the Net.

The decision to consolidate the RCM experience in a participatory foundation appeared to show that an awareness had been reached—within the local Milan community—that building the network society requires the presence of a variety of players: government organizations, private enterprise, and individual citizens. The RCM Participatory Foundation indeed looks like the kind of "new social enterprise" envisaged in "Community Networking Gets Interesting" (Civille 2000). However, five years after it was founded, it has to be admitted that such an awareness has not attained a satisfactory level either within local governments or in the private sector or, frankly speaking, among RCM members, who have joined the foundation in very limited numbers. So far we have only come across a few forward–looking individuals within certain local government organizations or at one of the few companies that became sponsors of the foundation. Their support for community networking—along with the determination of people like those mentioned in this chapter and the RCM staff, boosted by the enthusiasm of the students who succeed one another in the Civic Informatics Laboratory—have kept RCM alive until now. This does not address the problem posed by Davide, but it does make it possible to continue to seek a response, which, in our view, must spring from a theoretical grounding (what might be termed a model of sustainability) that is not abstract but rooted in practical experience.

A further open question is whether the RCM experience can be replicated elsewhere. At the outset, in the 1995–1997 period, in Lombardy and other parts of Italy, there was an outpouring of initiatives that explicitly drew inspiration from the experience of RCM and attempted to reproduce its success while adapting it to local needs. Some of these projects have now shut down. Others are barely surviving (though with some hope of revitalization). Many have turned into the institutional website of the municipality. Only a few are still active and vital CNs. In attempting to identify the key survival factors, I believe that the four genes discussed in this chapter must continue to play vital roles. We must focus on the ability to avoid falling into a fatal embrace with local government, remaining independent of it while maintaining open doors for dialogue and for ways to collaborate on specific projects with the public sector.

Acknowledgments

I would like to thank the people who responded to the RCM questionnaire; Philip Grew, the patient and precise reviewer of my faltering English; the RCM staff who supported this work with their tenacious, continuous, and indefatigable efforts; and the editors of this book.

Notes

1. A comparison of the CN experiences in Italy and other European countries is beyond the scope of this chapter; the interested reader is referred to De Cindio 2000.

2. In exchange, the CN represents an extraordinary playground for these students to learn about ICT that is not merely a technological playground but also an environment that cares about the needs and relations of its "users."

3. This aspect is, however, not managed by the staff alone but in cooperation with the moderators, according to guidelines that have evolved over the years but that cannot be explained here in detail.

4. The total number of citizens who have ever registered on RCM is actually nearly 15,000, with the difference due to the fact that, in the early years because of the cost of software licenses, those who had not logged on in more than a year were removed from the list of registered users. That also seemed in keeping with the idea of wanting a community of active citizens, although in hindsight that policy proved less reasonable than it seemed at the time. Often, those who had left RCM, especially at the time of the Internet boom and the rise of the Net economy, rediscovered RCM after a long hiatus and logged on again. Finding one's "old" account still active eases reentry.

5. However, this ratio is not very significant because RCM, unlike some other community networks run by municipalities, does not register as members only those who have their legal residence in the city. Such a policy would exclude, for example, the many students who come to town to attend classes at the university or people who live in the suburbs but work in the city. And the same holds true for the figures regarding the resident population.

6. RCM also makes it possible to open *private* areas that are accessible only to members who are part of an organization, association, or other group, either real or virtual, be it permanent or temporary—for example, a project workgroup. Such private areas represent the group's intranet.

7. We discuss this is detail later, in the section "Projects in Public Communication."

8. The Centro Idroscalo Sud was an arrival center that hosted new immigrants to Italy. The area was initially provided by the Province of Milan, while support services and

activities (from food to job-placement help) depended on volunteers. The problem arose when the province decided to use the area for a different purpose, namely, summer recreational activities.

9. In Italy, "free Internet" has meant that no paid subscription was required to connect to a provider, although substantial per-minute charges for local phone calls still applied.

10. Further information on the Scopri il Tesoro project and its origin in the context of RCM can be found in Casapulla, De Cindio, and Ripamonti 2001.

11. In Italian, *public communication* denotes communication between government bodies and citizens, in the widest sense, both as individuals and more generally as partners in the social pact who interact with government organizations.

12. In Italian, *galateo* (from an eponymous sixteenth-century bishop) is the generic term for good manners. In RCM, the word was applied to a localized version of the netiquette enshrined in the service agreement that all CN members must sign, obliging them to abide by certain rules, including tolerance for differing points of view. The role of Galateo in RCM's evolution is widely discussed in De Cindio et al. 2003.

13. This recommendation involves more than simply alleviating the weight of procedural obligations that inspired the moves made by successive center-left governments from 1996 to 2001, and the e-government program of the present right government. It was described effectively in the report of the president of the prestigious young industrialists' association Giovani Imprenditori (Garrone 2000).

14. Actually, as noted above, there are direct lines with some of the leading figures in city government. However, unlike the province's direct lines, which are linked from the official website, the city's direct lines are not linked from the official city site. Space would not allow us to go into the reasons here, but in the final analysis, this reflects a conscious choice on the part of the province, whereas the city's direct lines are isolated initiatives amidst a strategy that prefers broadcast communication through the official city website.

III Building a New Public Sphere in Cyberspace

11   Information Technology and the International Public Sphere

Craig Calhoun

Information technology (IT) and globalization have each been the object of enormous hope and considerable disappointment. So too is their combination in the notion of an international public sphere supported by the Internet and other communications media. This is basic to the dream of international civil society that has flourished since the early 1990s, with the collapse of communism and opening of capitalist markets. And indeed, such an international public sphere clearly already exists. Equally clearly, however, it has not yet provided the basis for cosmopolitan democracy its advocates have hoped.

The task of this chapter is to outline something of the stakes of thinking about an international public sphere, the role that IT can play in it, and some of the challenges that lie in the way of realizing its potential. I will discuss IT and the international public sphere against the background of globalization and the shifting bases of the production and dissemination of knowledge. I will not attempt to review the empirical specifics of where and how and by whom the Internet is used, or how public communication based on one technology compares to that based on others. While this would be useful and there are beginning to be interesting case studies to complement the usual journalistic anecdotes, social-science research on the Internet has barely started.[1] The present chapter does not offer findings so much as attempt to orient questions.

Globalization

Information technology has of course been an important basis for globalization. This did not start with the Internet, despite its hype. From the sextant to the map to the invention of calculus, the development of early modern navigation was centrally a matter of information technology—and the ships circulated information as well as goods and helped to link the globe in networks of exchange and control. Telegraphs, radio, and television, as well as trains, cars, and airplanes, all helped to establish links across space and shorten the time lags to action at a distance. The development of national and international highway infrastructures paved the way to flows of information long before the "information superhighway" existed. Colonial empires were pioneers in IT from at least the sixteenth century. They developed bureaucracies, accounting systems, file-management hardware and software, and both open and secret networks of communication. They also remind us that new forms of war figure centrally in the story of modern globalization—with new weaponry, certainly, but also military reliance on ever more complex systems of control and coordination managed by technologies that evolved quickly from carrier pigeons to coded telegraph messages to satellite transmissions. As the last suggests, too, globalization has all along included an element of surveillance, which has always been a matter of data management and analysis as much as observation, and which has benefited from technologies to improve these activities.

Old though some of the trends are, the last twenty years' innovations in computer and communications technologies have also been powerful. Modern financial markets are inconceivable without computer-mediated communication—and action. Not only are there nearly instant flows of money through global networks, but ever more complex forms of derivatives are driven by algorithms their "owners" never know and trading is done indirectly by software "robots" programmed by their human "supervisors." Satellite transmissions and electronic filing of stories speed up the flow of information through broadcast and print media. New Internet media complement older forms of circulation of public (and sometimes not-so-public) information. Migrants maintain global diasporic cultures and translocal communities partly by e-mail and websites. The Internet is an important support also for global social movements and for local social movements seeking global attention or support. It is important, though, not to imagine that with electronic help popular forces can easily get the jump on more centralized or elite powers—whether economic or political. For all the energy and innovation of global activism challenging neoliberalism or inequality, at least as much and often a good deal more resources are deployed in support of global capitalism. Nongovernmental organizations (NGOs) focus not just on human rights or the environment but on accountancy standards, corporate advocacy, and arbitration between firms. And IT is employed intensively in organizing global production processes as well as global markets. It makes possible not only just-in-time shipping but centralized control of manufacturing facilities that are physically dispersed throughout the world. What distinguishes the last thirty years or so, as Manuel Castells (1996, 1: 92) puts it, is the creation of "an economy with the capacity to work as a unit in real time on a planetary scale." This is a "global" rather than merely a "world" economy. It is also the basis for Castells's metaphor of the "network society," which refers not simply to the fact of global connections but also to the adaptive advantage of flexible, network-based forms of organization in relation to dynamic, global capitalism.

It is also important to note the extent to which global discussions of IT and its regulation have come to be embedded in security concerns. Especially since September 11, security (and military, intelligence, and police cooperation) have moved to the forefront of the agenda among those organizing interstate connections. This is likely to have long-term implications for the development of IT use, which is contingent in important ways on the legal-regulatory infrastructure created. This involves issues about security and surveillance as well as property rights, which are seldom openly debated in the public sphere.

Disease also figures prominently in the "dark side" of globalization. This is not just a matter of possible bioterrorism. More people die daily of AIDS than died in the World Trade Center attacks. And if the spread of deadly viruses from the less well developed (and thus less healthy and less vaccinated) world is a source of anxiety in rich countries, it is nonetheless the poor who suffer disproportionately from nearly all diseases. And disparities in access to treatment become one of the most dramatic faces of global inequality. Here too IT matters, though what we see most is the weakness of the global public sphere in spurring effective action. We see also the power of Western and especially American media. These have portrayed AIDS largely as a gay disease, thus adding a stigma to the difficulties of fighting it in the rest of the world—where homosexual contact is a minor vector compared to heterosexual transmission, drug use, and unsafe blood supplies—and as more or less "handled" by drugs available only at a cost prohibitive to much of the world.

In this context, it is worth noting that the most influential of electronic media is not yet the Internet or any form of computer-mediated communication but still television. Even its reach is not altogether global, but it comes close. Access to and use of the Internet are still much more uneven, and although usage of the Internet grows, it is less basic to shaping the broad "information background" to all public discourse. The different technologies are mutually intertwined, of course, not only with Internet sites run by television broadcasters but with news reports gathered by the Internet. Just as television often alerts people to stories they will read in newspapers, so an e-mail message can tell someone to turn on the TV or a TV show can send someone to the web for more detail.[2] Aside from inequalities of access, there may be even more telling inequalities in production of content for various media. Though access to the Internet is uneven, it does allow for point-to-point communication, dispersed access to common information resources, and relatively inexpensive posting of new content. Broadcast media remain almost completely one-directional, with broadcasters determining the form in which content appears and with the costs of competitive entry high. On the other hand, while more and more information is available on the Internet, there is a wealth of globally significant knowledge still accessible only in the libraries and computer data centers of rich countries. The results of most social-science research on the world's less developed countries, for example, are accessible only in the knowledge centers of the rich countries. Moreover, commercial sites tend to drown out nonprofit ones oriented to the public good, and search engines not only miss much of the web but generally relegate small-scale sites to their back pages.

Global news media are heavily controlled by a small number of Western corporations and public broadcasters from a few Western governments.[3] This is mitigated somewhat by the prevalence of national broadcasters, though without their own substantial news-gathering operations the global content these broadcasters can provide is limited to what they can acquire from the major global providers. One of the interesting sidebars to the post–September 11 "war on terrorism" was the emergence of Al Jazeera as an important global media player. This Arabic network not only broadcasts throughout the Arabic-speaking world, but it has become a key source of content for the major American networks and European broadcasters. Much Western commentary initially treated Al Jazeera with suspicion, viewing it as "an Arab voice" while the Western media were treated as neutral or universal. That Al Jazeera became a conduit for the messages of Osama bin Laden fueled this perception, but it may be more appropriate to see Al Jazeera as part of the emergence of a transnational Arabic-language public sphere.

All the electronic media, like books, newspapers, and the International Postal Union before them play a crucial role in extending communication beyond local, face-to-face contexts. They thus underwrite globalization. Again, though, there is a tendency in some of the speculative literature of early enthusiasts to imagine that the new media turn the tables on traditional inequality of access to information and effectiveness of communication more than they do. It is certainly true that the international activism of indigenous peoples, environmentalists, and opponents of the World Trade Organization (WTO) has been organized in new ways and with greater efficacy because of the Internet. It is equally certainly not the case that such use yet rivals the efficacy of information control by transnational corporations. Both the corporate control of much public content provision and the corporate use of IT to manage internal production and private financial transactions so far considerably outstrip insurgent and activist uses of the new technologies. This does not make the latter unimportant, but it should encourage a certain realism. As with other technologies, the ability to use IT varies not just with the potential of the technology but with the resources different users can invest.

The very ubiquity of IT has another curious effect on the global public sphere. It is part of a construction of globalization as an inevitable result of technological progress. From different national vantage points, the question is commonly posed not as whether to join in this globalization but as how to adapt to it. Challenges to the dominant Western—indeed American—neoliberal, capitalist forms appear simply as backward-looking traditionalism. This was perhaps especially true during the economic boom of the late 1990s; how visions of the future and struggle over capitalism will fare in less soaring economic times is unclear. But IT continues to play a double role—as the visible face of high technology and as part of the technical underpinning of a greater awareness of global trends.

In many countries around the world, the response is to try to adopt new technology as rapidly as possible, while simultaneously trying to protect traditional culture. Contemporary Indian politicians thus project their country as a potential IT superpower at the same time that they encourage a renewal of studying the Vedas and a more or less fundamentalist embrace of Hinduism. It is precisely the most culturally conservative party to lead the country in its modern history that announces the most high-tech economic plans—as part of its "Vision 2020" proposals. The very phrase "Vision 2020" is not uniquely Indian, however, having been employed in Malaysia and elsewhere. The common rhetoric pairs technology-grounded progress with protection or renewal of cultural traditions. The formula is old, being something of an update of the nineteenth-century Chinese response to the West: "Western learning for material progress, Eastern learning for spiritual values" (a phrase commonly summarized by the syllables *ti-yong*). But as the Qing emperors learned, it was hard to import railways and telegraphs without bringing Western values along. China's communist leaders worried about the same issue in the 1980s, and both their successors and some contributors to China's popular websites worry about the same thing today.[4] Even Canadian politicians echo the same theme, showing that anxiety about local identity has as much to do with American—that is, U.S.—power as with a clash between the West and the rest. As government officials told *Financial Times* reporters, "The country wants to become a lean global competitor while maintaining traditional local values" (Morrison and Warn 2001, 1).

Politicians presenting globalization as an irresistible force commonly embrace neoliberal policies as the necessary response. Global economic competition demands, citizens are told, that public-sector jobs be cut, taxes lowered, state-owned resources privatized. The same IT that potentially makes possible a more vigorous public sphere is cited as an example of global pressures before which public opinion should bow down; it is used to squelch dissent. Ironically perhaps, the IT industry itself often backs this neoliberal rhetoric, focusing on the image of freedom and seeing states and bureaucracies only as possible fetters on innovation (rather than also as embodiments of social achievements such as public education or health care). The result is to reduce the chances of the socially transformative and publicly engaged use of IT, while encouraging its domination and domestication by commercial interests.

Nonetheless, IT use does escape being harnessed entirely by capitalism. Some of this depends on slipping out of the net of property rights in order to enter the World Wide Web. In India, by some estimates, the majority of the people obtain access to the Internet illegally, from informal-sector

Internet vendors who establish hidden or black-market access to the system's backbone or trunk lines.[5] Without this—and a variety of other shady but creative adaptations around the world—IT access would be even more asymmetrically distributed than it is. But the solution is only partial. It enables e-mail and bulletin boards and access to public information. But it does not speak to the extent to which the provision of content on the web is itself ever more commercialized.

Both the flow of information and the financial value of Internet communications put IT on the agenda of government and multilateral regulators. Information flows on the Internet raise concerns about security, manipulation, and crises of unintended consequences (such as the financial flows that were central to the East Asian fiscal crisis of 1997). So far, there has been relatively little public discourse about the nature of this regulation. Indeed, nongovernmental advocates for the public interest have largely been excluded from the discussion. When the G7 powers established a working group on Internet policies in 2000, for example, they determined that each government would have one representative and that there would be a representative of each national private business establishment. Only under pressure did they agree to "observers" from less developed countries. Efforts to secure representation for the nonprofit sectors in the different countries failed. This brings up the basic issue of whether there is an effective way for nonbusiness civil-society interests to be heard. The open-source software movement has made remarkable strides, but advocates for this sort of vision of large-scale cooperation in the creative process, and of a more democratic approach to developing a technological infrastructure, are not significantly represented in core discussions of legal and political regulation. National public spheres and the nascent international public sphere alike are sharply challenged by the partnership of corporate powers and national governments, backed up by international agencies serving that partnership and a global culture heavily shaped by neoliberalism.

To the extent that there is a direct response to self-organized public communication, it comes mostly from nation-states. Though businesses are susceptible to campaigns focused on their public image (famously pioneered by the Nestlé boycott), they are much less directly attentive to public opinion when it is expressed in nonfinancial terms. It is the translation of opinion into either consumer purchasing patterns or capital investment patterns or occasionally the willingness of other firms to work cooperatively that matters. Likewise, multilateral organizations like the World Bank, the IMF, and the WTO can be challenged by public outcry, but are governed largely by states and operated along technocratic lines, with expertise conceived mainly within the terms of neoliberal ideology. Accordingly, it is a mistake for democrats to accept too readily the idea that the growth of a global civil society makes states unimportant. States still matter, they still wield considerable power, and this is at least in part a good thing, not least because they are the main locus for democracy.

It is common to speak of globalization as though the fact of worldwide interconnections meant that there was really a single, seamless whole.[6] I have done this to some extent here, but it can be misleading. Globalization looks different from different regions and localities in the world. It is both an opportunity for the European Union and a pressure behind European unification. The implications are more ambiguous in much of Africa, where access to the benefits of globalization has been minimal and the legacy of colonialism and other ills have in some cases been exacerbated by it. Instead of wondering whether states will lose their familiar power, for example, many Africans must wonder instead whether states will become strong enough to manage public services and unite countries. Likewise, senders and receivers of migrants must view migration differently. And while unequal access to IT is an issue everywhere, the inequality is between countries and regions as well as within them. And the term *access* can be misleading, since even countries that are in a good position to make access to the web universal may not be in a strong position to become suppliers of global information resources.

To a large extent, the notion of a single, uniform global culture or economy is an illusion encouraged by the way dominant Western media present information about the world. From other vantage points, the divergences are readily visible. Globalization is made up of a variety of different projects that clash with each other in varying degrees and combine in different ways in different places. Western dominance is contested. This is not to say that what happens elsewhere is simply survival or a response to Western-initiated trends; it is rather the creative development of alternative modernities (Gaonkar 2001). This is something of what has been at stake in clashes between Islamists and the West in recent years—not tradition versus modernity so much as struggle over whether Western trends can control the whole of the modern. Is the freedom to make pornography predominant in the content available on the web inherent in modernity, or a contingent choice the West has made in constructing modernity—not only in terms of sex and gender but in terms of minimally restricted commercialization? Moreover, Western-dominated globalization is not all of a piece—the WTO and the anti-WTO protests have both been Western-dominated. Neither is there simply a tension between the West and the rest, as though the latter were uniform. Regional and local differences still matter, along with religious, cultural, class, and other differences that crosscut regions. Even nationalism is commonly a response to globalization, not its other, something old and passing away.

Globalization is a heterogeneous process, in short, which produces multiple and overlapping layers of interconnection. It is a matter of enmities and rivalries as well as interdependence. Moreover, the other side of connectivity is exclusion. The more densely certain networks are woven together, the more difficult it is for outliers to find a way in.

International civil society has grown as part of globalization, but its enthusiasts must be careful not to overstate its strength. It is sometimes suggested that IT is a great equalizer, but as we have noted, IT is used by corporations at least as effectively as by protesters (if not a good deal more so). Describing the surge of global protest over capitalist hegemony, unequal development, and the environment, some writers seem almost to imply that the protesters outside the WTO meeting in Seattle came close to overpowering the global elite within. In fact, of course, they were able to get a message heard and to create a disruption but not to assume significant organizational power.

IT plays an important role, finally, in making it possible for globalization to combine decentralization and dispersal of activity with concentration of power (Calhoun 1992b). As Saskia Sassen (1996) notes, much of what official statistics present as global trade among seemingly independent nations is in fact coordinated production within individual global corporations. Carburetors may seem to be sold from Mexico to the United States, but this is just one link in Ford's new global assembly line, with computer-assisted control systems and financial management as important as computer-assisted design or robotics.

Networks and Knowledge

IT is powerful, but not all powerful. It is introduced into a world of existing social relations, culture, capitalism, and inequalities. These shape what will be made of it. So does the creativity of engineers, designers, and users.

So too, potentially, can the creative work of artists and others for whom the Internet provides a new medium for both production and circulation of work. Indeed, the aesthetic potential of IT is both important in itself, and potentially part of the contribution of IT to the public sphere. The latter is never simply a matter of rational-critical argument but also of cultural creativity; the reimagining of the nature of social relations can be as important as debate in the life of the public sphere. Through most of the twentieth century, for example, the public sphere joined an aesthetic and a distributive critique of capitalism, a bohemian discourse with the social-ist, hopes for a more beautiful world with hopes for a more egalitarian world. To a considerable extent this combination came unstuck in the 1990s (see the useful discussion in Boltanski and Chapiello 1999). Egalitarian ideals were tarred with the brush of defunct Soviet-style bureau-cratization and notions that government regulation was excessive even in the West. Conversely, capitalism appeared often in the aesthetically appealing guise of the high-tech corporate campus rather than the pollut-ing factory. For a time, at least, its paradigmatic occupation became website designer, and not only its economic but its aesthetic potentials seemed unlimited. There was more artistic freedom offered by the dot-coms than by government (and even universities looked awfully stodgy). How much of the changed attitude will survive the dot-com crash is unclear, but the example nonetheless illustrates the ways in which the revision of cultural images is important to the construction of public opin-ion. And of course, it was not an accident. The hybridization of Madison Avenue and Bellevue, Washington, was central to the dot-com era, and focused precisely on the revision of public opinion by aesthetic means.

Attempts by states and others to regulate the Internet and similar technologies may reflect purely bureaucratic concerns or may respond to such public discourse. A significant gap in this process, so far, is that IT has been the object of a great deal of speculation—often utopian but sometimes dystopian—and not much serious social research. Such research will advance best if there are more researchers with serious knowledge of both IT and social science. Such "cross-training" is not encouraged in contemporary universities, but it is not impossible. In any case, for the public to make informed choices about the develop-ment and deployment of IT—and perhaps about remedying inequalities in access or impacts—knowledge is crucial.

Sticking only to the American example (though versions of this process are widespread), several different changes are intertwined and are fundamentally changing the character of higher education. The changes are not evenly distributed, to be sure. Most especially, wealthy institutions have more capacity to shape their own futures—and to maintain attractive features of their current character. Thus it is not likely that Harvard University or Williams College will employ IT simply to cut costs, reduce faculty, or teach students online. They may use their "brand names" to offer profitable distance-education programs. But their endowments and social status will enable them to continue to serve a privileged segment of the student population with residential programs that reach far beyond the formal curricula and that include face-to-face relations among students and between them and the faculty. The options open to less well-endowed institutions are different, and so too the pressures shaping them. One reason we know less about the overall transformation of higher education is that researchers tend to be drawn from the upper tier of schools and reflect mainly on what has gone on in the institutions in which they were educated or work. But higher education in the United States is a highly differentiated system in which schools have different missions, student bodies, places in academic labor markets, and resources.

Colleges and universities have commonly maintained that even technical education was best pursued in the context of the broader liberal arts and sciences, that it was important to train citizens as well as technicians, and that students needed to develop critical-thinking skills for both roles. In relation to IT, many have pointed out the difference between mastering a specific software package or hardware configuration, both of which are likely to change quickly, and mastering the underlying principles that will enable students and workers to learn about new systems in the future. Absent a much greater social investment, though, this broader vision of higher education is inevitably somewhat elitist; it speaks less well to students worried about the fastest, surest course to a good job.

Traditional colleges and universities are expensive—and are under challenge from "rationalizers"—not only because they are inefficient, but because they bundle together a number of different activities and functions. They house libraries and sometimes publishing companies, counseling services and sports teams, computer centers and hospitals. They provide entertainment, housing, and at least implicitly dating services. One of the basic questions today is which institutions can—or should—maintain this bundling together of disparate activities. Perhaps most basically, the ideal of the university has combined the production and dissemination of knowledge, research, and teaching. Some efficiencies are available by unbundling these activities, and this is happening. Like many of the changes, it is happening within traditional institutions as well as in a redistribution of activities among institutions. Some faculty are able to negotiate privileged reductions in their teaching loads because of their research productivity; others make up the difference. The most extreme dimension of this trend is the rise in employment of temporary and part-time teachers, usually with low salaries, minimal benefits, and marginal status within the institutions. Though transformations in higher education are often described in terms of "privatization," this shift appears in public institutions as well, and market pressures are felt throughout the system.[7]

Indeed, profit and nonprofit orientations are being intermingled. Not-for-profit universities have established for-profit corporations to try to make money from online offerings. University presses long subsidized because of the academic value of their publications are being asked to pay their way as businesses. Charges for some library resources, especially those provided electronically, are becoming more widespread. The primary products of scholarly research—journal articles and books—are increasingly accessible only for a price. The institutions most immune from pressure are in fact not the public universities but the very well-endowed private ones. MIT and Princeton have thus, made their online offerings free—both seeing them as more valuable for public relations and alumni loyalty than as profit centers, and suggesting that there may not be as much profit in this kind of offering as is sometimes thought. On the other hand, such well-endowed institutions are also operated partly as for-profit businesses, not least when they get into joint ventures based on the inventions and innovations of their faculty.

In this as in other areas where IT is part of a larger change, inequalities are growing but masked. Not only individuals but institutions are unequal when facing technological innovation. Around the world, privatization of higher education is part of the more general process of reducing state support of social goods. This is encouraged by the neoliberal ideology dominant in contemporary globalization (Bourdieu 1998, 2001).[8] But it means that states—the institutions best placed to defend the gains workers and other popular forces have made in previous struggles—are instead abandoning them. Some of those struggles—such as for low-cost, equitably or perhaps meritocratically distributed public education—have been waged in part through the public sphere, with material pressures complemented by shifts in public opinion. The supporters of neoliberal capitalism have effectively dominated elite public opinion, including the ways in which the most powerful states perceive the implications of globalization. This means that debate in the broader public sphere is an important test for the capacity of civil society to resist the imperatives of capitalism. The debate influences not only current state actions but the availability of knowledge for future public discourse.

The Internet will always be a supplement to, not a replacement for, other connections. Those who already have power can make more effective immediate use of the technology—so those with less power have to work harder to make it effective on their side. The Internet thus makes it easier to find things out, but often harder to find out what we do not know. I do not mean simply that it adds to volume and creates new demands for the ability to discriminate and evaluate sources, though this is certainly true. I mean also that it makes new forms of surveillance possible that are inherently hard for ordinary people to observe and that may nonetheless dramatically enhance the control others have over their lives. Despite the fact that privacy issues have received more research and public attention than almost any other dimension of IT, surprisingly little public outcry has greeted U.S. government proposals—and actions—to reduce restrictions on such surveillance. People still seem to think mainly in terms of new information being gathered rather than recognizing the immense quantity of information already produced as by-products of computer use but (usually) not linked across datasets. The privacy label is thus partly misleading, since the issues involve not just "exposure" but control.

Control is also important in another way. It is usually unclear to users who is editorially shaping the content available on seemingly open public websites. China, for example, has a range of extremely lively web-based discussions about issues from international affairs to government corruption. Content that offends the government usually disappears quickly, however, and there is presumably also a good deal of self-censorship. The result is that sites apparently offering a glimpse of public opinion are skewed representations. Unlike a newspaper that can be read in certain ways based on the assumption that it is censored and its content controlled, websites give the impression of consisting simply of the spontaneous postings of the public. This does not mean that the web does not bring a gain in sharing information. Indeed, journalists on official Chinese newspapers have been known to anonymously post to the web stories censors would stop them from publishing—and these get some airing even if they are quickly censored. And, to complicate the matter further, the government sometimes tolerates web content that it would censor from print publication. The reason seems to be that it assumes that the Internet reaches a relatively elite part of the population within which it is willing to see issues aired. This may offer a kind of safety valve. It may be monitored by the government to see what its more publicly informed and vocal citizens think; it has the advantage that it does not seem as official as what appears in government-owned publications. Perhaps most basically, the government may simply recognize that it cannot effectively restrict all information from reaching this elite—but may still wish to restrict what reaches the broader population. In the information age, it may be all but impossible to stop information flows—including across borders—but it may be more possible to keep them relatively elite. In other settings, censorship may ultimately be less of a factor in determining the accessibility of information on the web than invisibility (because of the limits of search engines, the extent to which commercial sites push public ones to the margin, and the costs of advertising or maintaining links).

One argument has been that web-based "communities" are effective organizational counterparts to corporations, governments, and other more formally organized structures of power and action. There is some truth to this—organization is always crucial to making otherwise dispersed popular voices heard. Electronic communication is extremely effective at facilitating links among strangers—for example, facilitating both widely distributed protests and participation from widely distributed groups in demonstrations or other shared events. It is a useful vehicle for sharing information that can either motivate or inform action. At the same time, we need to note the ambiguity of the language of community in this regard. Writers seem to refer without clear distinction to dense networks of personal ties, broad but loosely linked categories of people linked by shared information, and IT users who derive their social connections from some other basis (say, trade-union membership) but then communicate partly online. If we mean the first of these, the most sociologically specific use of *community*, then communities are effective only on relatively small scales; density of connections—everyone knowing (and potentially trusting) everyone else—necessarily declines with scale. Precisely because social life began to be organized on ever-larger scales in the modern era, community could organize proportionately less of it. States, markets, and other kinds of connections among people came to predominate—even when people still valued community a great deal. Much of what IT facilitates is linkage among relative strangers—the second and third usages above—though I would hesitate to use the term *community* with its connotations of dense social networks. The term *community* is misleading, moreover, because it implies that collectivities formed in web-based discourse are somehow equivalent to local communities grounded in face-to-face relationships (Calhoun 1998). Here too the reality is that the Internet is most effective as a complement to face-to-face communication, not as a replacement for it. It empowers local activists who would otherwise find it harder to reach others with similar concerns in remote locations. It enables both lateral sharing of information and better access to information controlled by centralized providers (including government agencies). Here it is worth noting that how effective the technology is in this regard depends a great deal on institutional arrangements over which there can be political struggle. Are government agencies required to make all their data effectively accessible, for example? What laws and regulations govern public provision of data by other actors?

More generally, *community* is a misleading term for thinking about the Internet's role in social solidarity. It may be true, as William Mitchell (1995) puts it, that his keyboard is his café. Internet communications provide many of the functions that coffeehouses (and newspapers) played in Habermas's model of the eighteenth-century public sphere. At the same time, neither is necessarily best understood through the notion of community. Part of what Habermas described as important to coffeehouse society was precisely that it provided a setting for interactions among strangers, for discussions among those who were not knit to each other by communal ties. The same goes for various sorts of multiuser domains (MUDs) and is part of the basis for the creative identity work that Sherry Turkle (1997) has described. MUDs may evoke a sense of community for participants, and may be given metaphorical topographies complete with "neighborhoods." But it is also misleading to apply the warm, fuzzy language of the local without regard to scale. There is a crucial difference among MUDs that provide occasions for strangers to fantasize, listservs and websites that enable political organization among strangers, and web resources that provide supplemental communication channels for people also joined in directly interpersonal relationships. The three (and other variants) can shade into each other, but are distinct not just in conception but in implications. A particularly important part of the distinction comes with the difference between categorical identifications (categories of people with similar interests or identities) and network ties (more or less dense webs of actual relationships, especially multiplex ones) (White 1992; Calhoun 1992b, 2002). The latter join more or less "whole" people; the former tend to join people one issue or identity at a time. The former, however, transcend locality much more easily.

The point is not that one mode of interconnection is better or worse than the other, but that they have different implications. The Internet can make local community less isolated, or it can lead people to substitute online ties to relative strangers for interaction with neighbors. It can promote both enclaves and connectivity, nations and cosmopolitanism. Heavy reliance on the term *community* to describe computer-mediated groupings borrows from the warm and fuzzy connotations that the idea of community has in everyday life and especially in nostalgia. But it also obscures one of the most important potential roles for electronic communication, which is enhancing public discourse—a form of discourse that joins strangers and enables large collectivities to make informed choices about their institutions and their future.

The Idea of the Public Sphere

To say that a public exists is mainly to say that there is more or less open, self-organized communication among strangers. There are settings in which such public communication is minimal, in which strangers feel sharply constrained in what they can or should say to each other, or in which external regimentation of who may speak to whom or what may be the topics of communication prohibits self-organization of publics. So this minimal sense of publicness says a good deal.[9] It does not, however, give an adequate sense of the stakes of the idea of the public sphere. These focus not simply on the general existence of public communication, but on its capacity to guide social life.

The most famous study of the public sphere, Jürgen Habermas's (1989) *Structural Transformation of the Public Sphere*, focuses on the emergence in the eighteenth century of a widespread ideal—and partially successful actual practice—of open debate concerning questions about the public good and policies for pursuing it.[10] This debate was conducted by individuals with autonomous bases in civil society—that is, with their own sources of income and identity—but the debate achieved rationality to the extent that the wealth and identities of the individuals did not intrude on the argument itself. The public sphere was thus crucial to the capacity of civil society to influence the state; it was political, but not part of the state. Habermas (1989) describes the development of this political public sphere out of an earlier literary one, in which the formation of opinion about works of literature was elevated by rational-critical discourse. He also points to the importance of institutional supports for public communication, notably the newspaper and the coffeehouse."

In Habermas's analysis, however, the ideal of the public sphere was shown to mask a contradiction. It aspired equally to openness—in manner of communication and in entrance to the discourse itself—and to the critical use of reason to form opinion. Its successive structural transformations, however, reflected the extent to which expanding the scale of the public sphere led to a degeneration in the processes of opinion formation. Instead of individuals debating, public communication became increasingly a matter of organized interest groups—corporations, trade unions, political parties—using the techniques of advertising and mass communications. Opinion was formed less rationally on the basis of manipulation. The advent of opinion polls did nothing to arrest this, since they simply asked the opinion of discrete individuals without providing an occasion for different individuals to inform each other through discussion. Such opinions were less likely, therefore, to be based on knowledge. Indeed, opinion polls simply gave better information on people to those who would seek to influence or control them—treating them as "objects"—rather than enabling people to become better subjects of public discourse.

Behind both Habermas's optimistic account of the eighteenth century and his pessimistic account of subsequent transformations lie the same issues. Can public communication be a means of forming opinions based on reason and improved by critical discourse? Can these opinions then inform the creation or operation of social institutions and more generally the constitution of social life.[12] In other words, can ordinary people use their faculties for reason and communication to choose the nature of their lives together—even on a relatively large scale in which most are strangers to each other—rather than having this imposed on them by inherited tradition, political power, or economic wealth. For Habermas, the main issue was whether citizens could guide a state, which helps to explain why *public sphere* appears in the singular—it is the sum of the ways in which the open, rational-critical discourse of citizens at large can inform the (singular) state. The same broader questions can be asked of international public discourse, however, and with regard to influencing a multiplicity of states, of multilateral organizations, of quasi- or nongovernmental bodies, and indeed, of business corporations.

Communication among strangers in the public sphere thus appears as one of the various mechanisms by which social integration is achieved and social institutions are shaped and guided. Shared participation in public life itself can be a form of social solidarity, joining people in relation to each other and to the public projects they debate—even when they disagree about specifics. Among the various forms of social integration, public communication is distinctive because, more than any of the others, it offers the possibility of ordering collective life on the basis of reasoned choice. People are joined together by functional interdependence, as in markets, by subjection to political power, and by commonalities of culture. The public sphere has the potential to shape each of these other forms of connection, as well as offering a kind of connection of its own. It complements the realms of directly interpersonal relationships—family, friendship, neighborhood. These are open in varying degrees to choice and to construction through interpersonal communication. But they can join only modest numbers of people; they cannot organize relations among strangers. Moreover, when they steer affairs of state this is usually the illegitimate influence of one part of a polity over the rest. The public sphere distinctively offers the chance for the whole citizenry—or at least a large part of it—to participate in guiding the state, thus conferring legitimacy on it. This of course implies that legitimacy is based on the will of the people. While this is a predominant conception in the modern world, it is not the only possibility. Other approaches to legitimacy base it on divine will, on inheritance, or on the formal excellence of institutional arrangements. When legitimacy is based on the will of the people, though, a key question is how that will is formed. Is it a matter of inheritance or of a tradition that should be above question—as some proponents of ethnic nationalism would argue? Is it a matter of manipulation by those who can draw power from control over the media, or over jobs, or over the members of self-interested organizations? Or is this will of the people formed through discussion and debate among the people?

This is not the place to pursue questions of political theory, like how to balance unity and diversity, the sense of common commitment implied by the phrase "will of the people," and the need for tolerance and mutual engagement across lines of difference required by liberal democracy. But it is crucial to see that these questions are made pressing by any appeal to the public sphere as a basis for organizing life together. Take simply the relationship to nation as an example. Nationalist ideology commonly presents individuals as joined directly and identically to a common whole; differentiation appears as a threat to national unity. Such an ideology can have popular appeal and can be supported by masses of public communication—messages posted to both American and Chinese websites during the spy-plane crisis of 2000 demonstrated this. But this sort of public demonstration of unity and identity is different from public discourse in which rational-critical debate improves the quality of opinions, educates the participants, and forms a collective understanding of issues that advances beyond preexisting definitions of interests or identities.[13] Among other things, the mass version of popular nationalism is eminently open to manipulation by demagogues, the government, and other forces. Recall, indeed, that democracy can mean mass rule, not protection of rights, and that publicity and expansion of the media can be tactics in mobilizing such masses (and not just in Nazi Germany or Maoist China).

More or less open, self-organized public communication among strangers is evident in both mass nationalism and more rational-critical public discourse. The minimal definition of the public sphere does not adequately make the distinction (though to the extent that mass nationalism is manipulated by the state or others, it is not "self-organized"). It is recognizing the deeper stakes of the question of the public sphere that makes the tension between these two "ideal types" of public communication evident and important. And yet it should not be imagined that the realities to which they refer are completely distinct. There is no communication that is not also participation in the production or reproduction of culture. Even the most rational-critical of public debates, organized by the fairest rules of procedure and pursued in the least self-interested spirit, are thus conditioned by the cultural idioms in which they are conducted and contribute to the formation of common culture (as well as the recognition of cultural differences) among participants. Moreover, common culture is important in the commitment of participants to each other and to the process of public discourse. Recognizing the difference between simple affirmation of commonality and differentiated public debate should not lead us to imagine that the ideal of reasoned discourse is sufficient in itself to account for what goes on in any public sphere. Conversely, we should see also that popular nationalism (and other cultural or political traditions) is not immune from rational-critical discourse. It can be shaped and reshaped both by the culture-forming and the rational-critical dimensions of public discourse. Even when ideologues assert that there is one true and correct way to be American or Chinese or anything else, they tend always to offer distinct visions of that one and true way. This opens the possibility of debate even in the midst of affirmations of unity. And different nationalisms may incorporate greater recognition of internal diversity, of the importance of reason, or of debate as part of the self-understanding of the nation.

The existence of public communication, vital as it is, does not answer the questions we need to ask about public spheres. We need to know not only how active the communication is and how inclusive and open the participation is, but what the qualities of the communication are. We need to attend to the processes by which culture is produced and reproduced in public, not treat it as a mere inheritance or private product of individuals or small groups. We need to ask how responsive public opinion is to reasoned argument, how well any public sphere benefits from the potential for self-correction and collective education implicit in the possibilities of rational-critical discourse. And we need to inquire how committed participants are to the processes of public discourse and through it to each other. Finally, and not least of all, we need to ask how effectively the public opinion formed can in fact influence social institutions and wielders of economic, political, or indeed cultural power.

These questions should all be basic to inquiry into the implications of new information technology for public life and democracy. Various technologies have the potential to constrain or facilitate openness, reason, cultural creativity, self-organization, solidarity. This is as true internationally as domestically. Moreover, questions of unequal access, cultural diversity, and perhaps most basically, the multiplicity of agents of power and potential objects of public influence loom even larger in the global arena.

Conclusion

The implications of IT for the global public sphere are still being determined. Whether it will be put to use in ways that open and encourage public communication as much as in ways that facilitate commerce and control is an open question. If not, then web-based resistance to power—viruses, hacking, site flooding, and other IT and web-based strategies for attacking corporations, states, other users—may become more prominent. There is no perfect "firewall" between systems of public communication and infrastructural systems. Accordingly, the stakes are high should cyberterrorism become more prominent. At the same time, opportunities for democratic choice about how sociotechnical systems are organized are limited. And it is often the sense of being excluded from choices about the future than fans the flames of discontent.

Prospects for democratization of the global order depend crucially on the development of a global public sphere, as well as on attention to global inequities within the public discourse of individual societies. There are opportunities for activism. This need not always involve a leap to the truly global, but may involve the building of transnational communications networks on a regional scale—as has happened to some extent around Latin America and South Asia. It will be important for those who would open up the public sphere to figure out how to work within organizations (including corporations and states), not just against them or in seemingly separate and autonomous "communities." It may also be possible to *choose* at least some aspects of the transformation of colleges and universities instead of just letting it happen, and thus to choose to have stronger bases for producing and sharing knowledge to inform the public. In this regard, one of the most important actions may be to do real research to help replace the contest of anecdotes and speculations with a reasoned debate in the public sphere.

Notes

A draft of this chapter was presented to the International Sociological Association, Brisbane, Australia, July 11, 2002. An earlier version was presented at Directions and Implications of Advanced Computing 2000, Computer Professionals for Social Responsibility, Seattle, May 20, 2000.

1. See DiMaggio et al. 2001 for a useful review (though an overwhelmingly North American one). Even where there is serious research on the Internet, it is more likely to address the behavior of individual users than social processes or public communication as such, and it is commonly contained within national contexts (and within the global North). For a useful account of the research see Wellman 1999, as well as Wellmen and Haythornthwaite 2003, though this account remains heavily oriented to the processes of sociability. Important as this is, it is distinct from reorganization of power, the construction of more or less autopoetic systems, and the problems of design of complex technical infrastructures.

2. It is important to recognize, though, the extent to which broadcast media subsidize the provision of news by the Internet—because the latter is not yet autonomously profitable.

3. The literature on media concentration is huge; see, among the best examples (but still heavily U.S. focused), McChesney 1999 and Compaine and Gomery 2000.

4. For more on China's Internet-based public discourse and especially the interpenetration of domestic and international themes, see Yang 2002.

5. I am informed here by the work of Ravi Sundaram and colleagues in Serai, a research institute on IT at the Center for the Study of Developing Societies in New Delhi.

6. Interestingly, it is an illusion that informs critics as well as celebrants. In their influential book *Empire*, Michael Hardt and Antonio Negri (2000) present a picture of a fully sutured and self-sufficient dominant world order, one that lacks the internal contradictions to generate immanent transformation.

7. *Privatization* may be a more precise term for discussing changes in higher education in some other countries. In many of these cases, it is more closely correlated with a for-profit orientation than in the United States, which has a long history of private, but not-for-profit higher education. And in many of these cases, neoliberal state policies are leading to efforts not just to found new private institutions but to reduce public support for existing institutions.

8. A translation of the first essay in *Contre-feux II* appears in *Items and Issues*, 1(3), winter 2002 (available at www.ssrc.org).

9. Warner (2002) offers a more elaborate version of this minimal definition:

1. A public is self-organizing.
2. A public is a relation among strangers.
3. The address of public speech is both personal and impersonal.
4. A public is the social space created by the circulation of discourse.
5. Publics exist historically according to the temporality of their circulation.

For more history of the concept see Calhoun 2001a, 2001b.

10. For several critical analyses of the issues Habermas raises, see Calhoun 1992a.

11. A website imaginatively devoted to coffee includes a discussion of "Habermas, the coffee houses and the public sphere" (http://www.qmw.ac.uk/~english/personal/Coffeehome.html).

12. Habermas focuses mainly on political life and assumes the existence of a state to be influenced. Writing slightly earlier, Hannah Arendt (1958) emphasized the broader process of creating social institutions and also the moments of creation of states in acts of founding and revolutions.

13. For a study that addresses the interrelationships of the two dimensions, see Rajogopal 2001.

12   What Do We Need to Know about the Future We're Creating? Technobiographical Reflections

Howard Rheingold

A crucial turning point comes when one is able to acknowledge that modern technics, much more than politics as conventionally understood, now legislates the conditions of human existence. New technologies are institutionalized structures within an existing constitution that gives shape to a new polity, the technopolis in which we do increasingly live. For the most part, this constitution still evolves with little public scrutiny or debate. Shielded by the conviction that technology is neutral and tool-like, a whole new order is built—piecemeal, step by step, with the parts and pieces linked together in novel ways, without the slightest public awareness or opportunity to dispute the character of the changes underway. It is somnambulism (rather than determinism) that characterizes technological politics—on the left, right, and center equally.
—Langdon Winner, *Autonomous Technology*

Are we awake to the world we are building, or are we, as an old Sufi saying goes, merely asleep in life's waiting room?

The petroleum economy, aviation, nuclear power, biotechnology, lasers, organ transplants, telephone and television, and personal computer networks—today's technologies have put staggering amounts of power into the hands of millions. More power is on its way in the next several decades, as present scientific knowledge drives future technological capability. Do we know what to do with the powers over matter, mind, and life that tomorrow's technologies will grant us? If we do not already know the answers to these questions, what do we need to know before we can design, deploy, control, and live humanely and sustainably with the tools we are creating?

Like millions of others who came of age in the last half of the twentieth century, the evolution of technology is not just something I study; it has been the backdrop of my life. Interstate highways and the transformation of American life by the automobile were just shifting into high gear when I was born in 1947. When I was an infant, television and nuclear power were also in their infancy. I can remember using propeller-driven aircraft and vinyl record albums. I can remember black-and-white TV. Like most Americans, the foundation of my beliefs about the future was a strong faith in "progress"—the assurance that tomorrow will be different and better than today because of new technologies.

I am still immersed in technologies. They fascinate me. I make a good living using computers and networks to write about computers and networks. Somewhere along the way, I started spending hours of my day in front of a computer screen. But I have been paying more attention to the cracks in my worldview lately, especially the place where progress and somnambulism meet.

I am compelled to begin with a confession of not just my complicity in the creation of today's digital culture, but my outright seduction by high-tech tools. I am honor-bound to describe my love for mind-extending technologies before I can describe how I started to think more critically about tools, minds, and civilizations.

I speak now directly to others like myself who are admitted, even enthusiastic, technophiles. For that reason, I do not want anyone to mistake this for an orthodox neo-Luddite rant. I lack the certainty of the true believers—both the orthodox technophiles and the convinced technophobes. I confess up front that I know of no theology or ideology that will answer the questions I can no longer avoid asking.

Where are we going? Do we want to go there? Is there anything we can do about it? I have written this because I hope we can think together about where these questions lead. Perhaps there are solutions that can only be found by many of us, working together. I offer a brief technological auto-biography as a means of reflecting and discussing what humans do not yet know about our tools.

When Enlightenment Runs Out of Control, Nobody Notices

Thinking critically about the technosphere we inhabit, which defines who we are and dictates how we live and die, is scary—like thinking about performing surgery on yourself. Your internal denial alarms are going off already, I know. I entreat you to repress the urge to rise to the defense of penicillin and civilization, and consider for just a moment how I came to rethink my attitudes.

We are all partaking in, and many of us are helping to build, something that none of us understands. There are taboos against looking too critically at the real politics of technology. Although a relatively few people understand the urgency and relevance of the history of technologies, most people are not even aware that progress was not always our most important product.

One of the things that makes technology dangerous is that most people never learn where tools come from, what they were originally designed to do, and how people have evolved, appropriated, subverted, perverted, and augmented them from their original purposes and designs.

For the practical and irresistible reason that there is much money in selling tools and much less in critiquing them, the real and imagined benefits of technologies are trumpeted, while their histories and social impacts are not nearly as widely taught or discussed. Least discussed is how people think about certain things, because that way of thinking was invented by someone. The vast majority of the people who use technologies, and are affected by them, know little about the origins and provenance of the fundamental thinking tools we all benefit from—for example, the methods of rationality, the notion of progress, democratic self-governance, and the universal belief in the superiority of the scientific method to other ways of knowing.

That "science" equals "truth" is not viewed as a belief but as a fundamental assumption about the nature of reality. Few think of it as an invention—but as a mode of thinking, it has been the most world-changing technology of the past few world-changing centuries. A specific manner of systematically examining the world, extracting knowledge, and applying that knowledge to extend power, a system that was developed only a few hundred years ago, has been so extraordinarily successful that it has dominated our attention.

Our technologized culture shapes and fascinates us to the extent that we have ceased to perceive other ways of knowing and interacting with the world and each other. As Langdon Winner claims above, people in industrial, megatechnological civilization seem to sleepwalk through the world we have created, oblivious to the worlds that have been destroyed, rarely thinking about what new technologies will engender in years to come. I have long been one of the oblivious, but now I know I am oblivious.

One crashes into a fundamental paradox when one tries to determine whether one is sleepwalking, so I ask you to stipulate only that most people in the world are unaware of the true dimensions of the revolution that has taken place since the time of Descartes and Bacon. We know we live in a world of 747s and heart transplants and perpetual change, but we do not know—are not taught—how we got here. Knowing how we got here is particularly important now because civilization is facing a crisis about thinking about tools that was caused, in part, because we learned how to create tools for thinking.

People did not know how to think systematically about the material world until the seventeenth and eighteenth centuries, despite millennia of attempts by philosophers to understand the nature of energy and matter. In the sixteenth and seventeenth centuries, in an unpleasant era of plagues, witch burnings, Inquisitions, devastating religious wars and civil conflicts, a small number of European philosophers proposed that if we could discover a better method of thinking about the world—a systematic means of discovering truth—we could govern ourselves in a more equitable manner. That is, we could relieve the suffering of disease and hunger and improve the living conditions of many, if not all.

These thinkers postulated, not too many centuries ago, that the human condition could be improved by way of a magical mental operation that at that time was yet to be discovered. In their search for this mind magic, the founders of modern science drew their hints from the alchemic, hermetic, cabalist magical traditions of the past. The search for meaning in the stars or in the manipulation of magical symbols turned to the search for meaning in matter and the manipulation of mathematical symbols.

Newton's astrological speculations are forgotten, but every schoolchild learns what Newton discovered about gravity and motion. Science and technology seem to have trumped metaphysics, but it is important to know that metaphysical inquiry is what triggered the quest that led to science and technology. Rooted in Platonic transcendental idealism and Christian eschatology, with a strong tributary of Gnostic heresies, the notion that history has a direction prepared the way for the "new method" of recent centuries. Egyptians, Greeks, Hebrews, and Christians all contributed to the foundations of science, but the idea of scientific progress emerged as something wholly new. We take it for granted now, but the premise of this quest was a radically new view of human nature when it emerged, 400 years ago: humans are perfectible, are capable of discovering the means of our own perfection, and human institutions thereafter can be improved by perfected people. Our collective empirical understanding of nature can increase our knowledge, and from that knowledge, create better ways to live. This was the blueprint for the modern idea of progress, in its original form.

One key aspect of progress has been what Lewis Mumford called the invention of the "myth of the machine"—the mode of organizing and training people in hierarchies to perform tasks that add up to pyramids, empires, factories. When a system emerges that rewards everyone for treating individuals as components in a machine, some people are going to be crushed.

One of the reasons technology's shadow side is more or less invisible is because progress has been such a winner—although the growth of what Jacques Ellul called *la technique* has systematically created winners and losers. Another reason is that technology is magical. The mystical seekers of the sixteenth century found something in reality as potent as the alchemist's philosopher's stone had promised to be in imagination. Introducing rationalism and empiricism into human affairs and scientific enterprise was a noble vision, with many successes in the material world. A great deal of human misery has been relieved because those European thinkers began concocting this notion of perpetual discovery, perpetual change, perpetual improvement—and inventing tools for bringing about this transformation of the human condition. At the same time, a great deal of misery has been perpetrated by rational thinkers, using sophisticated tools.

Some claim that the nature of tools transforms us into components, but I consider technological determinism to be enervating and drearily lacking in free will. However, it must be kept in mind that thinking that we can improve on the ways we use technology is just what a rationally trained mind would suggest as an answer to suffering caused by technological civilization.

In response to that call for what came to be known as "the Enlightenment Project," thinkers including Descartes, Bacon, Newton, and Galileo applied themselves to the task of thinking in a wholly new manner. Between their individual insights, this small number of European intellectual adventurers came up with a "new method" that was extraordinarily successful for many (if not for those who labored in the infernal factories or suffered the effects of smog, pollution, industrial accidents, redundancy). The fundamentals of the new method are so simple that they seem self-evident, once you know them. First, doubt everything. Then gather evidence by examining the world and performing systematic experiments. Finally, formulate theories, preferably with mathematical formulas, that allow you to explain the evidence and predict the outcome of further experiments. In the beginning, few foresaw the limitations of this discovery. We can see now, however, how this transformation of human thought caused side effects that were not visible for centuries. And we have seen that the methods so powerfully predictive in the physical sciences did not turn out to be so amenable to the production of knowledge in the social sciences.

At the end of the twentieth century, it became easier to see that technological progress based on systematically gathered scientific knowledge, coupled with industrial capitalism (or socialism, for that matter), requires continuous growth, damages the environment that supports life, diminishes both biological and social diversity, and everywhere seems to move us toward societies in which humans learn how to be components in larger social machines. No matter how convenient it makes life for billions, this process of extracting resources, expanding power, and stimulating perpetual growth in energy consumption seems to be headed for ecological, political, and economic catastrophe within the next few decades, at most. In the last twenty years of unparalleled technological development the gap between rich and poor has become enormous and continues to grow. Desperation and ideology fuel war and terror. It is no longer as easy to assume that life will get better as technology marches on.

Although our present crisis is so threatening precisely because it plays out on the physical plane, where our bodies and other creatures live, it is a crisis of knowledge. We lack a crucial mental skill. I contend that our position today regarding the way we make decisions about technologies is similar to the dilemma that pre-Enlightenment scientists faced in the sixteenth century. We simply do not have a good method for thinking and making decisions about how to apply (and not apply) the powerful tools of rationality, the scientific method, reductionism, the combination of logic and efficiency embodied by technology. Cost-benefit analyses and economic simulations are insufficient methods for those who lose their way of life as a cost of providing benefits to others—those who live in lands where molybdenum or petroleum, forests or ores are to be found. The new way of thinking we now require is difficult to imagine precisely because it cannot be easily quantified or manipulated mechanically.

That we do not now know how to think publicly and make collective decisions about technology does not mean we are incapable of discovering a "new method" or new methods for thinking about technology. If ever our species needed thinkers of the caliber of Descartes and Newton, it is now, but first we need to think about a new way to think about technology. I strongly suspect that the solution must be collective—another Descartes or Newton will not be good enough this time. I am convinced that it helps to encourage a more widespread public discourse about the problem, in the hope that our process of thinking together can help lead to this future mindset. This mindset should ensure that the people who design and distribute tomorrow's technologies will do so with a more thorough knowledge of the systemic effects of their enterprise than their educations now provide.

We must be careful that we do not destroy what we set out to save. The assumption that there is a rational solution to every problem is at the heart of Enlightenment rationalism. Relentless and successful problem solving is what brought us from Mesopotamia to metropolis in five thousand years. Let us begin by not mistaking "thinking together" for "rushing for a solution." Perhaps the answer is not in the realm of "define problem → formulate solution." Perhaps we need to think/feel outside that frame. Without claiming I have an answer to the problems of technology, I would like to tell other technology lovers, technology designers, and technology users about a few of the things I have learned.

I have to start with my own fascination with technologies, especially those that amplify intellectual functions. I know that many people have fallen in love with the virtual life, as I have, and suspect that you and I are the people—the ones who are designing tomorrow's technologies—who most actively need to know about what I have been learning.

I think our compulsion and talent for changing our world and ourselves is hardwired in our frontal lobes and opposable thumbs; our extremities evolved to walk on and grasp the world, to roam it and use it. If the Devil is in the details, so is God, or at least the Demiurge. The seduction of digital technology in particular is not demonic, but Faustian. Faust did not sell his soul for ordinary wealth or power, but for the transformative development of progress, his and society's. Faust's problem was not in the nature of his goal, but in the coin he paid. All our stories these days are Faustian.

Seduction by Mind Amplifier

Like falling in love, my involvement with personal computer technology has been both a long slide and a series of abrupt, memorable, life-changing epiphanies. The first time I used WordStar to move a block of text, after ten years of retyping the entire page to switch two paragraphs, I was hooked. Then I saw the Alto, with its mice, windows, and point-and-click interface. I saw a need to tell an interesting story, about a group of dreamers and rebels who wanted to build mind amplifiers and who swam against the currents of mainstream computer industries and academic computer science. When I started digging into the history, I realized that a decent overview of the origins of personal computers would have to include something about Boole, Babbage, Turing, von Neumann, and Wiener. I ended up writing a book, *Tools for Thought* (1985). Looking back, I can see that I had begun the transformation from freelance writer to technology commentator—and that I had become a consumer, guinea pig, and (sometimes uncritical) advocate for the technological changes that were emerging from the information technology (IT) industries.

Over the past fifteen years, personal computer hardware, software, and ways of doing intellectual work have evolved far beyond the Alto. In 1984, I got my hands on a Macintosh and started playing with Macpaint. In Macpaint there is a tool that enables you to zoom in on a graphic and turn on and off the individual pixels that make up the details of a bit-mapped image. "Fat Bits" was the name of the pixel-twiddling tool in Macpaint. I think I sat down for three hours without getting up, as soon as I started playing with Macpaint and discovered Fat Bits.

Fat Bits was a kind of trance. Hours would go by and I could keep my consciousness focused at the pixel level. It was a type of abstraction exercise. My consciousness began to change. The Gutenberg trance began to change into another one. In some ways, the changes were instantaneous; in other ways, the changes took years. Yes, the screen became a kind of reality, an extension of my mind. A space that was both cognitive and social. I started spending most of the day there, and as I learned to use it, I learned to exercise my cognitive faculties in ways that took advantage of the screen-mind trance. Abstraction requires a certain amount of somnambulism: forget about all the detailed underpinnings, once you have clumped them into an abstraction; continually strive to change your focus to the next level of abstraction, where you can clump abstractions together to create the even higher levels. It is a breathtaking game but you have to remember you are playing it, or you run the risk of forfeiting part of your humanity. We all learn to build hierarchies of abstractions when we learn to put the intrinsically meaningless symbols of alphabetical characters into the higher-level abstractions of words (then forget thereafter that we are stringing together letters). We then use words as building blocks for the higher-yet levels of abstraction inherent in sentences, paragraphs, essays, and books.

A computer is a hierarchy of abstractions. At the bottom of the hierarchy is the electrical microcircuitry. As Claude Shannon demonstrated, on-and-off switches can be arranged in circuits that emulate the functions of Boolean algebra. Those arrangements of switches, which can be thought of as "and," "or," and "not" logical gates, constitute the first level of abstraction. The "machine language" of any computer is composed of these abstractions. Machine languages are clumped and processed through software compilers and interpreters and other virtual machines to become higher-level languages. Then those higher-level languages write the text display and windowing and mousing behaviors that make up the graphical user interface—the level of abstraction where personal computer users spend our time. Fat Bits zoomed in to an even higher level of abstraction, and today's state-of-the-art image-manipulation software, PhotoShop, is a toolkit of graphical abstractions, orders of magnitude more complex than 1984's Macpaint.

The particular entrancement induced by computer-based tools combines sensory entrancement via high-resolution media with abstraction languages that enable human minds to play with symbolic structures we are not able to manipulate by means of our unaugmented brains. A contemporary critic of computer technology, Sven Birkerts, in *The Gutenberg Elegies* (1994), noted this abstraction entrancement focused on computer screens. What such critics, and Birkerts in particular, fail to acknowledge is that abstraction entrancement did not begin with computers (he could have taken a hint from the title of his book). If you want to identify the culprit who shunted the human race into millennia of symbol intoxication, it was the person or persons unknown who created the alphabetic-phonetic alphabet in the vicinity of Sumer, around 5,000 years ago. Plato warned that the written word would destroy the traditions of memorization and direct teacher-to-student pedagogy, and Marshall McLuhan pointed out that the alphabet was an enabling technology for the Roman Empire. Every technology has a shadow, but I was too dazzled by the radiance of the benefits of computer-assisted abstraction to think about the shadows at that time.

Jumping into the Virtual World

Connecting my modem to my telephone was another epiphany that actually preceded my seduction by Macintosh. I was familiar with local area networks and servers from the Alto and Ethernet I had used at PARC, but I was not granted an ARPAnet account. I had stored and retrieved and printed documents on a network, but I had never used the computer as a communication device. As soon as I discovered that my mind amplifier could plug into other minds via a kind of groupmind amplifier, I spent the next fifteen years too enthralled to pay a great deal of attention to other effects the technology was having on me and the rest of the world.

It was an easy leap from the experience of my own empowerment to the conclusion, heartily supported by Engelbart (1963), and others, that personal computers and networks were empowering technologies. The answer to the question of whether these tools really empower individuals is "yes and no." There is no question that they added to my ability to think, communicate, and make a living. When something makes you happier and more prosperous, you are not strongly motivated to think critically about it.

In 1983 I bought a 300/1200-baud modem for $500 in order to ship text back and forth with a collaborator. I was helping write a book with a partner who worked at night. He insisted that I buy a modem and get an MCI mail account. I remember the exact moment of that epiphany. It came when I got to my computer, the first morning after activating my account, to see words, words, words streaming across the screen and onto my hard disk. At 1200 baud, it is possible to read it as it goes by. It did not take me long to start exploring BBSs and online services such as The Source. I wrote about those experiences in the last chapter of *Tools for Thought*. In 1985, I joined the Whole Earth Lectronic Link (WELL), and I have probably spent an average of four hours a day online ever since.

After more than a decade alone in my room, staring at a blank page in my typewriter (or, more recently, a blank file on a computer monitor), I was ripe for online communication. When I started out to be a writer, it had not occurred to me that I was sentencing myself to a life term in solitary confinement. My wife worked at her own jobs, outside the house. All the other people my age were going to offices, campuses, factories, or fields where they would see other humans (whether they liked them or not), hear the sound of other voices, feel somehow connected to others.

Like many inhabitants of modern civilization, my wife and I moved around the United States—Portland, Oregon, Boston, and New York—before settling in the San Francisco Bay Area in the early 1970s. After we moved to San Francisco, we changed houses and neighbors a half dozen times in the first ten years we were there. We got to know a few neighbors, and continued to see one or two of them after moving from the old neighborhood. A few friends from college were in the area. We did not belong to any organized religion. Like many others, we found that our mobility, the seclusion necessitated by my profession, and the social atomization of urban life left us with a dearth of social and intellectual affiliations.

Falling into social cyberspace was easy for me. I was sitting there in front of the computer for hours a day, anyway. It was not long before the modem had a dedicated telephone line. All I had to do was type a few keystrokes and I was connected to other people who were talking about everything under the sun. At first, I only did it in the evenings. I was fascinated by BBS culture. I still know two people I first met in 1984 via the Skateboard BBS. There were only about a dozen of us who regularly talked about life, art, jokes, and current events, via a BBS that ran off a PC in somebody's bedroom. However, it only took weeks before we started meeting regularly at a Chinese restaurant. BBS culture, however, is like a vast collection of small towns. No single online discussion offers much social or intellectual diversity. The Source was a much larger national service (later assimilated by CompuServe), but it cost as much as $15 an hour during prime time, and playing around with ideas online is no fun with the meter ticking.

My social isolation, fascination and dissatisfaction with BBSs, and inability to pay premium rates set me up for instant seduction when the WELL opened in 1985, offering a kind of freewheeling online salon of techies, writers, activists, deadheads, and other early adopters of technology culture—at $2 an hour. Where did the last seventeen years go? I had no idea at the time that reading, typing, thinking about, laughing at, crying over, and fretting over WELL postings would involve a significant amount, if not a majority, of my waking hours for more than a decade to come. I ended up traveling around the world to research the book I wrote about social cyberspaces, *The Virtual Community*, and traveling around it a half dozen more times after the book was published in 1993. Years of talking with people everywhere about this notion of virtual communities—an idea, I discovered, that many people find disturbing—pushed me to ask of myself some of the questions critics kept asking me in Tokyo and Sydney, Amsterdam and Vancouver, London and Stockholm.

The first such question I have been asked many times in many places is whether such groups are "really" communities. My answer is: "No, virtual communities are not 'really' communities, but it is important to extend the question." The same can be said of most apartment buildings, many neighborhoods, and all large cities. The question of what to do about increasing human alienation within the increasingly larger-and-faster-than-human environment is a serious one. People who communicate via computer networks definitely should be instructed about the danger of mistaking messages on computer screens for fully authentic human relationships. Similarly, we definitely need to be skeptical of claims that online discourse can effectively substitute for or revitalize the public sphere that was enclosed and fragmented by mass-media technology and public relations techniques. Every symbolic communication medium distances people in some ways while it connects them in others.

Two important qualifications must be considered before critiquing the phenomenon of virtual communities. First, for some people, online communication is a lifeline, a way of improving their quality of life, and one should think hard and long before appointing oneself the arbiter of whether it is healthy for an Alzheimer's caregiver, an AIDS patient, a quadriplegic, or a bright student in a remote location to spend time online. If one's critique does not take these people into account, there is the danger of doing real damage to the lives of people who might otherwise have no social life at all.

The second thing to keep in mind when critiquing virtual communities is that alienation is real and important but it did not begin with computers, nor should our critique end there. I would be the first to stipulate that in many cases, the availability of online social interaction can exacerbate the isolation and dehumanization of people who live in the modern world. If we are going to look unblinkingly at whether it is humane to support a world where more and more people spend more of our time driving single-passenger, petroleum-fueled vehicles through concrete landscapes to our cubicles inside big ugly buildings, where we spend our time staring at computer screens, manipulating symbols, and exercising our fingers— we need to look closely at the room, the building, the urban landscape, the entire civilization that computer screen is situated within, as well as questioning whether life in front of a screen is healthy.

The most important critiques of virtual communities are those that attack the validity of claims that many-to-many communication media have the potential for being used as a democratizing tool in the political sphere. Now that every desktop is potentially a printing press, a broad-casting station, and a place of assembly, has an important decentralization of the power to inform, witness, influence, and persuade taken place? Certainly, for the Serbian opposition who put their radio station B92 on the Net when the government shut down their broadcasts, and for the Zapatistas who effectively disseminated news and influenced world opin-ion via the Net, this claim is not wholly false. Minnesota's "E-democracy" project and the California Voter Foundation are excellent experiments. But whether computer bulletin boards, mailing lists, and e-mail can effectively counter the power of the global mass-media disinfotainment complex is a pragmatic question to ask.

I believe it is too early for a definitive answer. Indeed, a "definitive answer" may be impossible; it may be a matter of critical discussions rather than definitive answers, which are artifacts of our historical fascination with rationalism and science. The most intelligent critiques of this concept are Fernbach and Thompson's "Virtual Communities: Abort, Retry, Fail-ure?" (1995) and Langdon Winner's essay "Mythinformation," reprinted in his book *The Whale and the Reactor* (1986).

We should not close the books on the debate about the mental or social health of virtual communities and their relationship to the nonvirtual world. And neither should we stop at a shallow level of analysis. It is time to look at today's questions about digital life as instances of the same ques-tions Jacques Ellul and Lewis Mumford asked about technological civiliza-tion half a century ago, and which Marx, Weber, and Veblen dealt with even earlier.

It would be wrong to conclude that I am an uncritical enthusiast of virtual communities. Like all technologies, this medium has its shadow side, and there are ways to abuse it. Like all communication media, virtual communities enable people to misunderstand each other in new ways. Since the publication of the first edition of *The Virtual Community* in 1993, I have learned a great deal from my further experiences online and from the more intelligent critiques of the book. The MIT Press gave me the rare opportunity to amend my thinking in a long new chapter, including many more critical questions about the role of online social networks, in the 2000 edition. In general, I have learned two things. First, virtual communities are a subset of online social networks (Wellman and Guilia 1995). Most social networks have nothing to do with cyberspace, but the Internet provides an ideal medium for promoting social networks. Some but certainly not all social networks engender the kind of ongoing personal communications, caring, and offline activity that make the use of the word *community* appropriate, and not all social cyberspaces are pleasant, healthy, or productive.

If I had known about social-network analysis in 1993, I might have avoided nearly a decade of debate about whether virtual communities are real or not. In coming years, I believe the far more important questions will have to do with the nature of collective action in social cyberspaces, a more precise nomenclature (*community* is a notoriously slippery word) and a field amenable to social-science methodology.

From Thinking Tools to Thinking about Tools

It took years for me to understand the outlines of the problem and see that the problems of technology in which I began to suspect I shared complicity were inseparable from the powers granted me by my mastery of personal computers and online media. I still use and appreciate the same tools, but I was definitely more intoxicated back then with the sheer pace of change. A new world was emerging and it was fun, empowering, enriching—and most of all, cool.

When I was not hanging out online or writing about hanging out online, I maintained a professional interest in the evolution of computer technology. In 1990, I traveled from MIT and NASA to laboratories in Tokyo, London, and Grenoble, in order to research a book about a new computer technology that was threatening to create totally artificial worlds for people to pretend to inhabit: virtual reality. First, the computer came out of nowhere to dominate our lives. It looked like the next step might be for people to live inside the computer. In the process of writing my book *Virtual Reality* (1992), and in my reading of the book's reviews, I began to wonder whether the ultimate direction of personal computer development would really be the empowering mind amplification I had hoped for, or whether it might instead devolve into hypnotic disinfotainment. When someone can make a business out of selling everyone in the world a tool for telling them what else to buy next, do other potential applications for any new medium have a chance to compete?

At the time I was writing about virtual reality, I received an invitation from Kevin Kelly, who became the executive editor of the *Wired* magazine but was at that time the editor of the *Whole Earth Review*. I took over the job of editor of the *Whole Earth Review* when Kelly took off to write his book *Out of Control* (1995). Finding myself at the vortex of the Whole Earth community certainly accelerated my critical thinking about technology. I was immersed in an atmosphere that deliberately widened its focus from just the details of digital technology to include the biosphere and technologies of agriculture, energy, transportation, medicine, and urban planning.

Stewart Brand, the founder of *Wired* and the *Whole Earth Catalog* (1969)— the counterculture bestseller from which the magazine descended—was a biologist who shared my fascination with mind amplifiers. Indeed, when Douglas Engelbart produced his famous 1968 demonstration of the future of computer technology, his audiovisual coordinator was Stewart Brand. Brand's early writings about Xerox PARC helped steer me there, although I did not meet him for years to come. Brand's mentors, Ken Kesey and Gregory Bateson, were iconoclasts, pranksters, and whole-systems thinkers. Putting deep ecologists together with software engineers and questioning the fundamental premises of both camps was just the kind of thing Stewart Brand or Whole Earth would do. Over the years, the Whole Earth organization created cultural experiments such as the New Games Tournament, Cyberthon (a kind of geekstock for the protodigerati of 1992), the Hackers' Conference, and the WELL computer conferencing system.

Although "Access to Tools" was the magazine's slogan, the *Whole Earth Review* editorial staff certainly included several strong and knowledgeable advocates for radically different ways of thinking about technology. In fact, founder Stewart Brand became an adviser in the early

1980s to California's Governor Jerry Brown, who had created an "Office of Appropriate Technology."

The Whole Earth gang's funky old office in Sausalito was where I started thinking about where the technology I appreciated so much might all be going and where I began to suspect that a price of my technology intoxication was a kind of somnambulism regarding its dark side. I was outraged, during my tenure as editor, when William Irwin Thompson, in *The American Replacement of Nature* (1991, 44), accused Stewart Brand and me, by name, of being agents of the Zoroastrian demon of mindless mechanism. Richard Nilsen, Whole Earth's late "land-use" editor, put my face in the contradictions of ecology and technology every time I talked to him. Whenever people say "you can't stop progress," my friend J. Baldwin, Whole Earth's "tools guy" and a former student of Whole Earth guru R. Buckminster Fuller, advises asking the counterquestion: "progress toward WHAT?" One of my first issues of the *Whole Earth Review* was devoted to "Questioning Technology," an activity most people do not want to engage in, even as a thought experiment.

As soon as I finished editing *The Millennium Whole Earth Catalog*, the latest version of the decades-long succession of these catalogs, the World Wide Web came along, and I got sucked into a fascination within a fascination that consumed the next several years of my life. In the summer of 1994 I left Whole Earth and joined a young publishing enterprise, Wired Ventures, the publishers of *Wired* magazine. Kevin Kelly, ever my Mephistopheles, invited me to talk to the publisher of *Wired* about starting an online version, which was originally supposed to be called *@Wired* but ended up as *HotWired*, the first commercial webzine. I quit my job as *HotWired*'s executive editor because I wanted something more collaborative, a community rather than a publication. So I created a business plan, searched for and found $2 million in financing, launched *Electric Minds*, named by *Time* magazine as one of the ten best websites of 1996, lost financing when our backers found themselves in trouble, and folded the business in the summer of 1997.

In 1998, I teamed up with a company that turns cable television franchises into high-speed Internet service providers—we tried to test the notion that many-to-many communication media can help people build healthy local communities of the nonvirtual kind. I flew and ferried to Bainbridge Island, Washington, drove across the Arizona desert to Lake

Havasu City, and found that it took marketing budgets, legwork, and patience to make virtual communities work in small towns, under the sponsorship of cable stations. One of those communities I helped encourage still thrives, however: Palo Alto Online. In 1999 I designed virtual communities and online social networks for other clients, and in 2000 instigated a consultancy among a worldwide network of experienced virtual-community builders (http://www.rheingold.com/associates).

In retrospect, my career over the last fifteen years has been an unplanned curriculum in self-taught technology criticism—from the Institute of Noetic Sciences to Xerox PARC to *Whole Earth* to *Wired*, from *Tools for Thought* to *Virtual Reality* to *The Virtual Community*, to firsthand participation in the creation, rise, and fall of an Internet start-up, to direct work in civic community building as an online social-network consultant. I have shared my story as an observer of and participant in the digital revolution of the 1980s and 1990s, as a way of explaining some of what I have learned from reading and meeting people, and from getting my hands dirty (and burned) in pursuit of a few simple questions about technology: What are PCs and networks good for, and what are they bad for? Where are we going as individuals, communities, societies? Do we want to go there? Is there anything we can do about it?

Civilizing Virtual Communities

As Langdon Winner pointed out in his book *Autonomous Technology* (1978), the main question in the philosophy of technology now is whether to believe it is possible for humans to maximize the noble part and minimize the worst, whether technological progress is autonomous and therefore there is little we can do to influence it, or whether it is possible to separate the benefits from the liabilities. The evidence thus far is not good. I have been looking for examples of humans recognizing a problem caused by technological intervention in their lives, finding a solution, and making it work in action. Such people can be found, and they have much to say to us about what we need to know to find a solution that is democratic, humane, and workable. Right now, I think the first struggle is to get more than a tiny minority of people to recognize it is important to try to think together, as a civilization, about where technology came from, where it is going, and how to have a say in what happens next.

The social side of the Net has its shadow side, and it is not hard to find. I have seen that the relative anonymity of the medium, where nobody can see your face or hear your voice, has a disinhibiting function that cuts both ways—people who might not ordinarily be heard in oral discourse can contribute meaningfully, and people who might not ordinarily be rude to one's face can become frighteningly abusive online. As the Net has grown, the original norms of netiquette and collaborative, cooperative maintenance of an information commons that enriches everyone have been assaulted by waves of clueless newbies and sociopaths, spammers, charlatans, and loudmouths. Maintaining civility in the midst of the very conflicts we must solve together as citizens is not easy. The Net is the world's greatest source of information—misinformation and disinformation, community and character assassination—and we have very little but our own wits to sort out the valid from the bogus.

As with real-world communities, there is no single formula for success in virtual-community building, but there are several clear pitfalls, any one of which can cause the effort to fail. In order for a virtual community to succeed, the software must have a usable human interface, something that was not available until relatively recently. Unfortunately, many virtual-community organizers do not know better, or are sold on something by their investors and use older paradigms for online communication, which drives away those who have something to communicate but are not compelled to spend their time fiddling with technology. Another necessity for success is a clearly stated policy regarding online behavior that all participants must agree to. Having such a policy will not guarantee success, but not having such a policy probably guarantees failure.

Give people sensible rules and most of them will be very happy with that. Some communities will have very loose rules, some will be far more formal and controlled; the most important point of the exercise is that every participant agrees to a clear written statement of the rules before joining. People sometimes want to make up their own rules. If a subgroup wants a community with different rules, then they should formulate and agree on those rules and roll their own listserv, web conference, or IRC (chat) channel. A warning: "policy thrashing" over metaissues such as how to elect the people who make the rules can swallow up other forms of discourse. Face-to-face meetings are still far superior to online discussion for resolving conflicts and coming to agreement where consensus is not clear.

Most importantly, people who have had experience in dealing with online discourse need to participate, moderate, and host. Facilitating convivial and useful online discourse is a skill, one best learned through direct experience. Because behavior online tends to degenerate in the absence of conversational cues such as tone of voice, facial expression, or body language, it is necessary for experienced chatters or BBSers to model the behavior that the medium requires in order to maintain civility. Without a cadre of experienced users to help point out the pitfalls and the preferred paths, online populations are doomed to fall into the same cycles of flame, thrash, mindless chatter, and eventual dissolution.

The social and informational treasures of cyberspace are what drew me into the world of virtual communities. However, when I began to study the significance of these new media for our culture, I realized that the most important questions had to do with the political implications of global many-to-many media. Who would gain wealth and power? Who would lose?

Community Development in Cybersociety

The quality of community in tomorrow's wired world is an important concern. It is not, however, the first question we need to ask. The prefix *cyber*, from the Greek word for "steersman," implies that cybersociety will be steered in some manner. The first question to ask is: Who will be doing the steering?

Decades before computers existed, George Orwell and Aldous Huxley wrote about future dystopias where an elite, who use advanced communication tools to control the population, commands society. The malevolent dictator *Big Brother* and the paternalistic dictator Mustapha Mond used technologies of surveillance and persuasion to steer the societies of *Nineteen Eighty-Four* (Orwell [1949]) and *Brave New World* (Huxley [1932]). E.M. Forster, also writing years before digital technology emerged, wrote a novella, *The Machine Stops* (1963), that painted a future society steered by the machines themselves.

Today's world is a combination of all three visions, with a surprisingly democratic twist. The Orwellian portion is the invasion and commodification of privacy, aided and abetted by digital information-gathering and surveillance tools. The Huxley portion is the disinfotainment machinery that sells experiences, beliefs, issues, and candidates to a world that willingly pays for the illusion of information in the guise of entertainment.

The Forster part is the globalized economy, where liquid electronic capital has become detached from humanly recognizable goods and services and technology has taken over mediating more and more social relationships.

The global economy depends on a rapidly self-innovating technological infrastructure. Superheated economic competition requires the biggest players to concentrate massive resources on technology development. For these reasons, the only thing we can know with any degree of certainty about tomorrow's world is that technologies will be more powerful than they are today. And communication technologies, because of their ability to influence human perceptions and beliefs as well as their power to command and control automatic machinery, will continue to grow more powerful and persuasive, if not more true, authentic, and humane.

The democratic twist is that more people today have more to say about how their world is steered than at any other time in history. Structurally, the Internet has inverted the few-to-many architecture of the broadcast age, in which a small number of people were able to influence and shape the perceptions and beliefs of entire nations. In the many-to-many environment of the Net, every desktop is a printing press, a broadcasting station, and a place of assembly. Mass media will continue to exist and so will journalism, but these institutions will no longer monopolize attention and access to the attention of others.

It is not yet clear how this democratization of publishing power will translate into political change. The critical uncertainties today are whether the citizenry will learn to use the new tools to strengthen the public sphere and whether citizens are going to be any match for the concentrations of money, technology, and power emerging in the Internet era.

One important point of leverage where these critical uncertainties can be influenced is the role of journalism in civic affairs. If public broadcasting does not take the lead in this regard, it is difficult to see who will. In that respect I want to pose a couple of longer-term questions (Grossman and Minow 2001). First, how will new media affect the free and open discourse that forms the bedrock of democracy? Second, can professionally gathered news stories and civil-citizen discourse be blended in a way that enhances democracy? What is the role for traditional journalism in a world where the power to publish and communicate is radically diffused and disintermediated?

I am still hopeful that informed and committed people can influence the shape of tomorrow's cybersociety in a positive manner, although it has become increasingly clear that democratic outcomes will not emerge automatically. A humane and sustainable cybersociety will only come about if it is deliberately understood, discussed, and planned now—by a larger proportion of the population and not just the big business, media, or policy elites. Intelligent and democratic leadership is desperately needed at this historical moment, while the situation is still somewhat fluid. Ten years from now, the uncertainties will have resolved into one kind of power or another.

The public sphere is where people, through their communications, become citizens. The printing press did not cause democracy, but it made a literate population possible, and literate populations, who are free to communicate among one another, came up with the idea that they could govern themselves. As radio and television each had effects on the public sphere, so the Internet will affect democratic discourse in an evolving public sphere. However, I suspect that we simply do not yet know what form the public sphere will take in cyberspace. There certainly are strong signs that power and capital are moving swiftly to control and shape the way people use the emerging media.

Will the Internet strengthen civic life, community, and democracy, or will it weaken them? Failure to make the importance of this question clear to the public has been a shameful episode in the history of journalism. As one of the people who gets called for quotes on a daily basis, I can tell you that I have been talking about this issue for years, but all that ends up on the air or in print is something about porno or hackers or bomb recipes on the Internet. How do we introduce this truly important matter to popular discourse?

Because the public sphere depends on free communication and discussion of ideas, clearly this vital marketplace for political ideas can be powerfully influenced by changes in communications technology. According to the political philosopher Jürgen Habermas

When the public is large, this kind of communication requires certain means of dissemination and influence; today, newspapers and periodicals, radio and television are the media of the public sphere. . . . The term "public opinion" refers to the functions of criticism and control or organized state authority that the public exercises informally, as well as formally during periodic elections. Regulations concerning the publicness (or publicity [*Publizität*]) in its original meaning of state-related activities, as, for instance, the public accessibility required of legal proceedings, are also connected with this function of public opinion. To the public sphere as a sphere mediating between state and society, a sphere in which the public as the vehicle of publicness—the publicness that once had to win out against the secret politics of monarchs and that since then has permitted democratic control of state activity.

The sophisticated and wholesale manufacture of public opinion and the domination of popular media by electronic spectacles have damaged the public sphere, just as industrial pollution has damaged the biosphere. I believe the foundations of democracy have been eroded, for the reasons Neil Postman cited in *Amusing Ourselves to Death* (1986). The immense power of television as a broadcaster of emotion-laden images, combined with the ownership of more and more news media by fewer and fewer global entertainment conglomerates, has reduced much public discourse, including discussions of vital issues, to sound bites and images.

Opinion-shaping techniques originated in the print era but truly grew into their present degree of power during the era of broadcast media. Will citizen communications via the Internet be commodified, co-opted, or shaped? Have citizen forums been neutralized already, or were they never a threat to centralized control of public opinion? Are many-to-many media less easily manipulable than mass media, or does the manipulation simply come in a different form? Which way can the Internet go? When the present turbulence clears, who will have more power because of the Internet? Is there a concrete way of preserving a universally accessible public area in a rapidly privatizing Internet?

Civil society, a web of informal relationships that exist independently of government institutions or business organizations, is the social adhesive necessary to bind divergent communities of interest together into democratic societies. Until recently, the future of civil society in America and elsewhere was thought to be uncertain, gloomy even. However, around the world advocacy and action networks, community groups, and voluntary organizations are reemerging as a social force. Interestingly, many are beginning to utilize the Internet and other communication technologies to make their voices heard.

Can virtual communities help revitalize civil society, or are online debates nothing more than distracting simulations of authentic discourse? Enthusiasts—and I was one of the earliest—point at examples of many-to-many communication that appear to leverage power in the real world of politics. But how certain can we be, sitting at our desks, tapping on our keyboards, about the reality and limits of the Net's political effectiveness? Would you bet your liberty on it?

If, as citizens, we lose our freedom to communicate without fear of state censorship, then the Net's potential power to facilitate "electronic democracy" will stand revealed as a fatal illusion. Because the rights of citizens to communicate online are under direct political attack, Net activists are broadcasting action alerts, directing citizens' attention to the implications of proposed legislation, and furnishing contact information for key legislators on crucial votes. However, even if freedom of expression was not under attack, it is healthy to ask ourselves whether the kind of discourse facilitated by computer bulletin-board systems will bring together or further fragment the competing constituencies of the American republic.

Robert Putnam (2000b) has prominently claimed that the civil society that Alexis de Tocqueville (1990) noted 200 years ago in *Democracy in America* as the hallmark of the American experiment—the active involvement of citizens in voluntary associations for "the public good"—appears to be deteriorating. Is the Net really an effective answer to the mass hypnosis of the mass-media era? Talking at each other online seems to be at least marginally better than sitting stupefied in front of the tube, but we need to know how far, exactly, all that talk can carry us. Will worldwide Usenet discussions, up-to-the-minute legislative news listservs, World Wide Web pages, and e-mail chain-letter petitions add to civic life, or remove people from it?

The best critique of the democratic potential of virtual communities I have found so far is *"Computer-Mediated Communication and the American Collectivity: The Dimensions of Community within Cyberspace,"* a paper presented at the 1995 meeting of the International Communication Association by Jan Fernback and Brad Thompson (1995). This paper inspired me to sharpen my own critical perceptions regarding virtual communities.

Fernback and Thompson cite past outbreaks of technological utopianism to question the claim that online communications can strengthen civil society: "Citizenship via cyberspace has not proven to be the panacea for the problems of democratic representation within American society; although communities of interest have been formed and strengthened . . . and have demonstrated a sense of solidarity, they have nevertheless contributed to the fragmented cultural and political landscape of the United States."

The authors cite several arguments against believing in the democratizing power of virtual communities: the disjunction with geographically based neighborhoods can create phony communities, the cost of the technology and knowledge of how to use computers will always exclude much of society, and virtual communities are helping make direct, face-to-face conversation less common, among other arguments. Their conclusions are bleak: "It seems most likely that the virtual public sphere brought about by [computer-mediated communication] will serve a cathartic role, allowing the public to feel involved rather than to advance actual participation."

I believe the conclusion of their paper is wrong. I think there is time to prove the democratic potential of the medium by using it properly, as many authors in this book are now attempting. Electronic communications do not offer a utopia, but they do offer a unique channel for publishing and communicating, and the power to publish and communicate is fundamental to democracy. Communication media are necessary but not sufficient for self-governance and healthy societies. The important stuff still requires turning off the computer and braving the uncertainties of the offline world. When we are called to action through the virtual community, we need to keep in mind how much depends on whether we simply "feel involved" or whether we take the steps to actually participate in the lives of our neighbors, and in the civic life of our communities.

Online social networks constitute an important technology-enabled practice that has the potential to shape society. As a means of critical inquiry into how this technology affects our lives, I believe that it is more important to examine the nature of collective action in cyberspace than to debate whether virtual communities are real communities. The point is to understand how many-to-many media enable people to act together to create public goods or to behave destructively in more efficient ways.

As promised, this brief sketch of my own flirtation with technology has not presented any definitive answers. I hope that it has raised good questions. Just as we experienced the social changes associated with use of the personal computer in the 1980s and the changes enabled by the Internet in the 1990s, I believe we are at the threshold of a new technology that combines the powers and effects of mobile communications, pervasive computing, and peer-to-peer social networks. A new social sphere, new medium, new way of seeing the world will accompany the emergence of the new technology. Can we think critically about this next round of change in a way that maximizes our ability to influence it?

13   Libraries: The Information Commons of Civil Society

Nancy Kranich

For the first two-thirds of the twentieth century a powerful tide bore Americans
into ever deeper engagement in the life of their communities, but a few decades
ago—silently, without warning—that tide reversed and we were overtaken by a
treacherous rip current. Without at first noticing, we have been pulled apart from
one another and from our communities over the last third of the century
—Putnam, Bowling Alone

In this chapter, I discuss the importance of social capital as a catalyst to
rekindle civil society, as well as the key role of the library as an information commons for engaging citizens and encouraging participation in
community life. For more than two centuries, libraries have served communities in the United States and abroad as information commons. In that
role, they have helped promote an informed citizenry, offering safe spaces
for deliberation and exchange of a wide spectrum of ideas. For a democracy of the digital age to flourish, citizens need free and open access to
ideas more than ever. The salient tension of our times stems from those
barriers that deny citizens their full information rights. In the conclusion
to this chapter, I suggest an action agenda aimed at ensuring that everyone
has the opportunity to participate in a digital-age democracy.

Social Capital and Civil Society

To Vaclav Havel (1997) "Civil Society . . . means a society that makes
room for the richest possible self-structuring and the richest possible participation in public life." Civil society began to blossom in Havel's Czech
Republic over the last two decades. But in America, the associations and
activities that create the glue that strengthens civil society, notably

described by Alexis de Tocqueville in *Democracy in America*, (1838) have ensured a structure and climate for more than two centuries of active citizen participation in our democratic system. By the late twentieth century, however, journalists, political scientists, philanthropists, and citizens alike were documenting a declining public sphere, diminishing civic engagement, and eroding social capital. In response, social scientists have proposed new models to invigorate a weakened democracy and to encourage more active citizen involvement with governance. Among the most prominent voices is that of Benjamin Barber (1984, 148), who prescribes "strong democracy" as a remedy for incivility and apathy, where "active citizens govern themselves in the only form that is genuinely and completely democratic." Barber claims that "community grows out of participation and at the same time makes participation possible," and that "strong democracy is the politics of amateurs, where every [person] is compelled to encounter every other [person] without the intermediary of expertise" (p. 152). From his perspective, "Citizens are neighbors bound together neither by blood nor by contract but by their common concerns and common participation in the search for common solutions to common conflicts" (p. 219). In a later work, Barber calls for "a place for us in civil society, a place really for *us*, for what we share *and* who, in sharing we become. That place must be democratic: both public and free" (p. 38). David Mathews (1984, 1999; Mathews and McAfee, 2001) applies practical techniques to this active-citizenship model, engaging lay citizens in deliberation about issues of common concern. As president of the Kettering Foundation, he has developed a national network for civic forums, teaching citizens to frame issues, make choices, find common ground, and act in their community's best interest. James Fishkin (1995, 1997), has also helped pioneer this framework for citizen deliberation, joined by Daniel Yankelovich (1991, 1999) and his colleagues at Public Agenda. Harry Boyte, another political scientist instrumental in developing theories of active citizenship, has advanced new models for reinvigorating communities through the creation of free spaces or commons for public discourse and deliberation (see Boyte 1980, 1989; Boyte, Booth and Max 1986; Boyte and Evans 1986; Boyte and Kari 1996). These civil-society theorists were joined by a rash of other scholars in the last decade of the twentieth and into the early years of the twenty-first century (Edwards, Foley and Diani 2001; Ehrenberg 1999; Elkin and Soltan 1999; McConnell 1999; Seligman 1992; Verba, Scholzman and Brady 1995).

These and other scholars have documented and debated the state of civil society, both in the United States and abroad. Most notable is Robert Putnam, whose provocative article and bestselling book *Bowling Alone* (1995, 2000b) and his Saguaro Seminar, published as *Better Together* (2000a), have popularized the importance of reviving community by rebuilding social capital and increasing civic engagement.

The Information Commons

Information is essential to civic participation, and also encourages the development of civil society. When people are better informed, they are more likely to participate in policy discussions where they can communicate their ideas and concerns freely. Most importantly, citizens need civic commons where they can speak freely, discern different perspectives, share similar interests and concerns, and pursue what they believe is in their and the public's interest. Effective citizen action is possible when citizens develop the skills to gain access to information of all kinds and to put such information to effective use. Members of the community must have the real and virtual spaces to exchange ideas—ideas fundamental to democratic participation and civil society. Ultimately, discourse among informed citizens ensures civil society, and civil society provides the social capital necessary to achieve sovereignty of the people, by the people, and for the people.

Many of the theorists who focus their scholarship on new forms of citizen participation have recognized the importance of an information commons to bolster civic engagement. Boyte devotes a chapter of his book *Commonwealth* (1989) to the information age, elaborating the importance of schooling citizens in democracy by informing them about issues and utilizing public spaces to listen, negotiate, exchange, act, and hold officials accountable. Likewise, Hardt and Negro elaborate on the importance of the information commons to the evolution of the postmodern state and the emergence of new social movements in their book *Empire* (2000). With the rise of the Internet, commentators who focus on civil society in the digital age have identified the electronic information commons as underpinning equitable participation in a cyberdemocracy (Grossman 1995; Tsagarousianou, Tambini and Bryan 1998; Wilhelm 2000). Since 2000, civic-minded organizations have convened conferences and launched projects to design information commons for the digital age. Harry Boyte's Center for Democracy and Citizenship at the University of Minnesota hosted a New Information Commons Conference where participants from organizations such as the Project for Public Spaces and Libraries for the Future sketched out a plan for building new spaces by citizens in partnership with community organizations (Friedland and Boyte 2000). About the same time, the New America Foundation launched its Information Commons Project, directed by David Bollier, a prolific writer who focuses on intellectual property issues (Bollier 2001b). Bollier has also cofounded Public Knowledge, a nonprofit organization that will represent the public interest in intellectual property law and Internet policies. In the fall of 2001, the American Library Association sponsored a conference on the Information Commons, with commissioned papers on information equity, copyright and fair use, and public access, immediately followed by a similar meeting held at Duke University Law School's Center for the Public Domain, with papers on copyright and the information commons. Over just a two-year period, the role of the information commons has assumed a new dimension in the twentyfirst Century.

Libraries as Information Commons

Libraries provide the real and virtual spaces in communities for free and open exchange of ideas fundamental to democratic participation and civil society. In almost every school, college, and community, libraries in the Western world make knowledge and information available to all. They are the place where people can find differing opinions on controversial questions and dissent from current orthodoxy. Even beyond the United States, Canada, and Europe, and in emerging democracies, libraries serve as the source—often the sole source—for the pursuit of independent thought, critical attitudes, and in-depth information. And in so doing, they guard against the tyranny of ignorance, the Achilles heel of every democracy.

As community forums, many libraries present thoughtful, engaging, and enlightening programs about problems facing our democratic way of life—programs that have a vast potential to renew communities and encourage active citizenship. From librarians, we can learn how to identify and evaluate information that is essential for making decisions that affect the way we live, work, learn, and govern ourselves. Libraries are ideally suited to play a critical role in rekindling civic spirit by providing not only

information, but also the expanded opportunities for dialogue and deliberation that we need to make decisions about common concerns.

America's libraries, at the heart of every community, stand in defense of
freedom. Benjamin Franklin founded the first lending subscription library
even before he helped form the new republic. Franklin, James Madison,
and Thomas Jefferson were among the nation's founders who believed that
a free society must ensure the preservation and provision of accessible
knowledge for all its citizens. When they turned their attention to designing a government capable of preserving freedom for the citizenry, they
looked to an institution with the potential for realizing their ideal. For if
an informed public is the very foundation of American democracy, then
America's libraries are the cornerstone of that democracy. As Madison
(1822, 276) eloquently stated, "Knowledge will forever govern ignorance
and that people who mean to be their own governors must arm themselves
with the power that knowledge gives. A popular government without
popular information or means of acquiring it is but a prologue to a farce or
tragedy or perhaps both."

Benjamin Franklin's novel idea of sharing information resources was
a radical one. In the rest of the civilized world, libraries were the property
of the ruling classes and religious institutions. American democracy was
founded on the principles of freedom of information and the public's right
to know. America's libraries ensure the freedom of speech, the freedom to
read, the freedom to view. The mission of libraries is to provide the
resources the public needs to be well informed and to participate fully
in every aspect of the information society. In many parts of the world,
countries have adopted this centuries-old American tradition.

As libraries serve to prepare citizens for a lifetime of civic participation,
they also encourage the development of civil society. They provide the
information and the opportunities for dialogue that the public needs to
make decisions about common concerns. As community forums, they
encourage active citizenship and renew communities. Libraries build social
capital and encourage civic engagement by developing community partnerships, facilitating local dialogue, and disseminating local data.

Ever since their proliferation in the nineteenth century, American libraries
have played a key role in educating immigrants for citizenship. They have
also supported education by providing resources for curriculum-based and
lifelong learning. As the new millennium unfolds, a number of librarians

have published new texts underscoring the key role that libraries play in building civil society, paralleling the surge of social-science scholarship cited previously in this chapter. Redmond Kathleen Molz and Phyllis Dain (1999), faculty members at Columbia University, present a new history of the public library as a civic space, updated for the information age; Kathleen de la Peña McCook (2000), a professor at the University of South Florida, spells out the key role libraries play in community building; and Ronald McCabe (2001), a public library director in Wisconsin, provides a historic and theoretical framework for understanding the ways libraries enhance citizen involvement in renewing and strengthening communities. When millennial president of the American Library Association, I chose the theme of libraries: the cornerstone of democracy, which serves as the subject of a published collection of essays on equitable access and the public's right to know (Kranich 2001b).

Today, libraries throughout the United States, Canada, Europe, Australia, and beyond are undertaking a vast array of innovative, creative programs that support civil society and build social capital in their communities. They are convening groups to consider local issues and teach civic skills; building community information-literacy partnerships; coordinating local literacy training; hosting communitywide reading programs in cities like Chicago, Rochester, Seattle, Syracuse, and Buffalo; creating digital neighborhood directories that link residents and services; and partnering with local museums and public broadcasting stations. These collaborative efforts increase social capital—the glue that binds people together and enables them to build bridges to others.

According to Putnam (2000b, 341), "Just as one cannot restart a heart with one's remote control, one cannot jump-start republican citizenship without direct, face-to-face participation. Citizenship is not a spectator sport." The challenge for the information age is to find new ways to encourage citizens to participate in democracy and renew communities. Working closely with a rich and diverse array of citizens, libraries are a key institution that can help communities rekindle civil society and expand public participation in our democracy.

For centuries, libraries have served as the information commons in communities across America. They have offered free and open spaces to all—amateurs and experts alike. They embody many of the ideals of the public sphere envisioned by Jürgen Habermas (1992a; see also Calhoun

1992a). They are inclusive—offering universal service—and they encourage public participation and deliberation. In the digital age, libraries throughout the world serve communities as information commons within the public sphere: commons that promote economic well-being, global understanding, the advancement of learning, information literacy, digital inclusion, and public participation in the democratic process—essential ingredients of a civil society.

Libraries in the Digital Age

At the dawn of the information age, libraries are experiencing new vigor at the same time that they are helping rekindle civil society. Online or in person, today's libraries are more popular than ever. Polls estimate that more than two-thirds of the public uses America's libraries every year.

Why are America's 115,000 public, school, academic, and special libraries gaining in popularity? Libraries are the only place where an information commons is freely available for everyone in every community. Libraries provide communities with precise, replicable discovery tools and materials on every subject from all perspectives in a full range of formats and languages. Users can readily identify and link to these resources from home, work, or their local libraries and then borrow or copy them. Libraries also archive and preserve older titles. Best of all, professional librarians provide personalized help and training—in some cases twenty four hours a day, seven days a week. One innovative way libraries are cooperating around the world is the project undertaken by the Library of Congress, the British Library, and the National Library of Australia to provide round-the-clock reference service to English speakers wherever they reside.

Thanks to technology and worldwide collaboration, many of today's libraries have migrated from a state of scarcity to a state of abundance, transcending their geographic, legal, and political boundaries, with librarians serving as knowledge navigators and learning facilitators. What began in the 1950s as the automation of materials processing led to the deployment of computerized databases for locating information in the 1970s. More recently, libraries have offered direct public access to the Internet, supplemented by purchased commercial databases, plus unique local collections converted to digital formats, thereby creating digital libraries available anywhere, anytime. This capacity to deliver information directly and just-in-time to users helps connect collections and reference services directly to a population with an insatiable demand for information access. Over the years ahead, libraries will share more and more resources, offering seamless access to a rich collection of valuable, interesting resources. Experts will guide users precisely to the materials that meet their particular needs. It will no longer matter where digital content resides. All kinds of libraries, government agencies, and cultural institutions will work together with commercial and nonprofit producers to create, convert, index, archive, preserve, and make accessible digital resources. Several proposals to create national digital collections of cultural resources to enhance civil society have surfaced in recent years. One, the Digital Promise Project, recommends setting aside revenues from the auction of the publicy owned electromagnetic spectrum to finance digitization to enhance learning, encourage an informed citizenry, and make available the best of America's cultural resources (Grossman and Minow 2001). In the future, such projects will foster the creation of just-in-time virtual communities with such benefits as equitable access, reduced barriers of distance, timeliness, shared resources, and content delivery. But numerous impediments to equitable access face communities as they struggle to realize the true potential and power of the twenty first-century information society.

The Tendencies and Tensions of Public Access

Access to information is fragile. All sorts of barriers can restrict the public's access to ideas. Best known are blatant book-banning attempts. But every link in the information chain can either strengthen or weaken public access. The chain begins with information creators. Without doubt, the elite are far more likely to assume this role than those who are less advantaged. The marketplace for ideas is another key link in determining which voices will be heard—and which will be heard the loudest. But after the sale of an idea, information and knowledge are not used up or consumed like other commodities, even though many producers would prefer them to behave that way. They still have many chances to influence thought when they are collected, archived and preserved for future generations. Among the various barriers to sustained public access are classification, copyright or other licensing restrictions, funding, and filtering as well as other censoring actions. Any of these actions can limit the public's access to critical information and the opportunity to participate in civil society.

Because the information revolution has changed the way we live, learn, work, and govern, we simply cannot assume that libraries and other cultural institutions are capable of ensuring equitable access to all the resources and points of view that we desire. Access to abundance does not ensure access to diversity. Instead, we now have access to more and more of the same ideas, with alternatives marginalized more and more by such forces as corporate profiteering, political expediency, and the whimsy of the marketplace. The promise of new technologies is imperiled by powerful political and economic forces. Schement and Curtis (1995) argue that the tendencies and tensions of the information society stem directly from the organizing principles of industrialization and the realities of capitalism. These tensions confront the public as citizens struggle to reclaim the public sphere and their information rights in the digital age. Attempts to restrict the public's right to know and unfettered public access to information keep accelerating. Now more than ever we face serious threats to public access and the free flow of ideas. What is at stake is not only the basic and fundamental role of libraries as the information commons in our communities, but also the public's access to information and knowledge—the basic underpinnings of democracy.

The Information Rich and the Information Poor

The Internet promises to bridge the gap between the information haves and have-nots in our society. No longer divided by geographic, linguistic, or economic barriers, electronic information can span boundaries and reach into any neighborhood with just the click of a mouse. Truly, the dream of an equitable information society offers new hope for rekindling the democratic principles put forth by the founding fathers in the U.S. Constitution and by the authors of Article 19 of the International Declaration of Human Rights. Even if an American household cannot afford or chooses not to connect to the Internet, families have the option of logging on at a library or school. Under the universal-service provisions of the U.S. Telecommunications Act of 1996, nearly every community is now connected, thus ensuring an on-ramp to the information superhighway and an opportunity for all Americans to participate in their communities' economic, educational, social, political, and leisure activities.

The Clinton administration drew the nation's attention to the "digital divide" and the gap between the information rich and poor in America.

Recent research indicates that, despite a significant increase in computer ownership and overall usage, many low-income, minority, disabled, rural, older, and inner-city groups are falling behind in their ownership of computers and access to telecommunications networks (Benton Foundation, 1998; Novak and Hoffman 1998; U.S. National Telecommunications and Information Administration, 1995–2002). Beyond providing for the purchase of hardware and connectivity to the Internet, librarians and other public-interest groups have stepped into this gap to ensure public access to a broad array of information resources, promoting literacy in the twenty-first century and reducing barriers to intellectual freedom and fair use throughout the world. Particularly impressive is the work undertaken in this area beyond the United States by the International Federation of Library Associations (IFLA) through its Committees on Freedom of Access to Information and Free Expression (FAIFE) and Copyright and Other Legal Matters (IFLA/FAIFE, 2001).

The Digital-Content Divide

Into the milieu of this new century comes the Internet, with affordable and accessible content—content that was previously unavailable to many communities, both in the United States and abroad. Access to an abundance of information does not necessarily mean access to a diversity of sources. Cyberspace is sparse when it comes to local information, particularly for rural communities and those living at or near the poverty level. The vast majority of Internet sites are designed for people with average or advanced literacy levels. For the more than 20 percent of Americans whose reading levels limit them to poverty wages and for the thirty million Americans speaking a language other than English, few websites are readily comprehended (Children's Partnership, 2000). Residents of countries where English is not spoken are at even more of a disadvantage. Furthermore, ethnic and racial minorities are unlikely to find content about the uniqueness of their cultures. The Children's Partnership has estimated that at least fifty million Americans—roughly 20 percent—face a content-related barrier standing between them and the benefits of the Internet. That same study also indicates that adults want practical information focusing on local community, information at a basic literacy level, content for non–English speakers, and racial and ethnic cultural information. In addition, the study found that

Internet use among low-income Americans was for self-improvement, whether for online courses, job search, or other information. In short, the poor and marginalized individuals seek information that helps them with their day-to-day problems and enables them to participate as members of their democratic community.

An information commons is well suited to meet the needs of the populations cited by the Children's Partnership. Libraries and other community institutions can target websites and digitize materials of interest to special populations as part of the process of ensuring widespread participation in the information society. They can also create sites that are easy to navigate, translated into languages spoken by residents, and responsive to local needs. Information equity, a community priority, requires local organizations and institutions to join forces to bridge the digital-content divide.

Information Literacy in a Highly Mediated World

The public needs sophisticated information-literacy skills to succeed in the twenty-first century and to fulfill their roles as engaged citizens. Even those already proficient at finding, evaluating, and applying information to solve daily problems can be overwhelmed by the proliferation of information and the difficulty of sorting through it. To cope successfully, citizens must be able to identify, evaluate, apply, and communicate information efficiently, effectively, and responsibly. They will have to become information literate to flourish in the workplace as well as to carry out the day-to-day activities of citizens in a developed, democratic society. Many libraries now work in collaboration with community and education groups to identify information needs, initiate a dialogue aimed at encouraging a more information-literate populace, and facilitate the development of skills to utilize information strategically. Granted, the need for information-literacy skills has been around for generations. But the dawning of the information age forces the development of broader information skills if people are to separate the wheat from the chaff, the true from the untrue, the rumor from the real.

Registrations now exceed 560,000 per year at the U.S. Library of Congress Copyright Office. New book titles published annually in the United States have jumped more than 30 percent since 1990. Worldwide, publishing output has reached close to one million titles annually. More than 100,000 U.S. and 10,000 U.N. documents enter circulation annually, along with untold numbers of state, local, and international documents. Even more astounding is the exponential growth of the World Wide Web. A February 1999 study reported in *Nature* concluded there were about 800 million publicly available web pages, with about 15 trillion bytes of textual information and 180 million images weighing in at about 3 trillion bytes of data. The growth rate of the web is estimated to double every year, though some sources estimate this level of growth every six months (Lawrence and Giles 1998, 1999).

Not surprisingly, the complexity of finding, evaluating, and utilizing information in the electronic age has become a major challenge for the 60 percent of the American workforce that engages in some information-related activity. Librarians, teachers, and other professionals are needed more than ever to ensure that the public has the information-literacy skills it needs to live, learn, work, and govern in the digital age. In the contemporary environment of rapid technological change and proliferating information resources, communities face diverse, abundant information choices. The uncertain quality and expanding quantity of information pose large challenges for society. The sheer abundance of information will not in itself create a more informed citizenry without a complementary cluster of abilities necessary to use information effectively. Every community must promote the development of information-literate citizens, beginning at the elementary school level, progressing through high school and college, and commencing with adults through partnerships with community organizations (American Association of School Librarians and the Association for Educational Communication and Technology, 1998; American Library Association, 1989, 2000; Association of College and Research Libraries, Instruction Task Force, 2000; see also Marcoux 2001).

The Electoral Process

For years in the United States, the public has registered to vote and cast election ballots in libraries, schools, and community centers. Citizens attend local forums with candidates to learn more about their positions and voting records. They monitor the work of both elected and appointed officials through the reports housed in depositories of government information, where they also gather data to help them take positions on various issues facing their communities. During campaign seasons, citizens find voter guides and other relevant information about elections and referenda in libraries and other community organizations, and they engage with authors who write about political issues at locally sponsored events. They also seek local information about deadlines for voter registration, locations of polling places, and valuable electronic links to high-quality electoral information in print as well as on the web.

One key way libraries and other civic organizations support democratic action and citizen participation is through the development of electronic websites that guide users to valid and reliable information informing their choices about candidates and issues. Publicly accessible sites offer a comprehensive map of civic issues and the electoral process, including links to political-history sites, political search engines, candidates' voting records, campaign finance information, past election results and speeches, political statistics, media coverage, advocacy and lobby groups, and political-party platforms and conventions. Information must be available in a variety of media ranging from books and magazines to videos, audio recordings, and electronic resources that inform the public about the political process— resources that can be used either in libraries and community centers or outside with community groups and schoolchildren. Community and nonpartisan groups must collaborate to promote greater political participation in the digital age in conjunction with such groups as the League of Women Voters and a newer electronic organization—Project Vote Smart, which offers electronic access to candidate and voting information (Kranich 2000b, 2000c).

In March 2000, the Democratic Party of the state of Arizona pioneered a new frontier in America's oldest ritual. Over four days, members of the party cast ballots for their party's presidential candidate, many of them doing so electronically through the medium of the Internet. Total voter turnout increased from 13,000 in the primary of 1996 to 89,000 (even though only one candidate remained on the ballot); 40 percent cast Internet ballots. In Arizona, a major concern of the Democratic Party and voting-rights advocates was the potential for excluding voters who lacked computer access. To ensure that as many eligible Democrats could vote as possible, twenty-five Arizona public libraries served as polling places for electronic voting—a contemporary use of the information commons as civic spaces. "We think that there is something wonderfully symbolic about public libraries being used as polling places," said Gladys Ann Wells, State Librarian. She noted that "libraries have always been places where everyone in a community can find common ground, so it is logical that libraries would be places where people without computers could come to vote." Judy Register, Scottsdale City Librarian, added that "libraries are determined to play a leading role in helping people bridge the so-called 'digital divide.' Now, helping bridge this 'electoral divide' is a great use of the technology available in public libraries in Arizona."

Community Networks

Comparable to libraries, community networks, such as free nets, create channels of communication for public dialogue. The movement toward community networks reflects the desire for a democratic institution capable of recognizing the centrality of information access and communication to modern life. Community networks offer many of the services provided by libraries, including training, e-mail, web-page development, and small-business assistance. They also focus users on local assets and services, pulling together essential information and communication resources that might otherwise be difficult to identify or locate. Of special interest here, they offer opportunities for community institutions to collaborate and build partnerships in support of local-history projects, civic-education programs, and community enterprises, such as information and referral services, that might be overlooked by the commercial sector. Finally, community networks offer an exceptional opportunity to forge new roles locally for libraries as well as other public, educational, and cultural institutions and organizations in the digital age (Durrance et al. 2001; Durrance and Pettigrew 2000; Schuler 1997b; 1996a).

Government Information

Over the last decade, the persistent voice of librarians and public-interest groups and the promise of new technologies have improved access to government information. The result has been the promotion of the public's right to know along with the advancement of citizens' involvement in governance. A fifteen-year struggle to promote equitable and efficient access to government information culminated in the 1990s in the passage of the GPO Access Act, the Electronic Freedom of Information Act, and other statutes that strengthen public access in the digital age. Still, these victories are incomplete. Even though the public has benefited from ever more direct access to government records and documents, more and more data is slipping into private hands, getting classified under the guise of national security, or exempted from release under the Freedom of Information Act. Furthermore, a proposal before Congress to ensure permanent public access to electronic government documents has gone unheeded as links to important documents disappear unnoticed. So, while public access to government information produced at taxpayer expense is more freely available than ever before, the threat to public access persists. Even more vulnerable, state, local, and foreign electronic government information rarely falls under depository and other open-access statutes. Attempts to implement electronic government statutes could improve access, but may rely on the private sector for dissemination, resulting in higher prices, limited dissemination, and escape from the public domain. A civil society must be a transparent society with equal and ready access to government information if citizens are to trust, oversee, evaluate, and interact with public officials (Davis and Splichal 2000; Heanue 2001; Hernon, McClure, and Relyea 1996; see also American Library Association, 2002c).

Copyright and Fair Use

Against the promise of easy access to networked electronic information loom new technological protection measures. The ubiquity of digital information, the widespread use of networks, and the proliferation of the World Wide Web create new tensions in the intellectual property arena. The ease with which data may be copied impels information producers to seek ways of protecting their investments. Their intentions are perfectly understandable. Unfortunately, measures proposed to protect creators endanger users' fair-use rights to view, reproduce, and quote limited amounts of copyrighted materials. This high-stakes international policy debate might well result in a pay-per-view, or—even more chilling—a pay-per-slice digital-information economy where only those willing and able to pay can access electronic information. With librarians in the vanguard, the delicate balance between creators' and users' rights to information has been carefully negotiated for print materials over the past century. In the information age, however, the balance has tilted toward intellectual property owners. Should this imbalance persist, it will endanger free speech, the advancement of learning and research, the information commons, and the rekindling of civil society.

One statute in particular that places new limits on the public's access to information in the United States is the Digital Millennium Copyright Act of 1998, which criminalizes illegal use of digital materials for the first time and places additional limits on the rights of electronic information users. As a consequence, the widespread deployment of pay-per-view systems could effectively reduce libraries and other repositories of valuable knowledge to mere marketing platforms for content distributors. Fair use for electronic publications barely survived in this legislation as new restrictions were imposed on unauthorized access to technologically restricted work. The act prohibits the "circumvention" of any effective "technological protection measure" (TPMs) used by a copyright holder to restrict access to its material unless adverse affects on the fair use of any class of work can be demonstrated. Thus, the burden of proof rests with those seeking open access and the free flow of information.

Numerous attempts to regulate and restrict public access to information under the umbrella of intellectual property protection persist in Congress and in international tribunals. One in particular, a proposal to copyright databases in the United States, will safeguard investment rather than creativity for information companies and overturn over 200 years of information policy that has consistently supported unfettered access to factual information. Such an act will allow a producer or publisher unprecedented control over the uses of information, including factual information as well as government works. Even though the Supreme Court has held that constitutional copyright principles prohibit ownership of facts or works of the federal government and current copyright law already protects database companies, some producers continue to press hard for this over-broad protectionist legislation. Should they succeed, they will accomplish a radical departure from the current intellectual property framework that protects expression—not investment—and thereby endanger the doctrine of fair use. If these special interests prevail, a digital economy will emerge where the free flow of ideas is limited to the obsolescent world of print and photocopy machines, and where citizen discourse is relegated to the backseat of democracy (Bollier 2001a, 2001b, 2002; National Research Council, 2000; Vaidhyanathan 2001a, 2001b, 2001c; see also American Library Association, 2001d). Equally disturbing, precedents such as these set the tone for similar policy development in the European Union and through the World International Property Organization (WIPO).

Universal Service and Filtering

Since the early decades of the twentieth century, Americans have held the belief that maximum access to public information sources and channels of communication is necessary for political, economic, and social partici-pation in a vigorous civil society. Everyone must have access to informa-tion and communication networks in order to participate in democracy. Under the universal-service provisions of the U.S. Telecommunications Act of 1996 (Section 254), the Federal Communications Commission has authorized a program to ensure equitable access to telecommunications technologies by offering schools and libraries discounted rates that were once reserved for only the largest corporate customers. In this way, schools and libraries may be connected as a first step toward widespread public access. Known as the E-Rate, over $2 billion in discounts and grants is now earmarked annually for distribution from fees collected by long-distance phone carriers. In addition, the E-Rate helps bridge the digital divide by expanding access and connectivity to needy communities (EdLiNC, 2000; McClure and Bertot 2000; Urban Institute, 2000; see also American Library Association, 2002e). Still, it took some horse trading to gain acceptance for the E-Rate. Telecommunications companies agreed to this amendment to the 1996 Telecommunications Act in return for deregulation of their markets. Even so, several of the major carriers who benefited most from deregulation have tried to sabotage this program through court challenges and by highlighting the universal-service charge on consumer bills without explanation, thereby inciting the anger of their enormous customer base.

Where corporate attempts to stop the flow of subsidies to schools and libraries ended, Congress has added its own twists. A law passed in Decem-ber 2000, the Children's Internet Protection Act (CIPA), requires local schools and libraries to install filters to protect both children and adults from viewing obscenity and child pornography in order to receive E-Rate and other federal subsidies. Both the American Library Association (ALA) and the American Civil Liberties Union (ACLU) have brought suits to challenge the constitutionality of this law (American Library Association and the American Civil Liberties Union, 2001; see also American Library Association, 2002b). Attempts to tie federal funding to content restrictions raise serious constitutional questions similar to those brought forward in *ACLU v. Reno*, which succeeded in challenging the constitutionality of the Communications Decency Act. CIPA will impose federal regulations over local, community control of information access. First Amendment protections must extend to the digital sphere if we are to ensure open dialogue across the full spectrum of opinion in the information age.

Many states have proposed and some have passed similar laws to restrict Internet access in schools and libraries by mandating a filtering requirement in order for these institutions to receive state and local funding. Unfortunately, filters do more harm than good; they sweep too broadly, blocking only some of the sites with indecent materials while restricting access to legal and useful resources. Users complain that filters block such home pages as the Super Bowl XXX, the Mars Exploration site (MARSEXPL), swan migration in Alma, Wisconsin (swANALma), *Mother Jones* magazine, the National Rifle Association, the Quakers, thirty Congressional candidates, House Majority Leader Dick Armey, the American Association of University Women, Beanie Babies, and millions of other sites of legitimate interest. Filtering systems have trouble distinguishing between users who are six and sixteen years old; they apply the common denominator of the youngest users at the expense of all others. Furthermore, filters are not effective in blocking much material that some consider undesirable for children; they gives parents a false sense of security, leading them to believe that their children are protected from harm. Most importantly, they do not take the place of preferred routes that include the development of community-based Internet-access policies, user education programs, links to great sites (white/green lists), and safety guidelines.

The extraordinary benefits of Internet access are too often overshadowed by controversies fueled by groups who stoke imagined fears about the power of images and words in an effort to control access to information. According to a study by the National Coalition Against Censorship (1999), "The evidence of harm from Internet access at public institutions is at best equivocal, and the blunt-edged approach advocated by pro-censorship advocates ignores the individualized needs of children and their parents. Fortunately, most libraries have found ways of balancing the interests of all parties effectively, without censorship." Surely those relying on public institutions for connectivity deserve access rights equivalent to those enjoyed by consumers who can afford access at home, and should not be subjected to yet another digital-content divide (Kranich 2001a, 2000a; see also American Library Association, 2002a, 2002b, and Freedom to Read 2002).

The Tide of the Information Age

The emergence of personal computers and telecommunications technologies over the last twenty years has transformed information creation, transport, and dissemination industries from independent operators mostly involved with infrastructure to a highly integrated, multinational private sphere of megacompanies looking to optimize profits and dominate access to homes and businesses. Throughout the world, a period of deregulation and privatization has shifted the information policymaking arena to the private sector, where questions of the public interest are harder to raise.

What is at stake is not only the availability and affordability of information essential to the public interest, but also the very basis on which citizens' information needs are met. As communications and media industry giants stake their claims in cyberspace, the public interest must not be overlooked. The new information infrastructure must ensure free spaces that are filled by educational and research institutions, libraries, nonprofits, and governmental organizations charged with promoting and fulfilling public-policy goals. The new information commons must constitute a public sphere of free speech and open intellectual discourse that enhances democracy.

An Action Agenda for a Twenty-First-Century Information Commons

Everyone must have the opportunity to participate in a digital-age democracy. Citizens need safe gathering places where they can share interests and concerns, find information essential to civic involvement, and connect with fellow citizens. If the public's right to know is to be protected within a free-market global-information infrastructure, citizens must stand up and speak out to promote an information commons in the public interest. As Brian McConnell (1999, 125), former president of the Independent Sector, has warned, "The greatest dangers to civil society and democracy arise from neglect by the very citizens who expect privileges and rights without exercising responsibility to protect them."

Librarians are well positioned to lead the charge to ensure that citizens can exercise their twenty-first-century information rights. Why? Because librarians are committed to ensuring the free flow of information in our society and understand what is at stake. And they represent more than half of the country's adults as well as three-quarters of its children, who use libraries every year. They have extensive experience working with community groups in building social capital, strengthening civil society, and championing the public's information rights. Furthermore, librarians preserve the community's historic, cultural, political, and social record and provide free spaces for reflection and deliberation by local citizens.

Librarians must pick up the gauntlet and join forces with computer professionals, educators, cultural organizations, journalists, public officials, public-interest groups, and the general public to ensure that everyone has access to a free and open information commons. Neutrality will not work; the stakes are very high—namely, our democratic way of life that depends on an informed electorate. Working together in communities throughout the world, we must recognize the importance of an information commons to the advancement of civil society. We must be well informed about the issues and the players on all sides. We must undertake research that demonstrates the contributions of public access to the advancement of science and the arts. We must map public opinion.

We must compile anecdotes about the positive effects of access to information and the negative impact when access is denied. We must articulate the positive economic value of the social outcomes of the commons and how it outweighs the negative impacts on the market.

We must enter the struggle adequately armed. We must identify individuals and groups with common concerns, looking far beyond the normal sources for allies. We must build coalitions to promote public access, to extend our reach, to increase our strength and influence, and to galvanize grassroots action. We must seek opportunities to testify at relevant hearings and forums and urge that public-interest representatives be named to various task forces and advisory councils on information issues at the local, national, and international levels. We must support growth, connectivity, and digitization by local libraries, schools, and other cultural organizations and make their valuable resources readily available over the network.

We must focus more attention on the importance of the information commons and attempts to erode the public sphere. We must collect data about "Where's the harm?"; assemble facts and document the case; make the issues local; and use good examples, anecdotes, and stories. We must tell the story about why access to information helps and how the lack of it hurts.

We must take every opportunity to educate the public. We must develop a public-awareness action plan that mobilizes support, holds politicians accountable for their views, and encourages community involvement. To connect with citizens, we can circulate petitions and launch letter-writing campaigns; distribute flyers, buttons, and banners; develop a recognizable logo; organize special celebration days and events; sponsor lectures and events; mount exhibits; and commemorate Freedom of Information Day with award ceremonies and other events. We must also find citizens who will speak out about their concerns and communicate them to policymakers. And finally, we must establish local free nets and other communication vehicles to share community concerns, information, events, and opportunities.

Without a technologically sophisticated information commons in every community, the gulf between the information rich and the information poor will widen. If we are to revive communities and restore civic virtue and democratic participation, we must advocate for a public sphere with a rich, vibrant information commons—a commons where citizens are free to engage in civic life. Otherwise, we will endanger our most precious assets in a democratic society: our rights of free speech, inquiry, and self-governance.

14 The Soil of Cyberspace: Historical Archaeologies of the Blacksburg Electronic Village and the Seattle Community Network

David Silver

Using Benedikt's appropriately titled *Cyberspace: First Steps* (1991) as one bookend and Bell and Kennedy's equally appropriately titled *The Cybercultures Reader* (2000) as another, we find a decade's worth of rich scholarship in what is tentatively called cyberculture studies, Internet studies, or new-media studies. As the field of study continues to grow, patterns of approaches appear, beginning with journalistic descriptions in the early 1990s, a fascination with virtual communities and online identities in the mid-1990s, and critical explorations into issues of cultural diversity in the late 1990s (Bell 2001; Silver 2000a).

In the chapter that follows, I wish to suggest a new approach, one that borrows heavily from recent American studies and cultural studies scholarship, which, in turn, borrows from what is often referred to as "constructivist studies of technology." During the 1980s, historians of technology began examining technology within the culture and society that created it (Bijker, Hughes, and Pinch 1987; Corn 1986; Pacey 1983). As Downey (1998, 21) explains, constructivist studies of technology "make visible the diverse activities of individuals and groups involved in technological development, making it difficult to think of 'invention' and 'innovation' as singular events or fixed processes." Within such a framework, new technologies are neither positive, negative, nor neutral, but rather products of multiple agendas situated within a particular time and place.

Building on the work of the constructivists, American studies and cultural studies scholars have explored the social and cultural constructions of new and once-new communication technologies. For example, in the introduction to the influential anthology *Technoculture*, Penley and Ross (1991, xiv) note that technologies are not repressively foisted upon passive populations, any more than the power to realize their repressive potential is in the hands of a conspiring few. They are developed at any one time and place in accord with a complex set of existing rules or rational procedures, institutional histories, technical possibilities, and, last, but not least, popular desires. All kinds of negotiations are necessary to prepare the way for new technologies, many of which are not particularly useful or successful.

Surprisingly, while the field of cyberculture studies continues to grow, there are no book-length attempts to historically contextualize online culture. Although Abbate (1995) and Salus (1995) trace the historical development of the Internet, they stop short of addressing critically the cultural and social practices stemming from such developments. Conversely, while Dibbell's *My Tiny Life* (1998), Horn's *Cyberville* (1998), and Rheingold's *The Virtual Community* (1993) explore the cultural and social practices of specific online communities, they pay little, if any, attention to the historical development of such environments. Dibbell devotes a few pages to the history of multiuser domains, or MUDs, and exactly one page to the history of LambdaMOO, his book's site of inquiry; Horn offers no formal history of ECHO, an online community based in New York; and Rheingold provides a brief, cursory history of the WELL, a virtual community rooted in the San Francisco Bay Area. This reluctance to link culture with history is dangerous, for it casts the Net as a neutral, barren frontier: rootless, settlerless, waiting to be civilized.

In an attempt to lend proper context to the study of online cultures, this chapter traces the institutional histories of two of the best-known and most popular community networks: the Blacksburg Electronic Village (BEV) and the Seattle Community Network (SCN). Working under the assumption that cyberculture, like all forms of culture, is developed within a particular time and space and distributed and used via numerous cultural, economic, and political negotiations, I outline the community networks' initial inceptions, structural developments, and institutional contributions. I also examine the networks' implementation, focusing especially on community involvement, organizational structures, and content development. Throughout the chapter, I pay special attention to the respective roles, contributions, and interests of the projects' various partners. As I hope to reveal, although the BEV and the SCN share a common goal—to network a community—the ways and means by which they have sought to achieve that goal differ drastically, and have produced significantly different results.

I develop these histories from four major sources. First, I have consulted a number of online archives assembled by the networks' program and design teams. These archives include the BEV HistoryBase, the BEV Newsletter Archive, and the Seattle Community Network Association's Meetings Minutes Archives. Second, I have examined dozens of local and national newspaper and magazine articles that detail, among other topics, the networks' development. It is important to note at the outset, however, that while the organizers of the BEV made efforts to nurture and promote publicity, volunteers for the SCN seldom courted the press. Accordingly, articles on the SCN are far less numerous than those on the BEV. Third, I have drawn significantly from three studies on the two community networks: Cohill and Kavanaugh's *Community Networks: Lessons from Blacksburg, Virginia* (1997), an interesting yet particularly boosteresque account of the BEV; Schorger's Ph.D. dissertation, "A Qualitative Study of the Development and First Year of Implementation of the Blacksburg Electronic Village" (1997), an examination limited to the network's early origins and rooted in educational technology; and Schuler's *New Community Networks: Wired for Change* (1996a), a how-to manual on community networks with a minor focus on the SCN. Fourth, I have conducted a number of oral histories— both face to face and via e-mail—with key players from both networks.

The Blacksburg Electronic Village

The BEV is a test bed of services that will be demanded by customers in the future. —John W. Knapp, Jr., spokesman for Bell Atlantic (quoted in T. Farragher, "In Blacksburg, Va., There's No Wired Place Like Home")

The origins of the BEV are found in Virginia Polytechnic Institute and State University. In 1987, Virginia Tech, a university that hosts nationally ranked programs in computer science and engineering, jump-started its campuswide computer network. With a $16 million bond issue authorized by the General Assembly, the university constructed a state-of-the-art telecommunications system out of digitized telephone networks and high-speed modems. After the system was completed, Virginia Tech faculty, staff, and on-campus students enjoyed direct network access at a speed of 19,200 baud, a dramatic improvement over the then-normal 1200 baud (Bowden, Blythe, and Cohill 1997; Harrison 1995).

Two results followed. First, Chesapeake and Potomac Telephone of Virginia—now Bell Atlantic of Virginia—lost operation of the Virginia Tech telecommunications system, resulting in a considerable loss in revenue and a strained relationship between the two institutions (Bowden, Blythe, and Cohill 1997; Schorger 1997). Moreover, in turn, the town of Blacksburg lost a significant revenue tax. As Town Manager Ronald Secrist notes, "When C & P Telephone, now Bell Atlantic, was removed from providing telephone services on campus the loss in revenues in our consumer utility tax was upward of $90,000" (Schorger 1997, 32). The second result was widespread adoption of and increased demand for the network on the part of Virginia Tech students and faculty. Equipped with rocket-fast connection speeds, members of the Virginia Tech community spent a significant portion of the late 1980s online, e-mailing friends and colleagues, participating in mailing lists and bulletin boards for academic courses and social groups, and downloading documents, files, and programs from the university's mainframe computer (Harrison 1995; Rothenberg 1996).

Persistent requests from students and faculty for off-campus connectivity was the seed of the BEV. As Harrison (1995, A4) notes, "The electronic village project came about when local residents, most of them connected to the university, approached school officials about gaining access to a computer network off campus." (See also Blumenstyk 1997; Stepanek 1999.)

To solve the problem, the university, headed by Robert Heterick, then vice president for computing and information systems at Virginia Tech, considered a number of options. First, they investigated the possibility of working with the town of Blacksburg to propose a bond issue to construct a network. The idea garnered little interest. Second, Virginia Tech explored the option of partnering with a local cable television company, generating, again, sparse support. Finally, university officials considered renewing their ties with Bell Atlantic, which, in fall 1990, approached Virginia Tech to propose a campuswide telecommunications network. The university selected the third option and appointed Joseph Wiencko, then senior network consultant for Virginia Tech, to chair a series of meetings between the university and Bell Atlantic (Bowden, Blythe, and Cohill 1997; Schorger 1997).

On April 17, 1991, Wiencko delivered a presentation at Bell Atlantic's main office in Richmond, where the two parties agreed in principle to pursue what was then called the "Blacksburg Community Network." As Wiencko notes, "The main point of the presentation was to outline formation of a community network project that would serve as a test bed for industry and a stimulus for personal and regional enrichment for Blacksburg" (Schorger 1997, 33). Believing the project to be a window to tomorrow or, as described by John W. Knapp, Jr, a spokesperson for Bell Atlantic, a "test bed of services that will be demanded by customers in the future," the telephone company jumped at the opportunity (Farragher 1995, D1). With Bell Atlantic on board, Wiencko and his associates approached Mayor Roger Hedgepath and Secrist to invite the town to become a project partner. Hedgepath and Secrist were enthusiastic and secured the support of the town council (Huff and Syrcek 1997).

On January 20, 1992, a press conference was held at the Continuing Education Center on the campus of Virginia Tech. Accompanying Congressman Rick Boucher, representatives for the three project partners—Hugh Stallard, president of Bell Atlantic of Virginia; James McComas, president of Virginia Tech; and Hedgepath, mayor of Blacksburg—spoke to a standing-room-only audience and outlined their vision of the future. Judging from the official press release, the event focused on the project's uniqueness ("A university town nestled in the scenic Virginia mountains could become one of the nation's first 'electronic villages'") and on the collaborative efforts between the university, the town, and the telephone company (Blacksburg Electronic Village, 1992; Bowden, Blythe, and Cohill 1997; McCue and Rosenberg 1992; Schorger 1997). The conference concluded by announcing the launch of a comprehensive six-month feasibility study.

The largest local paper, the *Roanoke Times & World-News*, immediately championed the project. Two days before the press conference, a front-page article alerted readers about the project, exclaiming "this town may be the first in the country to be completely linked, house to house, business to business, by fiber optics" (Rosenberg 1992a; A1). A day after the press conference, the paper continued the celebration, publishing a glowing article on the project, remarking that "perhaps within just a few years every home, apartment, business and school in Blacksburg would be electronically linked with banks, pharmacies, grocery stores, libraries, stockmarkets and one another" (McCue and Rosenberg 1992, B1).

Led by Robert Morris of Bell Atlantic, the six-month feasibility study stretched to a year. Unfortunately, because the findings were never made public, the official results of the study are unclear.[1] There is, however, an online document titled "Why a Network in Blacksburg?" (Blacksburg Electronic Village 1995b), which is commonly featured in BEV press materials and public presentations. From this document, we can derive three main qualities that, in 1992, made the town of Blacksburg an ideal test site for Bell Atlantic. First, the town of Blacksburg is compact. Nestled in the foothills of the Blue Ridge Mountains, Blacksburg's 36,000 residents live within a small geographic area. Unlike metropolitan cities with their dispersed geographies and large populations, Blacksburg's small size and compact nature promote what sociologists call a relatively "closed community," an advantageous characteristic when attempting to establish a critical mass of participants. As the project developers note, "The most frequent social and cultural contacts by the people of Blacksburg are with other people in Blacksburg; most routine business transactions by residents are with local Blacksburg businesses."

The second quality was Virginia Tech. In addition to constructing the state-of-the-art telecommunications system in 1987, the university built a number of fully equipped computer labs distributed throughout campus. As Paul Gherman, a special assistant to the vice president for information systems at Virginia Tech, noted in 1992: "There are 15,000 to 17,000 computers on campus. We have more computers than telephones" (Watkins 1992, A26). As a result, the computer-literacy rate of Blacksburg residents was, in 1992, well above the national average. Further, accompanying the high computer-literacy rate was a high computer-ownership rate: "Because Virginia Tech is a large university in a relatively small town, it is likely that the per-capita usage rate of computers in Blacksburg is the highest of any town or city of Virginia; it is possibly the highest in the country or the world" (Blacksburg Electronic Village, 1995b; see also Heterick 1993; Holusha 1994).

The third quality making Blacksburg an ideal test site for a community network was the town's somewhat international composition. In addition to the approximately 1,500 international students enrolled at Virginia Tech in 1992, there were visiting faculty members from many countries. Seemingly uninterested in the multicultural flavor such an international community brings, the project partners were instead thrilled with the publicity such visitors could generate: "This international aspect is advantageous in disseminating, through individual user experiences, the ideas of community networking throughout the world" (Blacksburg Electronic Village, 1995b).

Apparently the three qualities were enough. On January 11, 1993, a second press conference was held, this time migrating from the university to the town's Municipal Building. Bell Atlantic President Hugh Stallard joined Boucher, McComas, and Hedgepath to announce the formation of a partnership to create "the most comprehensive 'electronic village' in the nation." Congressman Boucher added: "This is the first time a local government, major state university, and local telephone company have joined together for the purpose of making information services available for an entire community" (Blacksburg Electronic Village, 1993). Finally, Bell Atlantic reported that it had contributed over $6 million to the project, largely in the form of a digital switch for the town, an essential ingredient for a high-speed data network (Rosenberg 1993).

While a number of community networks began taking shape during the same time, the BEV was unique due to the nature of its partnership. As originally conceived and presented at the second press conference, the project brought together three entities, each assuming different yet complementary roles. First, Bell Atlantic was responsible for building and operating the network's infrastructure. This included upgrading switching equipment, constructing a fiber-optic backbone, and installing a network built primarily of ISDN lines and Ethernet that would cover both the campus and the town of Blacksburg. Further, Bell Atlantic installed internal wiring in several apartment complexes (approximately 450 individual apartment units), allowing occupants to link directly to the network via a T1 line. Finally, it connected the Blacksburg Public Library with high-speed network connections (Bowden, Blythe, and Cohill 1997; Chandrasekaran 1995; Holusha 1994; Zajac 1999).

Second, essentially fulfilling the role of project manager, Virginia Tech was responsible for both the development and assessment of the BEV. As agreed on, faculty, students, and staff from the university would develop the network, maintain its servers, package software and user-support guides, create local information resources, and handle user registration. Further, Virginia Tech's Student Telecommunications Society would serve as the network's guinea pigs, or beta group. They would also be in charge of assessment and coordinate several research groups from across the disciplines to assess the project (Bowden, Blythe, and Cohill 1997; Rosenberg 1992b).

And finally, the town of Blacksburg was responsible for community outreach and public relations. As originally conceived, community outreach would take the form of a series of presentations, seminars, and computer workshops conducted by the town for Blacksburg citizens, classrooms, and community groups. The town would also serve as a conduit through which members of the community could request particular services and resources. Finally, the town would be in charge of publicity, primarily in the form of public lectures and presentations to community groups ("BEV Project Partners," 1999; Bowden, Blythe, and Cohill 1997).

Directly following the second press conference and throughout 1993, the BEV rapidly took shape. In March, a beta version of the BEV software was developed and tested by a group of computer-savvy users, most of whom came from the Student Telecommunications Society, a Virginia Tech student organization consisting primarily of graduate students majoring in electrical engineering.[2] The testing process focused primarily on technical issues, including ease of software installation and configuration. As Patterson (1997, 55) notes, "to facilitate the evaluation effort, BEV designers gathered together a range of experts in computer-mediated communication systems from Virginia Tech." During the same period, Bell Atlantic installed Ethernet connections in four apartment complexes as well as ISDN lines throughout campus (Bowden, Blythe, and Cohill 1997; Martin 1997; Rosenberg 1992b).

By summer, things began to snowball. On July 1, members of the project formed the official BEV development group. As Schorger (1997, 37) notes,

The formation of this group gave a persona to BEV as well as staffing resources. Up to this point development had been on an ad hoc basis within the University community. . . . This changed when the BEV group was formed. Andrew Cohill, named the director of BEV at this time, and some members from a related project group [ERIS], at Virginia Tech, were brought in and became responsible for the development and implementation of BEV on a full time basis.

On October 25, with Cohill in charge, the group opened the BEV office, a small space located in the lobby of the Information Systems Building at Virginia Tech. Although the space was small and temporary, it was real. The BEV was in business, both online and offline.

Much of the next two years was spent fixing bugs, generating content, increasing access, and recruiting businesses. Indeed, the early sailing was not always smooth. Although the BEV software was beta tested a year earlier, the testers were computer-savvy students from Virginia Tech. As less computer-literate students and members of the town arrived, so did the headaches. As Madelyn Rosenberg (1994, NRV2), an assistant editor for the *Roanoke Times & World-News*, wrote in a March 1994 editorial, the BEV was anything but user-friendly: "'How's it going with BEV?' one [friend] asked when we met for darts last week. I made a faint hacking sound. She nodded. She's known BEV much longer than I have. 'Your frustrations are only beginning,' she said."

While Cohill and his team were busy fixing bugs, the town of Blacksburg began its efforts to increase community participation in the BEV. The Blacksburg Telecommunications Advisory Committee (BTAC), a citizens' committee originally formed in 1983 to address issues of poor cable television services, coordinated much of this work. On October 6, 1994, the BTAC approved the "Plan of Action for Putting Town on the BEV," a three-phase plan "to enhance communication amongst citizens and in particular to be proactive and a catalyst for empowering citizens to interact with their local government" (Blacksburg Electronic Village, 1995a). The first phase, contracted out to BizNet, a local Internet company, and implemented November 1, 1994, was titled "Town of Blacksburg Information" and provided timely information about the town of Blacksburg coupled with information on how to access town services. Among the avalanche of information included in this first phase were directories of Blacksburg boards, commissions, and town officials, extensive transportation guides, emergency response documents, and the agendas and minutes for a number of government meetings.

The second phase began on April 1, 1995. Titled "Electronic Access for Services and Feedback," the phase included putting online various town services that could be requested and downloaded electronically and setting up channels through which citizens could send electronic feedback to the Town Council. This process allowed citizens to request via the network police reports and vacation monitors, to reserve picnic shelters and camping grounds, and to notify the Department of Public Works of a dead animal or the need for a special pickup. Further, it allowed citizens to send electronically their ideas and opinions regarding town plans and ordinances to town officials. It never, however, considered how to ensure that those officials received, not to mention responded to, such ideas and opinions.

The third phase, titled "Electronic Application, Registration, and Payment for Town Services," would consist of various registrations and applications that citizens could complete electronically and send via computer to the appropriate town department for processing (Huff and Syrcek 1997; Blacksburg Electronic Village, 1995a). Originally slated to appear by 1996, the third stage has yet to be implemented.

In addition to fixing bugs and generating content, project developers worked to increase access to the network. The most significant event was moving the office from the university to the town. In October 1994, the BEV office moved into a space within the Virginia Tech Museum of Natural History, conveniently located on Main Street in downtown Blacksburg. As then–BEV operations manager Cortney V. Martin (1997, 237) observes, maintaining a physical presence was key to the project: "The Main Street location was a real boon to the project, and the number of walk-in customers increased. The Museum is a naturally inviting, people-friendly place that encouraged people to stop by and find out more about the BEV."

In addition to the access afforded by the Main Street office, the local library was perhaps the most instrumental factor in expanding participation. The Montgomery-Floyd Regional Library was involved in the BEV from the beginning. Steve Helm, computer specialist for the library, and Robert Heterick brainstormed possible collaborations in 1992; Bell Atlantic installed a powerful T1 line in the library in September 1993; and discussions between the library and the BEV group were common and fruitful throughout the early stages of the project. This involvement escalated in late 1993 when the library was awarded a 1993–1994 Library Services and Construction Act (LSCA) subgrant for $57,000. Complementing the equipment already donated by Bell Atlantic, the grant provided funds for ten computer workstations, necessary software and hardware, Ethernet connection fees, and a full-time librarian devoted to Internet training and assistance. Further, the project was extended a year with support from a $40,000 LSCA continuation subgrant for 1994–1995 (Cohill 1997; Helm 1994).

Complementing the new office and library access was a series of demonstrations and workshops for the community. Usually held at the library or at the New Media Center on the Virginia Tech campus, these events targeted particular groups, including government officials, children, schoolteachers, and, as we will see shortly, businesspeople. The workshops were designed not only to show potential users the network, but also to let them explore it. Further, the BEV project team conducted workshops outside the library and university, often visiting local schools, senior-citizen homes, and the local chapter of the Lions Club ("Blacksburg Electronic Village Classes Planned by Libraries," 1994; Cohill 1997; Foster 1994a; "Introduction to BEV Set at Library," 1994; Lindquist 1994).

Finally, in addition to handling technical troubleshooting, generating content, and increasing access, much of 1994–1995 was spent recruiting business. Indeed, commercial applications of the BEV were never far from the developers' thoughts, and members of the project team made extra efforts to recruit local businesses. This recruitment took two forms. First, in late 1994, the BEV group organized a series of hands-on workshops for local businesspeople. Taking place in a university computer lab, the four 2-hour seminars filled quickly, with many businesses asking to enroll up to fifteen of their employees. The second event that got local businesses on board came from the town. In the summer of 1995, the town of Blacksburg gave the BEV $15,000 in grant money to aid local businesses in creating websites. The grants were extremely successful, and within a few months the town of Blacksburg awarded forty-seven businesses funds ranging from $90 to $390 (Silver 1999, 2000b).

By the end of 1995, two years after its initial launch, the BEV had fully arrived. It gained international publicity, wired a significant portion of the town's citizens, services, and businesses, and secured many financial returns. During 1995 alone, the *Philadelphia Inquirer, Los Angeles Times,* and *Washington Post* featured articles on the network. Superlatives were difficult to avoid: the *Philadelphia Inquirer* called Blacksburg "perhaps America's most wired municipality" (Farragher 1995, D1); the *Los Angeles Times* caught Cohill remarking that "this is the most connected town in the world" (Harrison 1995, A4); and the *Washington Post* managed to hear Cohill call Blacksburg "without a doubt, the most computer-connected place, per capita, on the planet" (Chandrasekaran 1995, A12). Further, following a feature segment on the *NBC Nightly News with Tom Brokaw* a year earlier, the BEV was one of the main highlights in an hour-long Discovery Channel program on cyberspace shown in April 1995 ("Electronic Village Gets Discovered," 1995; Foster 1994b).

While publicity escalated offline, a community of users grew online. It grew quickly: in January 1995, three months after its initial launch, 300 town residents signed onto the BEV; by February, 400 users called the BEV home; and by April, 800 accounts were established. By its first anniversary in October, the BEV contained accounts for one-fourth of the town's 36,000 residents. By April 1995, one-third of Blacksburg residents participated in the BEV (Farragher 1995; Foster 1994a; Harrison 1995; Reed 1994; Schultz 1994).

Although the widespread publicity and early adoption of the BEV are impressive, the most dramatic development was commercial. As the *Wall Street Journal* notes, "The network has triggered a flurry of high-tech economic activity that exceeds what a town of 36,000 would normally support" (Choi 1996, B1). Symbolizing this flurry was the Corporate Research Center, a 120-acre commercial office complex dominated by high-tech industries. As the *Chicago Tribune* observes, "Most of the 11 brick offices are occupied by innovative start-ups spun off from Virginia Tech or drawn to the region by a tech-savvy workforce and fresh air" (Zajac 1999, C1). Indeed, by 1997, a mere three years after its initial launch, eighteen new Internet-related businesses opened in the Blacksburg area (Blumenstyk 1997).

Not to be left out, a number of Virginia Tech faculty members, working in conjunction with the BEV, were awarded substantial grants. As noted in the *Chronicle of Higher Education*, by 1997, Virginia Tech had received support for over ten BEV-related research projects, involving nearly forty faculty members and graduate students. In 1993, for example, a number of Virginia Tech computer scientists received a $449,088 grant from the National Science Foundation (NSF) for "Interactive Learning with a Digital Library in Computer Science." The following year, NSF awarded a planning grant of $99,824 to Virginia Tech, the BEV, and the Montgomery County Public Schools for "Planning for Virtual Schools in Electronic Villages," an attempt to develop and document an online school.

Significantly, the project called for a partnership with commercial education providers, including Scholastic Network, Inc., and Busch Entertainment. The principal investigators came from the departments of computer science, education, and communication studies. The next year, the Blacksburg Electronic Village, Incorporated was awarded a $266,710 grant from the U.S. Department of Commerce's Telecommunications and

Information Infrastructure Assistance Program (TIIAP) for "Building Community in Rural America—A Replicable Model for Community Networks" (Blumenstyk 1997; DeVaughn 1994; Milenky 1995).

And the grants kept coming. In 1996, the Network Infrastructure for Education of the National Science Foundation awarded the BEV a $151,493 grant for "Evaluation of the Impact of Computer Networking in K–12 Education Reform." The project, an attempt to assess the impact of network resources and learner-centered teaching strategies, as well as the role of networking for school-community interaction and involvement, was a collaboration between the BEV and Virginia Tech's College of Human Resources and Education. And finally, the U.S. Department of Commerce's Public Telecommunications Facilities Program awarded the BEV a $75,000 planning grant for "Meeting the Needs of Rural Health and Education: A Wireless Solution." The project supports an exploratory team to plan network connectivity and build educational content with community partners in nearby Smyth and Floyd Counties.[3]

The Seattle Community Network

[The SCN] redefines what neighborhood is. This kind of forum allows people to talk over the back fence with people of the same interests and concerns, rather than based on some geographic boundaries.

—David Kinne of Washington Ceasefire (quoted in S. Maier, "New Computer Network—The Talk of the Town")

Computer technology and progressive politics came together in 1983 with the formation of the Seattle chapter of Computer Professionals for Social Responsibility (CPSR). Originally conceived as an informal online discussion group at the Xerox Palo Alto Research Center in late 1981, CPSR was—and continues to be—a collection of computer professionals devoted to ensuring socially responsible applications of computer technologies. Beginning as an advisory group focused on increasing awareness of the risks associated with nuclear weapons and the Strategic Defense Initiative (SDI or "Star Wars"), CPSR extended and expanded on these efforts by sponsoring annual meetings and conferences. Fusing technology and politics, the conference themes, which continue today, include the following: Computers, Freedom, and Privacy; Directions and Implications in Advanced Computing; and

Participatory Design (Computer Professionals for Social Responsibility, "CPSR History," undated; Computer Professionals for Social Responsibility, "CPSR Timeline," 1998).

Among the nearly two dozen chapters, CPSR/Seattle is one of the most active, a result no doubt of the city's high-tech industries and progressive politics. Beginning in 1983, CPSR/Seattle established a diverse agenda of public awareness, community outreach, and policy. In turn, this agenda translated into a series of public talks and seminars, the formation of Computers for Activists, a group that provided high-tech help to nonprofit organizations, and the founding of a special-interest group focused on information-policy and information-privacy issues within the state of Washington ("Computer Professionals for Social Responsibility—Seattle Chapter," undated). It was not until 1990, however, that one of CPSR Seattle's members found a single project on which to focus their efforts collectively.

While the history of the BEV is rooted firmly in Virginia Tech, the origins of the SCN are found in the Seattle chapter of CPSR. In 1990, CPSR sponsored its biannual Directions and Implications of Advanced Computing (DIAC) symposium. Following the conference, the proceedings were published as *Directions and Implications of Advanced Computing: Proceedings from the DIAC '90 Conference*. Douglas Schuler, an engineer at Boeing, an active member of CPSR/Seattle, and, in 1990, a future chair of CPSR, read the proceedings and was particularly intrigued by "The Rainbow Pages: Building Community with Voice Technology," a paper submitted by Paul Resnick and Mel King. As Schuler (1993, online) recalls, "This paper had exciting insights on using computers for community development and communication. I looked deeper and discovered a small but growing world of community-based computer projects including pioneer systems such as Berkeley's Community Memory and Montana's Big Sky Telegraph."

On October 16, 1990, Schuler shared his interest in community networks at a CPSR/Seattle meeting at the home of member Jon Jacky. As part of his presentation, he discussed a number of community networking projects, including Community Memory and Big Sky Telegraph, as well as the Public Electronic Network (PEN) in Santa Monica, California, the New York Youth Network in New York, and the Cleveland Free-Net in Ohio. While no formal action took place, the presentation produced lively and sustained discussion. It also generated a community of activists and computer programmers—some who traveled from as far away as Portland, Oregon—interested in learning more (Schuler 1996b; Westrich 1997).

A few false starts and a little over a year later, Schuler reintroduced the idea of community networks at a January 1992 CPSR/Seattle meeting. Members watched "If It Plays in Peoria . . . ," a video about the Heartland Free-Net in Peoria, Illinois. Produced by the National Public Telecomputing Network, a nonprofit corporation located in Cleveland, Ohio, which served (until its bankruptcy in the late 1990s) as the parent organization for community networks around the world, the video examined the need for and potential benefits of community-run, community-built computer networks. According to Schuler, the video generated considerable excitement among those present, including Ken Gillgren, Randy Groves, Phil Harrison, Heather Holmback, Phil Hughes, Aki Namioka, Sharma Oliver, Lorraine Pozzi, and, of course, Schuler himself. Before the meeting adjourned, members voted unanimously to make the Seattle Community Network an official project of CPSR/Seattle (Schuler 1993, 1996a, 1996b).

Fueled by CPSR/Seattle members' interest, two crucial developments took shape. First, Lorraine Pozzi suggested a meeting with local activist groups and projects. After receiving resounding approval from the members, Pozzi, Schuler, and others approached Kay Bullitt, a long-time Seattle activist whose home often served as a political hub for progressive Seattleites. When Bullitt enthusiastically agreed to host an event, organizers sent invitations to over fifty local community leaders. The event was a huge success. Over forty guests, representing a diverse spectrum of Seattle, including public television station KCTS/9, Seattle Public Library, the University of Washington, and members of local educational, environmental, social services, and commercial communities, attended the spring event. According to Schuler (1996b), "Aki Namioka and I presented the vision of a free, public access computer system that would help a community keep in touch with itself. . . . Although the presentation was undoubtedly somewhat naive and there was some skepticism the mood was optimistic and many attendees at that early meeting are enthusiastic SCN supporters." Following the presentation, there was a free-flowing exchange of ideas as well as requests and commitments to become involved (Schuler 1996a, 1996b).

The second development was an offshoot of the first. Among the attending community leaders were Yvonne Chen and Jim Taylor of the Seattle

Public Library (SPL). Chen, the library's advocate for reference services, and Taylor, the coordinator of automated services, left the meeting convinced of the need to collaborate: "It complements our mission as a library," Chen remarked to her colleagues (Griest 1994, C1). Over the next seven months, Schuler and Groves met regularly with Chen and Taylor until a working agreement was reached. As we will see, collaborations between the SCN and the SPL made possible many of the network's early and sustained successes.

With a team of volunteers, interest from community activists and groups, and a working agreement with the SPL, CPSR/Seattle members spent the next two years focused on three activities: recruiting, organizing, and fundraising. While the origins of the BEV were conceptualized behind the closed doors of Bell Atlantic, members of the Seattle project opened the brainstorming process to the public. For example, the July 16, 1992, issue of the *Seattle Times* included a brief column on the nascent network. It read: "A Seattle Community Free Network? It's worked in other communities. The goal is to link local organizations and agencies electronically in build- ing a sense of civic involvement. The Seattle chapter of Computer Profes- sionals for Social Responsibility is looking into the concept. Call——for details" (Andrews 1992, B2).

Once brought together, the volunteers were organized into five com- mittees. These included the following: Outreach, responsible for general public relations, publicity, fundraising, and working with strategic part- ners; Services, in charge of working with information providers and design- ing the initial interface; Hardware/Software, responsible for all technical elements, including recommending, evaluating, and installing system soft- ware and debugging and maintaining the network; Policy, accountable for general principles and user policies; and Staff and Facilities, in charge of coordinating information providers, webmasters, and volunteers (Schuler 1996a, 1996b). As their name implies, none of the volunteers received financial remuneration.

In addition to the five committees, a coordinating council (often referred to as the steering committee) was established. The coordinating council consisted of an elected representative from each of the five committees and two members at large elected by all members.[4] The role of the coordinating council was "to respond quickly when necessary, to help determine strategic directions for the group, and to make recommendations" (Schuler 1996a,

358). Finally, an advisory board was formed and assigned "to help SCN think strategically on how better to make an impact in the community" (Schuler 1996b). Although more symbolic than active, the advisory board, initially made up of representatives from Seattle's progressive, educational, and governmental communities, helped to legitimize the project.

Complementing their recruitment and organizational efforts was a grassroots fundraising campaign. As an early flyer noted, traditional grant writing proved tricky and unproductive: "We have written several grants but seem to be in the Catch-22 of needing money to build a system and needing a system to get grant money" (Andrews 1993, D2). Instead, contributions came from within; 80 percent of the network's initial operating budget came from CPSR members, SCN volunteers, and individual donors. The rest arrived as financial and in-kind contributions from local software and Internet companies (Griest 1994).

During the same time, the volunteers worked to ensure tangible alliances and products. The first was a working agreement with the SPL, a result of seven months of discussions and negotiations. In essence, the SPL agreed to house SCN computers, provide a few phone lines for access, and distribute SCN brochures. Further, they agreed to provide the SCN with a small workspace within the library. Finally, and perhaps most importantly, the SPL installed SCN as a menu choice on its public-access system, affording visitors to the main library and its twenty-three neighborhood branches free and public access to the community network. In return, the SCN agreed to provide library visitors free computer training, e-mail accounts, and web space, as well as develop online content relevant to the libraries and their patrons (Schuler 1997, 1996a, 1996b).

The second product was a set of documents. Put together during a series of coordinating council meetings, the statement of principles serves not only to define what the SCN is but also what it hoped to become. According to Schuler (1996a, 339), the group process of coming up with a "shared vision" is absolutely essential, for that vision can and should be built into the network and its operations.

The statement of principles serves as a guiding set of commitments. Influenced heavily by the CPSR, the statement of principles privileges political ideologies over technological configurations and focuses on five commitments: to access; to service; to democracy; to the world community; and to the future. Accompanying the statement of principles was the policy statement. Written by the Policy Committee chaired by Aki Namioka, the policy statement would define what constitutes acceptable and unacceptable behavior within the SCN.

In January 1994, the SCN was launched as a pilot project. For the next six months, the SCN took what Schuler called a "shakedown cruise," an open yet closely monitored series of forums developed, in part, to test the system, look for and correct bugs, and build up online content, data, and information (Maier 1994, A1). In addition to testing the system, the pilot project was instrumental in building community. In early March, for example, the SCN joined Washington Ceasefire, a Seattle-based gun control coalition, to sponsor an electronic forum on violence. As reported in the *Seattle Post-Intelligencer*, the project sought to bridge the local with the national: "In addition to offering a 'bulletin board' for people to exchange ideas and comments on violence, the forum will provide a trove of local and national statistics, including a directory of organizations that work on violence issues and a calendar of community events" ("Discussion of Violence Goes On-line in Seattle," 1994, B2).

The importance of this forum cannot be underestimated. Because computer-savvy users are most likely to find advanced network errors and hard-to-find system bugs, most high-tech pilot projects, including the BEV, target high-tech users. The SCN took a different course by privileging community rather than technology. As David Kinne of "Washington Ceasefire" points out, communication, not communication technology, was the focus: "People from the south, north, Eastside—[people] who normally would not have any opportunity to meet each other and talk to each other—come together in this electronic forum. . . . It redefines what neighborhood is. This kind of forum allows people to talk over the back fence with people of the same interests and concerns, rather than based on some geographic boundaries" (Maier 1994, A1).

While still in the experimental stage, the project began to attract attention. Deeming it worthy of front-page attention, the *Seattle Post-Intelligencer* described the SCN as "a public computer exchange of ideas and information" and stressed its proactive, socially conscious nature: "The Seattle Community Network, two years in the making, started as a project of Computer Professionals for Social Responsibility, a group that promotes public access to computer information. The group hopes to 'demonstrate by example' that electronic highways needn't be the exclusive domain of government and big business" (Maier 1994, A1).

In June 1994, the project became available to the public. Hosted on a 386 donated by a local retailer, PCN Computer, run off of a UNIX operating system donated by BSDI, and wired through an Internet connection donated by Washington Library Network, the SCN was introduced to the public from within the downtown branch of the Seattle Public Library (Schuler 1996a, 1996b; Westrich 1997). Unlike the opening of the BEV, the inaugural launch was not a media spectacle. Further, unlike the event in Blacksburg, no representatives from multimillion-dollar corporations spoke in Seattle. Instead, Liz Stroup, the head librarian at the SPL, and Jim Street, the president of the Seattle City Council, delivered introductory speeches, followed by brief remarks from a few SCN volunteers and a short demonstration of the community network. The event concluded with three children using the SCN to send thank you e-mails to well-wishers. As Schuler (1996a, 344) notes, "Although other communities have launched their network with more fanfare (such as having the governor of the state or Vice President Al Gore cut a ribbon), the SCN community introduction was attended by nearly one hundred people and seemed perfectly appropriate for SCN."

Much of 1994 was focused on three activities besides the launching of the SCN: writing grants, upgrading hardware, and developing prototypical projects. Early in the year, the SCN partnered with the local Public Broadcasting System (PBS) affiliate KCTS/9 and Powerful Schools to submit a "Community-Wide Education and Information System" proposal to the Corporation of Public Broadcasting and USWest Foundation. In April, they were notified that their project, "Puget Soundings," had been awarded a $115,000 grant (Taylor 1994). Although the SCN received only a portion of the grant, it was enough to hire Nancy Kunitsugo to set up and host online community forums devoted to local issues and public education. First-year forums included "Ask the Governor" and "Teen Talk" (Schuler 1996a, 1996b).

As the network's traffic continued to grow, the once-trusty 386 became increasingly sluggish. In December, the coordinating council met and, based on a recommendation from the Hardware/Software Committee, purchased a Sun SPARCstation 5 for $5,000. After SCN's purchase of the high-end workstation, the local Sun Microsystem office, interested in the project, donated a Sun SLC, an even more powerful workstation (Schuler 1996a; Westrich 1997). Overnight, the SCN had become literally a new network.

Yet perhaps more important than the grant and the upgrade was the strategic partnership with a number of already-existing community projects, including Sustainable Seattle, the Homeless Network, and BaseCamp Seattle. Sustainable Seattle is a group of environmental activists formed in the early 1990s. Alarmed by what they perceived to be a steady degradation of Seattle's environmental settings, they drew up a list of indicators such as home gardening, the return of wild salmon to spawn, and participation in community arts. Interested in spreading the word, Sustainable Seattle approached the SCN, which offered service space to host a website. As Schuler notes, the SCN provides "an opportunity for activists acting as lay-scientists to publish important community data that other people or institutions have no interest in gathering or publishing" (Horvath, undated). Similarly, under the direction of Lorraine Pozzi, the SCN hosted the early versions of the Women's Homeless Network, an online center devoted to providing homeless women with civic and shelter-related resources.

Yet perhaps the most inspired project was BaseCamp Seattle, a "grassroots gateway" for Seattle-based feminists attending and interested in the United Nations Fourth World Conference on Women, which took place in Beijing in September 1995. A collaboration between WomensNet and the SCN, BaseCamp Seattle was at once a community, a series of workshops, an online discussion, and an informational archive. Before the conference in Beijing, BaseCamp Seattle sponsored a four-day miniconference at Seattle University. Combining political presentations with technological workshops, the project was an attempt to network like-minded activists and organizations and to listen proactively to marginalized voices (Gelernter 1995; Pozzi 1995). Aware of the forbidding cost of a trip to Beijing, BaseCamp Seattle organizers established a relatively low conference fee ($50) and offered free passes to the local miniconference for those willing to volunteer (Gelernter 1995). While in Beijing, BaseCamp Seattle hosted a number of Internet workshops and helped to provide electronic communications onsite. Finally, before, during, and after the conference in Beijing, BaseCamp Seattle sponsored online discussions focused on the eleven "Critical Areas of Concern," the official document governments were asked to ratify in Beijing.

As the network grew, so did its community. In July 1994, the network had over 700 registered users. By September, the population doubled to over 1,500 users. Six months later, it doubled again to over 3,000 users. By the end of 1995, over 6,500 users frequented the network. Within two years, the number doubled again, and in November 1997, there were over 13,000 registered users (Griest 1994; Schuler 1996b; Seattle Community Network 1996a). While project volunteers enthusiastically welcomed the growth of the network, it soon became too large to sustain under the limited nonprofit status of CPSR/Seattle, leading to the final chapter in our history.

By late 1995, the SCN had outgrown CPSR/Seattle in two important ways. The first was geographic. As Schuler (1996b) notes, "The organizers felt that SCN needed a regional focus and that the issues facing SCN were different (though usually complementary) than those facing CPSR." The second was financial. As noted in the "Seattle Community Network Association's Frequently Asked Questions List" (undated), the

Seattle community network was getting too big to be run as a project of the local chapter of Computer Professionals for Social Responsibility (CPSR), where it began. One of the problems is that the local chapter has an exemption from certain kinds of reporting via the national organization, but only if the chapter has an income from donations that is less than $25,000 in one year. SCN has been lucky to be able to draw more than that last year, and it looks like we're on track to do that or better this year.

SCN was getting like the tail wagging the dog. The solution was to establish the Seattle Community Network Association, or SCNA, a nonprofit organization with 501(c)(3) status. The SCNA, therefore, assumed the roles of both umbrella organization and fundraising arm, as reflected in its original mission statement: "SCNA provides, maintains and supports free community computing resources primarily to the citizens of the King County area. SCNA encourages community development and on-line citizenship by promoting equal and diverse access to technology and educating the public, including opinion leaders" (Seattle Community Network Association, undated). On July 28, 1995, volunteers for the SCN incorporated the Seattle Community Network Association.

A one-day retreat, attended by about fifteen volunteers, was held to hammer out the particulars. Significantly, it was decided that while use of the SCN would remain free, membership in the SCNA would require a fee. In turn, SCNA members would gain voting privileges and the right to run for office. Membership fees were established on a sliding scale, as indicated in the "Seattle Community Network Association's Frequently asked Questions List":

Standard Member	120.00
Sustaining Member	60.00
Basic Member	25.00
Low Income/Student	15.00

Later, in an attempt to be more inclusive, members of the SCNA board of directors changed the bylaws to allow an alternative membership fee based on service: "Resolved: 'Volunteers who have donated five (5) hours of recorded service to SCNA rendered within 30 days prior to application for SCNA membership will qualify to have the minimum cash contribution waived'" (Seattle Community Network, "SCNA Board Meeting Minutes," 1998). A year after its formation, the SCNA boasted nearly 1,000 members. On August 28, 1996, the first general meeting of the SCNA convened at the downtown branch of the SPL to hold general elections. While the meeting was open to the public, only SCNA members were allowed to vote. When the votes were tallied, Aki Namioka was elected president, Randy Groves treasurer, and Doug Schuler secretary (Schuler 1996b; Seattle Community Network, "SCNA First Meeting and Elections," 1996b). With an official governing body on board, the SCN assumed its current form. Further, by means of membership dues, it established a steady, albeit modest, revenue stream, an issue that has historically plagued community networks (see, for example, Cisler 1993). In 1999, for instance, the SCNA spent $500 publicizing its annual membership drive, returning approximately $8,500 in new membership fees (Seattle Community Network, "SCNA Board Meeting Minutes," 1999).

Conclusion

Long before users logged onto the BEV and the SCN, crucial negotiations took place. This chapter has attempted to trace these negotiations in order to shed light on the positions and priorities of our two community networks. As I have shown, the BEV was built largely as a collaborative project between Virginia Tech and Bell Atlantic of Virginia. In general, this community network was built from the top down: brainstormed behind the closed doors of Bell Atlantic, tested on a focus group consisting of computer-savvy graduate students from electrical engineering, and introduced as an already-existing network. While the town of Blacksburg had a nominal role in the development of the network, local businesses were welcomed aboard from the beginning and given small grants to be a part of the nascent network.

Conversely, lacking corporate sponsorship, the SCN was a product of a group of progressive-minded volunteers, many of whom came from the local branch of Computer Professionals for Social Responsibility. Seeking early collaboration with the Seattle Public Library, nonprofit organizations, and activist groups, the volunteers behind the SCN welcomed future users to become present designers, and built the network from the bottom up. Unlike those who established the BEV, which served as "a test bed of services that will be demanded by customers in the future," the developers of the SCN conceived their users as citizens rather than consumers. As such, early experiments like Sustainable Seattle, the Homeless Network, and Base-Camp Seattle focused on community involvement and civic engagement.

Similar to geographically based cities, online cities like the BEV and the SCN contain and reflect complex histories. These histories are important to uncover, for in many ways they inform and influence the kinds of interactions, communications, and communities that exist within them. To ignore such histories is to ignore the intricate cultural, economic, and political negotiations that make the community networks possible—negotiations that developers translate into what the Blacksburg Electronic Village and Seattle Community Network intended to be, have become, and could be in the future.

Notes

The research for this chapter was supported in part by a Nonprofit Sector Research Fund Dissertation Fellowship from the Aspen Institute. The author wishes to thank John Caughey for his helpful feedback and suggestions.

1. In an attempt to obtain the feasibility study, I emailed Dr. Andrea Kavanaugh, Director of Research of the BEV. She replied, "The feasibility study you mention is

not publicly available." (Personal correspondence with Andrea Kavanaugh, November 29, 1999.) Further, unlike the other interviews conducted by John Schorger for his dissertation, the one with Robert Morris is not public. When asked why, Schorger replied: "Robert Morris's interview is not available since he did not give permission for it to be released. I was able to interview him but could not release the interview." (Personal correspondence with John Schorger, December 6, 1999.) Finally, I emailed Robert Morris directly yet never received a reply.

2. For a discussion of the technical aspects of the BEV software, see Ward, 1997.

3. For additional information on many of the projects, see the broken-link infested "Blacksburg Electronic Village-Research," <http://www.bev.net/project/research/>.

4. Later, in October 1996, a representative from the Seattle Public Library was added. See "SCNA Board Meeting Minutes," <http://www.scn.org/scna/oct96min.html>.

15   Globalization and Media Democracy: The Case of Indymedia

Douglas Morris

The economic globalization that accelerated in the late twentieth century is generating a major transformation of capitalism. For the last century, powerful, nation-based corporations have dominated the international economic system. Now, a system is emerging that is increasingly dominated by transnational firms and their international neoliberal agencies such as the World Trade Organization (WTO) and International Monetary Fund/World Bank (IMF/WB) (Sklair 2000). The globalization of transnational capital has depended on a number of technological innovations—such as microprocessors and the Internet—that have provided the means to control vast networks of information and commerce. A synthesis of capitalism and technology, globalized technocapitalism (Kellner 2002), has changed the nature of technoscience (increasingly commercializing it), work, and organizations. Global technocapitalism, like previous forms of capitalism, continues to foster a great deal of alienation and suffering. In dialectical opposition, social movements are also globalizing, especially those already designed on network models of organization such as women's and environmental movements (Castells 2001; Leon, Burch, and Tamayo 2001). These two opposing trends in transnational society are mirrored in the centralized control of commercial news media and the formation of alternative-media networks.

The global-justice or antiglobalization movement burst into public attention during the protest in Seattle against the WTO in 1999.[1] Global-justice mobilizations gained increasing media coverage and public attention through protests in Washington, D.C., Melbourne, Prague, Quebec, and Genoa. The Seattle protest was an outgrowth of previous organizing efforts, most immediately preceded by the efforts of People's Global Action (PGA), an international network of activists against neoliberal globalization. PGA organized the J18 (June 18) Carnival against Capitalism protests internationally in summer 1999, and for several years prior (and continues actively today in Europe: see pgaconference.org). PGA combined major aspects of the global-justice mobilizations: protests in multiple cities, the carnival theme, grassroots democracy, and critique of globalization.

The history of antineoliberal globalization efforts goes back in the global South to protests against the IMF/WB starting in the mid-1980s and back further, considering the legacy of anticolonial struggles. With the Zapatista movement, activists began to successfully use the Internet to generate international support. Now, for social movements, the Internet has become a primary medium for outreach, organizing, and news.

The Seattle Independent Media Center (IMC) was created to report on the 1999 WTO protest. Inspired by the Seattle IMC, a network of local media centers, or "locals," have developed that use a sophisticated array of media practices to cover social-justice issues and movements.[2] While growing out of global-justice movement (GJM) coverage, the mission of the IMC network, Indymedia for short, includes reporting on a wide variety of social injustices, covering social-movement mobilizations, engaging in media activism, and embodying participatory democracy in its actions and media policies.

The mainstream media, dominated by politically conservative media conglomerates, have often portrayed GJM protests as violent and opposed to global progress. Since September 11, there have been attempts to liken some of the more radical GJM groups to terrorists. Through a network of volunteer street journalists and an online open-publishing system (anyone with access to the Internet can upload a story to the IMC newswires), Indymedia offers unique coverage of the GJM mobilizations and offers activists a space to voice their profound concerns. Indymedia is a forum for writers to express critical views about the severe consequences of economic globalization and to provide constructive editorials about the globalization of social justice and grassroots democracy. A growing readership and, perhaps ironically, some commercial media now rely on Indymedia as a primary news source on various social movement actions and issues not reported in other media.

While Indymedia web pages paint the picture of a fairly unified process, discussions with IMC participants revealed a wide variety of views about the nature of Indymedia. Participants' media philosophies include:

- Holding an objective journalistic stance
- Seeing Indymedia as reporting on GJMs as an activist press
- Interpreting Indymedia as an experiment in confederating local press efforts
- Envisioning Indymedia as a new online grassroots media experiment involving participants with diverse political views

Indymedia is all of these things and more. This is due in part to Indymedia's inclusive grassroots approach, inviting ever more diverse participants and views, and in part to the number of social movements that have influenced Indymedia's initial development.

This chapter is based on participant observation in Indymedia. The objective of the chapter, in a nutshell, is to discuss some of the main innovations and challenges in the organizing principles, practices, and flexible structures of Indymedia. A theoretical framework is presented at the end— a multiperspective approach, based on contemporary perspectives on the critical theory of the Frankfurt School.

A History of the Independent Media Centers

Since its launch in Seattle in November 1999, Indymedia has multiplied itself, rhizomatically branching out into a decentralized global network of media collectives. The Indymedia network now comprises nonlocal media working groups and over one hundred affiliated local media centers (96 active and 8 new IMCs approved as of October 2002, with over 60 more in formation). The network is very diverse. Media are created in over twenty languages across over thirty nations in various stages of technical development. Local, regional, and global organizing processes are engaged extensively over the Internet. A global media center, www.indymedia.org, and local IMC websites act as portals to the information, communications, media collectives, and projects of the network.[3]

Indymedia draws on the history and practices of several types of social movements. At least four main types of social movements can be identified as immediate sources of practices and strategies for Indymedia: grassroots media projects and the liberated/free-software, radical-democratic, and global-justice movements. Indymedia facilitators, individually and in small groups, creatively integrated aspects and practices of these movements into a diverse media network sharing common grassroots principles, practices, and resources. While these movements (internally diverse as they are) are common sources, additional factors are the diverse mix of movements unique to local political cultures.

Indymedia depends on volunteer programmers, or *techs*, who adapt free-software programming to IMC needs. Through donating endless hours of programming, techs incorporate the values of the free-software movement into the IMC culture. Indymedia's free-software practices are based on the Net hacker culture of both sharing of the source code of software and communally producing code. This policy is manifest in the software of the databases (a form of liberated, public technocapital—or democratic technology) underlying the interactive websites that are the backbone of the IMC network and in IMC collectives' consensual work processes.[4] Several Indymedia facilitators noted that IMC takes the same approach to freedom of media that free-software networks do to software (Arnison 2001).

Also foundational to Indymedia are practices developed in previous radical-media and online reporting projects (Downing et al. 2001). Halleck (2002) writes that "many different streams came together [in Indymedia]: the video activist community, the microradio pirates, the computer hacker/codewriters, the 'zine makers and the punk music world. These multi-media activists were ignited by several gatherings called The Next Five Minutes, organized by Geert Lovink, David Garcia and others in Amsterdam during the 1990s. These meetings provided a window on the possibilities of collaborative and participatory mega media events." The potential of online media was explored in various political venues in the 1990s, such as in the online media coverage by the CounterMedia during the 1996 Democratic presidential convention in Chicago and the work online in the mid-1990s to build Zapatista solidarity.

Indymedia activists mentioned that the Zapatista movement served as a major inspiration and concrete example of people coordinating their local collectives and actions with a diverse global community. On the founding of Indymedia, Chris Burnett recounts:

We were all very conscious at the time of this type of electronic resistance that took social, economic, and physical forms. . . . I remember being in Chicago for the 1996 Democratic National Convention, being impressed with CounterMedia. But I also remember having discussions about Zapatista solidarity work using the

Internet. . . . The Zapatista solidarity work brought people from all over the planet to work together in new ways, using the net for coordination and action (that I don't think happened in the same way with respect to Nicaragua solidarity work or anti-apartheid work in the 1980s).[5]

Directly antecedent to creating IMC was programming work to offer online coverage of the People's Global Action protests in June 1999. On the origins of the "active" software that runs many of the Indymedia websites, Matthew Arnison writes:

I was part of a team of media activists who built the website, and kept it live. The online activist media projects that influenced our work were in Chiapas, Europe, the Middle East, Australia, and the US. The free software called "active" that ran the original Indymedia website, which enabled automated multimedia open publishing, was written in Sydney by Community Activist Technology in the first half of 1999. We designed it for a mini-Indymedia-centre (of course we didn't have the name back then) that we set up to cover the Sydney protests as part of the J18 [June 18] global day of action against corporate tyranny.[6]

New Indymedia locals, including Seattle, have been created sometimes through networking among persons active in preexisting media projects. Initiators of the various media projects in Indymedia came from already-active groups: Paper Tiger, Deep Dish, Headwaters Video Collective, Sleeping Giant, Changing America, Speak Easy, Free Speech TV, and so on.[7]

Media activists started planning the Seattle IMC six months prior to the WTO protest. The aim was to cooperatively organize a media center that hosted many incoming media activists, over 300 people eventually, and supported the use of various types of media. Seattle IMC had a daily newspaper, thirty minutes of satellite TV every day, radio, miscellaneous other coverage, and the website. The website was intended from the start, but its details were decided only in the last few weeks.

In Seattle, the IMC provided extensive text, radio, and video coverage of the protests, offering a unique frame on an important watershed event in the history of modern social movements. During the WTO protest, the IMC coverage mixed accounts of the street battles with notes by local residents reporting outrage at having their neighborhoods gassed, editorial commentaries about the wrongs of the WTO, and pronouncements of success by protesters. Dorothy Kidd (2000) notes that international media campaigns, such as that around the Seattle WTO contest, include "old and new media—face-to-face communications, leafleting, and street art, along with radio, video, and websites—to organize with social justice movements at every level." This is a general practice in Indymedia now, with print newspapers, radio shows, and video for public-access TV being regularly created to widen outreach and participation of activists from various movements.

Interestingly, through the Internet, from the start, Indymedia has been an interactive, global, grassroots project. During the Seattle WTO protests, the IMC website often struggled with the load as the audience skyrocketed. Along with the techs feverishly working on the ground in Seattle, support—for help with installing, upgrading, and resuscitating the website several times during that week—was provided over the Internet from Sydney. Long-distance tech and editorial support has since become common practice in Indymedia.

Through its many forms of outreach, Indymedia is getting the word out about global-justice activism. According to the IMC technical collective, the new Seattle IMC website received over one million hits during its coverage of the November 1999 WTO protest. Internet traffic had grown to ten million hits during the anti-G-8 protests in Genoa in July 2001.

Since Seattle, IMCs have offered thorough coverage of many of the GJM mobilizations, such as those in Washington, D.C., Melbourne, Prague, Quebec, Genoa, and so on. On such protests, Smith (2001) writes, "Global Days of Action can cause major disruptions in numerous cities around the world with very little in the way of centralized, visible organizational structures. . . . The Internet has not only helped popularize these global days, but has also increased their potency." During GJM protests, it is not uncommon for notes to be posted to the network newswires from companion protests from around the world, expressing solidarity with the main protests. During the Genoa anti-G8 protest, the count was of over 200 solidarity protests in various cities—with many of those noted via posts to the IMC network.

Major protests are mobilization and networking sites, where dozens of IMC volunteers have gathered from many locals to offer coverage. Such confluences of effort lead to the translation of friendships formed in cyberspace to friendships sustained in comradeship in the press office and field, and vice versa. These events also introduce new volunteers to technical media skills, strategies for covering protests, and streetwise tactics of avoiding and dealing with tear gas and on-the-spot reporting. Indymedia is developing into not only a diverse global-media network, but also a committed network of journalists seasoned in the challenges of covering protests and activism.[8]

In addition to major global-justice mobilizations, the Indymedia network (global and various locals) has offered extensive coverage of actions and events such as May Day protests, the protests at the U.S. presidential political party conventions in Los Angeles and Philadelphia, the European Union protests in Nice and other cities, the World Social Forum (WSF) in Porto Alegre, Brazil, events after September 11 and the War on Terrorism, and the World Summit on Sustainable Development in Johannesburg, as well as a great variety of local issues.

As a new, decentralized people's media, the posts to the newswires were and still are in the larger protests rather "raw" news, live or nearly live from the streets—reported by cell phone as police rush and tear gas billows around, or by quickly uploaded audio and video at the nearby media centers, and even by text written sometimes midprotest at cybercafés. However raw the street news, editorial processes increasingly summarize multiple issues, story lines, and events (e.g., see the global and local website center-column features). The Indymedia network works in part as a global-justice movement press, but the wide variety of social-justice issues reported by Indymedia demonstrate its role in covering diverse peoples and movements fighting injustice and in providing a challenge to the corporate media's role in maintaining social inequality.

Indymedia Locals, Principles, Processes, and Network

IMC Locals

Developing a local online media center to cover a large protest, which mixes in-the-street coverage with background stories and analysis, is a pattern that has been repeated in forming dozens of IMC collectives by the efforts of local media activists. While a catalyzing reason for starting many IMCs has been to cover various protests, increasingly IMCs are formed to offer a local alternative press outlet using the Indymedia model of open publishing coordinated through grassroots processes.

The media producers of IMC, including full-timers, are volunteers, who take risks in their reporting. Through Internet-based communications and in face-to-face meetings locally (and in gatherings), the activists engage the media and process work of Indymedia in a generally collective manner. Indeed, early Indymedia activists explicitly drew on the cooperative, decentralist philosophies and practices of radical democratic movements. The lineage of such movements can be traced from those of radical labor in the nineteenth century to movements in the 1950s and 1960s, continuing to women's, radical peace, and left-green movements in the 1970s and 1980s. Indymedia's decision-making group-process roles and methods – such as facilitator, timekeeper, stack (list) keeping, mood checking, rotation of roles, and the consensus decision criteria used—are directly based in practices of recent radical-democratic movements.

Local IMC groups are generally independent collectives, not part of other media organizations. Some locals are based on the model of bringing together a network of local media projects and producers to cooperate in IMC work. Examples include Seattle, Vancouver, and a number of South American IMCs such as in Argentina and Brazil.

The work of Indymedia in large GJM mobilizations has been much noticed, informing coverage of events by alternative media and sometimes by corporate media. However, local coverage of a variety of issues is equally important and the bulk of organized media production is for such. Indymedia has generated a growing press "buzz" about the potential of new Net-based media.[9] Due to Indymedia's success in mobilizing coverage via the Net, and its unique mix of organizing strategies and mission, the network has grown quickly.

As of October, 2002, 104 IMC locals (96 active and 8 approved new IMCs) in over 30 countries comprised the network. By geographic region, the active IMCs include 2 IMCs in Africa (with 8 more requested), 4 in Asia, 6 in Australia and the Pacific, 12 in Central and South America, 21 in Europe, and 51 in North America above Mexico. The locations of the 8 newly approved IMCs (with over 60 requested) illustrate the growing diversity of the network: Andorra, Croatia, Istanbul, Nice (France), Peru, Poland, Springfield (Illinois), Winnipeg (Canada). Among the largest active "locals," geographically, are the Brazil, India, Russia, and South Africa IMCs, with the smallest being city-based IMCs (the main type in Canada and the United States), such as Melbourne, Australia, Victoria, British Columbia (Canada), and Madison, Wisconsin (U.S.).

A number of the large nation-level IMCs work through various local IMC groups. The Brazil IMC is a coalition of five locals within the country. IMC

Aotearoa (New Zealand) has two locals, Otautahi and Wellington, generating print projects. The U.K., German, and Italian IMC also use the model of numerous local IMC media collectives working through one national IMC website. For this reason, IMC locals are undercounted outside of North America. This undercounting may or may not become an issue as global network planning and decision-making processes develop. Another complication is that distinct IMC locals have formed that are subsets of an IMC having a larger geographic area (e.g., nation/city as in India and Mumbai IMCs, or region/city as in the Quebec and Montreal IMCs—interestingly, the Quebec IMC is more French based and Montreal is more English based). The complexity in Indymedia arises from having local control of the boundaries rather than system-level definitions. Through local control, different types of interlocal collaborations are developed that are suited to different contexts. However, there are networkwide standards for local membership, as is discussed next.

IMC Principles and Processes

IMC mission statements may differ in content between locals and change over time. The Seattle IMC mission statement reads:

The Independent Media Center is a grassroots organization committed to using media production and distribution as a tool for promoting social and economic justice. It is our goal to further the self-determination of people underrepresented in media production and content, and to illuminate and analyze local and global issues that impact ecosystems, communities and individuals. We seek to generate alternatives to the biases inherent in the corporate media controlled by profit, and to identify and create positive models for a sustainable and equitable society.[10]

This statement offers a clear sense of Indymedia as a democratic media project working for social and economic justice. The Boston IMC mission statement, which is by chance and legacy at the top of the global network home page (see indymedia.org), because an IMC participant from Boston put it there early on, reads: "Indymedia is a collective of independent media organizations and hundreds of journalists offering grassroots, noncorporate coverage. Indymedia is a democratic media outlet for the creation of radical, accurate, and passionate tellings of truth." This shorter, more emotionally evocative statement does not quite convey the media mission as clearly as the Seattle statement does. Neither the Seattle nor the Boston mission statement conveys *explicitly* the importance of decentralized,

consensus-based cooperative processes in Indymedia. Nor do these statements mention the open-publishing approach. Consensus processes and
open publishing are defining aspects of the network (and "the" key aspects
for some members). The Principles of Unity developed in 2001 aim to
articulate the grassroots democratic nature of the network.

Issues of Indymedia's goals, media policy, future development, network
structure, and decision processes were addressed at a meeting that took
place, April 28–29, 2001, at the twenty fifth annual "Press Freedom Conference" hosted by Project Censored in San Francisco.[11] The eighty
plus attending IMC participants came to consensus on criteria for approv-
ing new IMC locals. The criteria included statements of IMC network
Principles of Unity and local IMC collectives' membership criteria, which
were sections in a draft IMC Network charter. Chris Burnett, an early
participant in Indymedia, drafted a "Proposed Charter of the Confeder-
ated Network of Independent Media Centers," based on hundreds of
e-mail notes that discussed IMC principles and processes.[12] At the conference, various initiatives, which were stated in the draft charter, were
elaborated. The initiatives included editorial policies, an open-publishing
policy, and networkwide communication and decision-making guidelines. These were forwarded to the IMC listservs for development. Some
initiatives were eventually approved by ad hoc decision-making processes.
To date, the issue of a formal network decision-making process continues
to be debated.

Indymedia's media practices express the principles of unity—that is, the
principles guide media practices. The main principles include decentralized democracy and tolerance for diversity, open publishing and information flow, mutual support, and liberated software. These principles
generally parallel the four social-movement foundations for Indymedia
discussed above: the global-justice, media-activism, radical-democracy,
and free-software movements. In drawing inspiration from these democratic movements, a foundational principle for Indymedia is to coordinate
activities in a grassroots participatory manner, where democratic means
are part of the ends of the movement. That is, a foundational motivation
in Indymedia is a mission to create a global grassroots media democracy.
Sheri Herndon (2001), an organizer active in Indymedia from Seattle
onward, voices this mission (specifically in the context of antidemocratic
U.S. Federal Communications Commission policies): "What is our version

of the future of communications? . . . While we work hard at opening up the channels of communication and unleash the potential of handing over the means of communication to anyone who wants to become a media maker . . . there needs to be an information liberation manifesto." Herndon cites previous human rights statements, the Universal Declaration of Human Rights and the Adbusters' "Blueprint for a Revolution,"[13] which declares that we need a "Media Carta," where "Every human being has the 'right to communicate'—to receive and impart information through any media."

Indymedia expresses media democracy most directly through open publishing. Open publishing means that anybody with access to an Internet account can post news (in form of digital video, audio, or text files) to any of the network newswires. The IMCs are a network of open-publishing collectives in terms of content and policy. Open publishing also means that media creators and viewers can easily get involved in commenting, editing, highlighting stories, and even managing/facilitating the media production through Indymedia's open, (relatively) transparent grassroots media processes.

The practice of open publishing on IMC newswires is a formal policy in the network, adopted in summer 2001.[14] This posting policy enables people in general "to become the media." Not only may people become the media, but corporate interests are excluded. Part of the global-justice movement is anticapitalism. The exclusion of the profit motive is defined in an IMC unity principle that states that the IMCs must be not-for-profit. Hyde (2002) summarizes this participatory and anticorporate aspect of Indymedia: "Indymedias are restructuring the traditional news hierarchy. . . . The relationship between the sources, journalists, and readers is all that matters. In the Indymedia community, publishers, advertisers, and corporate interests are left out of the picture."

The global website and most of the local and project websites are portals, presenting links to many aspects of the network. The structures of the front pages of the Indymedia websites symbolically maintain the identity of IMC locals across very diverse societies. Ongoing internal debates are engaged over Indymedia website structures. Common elements of front-page design currently include a center column of news summaries (features), a newswire of local IMC features, a calendar of upcoming actions, and a long list of links to local IMC web pages and network information.

"Publish" links are prominently placed on most IMC home pages. Lawson and Gleason (2002) write about the variety of experiences in surfing IMC's open-publishing environment: "Indymedia sites [are] a mixed bag of thoughtful analyses, activist dispatches, on-the-street news items, rants, and reprinted media from unknown publications or organizations. Without a central editorial authority dispatching reporters (or fact-checking stories), readers are obliged to think critically as they are reading—to allow a story to provoke further research, further reading, and—perhaps—further writing." IMC posts have a comment function, which invites the sharing of opinions, which readers use to sometimes correct, affirm, or challenge points in posts.

The specifying of Indymedia policies is often done through IMC mailing lists, of which there are over 600 (many of them for local IMCs). The mailing lists, or e-mail listserves, are currently an important forum for coordinating media creation and local and network-level functions, such as legal issues, finance, large gatherings, and so on (particularly the various editorial, communications, process, and tech listserves). To date, the listserves are open to anyone interested. Over time various portals to Indymedia's processes have been developed, including the internal "process" (mostly static), "global," and "documentation"/"knowledge base" (very dynamic) websites.[15]

Through summer 2002, the IMC network globally had relatively informal decision-making and coordination processes. Early on, some argued that the Indymedia network was growing too fast. In late 2000, programmers placed a moratorium (essentially by decree) on accepting new IMC locals into the network (though dozens were in the formation stage). The moratorium was instituted due to a lack of a democratic process for setting up new IMCs and because the main IMC computer servers were overloaded. The moratorium was lifted in summer 2001 after policies for the formation of new IMCs were adopted.[16] The IMC unity principles and member criteria are points of agreement for all new IMCs-in-formation wishing to join the IMC network.

The Indymedia Network: Challenges and Innovations

As noted in an IMC FAQ and an overview for new IMC collectives, the IMC network is a loosely structured network, intentionally decentralized in its processes.[17] While Indymedia is an innovative media project in various ways, key elements of a successful network are needed (according to some) and are still in development.

There are a number of challenges for IMC in terms of planning and strategy:

1. *Decision making.* The IMC network has repeatedly failed in attempts to develop networkwide decision-making and planning processes. (See also Lovink and Riemens, chapter 6, this volume.) This is due to various factors, including the volunteer nature of the network, lack of funds, and many linguistic barriers (over twenty languages in use). The global extent of the network offers logistical barriers. At a level of principle, there is resistance to large collective processes, especially by the youth in the network. For instance, in September 2002, a plan to organize a series of regional gatherings for network planning was abandoned due to strong objections to the funding of travel grants by a corporate foundation. Indymedia may, by necessity, depend on donations, as the main source of funding, and develop creative efforts in online planning communications. For now, a density of communication processes is weaving the network together. Issues are addressed and decisions made in an ad hoc way, at times quite successfully and other times not.

2. *Global versus local.* There is a major difference in Indymedia between "globalizers" and "localizers." Globalizers seek to develop Indymedia as an alternative form of media practice, globally. Localizers see local media collectives as the fundamental mission of IMC and resist global projects. Some see a need to balance global working-group projects and local efforts. In practice, the GJM mobilizations and reporting are a fusion of local and global efforts. In general, it is possible that IMC may be finding a middle ground for now between little or no organization and a global system. To use a problematic but very suggestive metaphor: just as in industry there is just-in-time production and distribution, so in Indymedia there is just-in-time (or seat-of-the-pants) organizing of issue coverage and just-in-time crisis management at a network level. There are also unique experiments beyond the local in terms of media reporting occurring at regional levels. For instance, the Cyprus, Greek, and Turkish IMCs (some in formation) are cooperating to form a dialogue to cover issues of regional solidarity. As noted above, IMCs— such as those in Brazil, Aotearoa, and Germany—foster multiple local IMCs.

It is safe to say that Indymedia at this stage is developing an array of experiments in shared projects by locals.

3. *The role of organizers.* There is an uneasy opinion within Indymedia circles about the role of the very dedicated, talented participants who facilitate the functioning and growth of various aspects of the network. This issue is exacerbated by both of the above problems. The criticism has been made that the ongoing role of a small group of organizers performing key tasks centralizes power. Longtime facilitators may be gradually forming an inner circle, with a culture of understandings about what works best (or quickest or most strategically). This raises the classical organizational issue, Roberto Michels's (1962) iron law of oligarchy, which proposes that organizers, who arise out of a desire for a group to be effective, may develop eventually into an elite cultivating professional interests inside the movement. Not to emphasize these possibilities: Indymedia is working against the general social tendency of movement leaderships to develop activist "careers." There are no salaries, though a few stipends for legal and accounting work may be created. There is an informal practice of rotating listserve moderators (when there are moderators) and of rotating liaisons for global communications. There is an "organic" flow of coordinating effort in various projects as volunteers move on and new persons take over. However, unless balanced by regular planning and grassroots decision-making processes, the gradual development of experienced organizers with name recognition, many network ties, and hence power may be a serious future challenge for Indymedia as a grassroots network. Counter to such points are pragmatic arguments that organizers are simply required to facilitate something as technically and organizationally complex as Indymedia (Rabble 2002). The principle of sharing and often rotating key tasks is perhaps the best resolution to such a contradiction between grassroots policy and organizational needs.

4. *Challenges to unity principles.* Some types of locals challenge various Indymedia membership criteria and unity principles. The principle of open publishing is constrained in some European states that have strong regulations about civility in speech. The membership criteria stating there should be no affiliation with political parties is debated in some IMCs in Latin America, where the struggle against oppressive political structures by progressive political movements may be a necessary part of the fight for social

justice. As the Indymedia network matures, it is likely to be tested with the choice of accepting partial adherence to principles, redefining principles, or developing a way to enforce its principles, perhaps by severing ties with divergent locals.

5. *Digital divide.* It would seem that the digital divide has played a role in the distribution of Indymedia centers, in which half of the over 100 IMC locals are in Canada and the United States. According to a commonly cited source of online demographics, in Canada, the United States, and Northern European nations, for the most part, over 50 percent of people use the Net, whereas use is under 10 percent in most of Africa and Latin America.[18] However, there are political-cultural reasons for the high numbers of IMCs in the global North. Techs familiar with the setup of new IMCs cited security and collectivist cultures (vs. individualist cultures in Anglo-America). And, as noted, many IMCs outside of North America are organized on a nationwide scale. The pragmatics of smaller population sizes and densities are also a noted factor. The choice rests with local activists as to their local's initial geographic reach. The goal of crossing the digital divide in Indymedia is being pursued at a number of levels. Some IMCs—Philadelphia, Seattle, St. Louis—have created local media centers to offer media education and access. Techs and organizers sometimes travel to the global South to assist local media activists in the technical details of establishing IMCs. In one such effort, IMC techs have procured 100 computers for Indymedia collectives in the global South.

6. *Countermovement forces.* There is a history of direct suppression, legal harassment, and counterintelligence programs against radical-democratic social movements. Indymedia has experienced repeated arrests of its journalists, legal challenges (e.g., in Seattle and during the Quebec April 2001 protests), and confiscation of media materials and tools (e.g., during the Genoa protests in July 2001). Indymedia so far has responded to such problems with extensive press coverage of the issues (generating sympathetic press in other media) and with volunteer legal help. Some have claimed that several internal local IMC conflicts (e.g., the cases of IMC-Palestine and the Eugene and Portland IMCs created flame wars on IMC listserves in summer and fall 2002) are the result of counterintelligence activities. A conflict-resolution listserve has been initiated to deal with local conflicts.

7. *Aim of IMC reporting.* The IMC reporters who cover massive global-justice mobilizations (Seattle, Washington, D.C., Prague, Quebec, Genoa, and so on) often fail to cover one of the most important aspects of the mobilizations, the countersummits or social forums at each mobilization. This is partly due to a generation and "career" gap (the countersummit participants are older and often professionals). Another factor is radicalism, including alienation from the perception of reformism and institutionalization (in unions, NGOs, and social-movement organizations) of the GJM. There has been a general tendency, during large protests, to cover the drama of street conflict, arrests, and legal problems. There is some resistance to this trend in the network, with some reporters offering coverage emphasizing that the vast majority of protesters are nonviolent and that educational activities are engaged in people's forums. As noted, attention to local issues, various social movements, and political-economic analysis is increasing in the network.

There are many positive innovations in Indymedia. (See table 15.1.) Indymedia is unique in being a global volunteer grassroots media network of locals and media activists. Indymedia has benefited from and developed

Table 15.1
Innovations in Indymedia

Principles

1. *Global justice* Indymedia grew out of the emerging global social-justice movement that inegrates the social-justice concerns of many previous social movements.

2. *Grassroots democarcy* Indymedia is rather unique in being a cooperative global network of consensus-based media collectives.

3. *Open publishing* The "newswires" are open. Anyone can help run Indymedia. This allows a great deal of creative and social freedom in the discourses on Indymedia.

4. *Copyleft* A nonproprietary publishing criterion (no private ownership of intellectual property), copyleft, is used for both the code running Indymedia servers and for the original articles posted to Indymedia.

And, as discussed in the theory section below:

5. *Unity and diversity* Indymedia offers spaces to negotiate the dialectic of difference and unity, a fundamental challenge of a globalizing world.

Media Practices and Processes

6. *Interactivity* Dialogue and debate about stories is encouraged through a story-comment feature and the open wire. This is similar to a newsgroup process, but oriented toward news reporting.

Table 15.1

(continued)

---

7. *Online coordination*   Many discussions are conducted through listservs, chat rooms, and e-mail: at local and expanded (national, regional, and global) levels.

8. *Website design*   Most Indymedia Websites organize a wide variety of information helpful to activists and readers.

9. *Online documentation*   A documentation project (docs.indymedia.org) uses group authorware to enable cocreation of documents, including an index of Indymedia local histories, local organizing outlines, descriptions of various media projects, and so on.

Networking

10. *Network of networks*   Indymedia includes innovations at these levels and in these ways:

• *Locally.*   Indymedia locals are sometimes formed among networks of media activists and preexisting groups. Consensus decision-making processes are the norm, with specific tasks often conducted in more ad hoc and individualized ways.

• *Nationally.*   Media activists and multiple local media groups in various countries cooperate on press coverage. Exemplary cases include the Aotearoa (New Zealand), Brazil, and Germany IMCs.

• *Regionally.*   Regional working groups are emerging in Indymedia. Latin American IMCs dialogue about antiglobalization concerns. Activists in Greece-Cyprus-Turkey are exploring common issues. At-large mobilizations, involving dozens of IMC activists from many locals in the region, converge to share in making Indymedia and making media.

• *Globally.*   Indymedia is a primary medium of the global-justice movements, yet it is also more than this in adressing many social-justice and democratic issues at local through global levels.

11. *Media projects and working groups*   There are a number of ad hoc cooperative media projects, often involving many media activists working through the Internet, that create media for special events and in an ongoing way within specific media platforms—for example, text, radio, and video.

12. *Intermedia projects*   Media activists in various media are cooperating on media production across media platforms.

13. *Broad media networks*   Indymedia is participating in building broad alternative-media networks.

And as discussed in the theory section below:

14. *Alternative medias*   Indymedia is unique in serving, simultaneously, as a social-movement medium, a broad alternative social-justice medium, a network of local media centres, and a global forum for persons interested in global justice.

15. *Flexible, decentralized structure*   Indymedia is creating in its internal processes three structural elements needed for a successful decentralized network: strong local collectives, rich internal communication processes, and emerging networkwide decentralized decision-making and planning processes.

---

innovative principles, practices, and networking strategies for democratizing the Internet.

It should be emphasized that in the era of globalization via the Internet
(as opposed to slower forms of international exchange in previous eras),
Indymedia, as a global network of networks, is cutting new ground for grassroots, internetworked media production and politics. An important innovation in Indymedia at a broad scale of media networking is the interface of
activists using various types of alternative media, working in video, radio,
print, and online media. On a scale larger than Indymedia, some Indymedia
networkers and locals are branching out in widespread alternative-media
networking, and have actually done so for some time. Indymedia is often
discussed at media conferences and gatherings, such as the Press Freedom,
Underground Publishing, and Reclaim the Media conferences.

The visionaries and pragmatists in Indymedia are exploring many ways to
facilitate fruitful, democratic media on and off the Internet. In a nutshell,
through grassroots democratic practices and mutual support, Indymedia
activists are creating open media using free-software and media technologies. The Indymedia values and practices of decentralized media, online and
off, may increasingly inspire, vitalize, and challenge the work of left activists
and organizations to address the interconnection of justice issues and movements unfolding in the global-justice movement (and in other social-justice
fronts, of course: third-wave feminism (Collins 2000), the greens (Capra
and Spretnak 1984), and the globalization and interconnection of social
movements in general).

Theories of Media and Democracy

Media Centralization and Decentralization
Media conglomerates with conservative, pro-capitalist agendas, as in corporations controlled (or once controlled) by Rupert Murdoch, Ted Turner,
Conrad Black, Silvio Berlusconi, and so on, have formed to control much of
the world's media. The corporate domination of mainstream media has led
to a more widespread advocacy of a conservative political philosophy of
individualizing social problems and to a tendency to ignore radical and progressive issues and the social causes of problems (McChesney 1997, 1999).
Bagdikian (1997) notes that as of the year 2000 only six corporations
controlled most of what citizens saw, heard, and read in America. This is

exacerbated by the fact that the majority of corporate leaders are economically conservative, prioritizing profit making over all else.

Media conglomerates have been pursuing successfully a number of privatizing strategies such as vigorous lobbying for the deregulation of media-ownership regulations and for decreases in public media funding. Media corporations have pursued increasingly stringent ownership rights to intellectual property, leading to a loss of control by journalists, writers, and so on. This has resulted in a loss of depth and quality in the news and to a limitation of subjects addressed. While some interventions by owners are direct, corporate-media spin control is less obvious, as when employees learn to shape their coverage in favor of owners' biases. To make matters worse, in the mid- to late 1990s, many local community papers and radio stations in industrial societies (which expressed a wide range of political views) were purchased by conglomerates, some of which now control hundreds of local media "outlets."

Today, power is contested increasingly through symbolic means circulated through ever more pervasive information networks (Castells 1997). Social movements generally include ideological efforts that disseminate new social codes (values, ideals, and legitimations). Social movements in the industrial era, such as labor in the nineteenth century, were often grounded in struggles over material social inequalities and struggle for access to political participation, as in the suffrage movements, but depended on raising class consciousness and movement solidarity to succeed in mobilization efforts. In the early twentieth century, Gramsci (1971) argued that societies pervaded by a cultural hegemony (domination of society through ideology that favors elites) are best contested through counterhegemonic means (in a cultural "war of position"). As business interests have increasingly dominated politics, Melucci (1996) emphasizes that the global media industry has become a central battleground for social equality.

Corporate-media reproductions of dominant social codes now play a central role in structuring power relations today. For instance, Kellner (2001) criticizes the corporate media for promoting George W. Bush in the 2000 election, mostly defending his administration and ignoring his egregious faults after September 11. Also underplayed by the corporate media, after September 11, are the collapses of corporations such as Enron and Andersen, due to fraudulent accounting practices. As capital has internationalized, it has moved in various ways beyond the domains of national-level protective regulations (such as of workers and the environment) and actively suppressed such. The media conglomerates, at least in the United States, tend not to analyze transnational capital. The hegemony of media conglomerates dialectically inspires the formation of new alternative-media projects online to complement and extend the reach of existing political media.

An essential moment of democratization, as Castells (1997) notes, is the diversification of media. The Internet offers a variety of new-media possibilities. With a moderate level of resources or technocapital by the standards of advanced industrial society (a computer, Net access, and some technical literacy), many individuals and organizations are creating new media on the Internet. As a result, the Internet has increased and continues to increase the means and dialectical relations of both dominant and alternative social codes (Melucci 1996, 36–37).

Media that have moved online include various general alternative publications (e.g., in the United States: *Z Magazine*, *The Nation*), social-movement media (e.g., websites for Greenpeace, ILO, and so on), and the somewhat eroded field of independent local and regional media (which in the nineteenth and early twentieth centuries presented a wide array of political perspectives through independent community papers and radio stations). The Internet now allows a fourth type of alternative media: direct participation of citizens in making and sharing news via websites, newsgroups, listserves, informal e-mail networking, and so on. The new online media create places where a variety of otherwise silenced, marginalized voices may be heard. Many online media services now offer alternatives to corporate news. And, similar to Indymedia, there are various activist-oriented news websites and networks.[19] However, technology or media availability is not sufficient to ameliorate social inequality.

Political-economic practices that advance democracy are essential. Dyer-Witheford (1999) in *Cyber-Marx* emphasizes that addressing economic and political inequalities is a necessary basis for democratic culture, but that such struggles may be engaged in various quasi-independent beachheads such as redistributing income through living wages, creating universal communication networks, decentralizing social planning, and democratizing control of decisions about technoscientific development. The independent media online are creating global grassroots communication networks and social spaces for such democratic struggles.

Virtual Public Spheres

In early modern Europe, mass literacy became an essential condition for "civil society": a space of interactions, discourses, and ideas distinct from work, family, or newly emergent states. For Habermas (1989), a central moment of civil society was its "public sphere," where Enlightenment ideas were debated publicly in printed media, pubs, salons, and so on. Fraser (1989) argues that marginalized groups did not always have access to the dominant public spheres and the rhetoric of the Enlightenment. Hence, they developed alternative networks of discourse. While democracy, equality, justice, and freedom are central to the European Enlightenment (if only occasionally and imperfectly put into practice), similar principles are also discernible in other cultures and publics. For example, the Native American Iroquois confederacy practiced council decision making and held property as public. Women's networks have often relied on shared knowledge and cooperative practices. Golden age Islamic societies were the most progressive of their time in terms of social justice. Democratic principles, practices, and discourses have been created in various historical contexts. Discerning if and how varying social-justice practices may exemplify underlying universal possibilities or how seemingly irreconcilable concepts may require egalitarian multicultural dialogues is perhaps only now being appreciated.

In Habermas' analysis, in the eighteenth century, the bourgeois classes defeated the aristocracy and assumed power—eventually hegemony—partly through the mediating influence of the dominant public spheres. The bourgeois classes, seeking modes of governance and cultural understandings more compatible with their economic practices, embraced secular reason as a cultural ideology. Socially reflexive reason was translated into practices such as creating rational structures of administration and principles such as the popular sovereignty of "equals" as the basis of political legitimacy. After the bourgeoisie defeated the aristocracy and instituted capitalist relations of production and bureaucratic, parliamentary nation-states, new social contradictions emerged. Social movements of the nineteenth century—labor, suffragist, and national—engaged in liberation projects through using various public spheres. Similarly, in the middle twentieth century, movements used a variety of grassroots media and the mainstream mass media to spread political understandings and agendas.

Just as the print and mass media (and related political-economic transformations) enabled new political spheres and movements and new forms
of control, the new media of the Internet have made possible new "virtual
public spheres." The Internet opens up the possibility for movements and
individuals to create their own printing press, broadcast center, and communication network. But, through the Net, more global means of cultural
domination are possible. Just how the Internet will be used or constrained
is a point of ongoing struggle (Lessig 2001). To stick with discussing democratic trends, the new public spheres are informed by various constraints
and cultures, including: the reach of information technology and the
digital divide (in a nutshell: access and literacy); online cultures such as
pursuit of technical excellence and the hacker ethic of open sharing of
code and cooperative sharing of projects (Castells 2001); and in the case of
Indymedia—left press projects, communitarian social movements, and
consensus-based politics evolved from grassroots projects of the nineteenth century, some aspects of the movements of the 1960s (the civil
rights, new left, women's, and gay liberation movements), the 1980s
(radical antinuclear activists and left greens and continuing 1960s
movements), and the youth and movements of today.

For a widespread democratization of society and media, there is need for
both the critical rationalism of Habermas (1984) and LaClau and Mouffe's
(2001) celebration of difference.[20] As a foundation for democratic communication, Habermas proposes that undistorted communicative interactions
enable a deepened understanding of social-liberation potentials in a given
culture. A central aim of independent media is to provide authentic, true,
undistorted reporting informed by critical reason. LaClau and Mouffe
advocate an open toleration of difference as manifest in the multiple cultural bases in most societies today. It is important to note that a toleration
of diversity needs to be grounded in the principle of tolerance toward
groups/ideologies that are tolerant and intolerance of groups/ideologies
that are intolerant and oppressive (whether harsh exploiters like neoliberal
capitalists in sweatshops, imperial fascists like the Nazis, or militant fun-
damentalists like Al Qaeda). Just who will censure which excluders who are
oppressors is a fundamental debate—yet, notice progress in the formation
of the International Criminal Court.

Young (2000) argues that in a multicultural society, it is necessary to
engage in democratic politics in more inclusive ways. Linking a variety of

public spheres in democratic communication would best include both philosophical traditions of deliberation and the positive merits of narrative, rhetoric, and protest by marginalized communities. Similar to Dyer-Witheford, Young argues that an inclusive democracy needs to engage democratic communication practices, distributive justice, social-justice issues, recognition, and links to "international" concerns for global justice. In a similar vein, Fraser (1996) argues that recognition/identity (cultural issues) and redistribution (political-economic issues) are most effective, as democratic strategies, when pursued simultaneously. This points to the idea of global justice as an inclusive democracy of liberation from multiple types of oppression and positive democratic practices in various social spheres—cultural, political, economic (Collins 2000; Benhabib 1996).

In the celebration of diversity, if there is not a stand against oppression (capitalism, imperialism, racism, patriarchy, homophobia, environmental exploitation, and so on), then the principle of democracy as grounded in a social contract that balances the negative freedom from oppression (a libertarian ethic) with the positive freedom to pursue interests in cooperation with others (equality and democracy) will be severely undercut. Critical depth in rationality and acceptance of many cultures are realized democratically in communication practices in public spaces that both disfavor dominance and exclusion and favor tolerance and inclusion. The Indymedia network advocates both radical freedom and democracy through its unity principles. Indymedia activists struggle to enact these principles through decentralized, democratic practices and processes.

Following Tarrow (1995) on the three necessary structural elements of successful decentralized social movements in terms of political process, Indymedia may be seen as combining these factors: strong local collectives, rich internal communication processes, and emerging networkwide decentralized decision-making and planning processes. A breakdown in decision making often contributes to the failure of decentralized organizations. While Indymedia does have challenges and problems, already it is a model of what is possible in cyberspace.

The first part of this chapter considered some of the promising and problematic aspects of Indymedia. In short, the Indymedia network integrates online decentralized communication and coordination processes, mutual support in media projects, democratic technology, and open publishing. In accomplishing this (for a time), Indymedia is a rather unique instance of grassroots media democracy, interconnecting virtual public spheres across many languages and cultures, networked globally. More abstractly, Indymedia is both an effective online, decentralized media network using democratic technologies (cooperative open publishing) and a social space (movement networks and cultures) for global justice. Indymedia points the way to a more just future.

Conclusion

The centralization of corporate media has led to the increasing management of power through symbolic means. People's media on the Net give marginalized communities, progressive and traditional, a place to voice their concerns.

A critical social theory of media informed by the new social-movement theory of Castells and Melucci brings to light this dialectic: (1) editorial ignorance of social-justice issues in corporate media, whether willful or unconscious, based on various forms of conservative ideology (blaming the victim, locating the solution of social problems in individual actions and education, and so on), works to perpetuate a hegemony over, and pacification of, popular bases of potential resistance to oppression; (2) various alternative-media networks (formed effectively in the many-to-many connections of Internet media) circulate counterhegemonic critiques of domination, reporting on news that the mainstream corporate media ignores and on a variety of social-movement causes in increasingly diverse ways through the Internet. Alternative-media networks are now introducing and awakening larger publics to global-justice issues and actions.

Indymedia is a complex instance of alternative media. It is a unique integration of four types of alternative-media modalities. Indymedia works as

- A network for individual media activists and the general public
- Local media produced by local collectives
- A type of social-movement media covering the global-justice movement
- An alternative-media network, serving diverse movements and interests

Considering these media aspects, Indymedia is at the forefront of creating new multifaceted, decentralized virtual public spheres that advance democratic discourses and global-justice projects. Specific innovative aspects of Indymedia are outlined at the end of the second part of the chapter, titled "Indymedia Locals, Principles, Processes, and Networks."

Indymedia is a people's media in substance and process. Indymedia has increasingly rich media coverage of a wide variety of social- and global-justice issues. It is easy to self-publish there. Anyone can help run it. Indymedia activists are taking some steps not often seen—until the advent of the Internet and the creative struggle to interweave social movements globally in transformative resistance.

As Indymedia is cooperatively facilitated and based on liberated democratic technology (free-software and copyleft publishing of media), it is a realm of intensive democratic discourse, cooperative coordination, and public ownership. Indymedia, with all its growing pains and faults, is an example, in principle (if fallible in practice), of a holistic, direct democratic organization in its communications, economics, and internal politics. At the same time, Indymedia is part of a larger set of movements, including but not limited to the global-justice movement. In helping cocreate a decentralized participatory politics, a new nonpropriety media economy of collective information goods, and a multifaceted network of cultures, Indymedia is helping inspire a new social future for humanity and model a new postcapitalist set of social relations.

In conclusion, Indymedia is a significant, global decentralized network of public media spheres. Indymedia works to create democratic social relations and media production through open communication and collaborative coordination (comanagement) of group processes, mutual support in media collectives and networks, copyleft standards (coownership as public property), and open publishing (anyone can publish and participate in Indymedia). If Indymedia creates robust forms of these processes, continually refining them, it will have established a global, sustainable, grassroots democratic media network dedicated to realizing and reporting on global justice. This movement is early in the cycle of creation. Indymedia's organizing as a global network is incomplete. The network is only four years old. There are major challenges ahead. But much has been achieved already. If Indymedia continues to develop, its media transformation process toward social justice has the potential to widely inform interested publics. Partly through Indymedia, the global-justice movement has a way to define itself as such. Through Indymedia and independent grassroots media in general, we can create a more just and democratic future.

Notes

This chapter is based on: the author's longtime engagement in alternative-press projects; participant observation for over two years in various Indymedia meetings, Indymedia organizing listserves, Indymedia online working groups; study of Indymedia documents; discussions and interviews, online and off, with programmers, reporters, and networkers from a number of Indymedia local collectives (Chicago, Washington, D.C., Los Angeles, Minneapolis, New York, Quebec, Seattle, Italy, and more); and conversations with other independent journalists.

1. The term *global justice* is used in this chapter to designate the interaction of a wide array of social-movement causes (labor, antiracism, feminism, gay liberation, environmentalism, human rights, and so on). Networking among many movements in resistance to neoliberal globalization and institutions of domination in general is a characteristic of the global-justice movement. For a discussion of the emerging global-justice movements (or antiglobalization movements, a misnomer in the eyes of many global-justice activists), see *Naming the Enemy* by Amory Starr (2001) and *Globalization from Below* by Jeremy Brecher, Tim Costello, and Brendan Smith (2000). *One World* by William Greider (1998) is a powerful indictment of globalization. Z Mag online (http://www.zmag.org/CrisesCurEvts/Globalism/GlobalEcon.htm, linked from the Indymedia global front page) has extensive analyses of neoliberal economic liberalization and of the global-justice movement. The term *neoliberal* refers to the privatization agenda of international capitalism, which seeks to remove barriers to trade (such as tariffs and labor and environmental laws) through such instruments as the international treaties of the WTO, NAFTA, and the FTAA (if ratified) and the loan requirements of the IMF/WB.

2. IMC local collectives, or "locals," are groups of media activists who cooperate in the running of a geographically identified website (e.g., for the Italy IMC, the website is italia.indymedia.org) and associated multimedia. My thanks to Indymedia participants who have commented on this chapter. I apologize for the balance of North American and English-language-based examples. This will be adjusted through further research and collaboration. Additional work on the history, principles, and processes of Indymedia is documented online at the "Indymedia Documentation Site," docs.indymedia.org.

3. A survey of www.indymedia.org would complement the reading of this chapter.

4. On the Free Software Foundation, see http://www.gnu.org/. See these articles on the free-software origins of Indymedia programming: http://www.cat.org.au/maffew/cat/imc-rave.html and http://www.active.org. au/doc/active/goals.html.

5. For CounterMedia, see http://www.cpsr.cs.uchicago.edu/countermedia/. For more on the Zapatista rebellion and the views of Subcomandante Marcos, see Zapatismo in Cyberspace: http://www.utexas.edu/students/nave/cyber.html. The quote from

Chris Burns is from personal e-mail correspondence on September 28, 2002. Note: Quotes from e-mail correspondence used in this chapter have been approved by the writers.

6. The comments from Matthew Arnison in this chapter are based on personal e-mail correspondence, September 29–30, 2002.

7. See Halleck 2002 for further discussion of alternative-media precursors to Indymedia.

8. Related topics for further research include the following. As the global-justice movement grows, radical practices are being developed in various professions, trades, and needed services, such as action medical groups and legal support groups, which have also developed in support of GJM protests. See Kidd, forthcoming; Langman, Morris, and Zalewski 2003; and other forthcoming works by these authors. These works discuss manifestations of GJMs propagated by cyberactivism such as the GJM protests and Indymedia, as well as related events like the World Social Forum.

9. See "Stories about Indymedia": http://docs.indymedia.org/twiki/bin/view/Global/StoriesAboutIndymedia.

10. The Seattle IMC network mission statement was downloaded September 30, 2002, from http://seattle.indymedia.org/. The global IMC network mission statement was downloaded June 15, 2002, from the top of the "About Indymedia" web page, http://indymedia.org/about.php3.

11. See www.projectcensored.org.

12. See Principles of Unity, http://global.indymedia.org/front.php3?article_id = 330; the IMC network membership criteria, http://global.indymedia.org/front.php3?article_id = 331; and the draft IMC Charter, http://global.indymedia.org/front.php3?article_id = 198.

13. See "Blueprint for a Revolution," by Kalle Lasu, founder of Adbusters magazine: adbusters.org/magazine/23/blueprint.

14. See this definition of the IMC newswire open-publishing policy, "What is the www.indymedia.org newswire?" (the policy of which may vary in some locals): http://www.indymedia.org/fish.php3?file = www.indymedia.newswire. Also see Arnison 2001 for a discussion of open publishing.

15. See the IMC listserve, process, global, and documentation sites: http://lists.indymedia.org, http://process.indymedia.org, http://global.indymedia.org, and http://docs.indymedia.org.

16. For information on new IMCs, see "New IMC Information Space": http://newimc.indymedia.org/.

17. See "IMC FAQ," http://process.indymedia.org/faq.php3, and "IMC global overview," http://global.indymedia.org/front.php3?article_id-673.

18. For online Internet-use demographics, see Nua Internet Surveys: http://www. nua.net/surveys/how_many_online/index.html.

19. Progressive news services (in English) that could replace corporate news for many readers include commondreams.org, buzzflash.com, and alternet.org. There are also various precursor projects that have an online presence (such as the Media Alliance, media-alliance.org, and groups mentioned in the Indymedia history in the first section of this chapter). For examples of other activist-oriented radical media projects, see www.infoshop.org, Direct Action Media Network (damn.tao.ca), and webactive.com websites.

20. See Best and Kellner 1991 for discussion of various approaches to radical democracy and the relation of critical theories of modernity to postmodern theories of difference. On public spheres, also see Kellner 1997 and see Kellner's home page, with many essays on critical theory of media, technology, and democracy, http://www.gseis.ucla.edu/faculty/kellner/. Especially see "Techno-Politics, New Technologies, and the New Public Spheres." Online: http://www.gseis.ucla.edu/faculty/kellner/kellner.html

16   Prospects for a New Public Sphere

Peter Day and Douglas Schuler

In this book we have explored an expanding diversity of initiatives, activities, and approaches that form part of civil society's contribution and response to the network society. They represent images of society in stark contrast to the uncritical visions of competitiveness and profit offered up in the principles, norms, and practices found in the dominant visions of the network society. Embedded in the day-to-day lives of ordinary people from around the world, these extraordinary forms of social networking contribute to an emerging global civil society.

The community and civic infrastructures, applications, services, and artifacts outlined here are far removed from the technoeconomic credo that currently shapes the sanitized and homogeneous world of dot-coms and transnational corporate media. Social enterprises such as these illustrate the inventiveness, ingenuity, and resourcefulness of ordinary people, not-for-profits, voluntary-sector organizations, and community groups attempting to improve their social environments, often in the face of enormous odds.

Our intention is to illustrate the diverse nature of civil-society responses to global network-society developments conditioned by transnational corporate influences. Whether the diversity of such initiatives (and the advocacy networks that often accompany them) constitutes the emergence of a social-movement network in civil society is, as yet, unclear. The social enterprises presented here can but scratch the surface of such activities globally, but they do contribute to our understanding of social-networking activities in the network society. The rich picture of civil society to which each chapter contributes provides us with a better understanding of how information and communication technology (ICT) can and are being utilized as a social tool to build capacity and empower communities, groups, and individuals in the network society.

However, this book provides more than a simple collection of global civil-society narratives or case studies. Its prime contribution is to raise insights into the construction of an alternative vision of the network-society. Our intention is to frame a network-society discourse in which ordinary citizens participate in shaping their sociotechnical environments. While illustrating the diversity of ICT initiatives, projects, and experiments operated by community organizers, social activists, researchers, teachers, and not-for-profit organizations and groups globally, we have made every effort to retain a critical and analytic perspective on these emergent social developments.

Whether we achieve this goal is for others to judge. However, in attempting to meet that challenge, we endeavor to steer clear of the potential pitfalls of social forecasting that litter much of the information-society literature—that is, making extravagant claims based on much hype and little evidence.

Finally, while rejecting the revolutionary metaphor often attached to information- and network-society developments, we do portray the diversity of emergent initiatives and social engagement as evidence of civil-society action and advocacy. We present this as an indicator of an emerging grassroots potential and willingness to work for social change in the network society. They are, we believe, portents of embryonic social change: social networks in which information and knowledge are harnessed as key resources of communicative action, through which social goals can be achieved.

Networking the Information Society

It has been argued that global information-society developments require effective tripartite partnership between government, the private sector, and civil society to succeed (D'Orville 1999) yet most information-society policy development of the past decade has occurred to the exclusion of civil society in the policy processes. Even the U.N.-sponsored World Summit on the Information Society (WSIS), which is ostensibly open to global civil society, places barriers in the way of grassroots participation. The processes by which civil-society organizations can participate in the summit are cumbersome, difficult to understand, and poorly publicized with very few clear mechanisms for civic engagement and inclusion. To date, only groups and organizations with the resources or contacts to navigate through the bureaucratic maze surrounding WSIS have been able to register and participate.

Although policymakers view information as the key source of competitiveness, productivity, wealth, employment, and power, the emergence of networks as a means of communication and away of organizing society has led to the increased adoption of the term *network society* as a descriptor of current socioeconomic developments. Theoretically, the label is used to describe both the social and media networks shaping the prime mode of organization and most important structures of society (van Dijk 1999). In reality, however, the social networks with the most influence in shaping the structure and organization of modern society are those driven by transnational corporations (TNCs) and powerful nation-states. It is this manifestation of the network society, in which information is a key source of wealth and power, that increasingly represents the globalized world in which we live.

The unaccountable power and influence wielded by TNCs and international financial institutions such as the IMF, WTO, and the World Bank are often viewed as threats to cultural diversity and the nation-state (APEC, 2002). However, it is not simply the external dangers of the global marketplace that challenge national sovereignty and self-determination. Governments have been promoting a shift in power from public to private sector, through an ongoing process of public rationalization, since the Thatcher (U.K.) and Reagan (U.S.) governments of the 1980s.

This shift was facilitated in part by a popularist perception that the problems of unresponsive, hierarchical, public bureaucracies and monopolies could in some way be addressed by a more flexible approach in the private sector. Recent history has exposed this politically inspired myth for what it was: credo as profit-driven fabrication. Much of our governance, which although often unresponsive was at least partially transparent and accountable, is systematically being replaced by an opaque, undemocratic unresponsiveness of the private sector (Barber 2002). The chaotic state of the U.K. railway system bears testament to the potential for the dangerous inefficiency and ineffectiveness of the profit-driven approach found in this sector. The current process of rationalization and the growing bureaucratic apparatus and impenetrable policymaking authority of the G8 nations present a threat to the cornerstone of our democratic values.

Interestingly, while Thatcher and Reagan were waging their politicoeconomic battles of the 1980s, the technologies that would eventually underpin global communications and data exploitation of world markets by financial institutions and TNCs were being developed along a parallel track. As Barber points out, ICT has become inextricably associated with processes of globalization. Indeed, an argument can be made that ICT is a prerequisite of globalization:

In the unfettered high-tech global market, crucial democratic values become relics. Indeed, because globalization is correctly associated with new telecommunications technologies, the globalised and privatised information economy is constructed as an inevitable concomitant of postsovereign, postmodern society. (Barber 2002, 6)

Globalization and the Network Society

Expanding on these points, the authors in Part I highlight a range of issues and conditions resulting from the technoeconomic developments of the global network society. Oliver Boyd-Barrett, for example, focuses on links between trends in the communications industries and the governing global framework of neoliberal values. He casts doubt on the veracity of the digital-age metaphor by raising a fundamental question: If society has entered a new age, how does it differ qualitatively from its predecessor? Reinforcing the social significance of this question, he points to global rates of malnutrition, illiteracy, poor sanitation, and deaths from preventable diseases and highlights the absence of voice and influence that poor countries and people have in the face of global policymaking institutions.

Interestingly, the high rates of social exclusion reflected in Boyd-Barrett's presentation of U.N. *Human Development Report* (1998) statistics are mirrored in digital-divide statistics, where the richest 20 percent of the world's population has access to the majority of the world's ICT-related infrastructure, applications, and artifacts. The wealth of statistical data provided by Boyd-Barrett lends support to the idea that the digital divide reflects another form of social exclusion, and modern technological developments are simply symptomatic of evolving capitalism.

Evaluating the impact of globalization and communications media on contemporary society, Boyd-Barrett identifies three characteristics shaping the current epoch. First, these developments are inclusive; they involve almost all nation-states. Second, globalization is driven by Western-based TNCs. Third, this process is dependent to a large degree on the ICT sector. Illustrating how globalization has in the past tended to consolidate U.S.

global power, Boyd-Barrett concludes with a timely warning that any assessment of the conditions that might afford the formation of a global public sphere independent of state and corporate influence must be made against the backdrop of world power controlled by the United States and its allies.

While Boyd-Barrett provides insights into the structure and organization of the globalized techno economic network society, Gary Chapman offers contrasting visions. Echoing Boyd-Barrett's analysis of modern capitalist society, Chapman points to the dangers of unquestioning faith in the technological imperative. He argues that technology, and economic globalization have become the two chief determinants of life in the postindustrial world, where technoglobalism is rapidly engulfing world culture. By way of contrast, he then muses whether there might not be another way, in which technology could be adapted to meet human needs and interests. Pointing to the antiglobalization movement as an indicator, he presents a social perspective held by a disparate and yet growing number of people: that society could continue to emphasize social and cultural diversity and that this diversity could be reflected in the way people adopt and use technology.

Chapman suggests that identifying the role of civic society in cyberspace will mean balancing the technological imperative with our social imperative. It means explaining how the consumerized vision of the network society currently promoted and marketed by global media corporations and governments is not the only possible pathway to a network society. The technologies currently being designed to meet the profit-driven motives of TNCs in a homogenized world can also be utilized to meet the social agenda of a culturally diverse and inclusive network society.

Highlighting a bipolarity that has emerged in modern society, Chapman considers a number of key battlegrounds that will require people to behave as active citizens, rather than passive consumers, of the network society. The growing dissatisfaction with traditional politics globally is plain for all to see in the falling numbers of citizens participating in public elections. Chapman suggests that rather than adhering to the old formal frameworks of political engagement, a more dynamic basis of social organization is emerging.

By using ICT to communicate and share knowledge and experiences, it is becoming easier to identify allies and organize around ideas and issues. However, although the pieces for alternative global cultures have begun to emerge, they currently lack coherence. Chapman concludes that by using ICT as a tool to meet democratically determined human needs and interests, attempts to shape the network society will begin to find resonance in civic society.

Contemplating the human rights implications of global network-society governance, Cees J. Hamelink argues for international standards to protect against the harmful effects of technological developments and applications. In challenging the notion that an integrated global consumer market will enable all world citizens to share in the "good life," Hamelink reveals how the increasing global visibility of consumer goods has taken place against a backdrop of globalizing poverty, reinforcing the potential for conflict between rich and poor.

Mirroring Chapman's bipolarity thesis, Hamelink contends that a battle between the conflicting agendas of neoliberal globalization and humanitarianism is currently being waged, with the odds stacked heavily in favor of globalization. This is especially true in the communications arena, where an active humanitarian constituency has yet to emerge. Providing a timely warning for social activists globally, Hamelink cautions that despite the ability of the ad hoc coalitions involved in the antiglobalization networks to make decision makers sit up and take note, shaping an egalitarian and democratic network society will be an enormous, if not impossible, challenge. Underlining this sense of realism, he points to the unevenness of the world's communication resources. This unevenness is reflected in the gap between knowledge-rich and knowledge-poor nations and individuals and in the formidable power of the forces driving neoliberalism.

Such systems can only survive as long as people believe that they are in their best interests. Pointing to the growing vibrancy of local communities around the world, Hamelink suggests that the key prerequisite to achieving a humanitarian network society is a dynamic world civil society. To this end, a democratic world communication order should be placed squarely on the agenda of active communities and local initiatives everywhere.

Community Initiatives

Part II takes stock of issues raised by community activists/practitioners and participatory-action researchers from around the world. Although only a small cross-section of global-community initiatives are represented here, they provide a window through which we can observe the conditions in which a civil network society is emerging.

One of the most significant contribution's of public computing initiatives worldwide has been the attempts to address inequality in access to ICT (Clement and Shade 2000). However, as Kate Williams and Abdul Alkalimat make clear, the activities of many public computing sites lack are unknown in the public arena, and consequently tend to be overlooked at many levels of research, practice, and policy evolution.

In outlining the development of a methodological approach (which Williams and Alkalimat call "D6") that is intended to counter such social exclusion, the authors explain how the public computing movement has historically been associated with considerable democratic activity. In many local communities, for example, the provision of public access to ICT has been linked to the development of public communications platforms that enable information to be utilized as a resource for community organization and activities. Public computing spaces are social environments formed as the result of a confluence of social forces, institutions, and histories.

Utilizing the D6 method to identify and map four categories of public computing in Toledo, Ohio, the authors hypothesize three patterns of social environment. The first is that government sites are generally located randomly in terms of their proximity to rich and poor. The second is that commercial and university sites have a tendency to be situated according to market demand—that is, closer to people with higher incomes and to students. The third, and perhaps most interesting pattern for our purposes, is that community sites are likely to be located at opposing ends of the social spectrum: both rich and poor have community sites but not the middle strata.

Anticipating two further stages of their public computing research, Williams and Alkalimat argue that each category of public computing constitutes its own power dynamic, expressing a structural force through an aggregation of institutions, people, and spaces. The D6 method provides a useful tool for both civil-society policy and practice. Understanding the "cyberpower"—goal achievement through ICT utilization—of civil society will be more and more crucial to the nature of democracy in the network society.

Geert Lovink and Patrice Riemens argue that the commercialization of the Internet and the e-commerce and dot-com frenzy of the late 1990s, together with the privatizing deregulation approach of public policy, have endangered a once-vibrant "Digital City" in Amsterdam. Formed in 1994 against a background of public-media development in Amsterdam and amidst massive publicity, DDS rapidly attracted tens of thousands of users and became Europe's largest "free net."

However, although DDS became a huge networked community facility, it never was a community in its own right and only paid lip service to the aims of community building and development. Much of the massive membership growth at DDS is attributed to the attraction of free access to the global Internet, rather than to an interest in local information, communications, and networking. Still, the prime cause of DDS's success is ascribed to the freedoms that its users experienced, enabling a diverse range of subcultures to emerge.

Local researcher Peter van den Besselaar (2001), through longitudinal user-analysis profiles, demonstrated that by 1998 only around a quarter of active DDS inhabitants actually resided in Amsterdam. The fact that DDS lacked any clear sense of community ownership and was inhabited mostly by outsiders explains why users were content to let management direct the initiative's development unfettered.

The morphing of DDS from its humble grassroots, low-tech, and non-budget origins into a professional technobusiness was concluded at the peak of the e-commerce, dot-com feeding frenzy that took place in the 1990s. Plans to sell off the newly privatized enterprise were hit by the bursting of the new-economy bubble and the sudden emergence of competitive access and service providers, which severely undermined the DDS user base and consequently its value on the open market.

The shock waves generated by the social explosions that followed the economic crisis of December 2001, in Argentina changed the way civil society utilized ICT. Susana Finquelievich tracks the emergence of grassroots civic networks in Buenos Aires. As tens of thousands of people began to take to the streets, organizing themselves in grassroots networks known as neighborhood assemblies, a plethora of electronic forums and websites emerged to support these civil activities. The important point to note here is not that cyberspace was used to provide some alternative form of public communications space, but that it was used to provide additional communications space for civil communicative action. ICT was used, as both tool and process, to support in-person and face-to-face social engagement of real-world life, not to replace it.

The subsequent decline in real-world and online levels of civil-society activities in no way undermines or belittles the significance of the work still being conducted. The fact that neighborhood assemblies have been successful in assisting care centers for the elderly, providing food and shelter for street children, collecting medicines for public hospitals, as well as in many other areas of social need is significant. That ICT continues to be utilized to support these activities is important to us in providing context for and understanding the potential of these communication tools in civil society.

The symbiotic relationship between in-person and online communications, as illustrated in the neighborhood exchange clubs, is, as Finquelievich expounds, basic to the establishment of a new public sphere. The emergence of this public space exceeds the socially limited agenda of governments and TNCs. This form of social innovation contributes to the creation of a new associative concept of democratization, where, through operational solidarity, citizens contribute as direct participants in shaping the network society.

The chapter contributed by Veran Matic, which outlines the inspirational struggles of Radio B92 in the face of enormous state repression, concretizes the "human rights in the network society" issues raised by Hamelink. In this instance, however, the dangers facing civil society and democracy came not in the form of TNCs and globalization but from an abuse of power exercised by autocratic state officials.

The B92 story is an illustration of how independent media can become a catalyst for social reform and change. It is a chronicle of how human creativity, innovation, and determination found ways to maintain a free flow of credible information against enormous odds. It is testament to the power of the open communication of ideas and to the way such communication can result in social mobilization that can topple even the most repressive and tyrannical of state regimes. Of course, not all struggles facing civil society will be this stark. The nature of each struggle will be determined by the social environment in which it occurs.

Scott S. Robinson adopts a normative approach to citizen participation, which he applies to the telecenter movement that has emerged in Latin America in recent years. Providing insights into the experiences of migrant workers and their families in the remittance economies of Central America as well as into the operations of the transnational corporations and financial institutions that prey on migrants, Robinson presents a sustainable vision of telecenters working in partnership with microbanks for the good of local and diasporic communities.

In Central America many people have no telephone or personal computers at home, or for that matter, the credit to purchase such basic components of the network society. Community telecenters have the potential to provide affordable and community-relevant digital services. However, as Robinson explains, telecenters face barriers to their sustainability from a number of quarters—commercial ISP and telecommunications service providers, computer hardware and software producers, public and government agencies.

Robinson suggests that linking telecenters with microbanks can provide a form of cheap communication between the eighteen million Mexicans living in the United States and their families in Mexico, as well as inexpensive ways for migrant workers in the United States to send remittance monies to their families south of the border. Fees for processing money transfers will contribute to the financing of the telecenters and microbanks, ensuring their sustainability.

Although this system is still currently a vision, Robinson points the reader to many initiatives that appear to indicate that such mutuality between telecenters and microbanks is not far removed from becoming a reality. As with the Argentine neighborhood assemblies and exchange networks, Robinson's vision is indicative of the abundance of creativity, imagination, and social innovation that exists in civil society.

Finally in part II, Fiorella de Cindio provides a candidly critical evaluation of the development and progress of Rete Civica di Milano (RCM) and its cross-sectoral approach (public-, private-, and voluntary-sector partnerships) to community networking. Outlining a number of community projects hosted by RCM, de Cindio establishes community links at a variety of levels. Voluntary-sector projects such an association for drug addicts and immigrants, a social-solidarity umbrella organization, and a local social research forum stand alongside innovative educational and learning initiatives and cultural forums.

To maintain its independence in the public sector, RCM intentionally avoided cultivating formal relations with local government. However, it has been successful in developing electronic "direct line" links between politicians, government officials, and local citizens. Although their function is not clearly understood by the general public yet, the direct lines represent an innovative attempt to promote democratic communications in the city.

There can be little doubt that RCM has done much to achieve its three basic goals since its birth in 1994: the goals of providing citizens with access to the Net, offering a shared field for mutual cooperation in the community, and affirming the right to citizenship in the network society. It has been incredibly successful in raising the profile of ICT within a range of community contexts. Where many similar networked initiatives failed, RCM continues to innovate socially, which helps explain its continued sustainability.

However, as de Cindio recognizes, levels of civic awareness are not as high as they might be or need to be. If RCM is to move beyond the stage of interesting social experiment and achieve the model of sustainability to which De Cindio refers, then the RCM Participatory Foundation might need to reconsider what she calls the civic-engagement gene.

Taking RCM out of the social laboratory and developing an understanding of the practices of the social networks of Milan's local communities might be considered as the next stage. If participatory capacity-building and community-development activities are adopted, the stated belief that citizens are "owners of a sovereignty" and therefore entitled to play an active role in shaping the network society might be realized at RCM.

Building a New Public Sphere In Cyberspace

Part III considers the development of a new public sphere for social and environmental progress in cyberspace. The dynamic and changing nature of the medium and its promise of inexpensive and universal access to information and communication suggest rich potential for civic uses. However, obstacles to the construction of such a public sphere can be great. The first two chapters of part III raise issues of a general nature, while the final three chapters examine the contribution of public libraries, community networks, and independent media centers to public spheres in the network society.

Although the Internet can be utilized to provide important support for a wide variety of social movements and civil-society organizations and community groups, Craig Calhoun cautions that ICTs will not automatically lead to the triumph of popular social forces over neoliberal power bases. He argues that although the Internet has enabled international activists, indigenous peoples, environmentalists, and opponents of the WTO to organize in new and effective ways, such efforts are exceeded by the uses to which transnational corporations put the same technology and applications. Recognizing the importance of the Internet to social movement activists, Calhoun calls for a sense of realism, pointing out that IT use often varies depending on the resources different users are able to invest.

Developing this point further, Calhoun reasons that international civil society has grown as part of globalization and that its enthusiasts should avoid overstating its strength, especially in terms of ICT. One of the main strengths of ICT for neoliberal globalization, he argues, is that it facilitates both decentralization and dispersal of activity and concentration of power. Consequently, countering this will require a new vision of social relations. It is not simply enough to respond to Western-initiated trends in survival mode. For Calhoun, global civil society must be creative in its development of alternative modernities.

Research showing how and in what context ICT affects the relationships between civil society and the broader social environment is crucial to the development of these alternative modernities. Public spheres in the global network society present opportunities for social activism across a range of spatial levels. But sound research will be crucial in informing the development of alternative modernities. Consequently, the development of meaningful links between academic researchers and civil-society practitioners and policymakers should be recognized as a crucial step in this process.

Another author promoting the need to develop a critical understanding of how ICTs affect our lives is Howard Rheingold, who emphasizes the importance of examining the nature of collective action in cyberspace. In a reflective reassessment, the self-confessed technophile critically reappraises his "love affair" with new technologies.

Challenging a fundamental public assumption that "science" equals "truth," Rheingold criticizes technological determinism for suppressing free will and promoting a lack of public understanding of the social meanings of technology and its applications. He proposes that this has led to a crisis of knowledge and an inability to think publicly and make collective, substantive decisions about technology and its role in the network society. Suggesting that solutions to this situation will be found collectively through widespread public discourse, Rheingold argues that it is time to prove the democratic potential of ICT.

Questioning whether Internet applications contribute to civic life or remove people from it, he reasons that it is not enough to get involved through online activism. Communications media are necessary but not sufficient for vibrant, self-governing societies. In the network society, the "important stuff" still occurs in the civic life of our communities and in the lives of our neighbors. It is here—where participation is important—that ICT could provide another platform for social engagement. But as Rheingold observes, this will only be a subset of real-world social networks.

Nancy Kranich contemplates the modern-day public sphere in terms of real and virtual spaces where community members can exchange ideas. These information commons are, she argues, fundamental to democratic participation in the network society. Grounding her thesis in concepts of social capital and civil society, Kranich contends that information underpins civic participation and facilitates the development of civil society: a better-informed citizenry is more likely to engage in policy discussion and communicate their ideas and concerns freely.

Outlining her views on the information commons, she discusses plans for building new spaces by partnerships of citizens and community organizations. Public libraries, she argues, are ideally placed to contribute to such activities. They have historically provided community spaces for the free and open exchange of ideas, making information and knowledge available to everyone. Kranich makes a convincing case, which illustrates the enormous contributions public libraries have made to community life over the years. She cites many examples of how libraries, often acting as community forums, have contributed to and stimulated the processes of independent thought development so crucial to the public sphere. The community and capacity-building initiatives fostered by libraries include: civic-skills teaching, community information-literacy partnerships, communitywide reading programs, digital neighborhood directories, and public-access ICT schemes.

However, these significant social activities and services are under threat. Deregulation and privatization have shifted information policymaking into the private arena and clouded issues of public interest. As transnational communications and media corporations compete for domination of cyberspace, the public interest is in danger of being neglected. To counter this neglect, educational and research institutions, libraries, nonprofits, and community networks must be guaranteed free space in the new information infrastructures. The information commons, she argues, must constitute a public sphere of free speech and open discourse to enhance democracy.

Our rights of free speech, inquiry, and self-governance are dependent on a culturally rich and socially vibrant information commons.

Employing a social-constructivist perspective on the information infrastructure in the network society, David Silver compares and contrasts two differing approaches to community networking in the United States. Although both initiatives are grounded in a common goal—that is, "to network a community"—the methods adopted to achieve this aim are markedly different and produce quite distinct outcomes. Silver confirms the notion put forward by Williams and Alkalimat that community networks are social environments whose form depends on the specific pattern of social forces, organizations, and histories that shape them. In a critical evaluation of the top-down and bottom-up approaches adopted by the community networks, Silver challenges what he calls a "prevailing and dangerous hypothesis"—the neutrality of the Internet.

Successful in obtaining support from a wide range of public- and private-sector funding agencies, Blacksburg Electronic Village (BEV) adopted a top-down approach. Network-design strategies took place behind closed doors at Bell Atlantic, while computer-literate electrical engineering students from Virginia Tech tested the network. Despite an emphasis on the potential advantages of civic-based community building, from very early on the intention appears to have been one of promoting the construction of a commercially driven online community. Although the project has been promoted as a socially collaborative initiative, the people of Blacksburg have actually had little input into its design, implementation, and development processes.

By way of contrast, the Seattle Community Network (SCN) receives no corporate sponsorship to achieve sustainability. Attempting to ground the initiative in the local community, the SCN project team adopted participatory-design techniques and encouraged local people to collaborate in the design and building processes of the network. Local community organizations were introduced to SCN through a range of workshops and outreach programs.

Intended initially as a community-development tool, the network evolved through the efforts of a group of progressive local volunteers. They have benefited from the support of and association with the Seattle Public Library and a range of local nonprofit organizations and activist groups. SCN is free of charge to local residents and is available to people without Internet access at home through Seattle public libraries.

It was in the same part of the United States during the 1999 WTO demonstrations, that the Seattle Independent Media Center (IMC) or Indymedia sprang to public prominence. Critically assessing the main characteristics, processes, and challenges to this global network of media collectives, Douglas Morris asserts that alternative-media networks stimulate public awareness of global-justice issues and actions. Indymedia, he argues, forms part of a broader set of social movements contributing to the development of participatory politics, nonproprietary and collective information products, and a multifaceted network of cultures. A consequence of these diverse activities has been the creation of decentralized virtual public spheres, locally and globally, in which democratic discourse is advanced.

Although clearly still in its infancy and facing significant challenges as it evolves, the democratic media associated with Indymedia are tools that can be utilized to raise awareness and inform an increasingly receptive public on social justice issues. Indymedia provides an alternative to the expansion and centralization of transnational media corporations. The vitality and vibrancy of its practices and principles, together with the participatory networking of grassroots activism have much to contribute to the development of public spheres through which civil society can begin to collectively shape the network society.

Networks of Awareness, Advocacy, and Action

Although this book has highlighted a range of civil-society ICT initiatives, we have deliberately steered clear of attempting to construct a typology of them. We have taken this approach for two reasons: first, because we are not convinced that trying to force these initiatives into convenient-sized packages with neat labels on them contributes to the discourse in any positive manner, and second, because the cross-section of ICT initiatives illustrated here only reflects a small proportion of the diversity of such social enterprises. Just as community and culture differs according to social environments, so too do civil society initiatives. Of course there are strong commonalities, but as was seen in the earlier chapters, there are also significant differences. Rather than providing hard-and-fast definitions, we have sought, through an illustration of diversity, to explain what these initiatives are, why and how they emerged, and what they seek to achieve.

Peter Day and Douglas Schuler

Although such insights aid our understanding of civil society in the age of networks, they also raise other questions, to which we now turn: Why are civil society ICT initiatives significant? How might their influence be felt in the current neoliberal network society? Does the growth in numbers and diversity of civil-society ICT initiatives globally represent the emergence of a global civil-society social movement?

To address these questions we frame our deliberations in the context of social-network theory (Wellman 1999). We find this framework useful not only because we seek to understand these social phenomena within the broader context of the network society, but also because we are investigating the conditions and communicative relationships that surround these social environments. In pursuing this investigation, we were mindful that issues of agency and political opportunities are central to understanding the evolution of social relationships. The simplistic assumption that global civil-society activities and social movements will automatically emerge out of economic globalization or revolutions in communications technologies ignores both.

It is too early to state with certainty that the initiatives we introduce here are representative of a transnational civil-society social movement. We do, however, present them as indicators of an emerging grassroots potential and openness to social change in the network society. Insight into the way initiatives, groups, and networks emerge and are legitimized is central to understanding the politics of civil society and consequently crucial to understanding successful networking. This is of relevance to us in developing knowledge of such practices in the global network society because transnational civil society is "an area of struggle, a fragmented and contested area" (Keck and Sikkink 1998, 33).

Network theory provides a framework for change through which the preferences and identities of actors engaged in social activities can be mutually transformed by interaction with others. Keck and Sikkink suggest that the voluntary and horizontal nature of networks means that the motivational force for actor participation is an anticipated mutuality of learning, respect, and benefits. Networking therefore has the potential to provide civil society with both a vehicle for communicative and political exchange and the potential for mutual transformation of participants.

However, not all social networking is conducted in a spirit of mutuality and reciprocity. Civil society is often forced to network under conditions of power imbalance, where the public and commercial sectors exercise influence that affects their ability to shape social developments. This is especially true in the network society, as was seen the chapters by Boyd-Barrett, Chapman, Hamelink, Calhoun, and Rheingold, where the power exercised in networks followed from the resources that the public and commercial sectors owned.

In the network society, the contested and fragmented area of struggle to which Keck and Sikkink refer occurs in the interaction within and between civil-society groups, institutions, and governments at many levels. The extent to which civil society can identify and influence targets vulnerable to material and moral leverage, so that the future direction of the policy discourse might be shaped by civil society, remains to be seen. However, the effectiveness of networks is dependent on their density and strength, and much will depend on the number and size of organizations in civil-society networks and on the regularity and quality of their exchanges (Keck and Sikkink 1998). Communicative interaction is crucial to successful networking, and the development of social-network analysis (Degenne and Forse 1999; Wasserman and Faust 1994) as both participatory-action research method and civil-society development tool will be of interest to the future of effective civil-society networking—locally, nationally, and globally.

Challenges

The work presented in this book is simultaneously a product of today's ICT environment and a shaper of tomorrow's. Insofar as this work attempts to shift focus and power downward and laterally through its insistence on universal access and community control, it implicitly threatens the status quo with its established (though dynamic) modalities of control. However, as Calhoun points out, though the strength of these established modalities of control should not be underestimated, neither should the case for the use of ICT by community and advocacy/action networks be overstated. Nonetheless, on a profound level some threats to established systems of institutional control might now exist. If this is indeed the case, the consequences of unraveled state systems might be severe. But the effects of community networks and other grassroots forms of democratized communication are likely to be anticipated and mitigated by organizations with vast resources.

What is the nature of these challenges? And how can they be met effectively? The first threat comes from the side effects of vast media empires going about their daily business of gaining market share and of governments setting

ICT policies that ignore or devalue civil society. For example, as a response to the September 11, 2001, atrocity, the U.S. federal government removed an immense amount of public information from its websites, regardless of whether such information was of import to civil society and citizens in general. It is worth remembering that when one is sleeping in the same bed as titans, the simplest shift of position can be fatal. Consequently, while trying to adopt a sufficiently cautious and critically reflective attitude, without becoming unduly paranoid, we need to entertain the unpleasant possibility that efforts like those in this book will be *actively* targeted in the future if they are perceived as a threat. The FBI's domestic COINTELPRO ("counterintelligence programs") program, for example, spent millions of dollars covertly interfering with civil rights, the peace movement, and other political activism from 1956 to 1971. More recently FBI agents, looking for extensive logs on everybody who had visited the IMC website, visited IMC activists in Seattle. Unfortunately, there was no outcry among other media outlets in Seattle whose rights under the First Amendment might also be at risk.

Many of the challenges to our enterprises are not so nefarious. Some arise from within our own ranks, and it is not so easy to point fingers at others if we do not rise to the occasion ourselves. These inherent challenges include our difficulty to describe our own work and vision in a compelling way. As social innovators we have a responsibility to make our work compelling. The onus is on us to ensure that we get our vision across to as many people, in as many social spheres, as possible. In other words, it is not enough to do "the right thing"—we have to convince others that we are doing "the right thing" and that they have an important contribution to make also.

Prospects for Success

Success is, in itself, an elusive term to define or come to understand. Success presumably entails reaching all of our goals. But our goals are diffuse, impossible to specify precisely, and possibly contradictory. Are we looking for success tomorrow, next week, or at some nebulous time in the distant future when success becomes finally established as a permanent condition? Is success a description of a utopia where no wrong occurs, no violence is visited on people or other forms of life, or does success mean that some pain is avoided, some scars are healed, some progress is made toward reducing misery? Whether the impossibility of utopia is regrettable or simply a basic fact of human existence makes little difference here. We are concerned about trajectories, the directions that we are heading in as a powerful constituent of an ecosystem, and about possible ways to intervene.

ICT (as well as the social systems it is embedded in) enables voices to travel great distances. Generally this means that some voices travel farther than others and are heard by greater numbers of people. When the information and communication environment is entirely one directional, it becomes as unalterable as the weather. Paraphrasing Mark Twain's remark on the weather, one can talk about it but one cannot do anything about it. Control over the content and distribution of information is an awesome power. For one thing, it makes propaganda eminently more possible. The unremitting pounding of a single point of view can help build the necessary hatred and fear to approve the preemptive invasion of a country. Technology, of course, can aid immeasurably with this process—for example, through the then-new miracle of radio, Hitler was able to send his message continuously and simultaneously all over Germany.

Regardless of the ultimate destination, it seems clear that success of the work and the ideas presented in this book will mean increasing influence in the world (both locally and globally?). We believe that a public airing and cross-fertilization of new ideas will be indispensable to any democratization of the Internet and other ICT systems. A large part of our motivation for this book has been our desire to publicize such ideas and make them available for thoughtful consideration, in practice and policy as well as in academia. Another motive has been to show that there is no geographic monopoly on these ideas; indeed they are emerging and developing much faster than we as observers and as editors of this book can absorb. The efforts of our collaborators in this book will need to be integrated with the vast array of other activities and initiatives around the world if additional influence is to be attained globally.

Some of this integration will occur at the organizational level; groups will undoubtedly coalesce—often across traditional borders—over shared ideas, and these groups may be able to institutionalize and facilitate additional work and thinking. Moreover, as Keck and Sikkink (1998) make clear, forming new organizations may not be the key idea or catalyst for social action and progress. Discussion, as is increasingly taking place in electronic mailing lists, chat rooms, and so on, is helping to promote the development of shared vocabularies and shared agendas that are necessary for group mobilization around issues. Shared understanding—particularly around basic principles—may, in fact, be more immune to the challenges discussed in the previous section.

These new groups and issue-oriented communities also need to consciously regard themselves as players in a dynamic and complex issue space in which they will likely need to coexist to see their long-term visions become real. Such social movements, Keck and Sikkink report, are no longer limited to relatively simple messages but are increasingly capable of constructing more complex and insightful programs that present in detail the type of world they would like to see. In addition, the large numbers of people involved and interested in preventing war, protesting human rights abuses, or celebrating Earth Day may be capable of massive coordinated actions, on scales unimaginable before networked communication. These communities might be able to work with the open-source community to develop sociotechnical platforms that they can distribute worldwide, much along the lines of the IMC model.

The constitution of the "network society" is such that nearly all of us are connected to nearly all of us in some way or another. We all coexist in the ecosystem of the natural world and in the social "ecosystem" of our information and communication spheres and through our actions on the social and natural environments. Although we are all connected, we are not necessarily connected directly; we are configured into a network or web of relationships. "Communities" in such a world web can coalesce around shared interests, values, principles, aims, or other viewpoints. Religions demonstrate this reality, as do national identities (or "imagined communities," as Anderson (1983) calls them). By using the work in this book as background, we can see that new, overarching paradigms that can integrate many views of thinking in a nonhierarchical network fashion may be the next step in the evolution of the conscious development of ICT for the amelioration of social and other problems.

Schuler (2002), for example, has started a "Pattern Language for Living Communication" project. This project is designed to collect the knowledge and wisdom of people involved with these issues and make them available in an online (and print) format that will help people more easily find and adopt suggestions relevant to their work. Similarly, Schuler (2001) has also written on the idea of "civic intelligence," which attempts to provide an overarching concept that both describes current efforts and, hopefully, motivates future ones.

Unlike many previous "utopian" projects that ignored social realities, efforts to cultivate civic intelligence must be more pragmatic. This will require recognizing the factors that promote innovation and acting on them by developing programs that incorporate them. It is also possible for community practitioners and researchers to help develop and promote the factors themselves. Basalla (1988) suggests that three preconditions for the success of technological innovation exist:

1. Existing models to extend and build on
2. Social environments that value the innovation
3. Intents, skills, etc. of innovator

To these three preconditions we would add a fourth:

4. Adequate resources for innovator

This fourth factor acknowledges the important role of resources for promoting innovation. Although the innovations we are considering are primarily social and secondarily technological, Basalla's observations are pertinent. A civic intelligence would help promote social innovation by helping to ensure that each of the preconditions were met. In fact, civic intelligence can be viewed as a way of guaranteeing that these preconditions are continuously improved and strengthened and made to reflect abiding human values. In terms of Basalla's preconditions, a civic-intelligence orientation would help foster a social environment that values civic-intelligence innovations, motivate the creation and marketing of suitable models, inspire and educate potential innovators, and identify and distribute resources.

Presenting the preconditions for sociotechnical innovation in a framework of design criteria for community ICT initiatives, Day echoes Schuler's civic-intelligence approach (2001, 2002). Attempting to link theory with practice for socially constructive purposes, Day is actively engaged in establishing a global network of community ICT academics/practitioners. The purpose of the network is to stimulate the development of an open-source knowledge base related to community ICT initiatives. The intention is to help communities from all over the world draw from and contribute to a dynamic and participatory knowledge base, similar to the notion of "civic intelligence" referred to above. To this end, Go.ItiRA was launched in Rockhampton, Central Queensland, in the summer of 2002, with a view to stimulating collaboration and cooperation between academia and community practice globally (Marshall, Taylor, and MacPherson 2002).

Thoughts for the Future

Part of our current task includes more fully understanding the nature and power of civic and social communications. Historically this has mostly occurred at a local level; most of the communication encountered during one's life was among people who lived in close proximity. Now globalization, bolstered by commerce, cheap travel, and communication, increases the distance that messages we encounter are likely to have traveled. It is therefore imperative to support the kind of experimentation and collaborations between academia, activists, and community members outlined in the pages of this book and to acknowledge the common themes that emerge. With these common themes in mind, we offer a number of recommendations to promote the support of socially innovative civic ICT initiatives.

First, there is an urgent need to make policy more responsive to the needs of local citizens. It is therefore imperative that we create a meaningful, equitable, and inclusive dialogue between (civic/community) policymakers, practitioners, and researchers. Based on principles of mutuality, reciprocity, and trust, this dialogue should facilitate the exploration of ways to identify and respond to the needs of citizens in the network society. One means by which such civic dialogues can be informed is through new research approaches that engage communities and civic networks in socially meaningful ways. Consequently, a second recommendation would involve the public funding of new and innovative research that improves our understanding and knowledge of the diversity of cultures, values, belief systems, and needs found throughout global civic society. Finally, we draw attention to the notion of civic intelligence not as an abstract concept but as an organic and living project to which and from which civic societies from around the world can contribute and draw, as their experiences and needs permit. Through the utilization of civic intelligence as a sociocultural knowledge base that informs policy, practice, and research, people in their localities, by means of communicative action, can shape network societies.

The linkages that our work favors are not typically those that businesses in the developed world can exploit to get their job done faster and more efficiently. In our opinion, enough attention has been given to that sector already. We are concerned with two other areas: the connections that need to be made *within* communities that are increasingly marginalized and left behind, and the connections that are to be made *across* traditional boundaries—economic, cultural, geographic, ethnic. These connections should be established not for the purpose of assimilating or selling but for the purpose of understanding and of providing mutual aid and support.

It is unclear how soon we will be able to ascertain whether these new developments signal something profound historically or if they ultimately become known merely as historical footnotes. We now know that ordinary people are capable of conceiving—and achieving—extraordinary things with very few resources. While current institutions, notably governments and businesses, often fail to address or even recognize what needs to be done, the civic sector may step in and fill this void. It certainly will not be a trivial undertaking. We await the future with anticipation—and hope.

References

Abbate, J. 1995. *Inventing the Internet.* Cambridge, MA: MIT Press.

Adilkno. 1998. *Media Archive.* New York: Autonomedia.

Africana Studies 4900. 2002. "'Cyberspace and the Black Experience,' at University of Toledo." *Chronicle of Higher Education,* A18.

Agre, P., and Schuler, D., eds. 1997. *Reinventing Technology, Rediscovering Community: Critical Explorations of Computing as a Social Practice.* Greenwich, CT: Ablex.

Alger, D. 2000. *Megamedia.* Lanham, MD: Rowman and Littlefield.

Alkalimat, A., and Williams, K. 2001. "Social Capital and Cyberpower in the African American Community: A Case Study of a Community Technology in the Dual City." In L. M. Keeble and B. D. Loader, eds., *Community Informatics: Community Development through the Use of Information and Communications Technologies.* London: Routledge. http://www.communitytechnology.org/cyberpower

American Association of School Librarians and the Association for Educational Communication and Technology. 1998. *Information Power: Building Partnerships for Learning.* Chicago: American Library Association.

American Library Association. 1989. *Presidential Committee on Information Literacy Report.* Chicago: American Library Association. http://www.ala.org/acrl/nili/ilit1st.html

American Library Association. 2000. *A Library Advocate's Guide to Building Information Literate Communities.* Chicago: American Library Association. http://www.ala.org/pio/advocacy/informationliteracy.pdf

American Library Association. 2002a. Office of Intellectual Freedom Website. Chicago: American Library Association. http://www.ala.org/oif.html

American Library Association. 2002b. Office of Intellectual Freedom Website on CIPA. Chicago: American Library Association. http://www.ala.org/cipa/

American Library Association. 2002c. Washington Office Website on Access to Government Information. Washington, DC: American Library Association. http://www.ala.org/washoff/governmentinfo.html

American Library Association. 2002d. Washington Office Website on Copyright. Washington, DC: American Library Association. http://www.ala.org/washoff/copyright.html

American Library Association. 2002e. Washington Office Website on the Digital Divide. Washington, DC: American Library Association. http://www.ala.org/washoff/e-rate.html

American Library Association and the American Civil Liberties Union. 2001, March 20. *American Library Association v. the United States of America, and Multnomah County, et al. v. the United States of America: Complaints for Declaratory and Injunctive Relief.* Chicago: American Library Association; New York: American Civil Liberties Union.

Anderson, B. 1983. *Imagined Communities.* London: Verso.

Andrews, P. 1992, June 16. "PC Prices Take a Cold Dive as Competition Heats Up." *Seattle Times*, B2.

Andrews, P. 1993, June 15. "Internet Offers Inexpensive, Global Communications Link." *Seattle Times*, D2.

APEC. 2002. *Globalisation Guide.org.* http://www.globalisationguide.org/

Arendt, H. 1958. *The Human Condition.* Chicago: University of Chicago Press.

Arnison, M. 2001. "Open Publishing Is the Same as Free Software." *Community Activist Technology* website, March 2001. http://cat.org.au/maffew/cat/openpub.html, accessed September 30, 2002.

Arroyo, D. 2000. "Estado y sociedad civil en el proceso de descentralización." In *Municipios, democratización y derechos humanos.* Buenos Aires: CODESEDH.

Arroyo, D., and Filmus, D. 1997. "El Perfil de las ONGs en Argentina." *FLACSO, EUDEBA.* Buenos Aires: World Bank.

Artopoulos, A. 1998. "El futuro llegó hace rato . . . : usos alternativos de la informática centralizada en espacios urbanos." In S. Finquelievich and E. Schiavo, eds., *La ciudad y sus TIC.* Buenos Aires: Editor Universidad de Quilmes.

Askins, J. 1994, May 1. "Information Highway Has Roadblocks." *Roanoke Times & World-News*, B3.

Association of College and Research Libraries, Instruction Task Force. 2000. *Information Literacy Competency Standards for Higher Education.* Chicago: American Library Association. http://www.ala.org/acrl/ilcomstan.html

Babe, R. E. 1997. Telecommunications: From old to new models of control. In O. Boyd-Barrett (ed.), *MA in Mass Communications* (Module 10, Unit 60). Leicester, U.K.: Centre for Mass Communications Research, University of Leicester.

Bagdikian, B. 1997. *The Media Monopoly.* 5th ed. Boston: Beacon Press.

Barber, B. 1984. *Strong Democracy.* Berkeley: University of California Press.

Barber, B. 1998. *A Place for Us: How to Make Society Civil and Strong.* New York: Hill and Wang.

Barber, B. 2002. Globalizing Democracy. *The American Prospect,* 11(20): 858. http://www.prospect.org/print/V11/20/barber-b.html

Basalla, G. 1988. *Evolution of Technology.* Cambridge: Cambridge University Press.

Beamish, A. 1995. "Communities On-line: A Study of Community-Based Computer Networks." Unpublished M. A. thesis, Department of Urban Studies and Planning, MIT, Cambridge, MA.

Bell, D. 2001. *An Introduction to Cybercultures.* London: Routledge.

Bell, D., and Kennedy, B., eds. 2000. *The Cybercultures Reader.* London: Routledge.

Bellezza, E., and Florian, F. 2001. *Le Fondazioni del Terzo Millennio: Pubblico e Provato per il non-profit.* Florence, Italy: Passigli Editori. (In Italian.)

Benedikt, M., ed. 1991. *Cyberspace: First Steps.* Cambridge, MA: MIT Press.

Benhabib, S. 1996. *Democracy and Difference: Contesting Boundaries of the Political.* Princeton, NJ: Princeton University Press.

Benton Foundation. 1998. *What's Going On, Losing Ground Bit by Bit: Low-Income Communities in the Information Age.* Washington, DC: Benton Foundation. http://www.benton.org/Library/Low-Income/

Bertot, J., and McClure, C. 2000. Public Libraries and the Internet 2000: Summary Findings and Data Tables. Washington, DC: U.S. National Commission on Libraries and Information Science. http://www.nclis.gov/statsurv/2000plo.pdf

Best, S., and Kellner, D. 1991. *Postmodern Theory: Critical Interrogations.* New York: Guilford Press.

Bijker, W., Hughes, T., and Pinch, T., eds. 1987. *The Social Construction of Technological Systems: New Directions in the Sociology and History of Technology.* Cambridge, MA: MIT Press.

Birkerts, S. 1994. *The Gutenberg Elegies: The Fate of Reading in an Electronic Age.* Winchester, MA: Faber and Faber.

Bishop, A., ed. 1993. *Emerging Communities: Integrating Networking Information into Library Services.* Urbana: Graduate School of Library and Information Science, University of Illinois at Urbana-Champaign.

Bishop, M. 2001, June 16. "The New Wealth of Nations." *The Economist.*

Blacksburg Electronic Village. 1992, January 20. "Blacksburg, Tech, C & P Telephone, Explore 'Electronic Village' Concept." Press release.

Blacksburg Electronic Village. 1993, January 11. "America's First Electronic Village to Become a Reality." Press release.

Blacksburg Electronic Village. 1995a. "Plan of Action for Putting Town on the BEV." http://www.bev.net/project/townprop.html

Blacksburg Electronic Village. 1995b. "Why a Network in Blacksburg?" http://www.bev.net/project/vision95/Why.html

Blacksburg Electronic Village. 1998. "Blacksburg Electronic Village—Research." http://www.bev.net/project/research/

Blacksburg Electronic Village. 1999. "BEV Project Partners." http://www.bev.net/project/partners.html

"Blacksburg Electronic Village Classes Planned by Libraries." 1994, March 18. *Roanoke Times & World-News*, NRV2.

Blomberg, J., and Kensing, F. 1998. "Participatory Design: Issues and Concerns." Special issue on participatory design. *Computer-supported cooperative work: The Journal of Collaborative Computing*, 7(3–4): 167–185.

Blumenstyk, G. 1997, January 17. "An Experiment in 'Virtual Community' Takes Shape in Blacksburg, Va." *Chronicle of Higher Education*, A24–A26.

Bollier, D. 2001a. "Can the Information Commons Be Saved: How Intellectual Property Policies Are Eroding Democratic Culture and Some Strategies for Asserting the Public Interest." *What's New?* Washington, DC: Center for Arts and Culture. http://www.culturalpolicy.org/whatsnew/Bollier.pdf

Bollier, D. 2001b. *Public Assets, Private Assets: Reclaiming the American Commons in an Age of Market Enclosure.* Washington, DC: New America Foundation.

Bollier, D. 2002. *Silent Theft: The Private Plunder of Our Common Wealth.* New York: Routledge.

Boltanski, L., and Chapiello, E. 1999. *Le nouvel esprit du capitalisme.* Paris: Gallimard.

Bourdieu, P. 1998. *Acts of Resistance.* New York: New Press.

Bourdieu, P. 2001. *Contre-feux II.* Paris: Raisons d'Agir.

Bowden, P., Blythe, E., and Cohill, A. 1997. "A Brief History of the Blacksburg Electronic Village." In A. Cohill and A. Kavanaugh, eds., *Community Networks: Lessons from Blacksburg, Virginia*, 15–28. Norwood, MA: Artech House.

Boyd-Barrett, O. 1998. Media Imperialism Reformulated. In D. Kishan Thussu, ed., *Electronic Empires*, 157–176. London: Edward Arnold.

Boyd-Barrett, O. 1999. Trends in World Communication. *Global Dialogue*, 1(1): 58–69.

Boyd-Barrett, O. 2001. World Information Orders. In W. Gudykunst and B. Mody, eds., *Handbook of International and Intercultural Communication*, Thousand Oaks, CA: Sage.

Boyd-Barrett, O. Forthcoming. Cyberspace and the Global Public Sphere. In Peter Day and Douglas Schuler, eds., *Community Practice in the Network Society: Local Action/Global Interaction*. London: Routledge.

Boyte, H. 1980. *The Backyard Revolution: Understanding the New Citizen Movement*. Philadelphia: Temple University Press.

Boyte, H. 1989. *Commonwealth: A Return to Citizen Politics*. New York: Free Press.

Boyte, H., Booth, H., and Max, S. 1986. *Citizen Action and the New American Populism*. Philadelphia: Temple University Press.

Boyte, H., and Evans, S. 1986. *Free Spaces: The Sources of Democratic Change in America*. New York: Harper and Row.

Boyte, H., and Kari, N. 1996. *Building America: The Democratic Promise of Public Work*. Philadelphia: Temple University Press.

Brand, S. 1987. *The Media Lab: Inventing the Future at MIT*. New York: Viking Press.

Bray, H. 2002, July 22. "A Nice Little Café with a Window on the World." *Boston Globe*, C2.

Brecher, J., Costello, T., and Smith, B. 2000. *Globalization from Below: The Power of Solidarity*. Cambridge, MA: South End Press.

Briefs, U., Ciborra, C., and Schneider L., eds. 1983. *Systems Design for, with and by the Users*. Amsterdam: North-Holland.

Brooks, R. 2002. *Flesh and Machines: How Robots Will Change Us*. New York: Pantheon Books.

Brown, R. 1990. *Sudan's Other Economy: Migrants's Remittances, Capital Flight and Their Policy Implications*. The Hague: Institute of Social Studies.

Calhoun, C. 1992a. *Habermas and the Public Square*. Cambridge, MA: MIT Press.

Calhoun, C. 1992b "The Infrastructure of Modernity: Indirect Relationships, Information Technology, and Social Integration." In H. Haferkamp and N. J. Smelser, eds., *Social Change and Modernity*, 205–236. Berkeley: University of California Press.

Calhoun, C. 1998. "Community without Propinquity Revisited: Communications Technology and the Transformation of the Urban Public Sphere." *Sociological Inquiry*, 68 (3): 373–397.

Calhoun, C. 2001a. "Civil Society/Public Sphere: History of the Concepts, 1897–1903." In *International Encyclopedia of the Social and Behavioral Sciences*. Amsterdam: Elsevier.

Calhoun, C. 2001b. "Public Sphere: 19th and 20th Century History." In *International Encyclopedia of the Social and Behavioral Sciences*, 12595–12599. Amsterdam: Elsevier.

Calhoun, C. 2002. "Imagining Solidarity: Cosmopolitanism, Constitutional Patriotism, and the Public Sphere." *Public Culture*, 14(1): 147–172.

Capra, F., and Spretnak, C. 1984. *Green Politics: The Global Promise*. New York: Dutton.

Casapulla, G., De Cindio, F., Gentile, O., and Sonnante, L. 1998. "A Citizen-Driven Civic Network as Stimulating Context for Designing On-line Public Services." In R. Henderson Chatfield, S. Kuhn, and M. Muller, eds., *Proceedings of the Fifth Biennial Participatory Design Conference "Broadening Participation"*. Palo Alto, CA: Computer Professionals for Social Responsibility.

Casapulla, G., De Cindio, F., and Ripamonti, L. 2001. "Community Networks and Access for All in the Era of the Free Internet: 'Discover the Treasure' of the Community." In L. Keeble and B. D. Loader, eds., *Community Informatics: Shaping Computer-Mediated Social Relations*. London: Routledge.

Castells, M. 1989. *The Informational City: Information Technology, Economic Restructuring, and the Urban-Regional Process*. Oxford: Blackwell.

Castells, M. 1996. *The Rise of the Network Society, Vol. 1: The Information Age: Economy, Society and Culture*. Oxford: Blackwell.

Castells, M. 1997. *The Power of Identity, Vol. 2: The Information Age: Economy, Society and Culture*. Oxford: Blackwell.

Castells, M. 1998. *End of Millennium, Vol. 3: The Information Age: Economy, Society and Culture*. Oxford: Blackwell.

Castells, M. 1999. "The Informational City Is a Dual City: Can It Be Reversed?" In D. A. Schön, B. Sanyal, and W. J. Mitchell, eds., *High Technology and Low-Income Communities: Prospects for the Positive Use of Advanced Information Technology*, 25–42. Cambridge, MA: MIT Press. http://web.mit.edu/sap/www/colloquium96/papers/1castells.html

Castells, M. 2001. *The Internet Galaxy*. Oxford: Oxford University Press.

Castells, M., and Hall, P. 1994. *Technopoles of the World: The Making of Twenty-First Century Industrial Complexes*. London: Routledge.

Center for Civic Networking. 1993. *A National Strategy for Civic Networking: A Vision of Change*. gopher://gopher.civic.net:2400/11/ssnational_strat

Centrinity. 2002. *FirstClass 7 Administrator's Guide*. <www.centrinity.com>

Chandrasekaran, R. 1995, April 11. "In Virginia, a Virtual Community Tries Plugging into Itself." *Washington Post*, A1.

Children's Partnership. 2000. *Online Content for Low-Income and Underserved Americans: The Digital Divide's New Frontier—A Strategic Audit of Activities and Opportunities.* Washington, DC: Children's Partnership. http://www.childrenspartnership.org/pub/low_income/index.html

Choi, A. 1996, June 3. "Towns 'Get Wired' to Spur Development." *Wall Street Journal*, B1.

Chow, C., Ellis, J., Mark, J., and Wise, B. 1998. *Impact of CTCNet Affiliates: Findings from a National Survey of Users of Community Technology Centers*. Newton, MA: Community Technology Centers Network/Educational Development Center. http://www.ctcnet.org/impact98.htm

Chow, C., Ellis, J., Walker, G., and Wise, B. 2000. *Who Goes There? Longitudinal Case Studies of Twelve Users of Community Technology Centers*. Newton, MA: Community Technology Centers Network/Educational Development Center, Inc. http://www.ctcnet.org/publics.html

Cisler, S. 1993. *Community Computer Networks: Building Electronic Greenbelts.* http://home.inreach.com/cisler/greenbelts.html

Città Slow, 2002. Slow Cities website. http://www.cittaslow.stratos.it/, accessed April 5, 2002.

Civille, R. 2000. *Community Networks Get Interesting: A Synthesis of Issues, Findings and Recommendations.* Report of the Art Portalis Project Strategic Planning Retreat, Center for Civic Networking. http://www.civic.net/ccn.html

Clement, A., and Shade, L. 2000. "The Access Rainbow: Conceptualizing Universal Access to the Information/Communications Infrastructure." In M. Gurstein, ed., *Community Informatics: Enabling Communities with Information and Communications Technologies*. Hershey, PA: Idea Group Publishing.

Cohill, A. 1994, April 3. "Electronic Village Still in Experimental Stage." *Roanoke Times & World-News*, NRV2.

Cohill, A. 1997. "Success Factors of the Blacksburg Electronic Village." In A. Cohill and A. Kavanaugh, eds., *Community Networks: Lessons from Blacksburg, Virginia*, 297–318. Norwood, MA: Artech House.

Cohill, A., and Kavanaugh, A., eds. 1997. *Community Networks: Lessons from Blacksburg, Virginia*. Norwood, MA: Artech House.

Collins, P. 2000. *Black Feminist Thought: Knowledge, Consciousness, and the Politics of Empowerment*. New York: Routledge.

Compaine, B., and Gomery, D. 2000. *Who Owns the Media: Competition and Concentration in the Mass Media Industry*. 3rd ed. Mahwah, NJ: Erlbaum.

Computer Professionals for Social Responsibility. 1998. "CPSR Timeline." Palo Alto, CA: Computer Professionals for Social Responsibility. http://www.cpsr.org/cpsr/timeline.html

Computer Professionals for Social Responsibility. Undated. "CPSR History." Palo Alto, CA: Computer Professionals for Social Responsibility. http://www.cpsr.org/cpsr/history.html

"Computer Professionals for Social Responsibility—Seattle Chapter." Undated. http://www.scn.org/cpsr/aboutsea.html

Corn, J., ed. 1986. *Imagining Tomorrow: History, Technology, and the American Future*. Cambridge, MA: MIT Press.

Curran, J., and Park, M. 2000. *De-westernizing Media Studies*. London: Routledge

Czitrom, D. J. 1982. *Media and the American Mind: From Morse to McLuhan*. Chapel Hill: University of North Carolina Press.

Davis, C., and Splichal, S., eds. 2000. *Access Denied: Freedom of Information in the Information Age*. Ames: Iowa State University Press.

Day, P. 2001a. "Designing Democratic Community Networks: Involving Communities through Civil Participation." In M. Tanabe, P. Van den Besselaar, and T. Ishida, eds., *Digital Cities II: Computational and Sociological Approaches*, 86–100. Berlin: Springer.

Day, P. 2001b. "The Network Community: Policies for a Participative Information Society," unpublished doctoral dissertation. Brighton & Hove: University of Brighton.

Day, P. 2002a. Community Informatics—Policy, Partnership and Practice. In S. Marshall, W. Taylor, and C. Mac Pherson, eds., *Using IT: Making IT Happen*, 1–11. Proceedings of IT in Regional Areas Conference 2002. Rockhampton, Central Queensland: Central Queensland University.

Day, P. 2002b. "Participatory Community Practice in the Network Society—A Position Paper." Participatory Design of Information/Communication Infrastructures Workshop at the "Shaping the Network Society" symposium (DIAC 2002), Seattle, May 16–19. http://www.fis.utoronto.ca/research.iprp/pdworkshop/private/peterday.html

Day, P., and Schuler, D., eds. 2004. *Community Practice in the Network Society: Local Action / Global Interaction*. London: Routledge.

De Cindio, F. 2000. "Community Networks for Reinventing Citizenship and Democracy". In M. Gurstein, ed., *Community Informatics: Enabling Communities with Information and Communications Technologies*. Hershey, PA: Idea Publishing Group.

De Cindio, F., De Michelis, G., Pomello, L., and Simone, C. 1983. "Conditions and Tools for an Effective Negotiation during the Organization/Information Systems Design Process." In *U. Briefs, C. Ciborra, and L. Schneider, eds., Systems Design for, with and by the Users*. Amsterdam: North-Holland.

De Cindio, F., De Michelis, G., and Simone, C. 1992. "The Communication Disciplines of CHAOS." In *Concurrency and Nets*. K. Voss, H. Genrich, and G. Rozenberg, eds., Berlin: Springer Verlag. Also in: D. Marca and G. Bock, eds., *Groupware: Software for Computer-Supported Cooperative Work*. pp. 115–139. Washington: IEEE Comp. Society Press.

De Cindio, F., De Michelis, G., Simone, C., Vassallo, R., and Zanaboni, A. 1986. "CHAOS as a Coordination Technology." *Proceedings of First Computer Supported Cooperative Work Conference*. New York: ACM Press.

De Cindio, F., Gentile, O., Grew, P., and Redolfi, D. Forthcoming. *Community Networks: Rules of Behavior and Social Structure*.

De Cindio, F., and Serra, A., eds. 1997. *Proceedings of the First European Conference on Community Networking: "Put People First."* Milan, Italy: AIREC. http://www.retecivica.milano.it/ecn97

De Cindio, F., and Simone, C. 1985. "Women and work in the age of computers: (many problems), one opportunity, two challanges. In A. Olerup, L. Schneider, and E. Monod, eds. *Women, Work and Computerization: Opportunities and Disadvantages*, 195–203. Amsterdam: Elsevier/North Holland.

De Cindio, F., Sonnante, L., and Cannada, V. 1997. "From the Milano Community Networks (RCM) to the Association of Civic Networking—Lombardia (AIReC)." In F. De Cindio and A. Serra, eds., *Proceedings of the First European Conference on Community Networking*. Milan, Italy: AIREC.

Degenne, A., and Forse, M. 1999. *Introducing Social Networks*. London: Sage.

De Kerchkove, D. 1998, May 21. Keynote Speech at TeleComNet Conference, Milan, Italy.

Dertouzos, M. 1997. *What Will Be: How the New World of Information Will Change Our Lives*. San Francisco: HarperEdge.

Dertouzos, M. 2001. *The Unfinished Revolution: Human-Centered Computers and What They Can Do for Us*. New York: HarperCollins.

DeVaughn, M. 1994, October 13. "Grant Bringing Info Highway Straight to Pupils." Roanoke Times & World-News, A1.

Dibbell, J. 1998. *My Tiny Life: Crime and Passion in a Virtual World*. New York: Henry Holt.

Digital Divide Network. 2002, July 11. *Bringing a Nation Online: The Importance of Federal Leadership*. http://www.digitaldividenetwork.org/content/stories/index.cfm? key = 248, accessed August 22, 2002.

Digital Promise. (2002). The website for Digital Promise is at <http://www. digitalpromise.org>. The text of the Digital Opportunity Investment Trust Act is at <http://www.digitalpromise.org/senate_bill.asp>. Both pages accessed June 27, 2002.

DiMaggio, P., and Hargittai, E. 2001. *From the "Digital Divide" to "Digital Inequality": Studying Internet Use as Penetration Increases*. Princeton, NJ: Center for Arts and Culture Policy Studies, Princeton University.

DiMaggio, P., Hargittai, E., Neuman, W., and Robinson, J. 2001. "Social Implications of the Internet." *Annual Review of Sociology*, 27: 307–355.

"Discussion of Violence Goes On-line in Seattle." 1994, February 28. *Seattle Post-Intelligencer*, B2.

D'Orville, H. 1999. *Towards the Global Knowledge and Information Society—The Challenges for Development and Co-operation*. http://www.undp.org/info21/public/ pb-challenge.html

Downey, G. 1998. *The Machine in Me: An Anthropologist Sits among Computer Engineers*. New York: Routledge.

Downing, J., with Villareal Ford, T., Gil, G., and Stein, L. 2001. *Radical Media: Rebellious Communication and Social Movements*. Thousand Oaks, CA: Sage.

Drumm, J., and Groom, J. 1998. The Cybermobile Rolls onto Capitol Hill. *Computers in Libraries*, 18(10): 18–19.

Durrance, J., and Pettigrew, K. 2000, February 1. "Community Information: The Technological Touch." *Library Journal*, 125: 244–246.

Durrance, J., Pettigrew, K., Jourdan, M., and Scheuerer, K. 2001. "Libraries and Civil Society." In N. Kranich, ed. *Libraries and Democracy: The Cornerstones of Liberty*, 49–59. Chicago: American Library Association.

Dyer-Witheford, N. 1999. *Cyber-Marx: Cycles and Circuits of Struggle in High-Technology Capitalism*. Chicago: University of Illinois Press.

Economic Resource Centre for Overseas Filipinos. 2001. Working paper prepared for the Seminar Workshop on Identifying Effective Economic Linkages between Overseas Filipinos and the Rural Communities in the Philippines, Geneva. www.ercof.org: 8080/ercof/ContentLoader?page = workingPaper.erc

EdLiNC. 2000, July 10. *E-Rate: Keeping the Promise to Connect Kids and Communities to the Future.* Washington, DC: The Education and Libraries Networks Coalition (EdLiNC). http://www.edlinc.org/pubs/eratereport2.html

Edwards, B., Foley, M., and Diani, M., eds. 2001. *Beyond Tocqueville: Civil Society and the Social Capital Debate in Comparative Perspective.* Hanover, NH: University Press of New England.

Ehrenberg, J. 1999. *Civil Society: The Critical History of an Idea.* New York: New York University Press.

Einhorn, B., with Keliher, M. 2000, June 26. "Taiwan: Hitching a Ride on the Wireless Web." *Business Week,* 24.

"Electronic Village Gets Discovered." 1995, April 4. *Roanoke Times & World-News,* NRV3.

Elkin, S., and Soltan, K., eds. 1999. *Citizen Competence and Democratic Institutions.* University Park: Pennsylvania State University Press.

Emling, S. 2002, February 16. "Internet Coming to a Corner Near You?" *The Toledo Blade,* D2.

Engelbart, D. 1963. "A Conceptual Framework for the Augmentation of a Man's Intellect." In P. W. Howerton and D. C. Weeks, eds., *Vistas in Information Handling,* vol. 1. Washington, DC: Spartan Books.

Evers, J. 2001, July 6. *Modified Game Consoles to Narrow Digital Divide.* CNN.com, http://www.cnn.com/2001/TECH/industry/07/06/consoles.divide.idg, accessed April 5, 2002.

Falk, R. 1993. "The Making of Global Citizenship." In J. Brecher, J. Childs, and J. Cutler, eds., *Global Visions: Beyond the New World Order,* 39–50. Boston: South End Press.

Farragher, T. 1995, May 14. "In Blacksburg, Va., There's No Wired Place Like Home." *Philadelphia Inquirer,* D1.

Farrington, C., and Pine, E. 1997. "Community Memory: A Case Study in Community Communication." In P. E. Agre and D. Schuler, eds., *Reinventing Technology, Rediscovering Community: Critical Explorations of Computing as a Social Practice,* 219–227. Greenwich, CT: Ablex.

Fernández, H., and Angel, L. 2000, November 7. "Las redes ciudadanas maduran." Editorial Nº 240 de Enredando de fecha, http://www.enredando.com

Fernández-Vega, C. 2002, Septemeber 30. "Remesas: millonario negocio a costa de los migrantes." *La Jornada,* (Mexico), 26. www.lajornada.unam.mx

Fernback, J., and Thompson, B. "Virtual Communities: Abort, Retry, Failure?" Presented as "Computer-mediated Communication and the American Collectivity" at the Annual Meeting of the International Communication Association, Albuquerque, New Mexico.

Financial Times. 2001. *FT500—Global 500 Data*. FT.com, http://www.ft.com London: Financial Times.

Finquelievich, S. 2000. "ICT and Local Governance: A View from the South." In Mi. Gurstein, ed., *Community Informatics: Enabling Communities with Information and Communication Technologies*. Hershey, PA: Idea Group Publishing.

Finquelievich, S. 2002. *Hacia una nueva ciudadanía: Argentina y sus TICs*. In ENREDANDO, http://www.enredando.com, week of February 5–February 11, 2002.

Finquelievich, S., ed. 2000. *¡Ciudadanos, a la Red!* Buenos Aires: Ed. La Crujía.

Finquelievich, S., and Schiavo, E., eds. 1998. *La ciudad y sus TICs*. Buenos Aires: Ed. Universidad de Quilmes, Colección Ciencia, Tecnología y Sociedad.

Fishkin, J. 1995. *The Voice of the People: Public Opinion and Democracy*. New Haven, CT: Yale University Press.

Fishkin, J. 1997. *Democracy and Deliberation: New Directions for Democratic Reform*. New Haven, CT: Yale University Press.

Forster, E. M. 1963. *"The Machine Stops."* In A. Lewis, ed. *Of Men and Machines*. p.261–291. New york: E. P. Dutton.

Foster, S. 1994a, January 15. "A Ride on Electronic Street." *Roanoke Times & World-News*, NRV1.

Foster, S. 1994b, April 4. "TV Turns Attention to Electronic Village." *Roanoke Times & World-News*, NRV1.

Fraser, N. 1989. *Unruly Practices: Power, Discourse, and Gender in Contemporary Social Theory*. Minneapolis: University of Minnesota Press.

Fraser, N. 1996. *Justice Interruptus: Critical Reflections on the "Postsocialist" Condition*. London: Routledge.

Frasier, N. 1988. In C. Calhoun, ed. *Habermas and the Public Square*. Cambridge, MA: MIT Press.

Freedom to Read Foundation. 2002. Website. Chicago: Freedom to Read Foundation. http://www.ftrf.org/index.html

Friedland, L., and Boyte, H. 2000, January. "The New Information Commons: Community Information Partnerships and Civic Change." Minneapolis: Center for Democracy and Citizenship, Hubert Humphrey Institute, University of Minnesota. http://www.publicwork.org/pdf/workingpapers/New%20information%20commons.pdf

"FT 100/200 Scoreboard." 2001, June 8. *BusinessWeek Online.*

Gammeltoft, P. 2002, August. *Remittances and Other Financial Flows to Developing Countries.* Copenhagen, Centre for Development Research. www.cdr.dk/working_papers/02-11-abs.htm

Gaonkar, D. P., ed. 2001. *Alternative Modernities.* Durham, NC: Duke University Press.

Garrone, E. 2000, June 9–10. "Dalla new economy alla new society—Miti e realtà di una rivoluzione in corso." *Proceedings of the Conference Held in Santa Margherita Ligure.* Rome: Confindustria. (In Italian.)

Gelernter, C. 1995, August 21. "Women Send Message of Concerns to Beijing." *Seattle Times,* F1.

Gershenfeld, N. 1999. *When Things Start to Think.* New York: Henry Holt.

Gilder, G. 2000. *Telecosm: How Infinite Bandwidth Will Revolutionize Our World.* New York: Free Press.

Gordon, A., Gordon, M., Moore, E., and Boyd, A. 2002. *Support for Public Access Computing Widespread and Strong.* Seattle: Bill and Melinda Gates Foundation. http://www.gatesfoundation.org/libraries/uslibraryprogram/evaluation/default1.htm

Gore, A. 1994, March 21. Address at the Conference of the International Telecommunications Union Buenos Aires. http://www.interesting-people.org/archives/interesting-people/199403/msg00112.html

Graham, S., and Simon, M. 1996. *Telecommunications and the City: Electronic Spaces, Urban Places, New York: Routledge.*

Gramsci, A. 1971. *Prison Notebooks.* New York: International Publishers.

Greider, W. 1998. *One World, Ready or Not: The Manic Logic of Global Capitalism.* New York: Simon and Schuster.

Griest, S. 1994, July 21. "Volunteers Help Widen Access to Information Superhighway." *Seattle Post-Intelligencer,* C1.

Grossman, L. 1995. *The Electronic Republic: The Transformation of American Democracy.* New York: Viking.

Grossman, L., and Minow, N., eds. 2001. *A Digital Gift to the Nation: Fulfilling the Promise of the Digital and Internet Age.* New York: Century Foundation Press.

Gurstein, M. 2000. "Community Informatics: Enabling Communities' Uses of Information and Communications Technology." In M. Gurstein, ed., *Community Informatics: Enabling Communities with Information and Communications Technologies.* Hershey, PA: Idea Group Publishing.

Habermas, J. 1984. *The Theory of Communicative Action, Vol. 1: Reason and the Rationalization of Society*. Boston: Beacon Press.

Habermas, J. 1989. *The Structural Transformation of the Public Sphere: An Inquiry into a Category of Bourgeois Society*. Cambridge, MA: MIT Press.

Habermas, J. 1998, winter. "The European Nation-State: On the Past and Future of Sovereignty and Citizenship." *Public Culture,* 10(2).

Halleck, D. 2002. *Hand-Held Visions: The Impossible Possibilities of Community Media*. New York: Fordham University Press.

Hamelink, C. 1994. *Trends in World Communication*. Penang, Malaysia: Southbound Publishers.

Hamelink, C. 2000. *The Ethics of Cyberspace*. London: Sage.

Hamilton, D. 2002. "Sustainability of a Community Technology Center: Action Research at the Murchison Center." Unpublished M.L.S. thesis, Africana Studies, University of Toledo, Toledo, OH.

Hardt, M., and Negri, A. 2000. *Empire*. Cambridge, MA: Harvard University Press.

Harrison, E. 1995, May 16. "Virtual Village Opens Up Alternate Reality for Townspeople." *Los Angeles Times,* A4.

Hart, K. 2000. *The Memory Bank: Money in an Unequal World*. London: Profile Books.

Havel, Vaclev. 1997, December 9. "State of the Republic." Presidential address to the Parliament and Senate of the Czech Republic as quoted in: Jean Bethke Elshtain, "Families and Civic Goods: Connecting Private Lives and Civic Goods," http://www2.duq.edu/familyinstitute/templates/features/conference/elshtain.html

Heanue, A. 2001. "In Support of Democracy: The Library Role in Public Access to Government Information." In N. Kranich, ed., *Libraries and Democracy: The Cornerstones of Liberty,* 121–128. Chicago: American Library Association.

Helm, S. 1994, October–December. "Public Access to the Internet: The Blacksburg Experience." *Virginian Librarian,* 10–14.

Herman, E., and McChesney, R. 1997. *The Global Media: The New Missionaries of Corporate Capitalism*. London: Cassell.

Herndon, S. 2001. "Future of Communications: Information Liberation Manifesto and Strategy Needed." Post to public imc-process mailing list, December 16, 2001, http://lists.indymedia.org/mailman/public/imc-process/2001-December/002158.html

Hernon, P., McClure, C., and Relyea, H., eds. 1996. *Federal Information Policies in the 1990s: Views and Perspectives*. Norwood, NJ: Ablex.

Heterick, R. C. 1993, June. "The Blacksburg Electronic Village: A Field of Dreams." *Information Technology and Libraries*, 240–242.

Hodges, D. 2000. *Class Politics in the Information Age*. Urbana: University of Illinois Press.

Holsendolph, E. 2001, December 12. "Cyberbus Brings Computing to Neighborhoods." *The Atlanta Journal and The Atlanta*, Constitution p. D6.

Holusha, J. 1994, January 16. "Virginia's Electronic Village." *New York Times*, F9.

Homer-Dixon, T., Boutwell, J., and Rathjens, G. 1993, February. "Environmental Change and Violent Conflict." *Scientific American*, 38–45.

Horn, S. 1998. *Cyberville: Clicks, Culture, and the Creation of an Online Town*. New York: Warner Books.

Horrigan, J. 2001. *Online Communities: Networks That Nurture Long-Distance Relationships and Local Ties*. Washington, DC: Pew Internet and American Life Project. http://www.pewinternet.org/reports/index.asp

Horvath, J. Undated. "Community Networking: A Network of Sustainable Communities." Telepolis. http://www.heise.de/tp/english/special/pol/8024/1.html.

Huff, S. W., and Syrcek, B. 1997. "Town Government in Cyberspace." In A. Cohill and A. Kavanaugh, eds., *Community Networks: Lessons from Blacksburg, Virginia* 73–87. Norwood, MA: Artech House.

Hyde, G. 2002, April. "Independent Media Centers: Cyber-Subversion and the Alternative Press." *First Monday*, 7(4). http://firstmonday.org/issues/issue7_4/hyde/index.html.

Information Technology Indicators Residential Survey. 2000. Conducted for City of Seattle Department of Information Technology by Northwest Research Group, Inc. http://www.cityofseattle.net/tech/indicators/Residential_Survey_Report.pdf

International Federation of Library Associations, Committee on Freedom of Access to Information and Free Expression. (IFLA/FAIFE). 2001. *World Report*. Copenhagen: IFLA/FAIFE.

Internet Access in U.S. Public Schools and Classrooms: 1994–2001. Washington, DC: U.S. Department of Education, Office of Educational Research and Improvement. http://nces.ed.gov/pubsearch/pubsinfo.asp?pubid-2001071

"Introduction to BEV Set at Library." 1994, April 12. *Roanoke Times & World-News*, NRV6.

Ipsos-Reid. 2001. *The Face of the Web*. New York: Ipsos-Reid.

Jongma, A. J., and Schmid, A. P. 1994. *Monitoring Human Rights: Manual for Accessing Country Performance*. Leiden: Interdisciplinary Research Program on Root Causes of Human Rights Violations, Faculty of Social Sciences, Leiden University.

Jordan, T. 1999. *Cyberpower: The Culture and Politics of Cyberspace and the Internet*. London: Routledge.

Joseph, M. 2001, July 19. "Tech's Still Got IT Made in India." *Wired News*, www.wired.com/news/business/0,1367,45192,00,html

Joy, B. 2000, April. "Why the Future Doesn't Need Us." *Wired*. http://www.wired.com/wired/archive/8.04/joy_pr.html, accessed March 22, 2002.

Kahn, J., and Andrews, E. 2001, August 20. "World's Economy Slows to a Walk in Rare Lock Step." *The New York Times*, A1, Col. 6.

Keck, M., and Sikkink, K. 1998. *Activists beyond Borders: Advocacy Networks in International Politics*. Ithaca, NY: Cornell University Press.

Keeble, L., and Loader, B., eds. 2001. *Community Informatics: Shaping Computer-Mediated Social Relations*. London: Routledge.

Kellner, D. 1997, fall. "Intellectuals, the New Public Spheres and Techno-Politics." *New Political Science*, 169–188. www.gseis.ucla.edu/courses/ed253a/newDK/intell.htm

Kellner, D. 2001. *Grand Theft 2000: Media Spectacle and a Stolen Election*. Lanham, MD: Rowman and Littlefield.

Kellner, D. 2002. "Theorizing Globalization." *Sociological Theory*, 20(3) http://www. gseis.ucla.edu/faculty/kellner/papers/theoryglob.htm

Kelly, K. 1995. *Out of Control: The New Biology of Machines, Social Systems and the Economic World*. Cambridge, MA: Perseus.

Kelly, K. 1998. *New Rules for the New Economy: 10 Radical Strategies for a Connected World*. New York: Viking Press. http://www.kk.org/newrules/

Kidd, D. 2000. *International Media Campaigns Win Victories*. Media Alliance website, http://www.media-alliance.org/mediafile/19–1/international.html.

Kidd, D. 2003. "Become the Media The Global IMC Movement." In A. Opel and D. Pompper, eds., *Representing Resistance: Media, Civil Disobedience and the Global Justice Movement, 224–240*. Westport, CT: Greenwood.

Klare, M. 2001, July 23/30. "Energy Imperialism." *The Nation*, 5–6.

Kleiner, A., and Farris, E. 2002. "Internet Access in U.S. Public Schools and Classrooms: 1994–2001." U.S. Department of Education, National Center for Educational Statistics. http://nces.ed.gov/pubs2002/2002018.pdf

Kominski, R., and Newburger, E. 1999. "Access Denied: Changes in Computer Ownership and Use, 1984–1997." Paper presented at the annual meeting of the American Sociological Association, Chicago. (August 1999) http://www.census.gov/population/socdemo/computer/confpap99.pdf

Kranich, N. 2000a, fall. "Assessing Internet Access: The Public Library Meets the First Amendment in the Information Age." *Media Studies Journal*, 14(3): 42–45.

Kranich, N. 2000b, May. "Libraries, the New Media, and the Political Process." *iMP: Information Impacts Magazine*. http://www.cisp.org/imp/may_2000/05_00kranich.htm

Kranich, N. 2000c, August. "Smart Voting Starts at Your Library." *American Libraries*, 13(3). www.ala.org/Content/NavigationMenu/Our_Association/Offices/Public_Information/Available_PIO_Materials/Smart_voting_starts_@_your_library.htm

Kranich, N. 2001a, June. "Why Filters Won't Protect Our Children: Libraries, Democracy, and Access." *imp: Information Impacts Magazine*. http://www.cisp.org/imp/june_2001/06_01kranich.htm

Kranich, N., ed. 2001b. *Libraries and Democracy: The Cornerstones of Liberty*. Chicago: American Library Association.

Kurzweil, R. 1999. *The Age of Spiritual Machines: When Computers Exceed Human Intelligence*. New York: Viking Press.

LaClau, E., and Mouffe, C. 2001. *Hegemony and Socialist Strategy: Towards a Radical Democratic Politics. 2nd ed.* London: Verso Books.

Lago Martínez, S., and Jara, A. 2000, September 29,30. "Un ensayo sobre los movimientos sociales en la sociedad de la información." International Seminar *Lo urbano en el Pensamiento Social*, Instituto de Investigaciones Gino Germani, Buenos Aires.

Langman, L., Morris, D., and Zalewski, J. 2003. "Cyberactivism and Alternative Globalization Movements." In W. A. Dunaway, ed., *The 21st Century World-System: Systemic Crises and Antisystemic Resistance*. Westport, CT: Greenwood Press.

Lawrence, S., and Giles, C. 1998, April 3. "Searching the World Wide Web." *Science*, 280: 98–100.

Lawrence, S., and Giles, C. 1999, July 8. "Accessibility of Information on the Web." *Nature*, 400: 107–109.

Lawson, J., and Gleason, S. 2002, February. "Democracy and the War on Dissent." *Z Magazine*, 15(2): 12–14. http://www.zmag.org/Zmag/articles/february02lawson-gleason.htm

Lee, E. 1997. *"The Labour Movement and the Internet: The New Internationalism."* In A. Lipow, series ed., *Labour and Society International*. London: Pluto Press.

Leon, O., Burch, S., and Tamayo, E. 2001. *Social Movements on the Net*. Quito: Agencia Latinoamericana de Informacion.

Lessig, L. 2002. *The Future of Ideas: The Fate of the Commons in a Connected World*. New York: Random House.

Lévy, P. 1997. *Collective Intelligence: Mankind's Emerging World in Cyberspace*. Trans. R. Bonnonno. New York: Plenum Press.

Lévy, P. 1998. *Becoming Virtual: Reality in the Digital Age*. Trans. R. Bonnonno. New York: Plenum Press.

Lévy, P. 2001. *Cyberculture*. Minneapolis: University of Minnesota Press.

Levy, S. 1998, November 9. "The Hottest New Tech Cities" (cover story and sidebars). *Newsweek*, 44–56.

Lichterman, P. 1996. *The Search for Political Community: American Activists Reinventing Commitment*. Cambridge: Cambridge University Press.

Lindquist, R. 1994, November 30. "Computer Class Aimed at Removing Fear of Technology." *Roanoke Times & World-News*, NRV3.

Loader, B., ed. 1998. *Cyberspace Divide: Equality, Agency, and Policy in the Information Society*. London: Routledge.

Ludmer, J. Undated. *ARGENTINA, EN LA SERIE DE SEATTLE, La multitud entra en acción*. http://www.clarin.com/suplementos/cultura/2002-01-19/u-00201.htm

Luisi, P. 2001. "Tre buoni motivi per considerare finita la rete civica (così come l'abbiamo sempre considerata)." *Quaderni di Comunicazione Pubblica*, 5. Bologna, Italy: CLUEB. (In Italian.)

Lukes, S. 1993. "Five Fables about Human Rights." In S. Shute, and S. Hurley, eds., *On Human Rights*. New York: Basic Books.

Lyman, S., ed. 1995. *Social Movements: Critiques, Concepts, Case Studies*. Philadelphia: Temple University Press.

Madison, James. 1822. Letter to W. T. Barry, August 4, 1822. In *Letters and Other Writings of James Madison*, published by order of Congress. 4 volumes. Edited by Philip R. Fendall. Philadelphia: Lippincott, 1865, v. 3.

Maier, S. 1994, January 4. "New Computer Network—The Talk of the Town." *Seattle Post-Intelligencer*, A1.

Marcoux, E. 2001. "Information Literacy for the Twenty-First-Century Citizen." In N. Kranich, ed. *Libraries and Democracy: The Cornerstones of Liberty*, 70–80. Chicago: American Library Association.

Mark, J., Cornebise, J., and Wahl, E. 1997. *Community Technology Centers: Impact on Individual Participants and Their Communities.* Newton, MA: Education Development Center. http://www.ctcnet.org/eval.html

Markoff, J., and Lohr, S. 2002, September 29. "Intel's Big Bet Turns Iffy." *New York Times.* http://www.nytimes.com/2002/09/29/technology/circuits/29CHIP.html, accessed September 29, 2002.

Marshall, S., Taylor, W., and MacPherson, C., eds. 2002. "Using IT: Making IT Happen." *Proceedings of IT in Regional Areas Conference 2002.* Rockhampton, Central Queensland: Central Queensland University.

Martin, C. V. 1997. "Managing Information in a Community Network." In A. Cohill and A. Kavanaugh, eds., *Community Networks: Lessons from Blacksburg, Virginia,* 235–276. Norwood, MA: Artech House.

Mathews, D. 1984, March. "The Public in Practice and Theory." *Public Administration Review,* 44, special issue: 120–125.

Mathews, D. 1999. *Politics for People.* 2nd ed. Champaign: University of Illinois Press.

Mathews, D., and McAfee, N. 2001. *Making Choices Together: The Power of Public Deliberation.* Dayton, OH: Charles F. Kettering Foundation.

McCabe, R. 2001. *Civic Librarianship: Renewing the Social Mission of the Public Library.* Lanham, MD: Scarecrow Press.

McChesney, R. 1997. *Corporate Media and the Threat to Democracy.* New York: Seven Stories Press.

McChesney, R. 1999. *Rich Media, Poor Democracy: Communication Politics in Dubious Times—The History of Communication.* Urbana: University of Illinois Press.

McClure, C., and Bertot, J. 2000, August. *Public Library Internet Services: Impacts on the Digital Divide.* Washington, DC: American Library Association Office of Information Technology Policy. http://www.ala.org/oitp/e-ratestage1.pdf

Miani, M. 2000. "The Institutionalization of Civic Networks: The Case of Italian Digital Cities." Presented at the Second Euricom Colloquium Electronic Networks & Democracy, University of Nijmegen, October 2002. http://baserv.uci.kun.nl/~jankov/Euricom/papers/Miani.pdf

McConnell, B. 1999. *Civil Society: The Underpinnings of American Democracy.* Hanover, NH: University Press of New England.

McCook, K. 2000. *A Place at the Table: Participating in Community Building.* Chicago: American Library Association.

McCue, C., and Rosenberg, M. 1992, January 21. "Electronic Future Planned." *Roanoke Times & World-News*, B1.

McGreevy, M. 2002. "First Saturday: Mobilizing a Community for Achievement and Empowerment." Unpublished M.L.S. thesis, Africana Studies, University of Toledo, Toledo, OH.

McKeown, K. 1991. *Social Norms and Implications of Santa Monica's PEN* (*Public Electronic Network*). Website, http://www.mckeown.net/PENaddress.html, accessed July 31, 2002.

McLuhan, M. 1964. *Understanding Media*. New York: Signet Books.

Melucci, A. 1996. *Challenging Codes: Collective Action in the Information Age*. Cambridge: Cambridge University Press.

Micelli S. 2001. *Imprese, reti e comunità virtuali*. Milan, Italy: ETAS. (In Italian.)

Michels, R. 1962. *Political Parties: A Sociological Study of the Oligarchical Tendencies of Modern Democracy*. London: Collier-Macmillan.

Milenky, E. 1995, October 21. "Electronic Village Growing into County." *Roanoke Times & World-News*, NRV1.

Miller, S. 1996. *Civilizing Cyberspace: Policy, Power, and the Information Superhighway*. New York: ACM Press.

Mitchell, W. 1998. *City of Bits*. Cambridge, MA: MIT Press.

Mitchell, W. 1999. *E-topia: "Urban Life, Jim—But Not as We Know It."* Cambridge, MA: MIT Press.

Molz, R., and Dain, P. 1999. *Civic Space/Cyberspace: The American Public Library in the Digital Age*. Cambridge, MA: MIT Press.

Moore, N. 2000. "The International Framework of Information Policies." In D. Law, and J. Elkin, eds., *Managing Information*, 1–19. Open University Press.

Moravec, H. 1998. *Robot: Mere Machine to Transcendent Mind*. Oxford: Oxford University Press.

Morrison, S., and Warn, K. 2001, June 11. "Liberals Strive to Sharpen Competitive Edge." *Financial Times*, "Canada Survey," 1–2.

Moskowitz, R. 2000. *PKI at a Crossroads*. www.networkcomputing.com/1108/1108colmoskowitz.html

Munoz, L. 2001, March 24. "Diversity in Oscars Still Elusive." *Los Angeles Times*, A1

National Coalition against Censorship. 1999. *The Cyber-Library: Legal and Policy Issues Facing Public Libraries in the High-Tech Era*. New York: NCAC. http://www.ncac.org/issues/sex_censorship.html

National Foreign Intelligence Board. 2000. *Global Trends 2015: A Dialogue about the Future with Nongovernment Experts*. GPO stock number 041-015-00211-2, published on CIA website, www.cia.gov/cia/publications/globaltrends2015.

National Research Council (NRC). 1999. *Being Fluent with Information Technology*. Washington, DC: National Academy Press. http://www.nap.edu/catalog/6482.html

National Research Council, Committee on Intellectual Property Rights and the Emerging Information Infrastructure. 2000. *The Digital Dilemma: Intellectual Property in the Information Age*. Washington, DC: National Academy Press.

National Telecommunications and Information Administration (NTIA). 1995. *Falling through the Net: A Survey of "Have Nots" in Rural and Urban America*. Washington, DC: U.S. Department of Commerce. http://www.ntia.doc.gov/ntiahome/fallingthru.html

National Telecommunications and Information Administration (NTIA). 1998. *Falling through the Net II: New Data on the Digital Divide*. Washington, DC: U.S. Department of Commerce.

National Telecommunications and Information Administration (NTIA). 1999a. *Falling through the Net: Defining the Digital Divide: A Report on the Telecommunications and Information Technology Gap in America*. Washington, DC: U.S. Department of Commerce. http://www.ntia.doc.gov/ntiahome/fttn99/FTTN.pdf

National Telecommunications and Information Administration (NTIA). 1999b. *Falling through the Net III: New Data on the Digital Divide*. Washington, DC: U.S. Department of Commerce.

National Telecommunications and Information Administration (NTIA). 2000. *Falling through the Net: Toward Digital Inclusion: A Report on Americans' Access to Technology Tools*. Washington, DC: U.S. Department of Commerce. http://search.ntia.doc.gov/pdf/fttn00.pdf

National Telecommunications and Information Administration (NTIA). 2002. *A Nation Online: How Americans Are Expanding Their Use of the Internet*. Washington, DC: U.S. Department of Commerce. http://www.ntia.doc.gov/ntiahome/dn

Negroponte, N. 1995. *Being Digital*. New York: Knopf.

Network Appliance. Undated. *Toledo Public Schools: NetApp Scores an A+ for Improving Content Delivery*. http://www.netapp.com/case_studies/toledo.html

Norris, P. 2001. *Digital Divide: Civic Engagement, Information Poverty and the Internet Worldwide*. Cambridge: Cambridge University Press.

Novak, T., and Hoffman, D. 1998, February 2. *Bridging the Digital Divide: The Impact of Race on Computer Access and Internet Use*. Nashville, TN: Vanderbilt University. http://www2000.ogsm.vanderbilt.edu/papers/race/science.html

O'Connell, J. 2001, August 19. "What's in a Trade Statistic? Less and Less." *Los Angeles Times*, M2.

OMB Watch. Website. Washington, DC: OMB Watch. http://www.ombwatch.org/

Orwell, G. 1949. *Nineteen Eighty-Four*. New York: Harcourt, Brace and Company

Osvaldo, L., Burch, S., and Tamayo, E. 2001. *Social Movements on the Net*. Quito: Agencia Latinoamericana de Información—IDRC.

Pacey, A. 1983. *The Culture of Technology*. Oxford: Blackwell.

Pan, E., and Arora, A. 1999, August 9. "Sending AOL a Message." *Newsweek*, 51.

Pantic, D. 1999, Fall. "Independent media in Serbia—Ten Years After" *Media Studies Journal*, 13(3).

Patterson, S. 1997. "Evaluating the Blacksburg Electronic Village." In A. Cohill and A. Kavanaugh, eds., *Community Networks: Lessons from Blacksburg, Virginia*, 55–71. Norwood, MA: Artech House.

Penley, P., and Ross, A. 1991. "Introduction." In C. Penley and A. Ross, eds., *Technoculture*, viii–xvii. Minneapolis: University of Minnesota Press.

Perelman, M. 1998. *Class Warfare in the Information Age*. New York: St. Martin's Press.

Petri C. 1977. "Comunication Disciplines." In B. Shaw, ed., *Proceedings of the Joint IBM–University of Newcastle upon Tyne Seminar*. Newcastle upon Tyne, UK: Computing Lab.

Poster, M. 1995. *CyberDemocracy: Internet and the Public Sphere*. University of California, Irvine. http://www.hnet.uci.edu/mposter/writings/democ.htm

Postman, N. 1986. *Amusing Ourselves to Death: Public Discourse in the Age of Show Business*. New York: Penguin.

Pozzi, L. 1995. "Grassroots Gathering in Pacific Northwest." *Sea Change*. http://www.igc.apc.org/vsister/sea/one/beijing.html

Prince and Cooke 2002. Online newsletter. http://www.princecooke.com/comletter/newsletters/comLetter_20_05_2002.asp

Putnam, R. 1995, January. "Bowling Alone: America's Declining Social Capital." *Journal of Democracy* 6(1) 65–78.

Putnam, R. 2000a, December. *Better Together: The Report of the Saguaro Seminar: Civic Engagement in America*. Cambridge, MA: Kennedy School of Government, Harvard University.

Putnam, R. 2000b. *Bowling Alone: The Collapse and Revival of American Community*. New York: Simon and Schuster.

Quasimodo, S. 1959. Quasimodo's Nobel Prize acceptance speech can be found at http://www.nobel.se/literature/laureates/1959/quasimodo-acceptance.html, accessed April 5, 2002.

Rabble. 2002, March 20. *Indymedia and the Role of the Organizers.* Online at AnarchoGeek, http://anarchogeek.protest.net/archives/000005.html.

Rajogopal, A. 2001. *Politics after Television: Religious Nationalism and the Reshaping of the Indian Public.* Cambridge: Cambridge University Press.

Ramirez, P. 2001. *Remittances as a Development Tool: A Regional Conference, Multilateral Investment Fund, Interamerican Development Bank.* www.iadb.org/mif/eng/conferences/pdf/pilarramirez.pdf

Reed, D. 1994, October 26. "Happy 1st Birthday to Blacksburg Electronic Village." *Roanoke Times & World-News*, C1.

Rheingold, H. 1985. *Tools for Thought.* New York: Simon and Schuster.

Rheingold, H. 1992. *Virtual Reality.* New York: Touchstone.

Rheingold, H. 1993. *The Virtual Community: Homesteading on the Electronic Frontier.* Reading, MA: Addison-Wesley.

Rheingold, H. 2000. *The Virtual Community: Homesteading on the Electronic Frontier.* 2nd ed. Cambridge, MA: MIT Press.

Rifkin, J. 2000. *The Age of Access: The New Culture of Hypercapitalism, Where All of Life Is a Paid-For Experience.* New York: Penguin Putnam.

Rodotá, S. 2000. *Tecnopolítica: La democracia y las nuevas tecnologías de comunicación.* Buenos Aires: Losada.

Ronfeldt, D., and Martinez, A. 1997. "A Comment on the Zapatista 'Netwar.'" In J. Arquilla and D. Ronfeldt, eds., *In Athena's Camp: Preparing for Conflict in the Information Age*, 369–391. Santa Monica, CA: RAND.

Rosenberg, M. 1992a, January 18. "Plan Would Change Fiber of Blacksburg." *Roanoke Times & World-News*, A1.

Rosenberg, M. 1992b, September 3. "Blacksburg Users Anticipate Linking as 'Computer Village.'" *Roanoke Times & World-News*, NRC1, NRC11.

Rosenberg, M. 1993, January 12. "'Electronic Village' Proponents Meet to Gaze at Future." *Roanoke Times & World-News*, NRC1.

Rosenberg, M. 1994, March 20. "In BEV, Loose Slips Sink Computers." *Roanoke Times & World-News*, NRV2.

Rothenberg, R. 1996, February. "Life in Cyburbia." *Esquire*, 56–63.

Ryan, M. 1998. *Global Competition and the Politics of Intellectual Property*. Washington, DC: Brookings Institution Press.

Sager, I. 1999, June 21. "Big Blue at Your Service." *Business Week*, 130–132.

Salus, P. 1995. *Casting the Net: From ARPANET to Internet and Beyond*. Reading, MA: Addison-Wesley.

Sassen, S. 1996. *Losing Control?* New York: Columbia University Press.

Sassen, S., ed. 2002. *Global Networks, Linked Cities*. New York: Routledge.

Schement, J., and Curtis, T. 1995. *Tendencies and Tensions in the Information Age*. New Brunswick, NJ: Transaction.

Schiller, D. 1999. *Digital Capitalism: Networking the Global Market System*. Cambridge, MA: MIT Press.

Schön, D., Sanyal, B., and Mitchell, W. 1999. *High Technology and Low-Income Communities: Prospects for the Positive Use of Advanced Information Technology*. Cambridge, MA: MIT Press.

Schorger, J. 1997. "A Qualitative Study of the Development and First Year of Implementation of the Blacksburg Electronic Village." Unpublished doctoral dissertation, Education Curriculum and Instruction, Virginia Polytechnic Institute and State University.

Schuler, D. 1993. "The Seattle Community Network." *CPSR Newsletter* 11(2). http://www.cpsr.org/publications/newsletters/issues/1993/Summer1993/schuler.html

Schuler, D. 1994. "Community Networks: Building a New Participatory Medium." *Communications of the ACM*, 37(1): 39–51.

Schuler, D. 1995, December. "Creating Public Space in Cyberspace: The Rise of the New Community Networks." *Internet World*. http://www.scn.org/ip/commnet/iwdec.html

Schuler, D. 1996a. *New Community Networks: Wired for Change*. New York: ACM Press.

Schuler, D. 1996b. "The Seattle Community Network: A Brief Informal History (June 1989 to April 1996)." Unpublished manuscript. http://www.scn.org/commnet/scn-history-schuler.html

Schuler, D. 1997a. "Community Computer Networks: An Opportunity for Collaboration among Democratic Technology Practitioners and Researchers." *Proceedings of Technology and Democracy—Comparative Perspectives*. Oslo, Norway: Center for Technology, and Culture, University of Oslo.

Schuler, D. 1997b, September. "Let's Partner as Patriots: The Future of Democracy May Lie in Linking Libraries with Community Networks." *American Libraries* 28(8): 60–62.

Schuler, D. 2000. "New Communities and New Community Networks." In M. Gurstein, ed., *Community Informatics: Enabling Communities with Information and Communications Technologies*. Hershey, PA: Idea Group Publishing.

Schuler, D. 2001. "Cultivating Society's Civil Intelligence: Patterns for a new 'World Brain.'" *Information, Communication and Society*, 4(2): 157–181.

Schuler, D. 2002. "A Pattern Language for Living Communication: A Global Participatory Project." *Proceedings of PDC '02*. Palo Alto, CA: Computer Professionals for Social Responsibility.

Schuler, D., and McClellan, J. 1999. *Public Space in Cyberspace: Library Advocacy in the Information Age*. New York: Libraries for the Future.

Schuler, D., and Namioka, A., eds. 1993. *Participatory Design: Principles and Practices*. Hillsdale, NJ: Erlbaum.

Schultz, J. 1994, February 10. "A Town's High-Technology Leap: A Computer Network in Blacksburg Has Linked City Hall to Schools to Residents." *Virginian-Pilot*, D3.

Sclove, R. 1995. *Democracy and Technology*. London: Guilford Press.

Seattle Community Network. 1996a, March. "Time of Growth." *SCN Access*. http://www.scn.org/newsletter/3.95news.html

Seattle Community Network. 1996b, August. "SCNA First Meeting and Elections." *SCN Access*. http://www.scn.org/newsletter/8.95news.html

Seattle Community Network. 1996c, October 9. "SCNA Board Meeting Minutes." http://www.scn.org/scna/oct96min.html

Seattle Community Network. 1998, March 11. "SCNA Board Meeting Minutes." http://www.scn.org/scna/mar98min.html

Seattle Community Network. 1999, June 9. "SCNA Board Meeting Minutes." http://www.scn.org/scna/bd99jun.html

Seattle Community Network Association. Undated. "Seattle Community Network Association's Frequently Asked Questions List." http://www.scn.org/scna/faq.txt

Seattle Statement. 2000. www.scn.org/cpsr/diac-00/seattle-statement.html

Seligman, B. 1992. *The Idea of Civil Society*. New York: Free Press.

Shanker, T. 2001, August 19. "Global Arms Sales Rise Again: The U.S. Leads the Pack." *New York Times*,

Shuman, M. 1994. *Towards a Global Village: International Community Development Initiatives*. London: Pluto Press.

Silver, D. 1999. "Localizing the Global Village: Lessons from the Blacksburg Electronic Village." In R. B. Browne and M. W. Fishwick, eds., *The Global Village: Dead or Alive?*, 79–92. Bowling Green, OH: Popular Press.

Silver, D. 2000a. "Looking Backwards, Looking Forward: Cyberculture Studies 1990–2000." In D. Gauntlett, ed., *Web.Studies: Rewiring Media Studies for the Digital Age*, 19–30. London: Edward Arnold.

Silver, D. 2000b. "Margins in the Wires: Looking for Race, Gender, and Sexuality in the Blacksburg Electronic Village." In B. E. Kolko, L. Nakamura, and G. B. Rodman, eds., *Race in Cyberspace*, 133–150. New York: Routledge.

Silvia, L., and Jara, A. 2001. "Nuevos interrogantes sobre los movimientos sociales antiglobalización: de Seattle a Porto Alegre." 1st Conferencia Regional de la Asociación Internacional de Sociología en América Latina, Venezuela, 7 al 11 de mayo de 2001.

Sklair, L. 2000. *The Transnational Capitalist Class*. Boston: Blackwell.

Slow Food. 2002. http://www.slowfood.com, accessed April 5, 2002. See also the website for Slow Food USA, http://www.slowfoodusa.org/, accessed April 5, 2002.

Smith, J. 2001, spring. "Cyber Subversion in the Information Economy." *Dissent*, 48(2): 48–52.

Sofranko, S. J., and Idris, K. 1999. "Use of Overseas Migrants' Remittances to the Extended Family for Business Investment, A Research Note." Rural Sociology, 64(3): 464–481.

Starr, A. 2001. *Naming the Enemy: Anti-Corporate Movements Confront Globalization*. London: Zed Books.

Stepanek, M. 1999, October 4. "A Small Town Reveals America's Digital Divide." *Business Week*, 185–188.

Tanner, A. 2001, July 13. "Activists Embrace Web in Anti-Globalization Drive." Reuters, http://www.globalexchange.org/economy/rulemakers/reuters071301.html, accessed April 5, 2002

Tarrow, S. 1995. *Power in Movement: Social Movements and Contentious Politics*. Cambridge: Cambridge University Press.

Taylor, C. 1994, April 21. "KCTS Awarded Grant for Online Project." *Seattle Times*, B3.

Thompson, J. 1995. *The Media and Modernity: A Social Theory of the Media*. Stanford, CA: Stanford University Press.

The Economist. 1999, March 18. "Data Mining."

The Economist. 2000, April 6. "Monopoly Money."

The Economist. 2001, August 9. "The Great Chip Glut."

Thompson, W. 1991. *The American Replacement of Nature*. New York: Bantam.

Thussu, D. 1998. Infotainment International: A View from the South. In D. Kishan Thussu, ed., *Electronic Empires*, 63–82. London: Edward Arnold.

Tocqueville, A. de [1835–1840] 1990. *Democracy in America*. New York: Vintage Books.

Toffler, A. 1980. *The Third Wave*. New York: William Morrow.

Toffler, A., and Toffler, H. 1995. *Creating a New Civilization: The Politics of the Third Wave*. Atlanta: Turner.

"Toledo Public Schools: NetApp Scores an A+ for Improving Content Delivery." 2000. Network Appliance, Inc. http://www.netapp.com/case_studies/toledo.html

Tsagarousianou, R., Tambini, D., and Bryan, C., eds. 1998. *Cyberdemocracy: Technology, Cities, and Civic Networks*. New York: Routledge.

Turkel, T. 2002, July 19. "Where Tech Meets Design." *Portland Press Herald*, C1.

Turkle, S. 1997. *Life on the Screen*. New York: Touchstone.

United Nations Development Program (UNDP). 1998. *Human Development Report 1998*. New York: Oxford University Press.

United Nations Development Program (UNDP). 1999. *Human Development Report 1999*. New York: Oxford University Press.

United Nations Development Program (UNDP). 2000. *Human Development Report 2000*. New York: Oxford University Press.

Urban Institute. 2000. *E-Rate and the Digital Divide: A Preliminary Analysis from the Integrated Studies of Educational Technology*. Washington, DC: Urban Institute. http://www.urban.org/pdfs/erate_FR921.pdf

U.S. National Telecommunications and Information Administration. 1995, 1998, 1999, 2000, 2002. *Falling through the Net: Defining the Digital Divide*. Washington, DC: U.S. Department of Commerce. http://search.ntia.doc.gov/pdf/fttn00.pdf

Vaidhyanathan, S. 2001a. "Copyright and Democracy: Its Implications for the Public's Right to Know." In N. Kranich, *Libraries and Democracy: The Cornerstones of Liberty*, 155–165. Chicago: American Library Association.

Vaidhyanathan, S. 2001b. *Copyrights and Copywrongs: The Rise of Intellectual Property and How It Threatens Creativity*. New York: New York University Press.

Vaidhyanathan, S. 2001c, June 22. "Cultural Policy and the Art of Commerce." *Chronicle of Higher Education*, B7.

van den Besselaar, P. 2001. "E-community versus E-commerce: The Rise and Decline of the Amsterdam Digital City." *AI & Society: The Journal for Human-Centred Systems and Machine Intelligence*, 15(3): 280–288.

Van den Besselaar, P., Tanabe, M., and Ishida, T. 2002. "Introduction: Digital Cities Research and Open Issues." *Lecture Notes in Computer Science* 2362: 1–9. Accessed via http://www.swi.psy.uva.nl/usr/peter/peter.html.

van Dijk, J. 1999. *The Network Society*. London: Sage.

Verba, S., Scholzman, K., and Brady, H. 1995. *Voice and Equality: Civic Voluntarism in American Politics*. Cambridge, MA: Harvard University Press.

Victor, D. 2001, August 19. "A Deal Rescuing Nothing." *Los Angeles Times*, M1.

Vieira, L. 2001. *Os argonautas da cidadania: A sociedade civil na globalizaçao*. Rio de Janeiro: Ed. Record.

Walch, J. 1999. *In the Net: An Internet Guide for Activists*. London: Zed Books.

Ward, L. 1997. "Community Network Technology." In A. Cohill and A. Kavanaugh, eds., *Community Networks: Lessons from Blacksburg, Virginia*, 159–234. Norwood, MA: Artech House.

Warner, M. 2002. *Publics and Counterpublics*. Cambridge, MA: Zone Books.

Wasserman, S., and Faust, K. 1994. *Social Network Analysis: Methods and Applications*. Cambridge: Cambridge University Press.

Watkins, B. 1992, May 6. "Virginia Tech Forms Partnership to Study an 'Electronic Village.'" *Chronicle of Higher Education*, A26.

Wellman, B., ed. 1999. *Networks in the Global Village: Life in Contemporary Communities*. Boulder, CO: Westview Press.

Wellman, B., and Giulia, J. 1995. "Netsurfers Don't Ride Alone." In *Communities in Cyberspace*, M. Smith, and P. Kollock, eds., 167–194. London: Routledge.

Wellman, B., and Haythornthwaite, C., eds. 2003. *The Internet in Everyday Life*. Cambridge, MA: Blackwell.

Wells, H. G. 1933. *The Shape of Things to Come*. London: Hutchinson.

Westley, G. 2001, August. *Can Financial Market Policies Reduce Income Equality?* Sustainable Development Department Best Practices Series MSM-112. Washington, DC: Interamerican Development Bank.

Westrich, K. 1997. "Seattle's Community Connection." *Network*, 6(12): 125–129.

White, H. 1992. *Identity and Control*. Princeton, NJ: Princeton University Press.

Wilhelm, A. 2000. *Democracy in the Digital Age: Challenges to Political Life in Cyberspace*. New York: Routledge.

Williams, K. 2000. "Library Computers Bridging the Digital Divide: An Illustration of the Usefulness of Geographic Information System." Unpublished manuscript. Available from the author.

Williams, K. 2001. "What Is the Digital Divide?" In *Working Papers from the d3 Workshop*, University of Michigan, Ann Arbor. http://www.umich.edu/~katewill

Williams, K. 2003. *Literacy and Computer Literacy: Analyzing the NRC's "Being Fluent with Information Technology."* Journal of Literacy and Technology, 3(1).

Winner, L. 1978. *Autonomous Technology: Technics-out-of-Control as a Theme in Political Thought.* Cambridge, MA: MIT Press.

Winner, L. 1986. *The Whale and Reactor.* Chicago: University of Chicago Press.

Winograd, T., and Flores, F. 1986. *Understanding Computers and Cognition. A New Foundation for Design.* Norwood, NJ: Ablex.

Winseck, D. 1998. *Reconvergence: A Political Economy of Telecommunications.* Hampton, NJ: Hampton Press.

World Bank, Public-Private Infrastructure Advisory Facility. Undated. *Tapping Financial Remittances for Infrastructure Development: The case of Mexico.* Wbln0018.worldbank.org/ppiaf/activity.nsf/files/MEXICO.pdf/$FILE/MEXICO.pdf

Yang, G. 2003. "Online Chinese Cultural Spaces as Spaces of Visibility." *Media, Culture, and Society.*

Yankelovich, D. 1991. *Coming to Public Judgment: Making Democracy Work in a Complex World.* Syracuse, NY: Syracuse University Press.

Yankelovich, D. 1999. *The Magic of Dialogue.* New York: Simon and Schuster.

Yang, G. 2003. "The Internet and the Rise of a Transnational Chinese Cultural Sphere." *Media, Culture & Society* 25(4): 469–490.

Young, I. 2000. *Inclusion and Democracy.* Oxford: Oxford University Press.

Zajac, A. 1999, April 5. "Notes from a Wired Community: As Evanston's Cyber-Town Project Gets Under Way, It Can Find Guidance in Virginia." *Chicago Tribune*, C1.

Zelip, B. 2002. "Black People's Hair: The Digitization of Popular Culture." Unpublished M.L.S. thesis, Africana Studies, University of Toledo, Toledo, OH.

Contributors

Abdul Alkalimat is professor of sociology and director of Africana Studies at the University of Toledo, Ohio, where he engineered the only known Internet-based course taught from Africa to students in the United States. He moderates the largest African-American Studies discussion list, H-Afro-Am, and created and maintains two research websites, one on Malcolm X and one on eBlack Studies. He recently moved his "Introduction to Afro-American Studies: A Peoples College Primer," for thirty years the most widely used black studies curriculum, onto this website.

Oliver Boyd-Barrett is professor, Department of Communication, California State Polytechnic University, Pomona. His classes include propaganda and public opinion, political economy of mass communication, communications theory, and communications research. Boyd-Barrett has published extensively on issues to do with international communications, notably about international and national news agencies. He has pioneered the application of distance-learning techniques to the study of mass communications, at the Open University, U.K., and the Center for Mass Communications Research at the University of Leicester, U.K. He is currently researching media coverage of the "war on terrorism."

Craig Calhoun is president of the Social Science Research Council and professor of sociology and history at New York University. Calhoun received his doctorate from Oxford University and taught at the University of North Carolina, Chapel Hill, from 1977 to 1996. His books include *Nationalism* (University of Minnesota Press, 1997), *Neither Gods Nor Emperors: Students and the Struggle for Democracy in China* (University of California Press, 1994), *Critical Social Theory: Culture, History and the Challenge of Difference* (Blackwell, 1995), and *The Public Sphere* (Norton, forthcoming). He is also the editor-in-chief of the *Oxford Dictionary of the Social Sciences*, coeditor for international and area studies of the *International Encyclopedia of Social and Behavioral Sciences*, and editor of *Understanding September 11th* (New Press, 2002). Calhoun works especially on issues of democracy, social movements, and social solidarity in the contexts of technological and social change.

Gary Chapman   is director of The 21st Century Project at the Lyndon Baines Johnson School of Public Affairs in the Graduate School of Public Policy at the University of Texas at Austin. He is a visiting professor at the LBJ School, and also associate director of the University of Texas's Telecommunications and Information Policy Institute. For six years Chapman wrote the internationally syndicated, biweekly newspaper column on technology and society called "Digital Nation," published in and syndicated by the *Los Angeles Times*. He is now a regular columnist for the *Austin American-Statesman*. He serves on the selection committee for the Turing Award, the world's highest award in computer science. He is the former longtime executive director of the national public-interest organization Computer Professionals for Social Responsibility. He was educated at Occidental College in Los Angeles and at Stanford University, and he is also a former member of the U.S. Army Special Forces, or "Green Berets."

Peter Day   is a senior lecturer in the Faculty of Management and Information Sciences at the University of Brighton, U.K., and teaches across a wide range of network-society-related subjects, including community informatics, communications and development, and information and communications policy. He is also a senior research fellow in the Faculty of Informatics and Communication at Central Queensland University, Australia. Coauthor of the IBM/CDF-sponsored *COMMIT Report* which critically evaluated cross-sectoral community ICT initiatives in the U.K., Day has researched the area of community ICT practice extensively. He is a director of the Sussex Community Internet Project (SCIP) in Brighton and Hove, U.K., and a vice president of Go.ITiRA. Day has also just completed coediting (with Douglas Schuler) *Community Practice in the Network Society: Local Action / Global Interaction.*

Fiorella de Cindio   is associate professor of programming languages at the State University of Milan. Her research interests includes Petri nets as concurrency theory, programming languages (namely, object-oriented and distributed programming languages), and the applications of ICT to support life and work within social and office systems. In this last effort, in the 1980s De Cindio did action research and education on workers' participation in systems design, then was a member of the team that conceived and developed one of the first CSCW prototypes (Commitment Handling Active Office System or CHAOS). In 1994, she initiated the Civic Networking Laboratory, for which she is now responsible, and, in that framework, the founding of the Milan Community Network (Rete Civica di Milano or RCM), which is now a Participatory Foundation.

Susana Finquelievich   born in Buenos Aires, Argentina, is an architect and urbanist and has a Ph.D. in urban sociology. She is the head of the Department of Urban Studies at the Research Institute Gino Germani, University of Buenos Aires, and coordinates a research team that works on Internet and society. Finquelievich has published seven books on this subject, plus over a hundred papers in national and international journals. She is formerly president of the Global Community Networking Partnership.

Cees J. Hamelink   is professor of international communication at the University of Amsterdam and professor of media, religion and culture at the Vrije University in Amsterdam. He studied moral philosophy and psychology at the University of Amsterdam, where he graduated in 1968 and obtained his Ph.D. in 1975. Hamelink is the editor-in-chief of the *International Journal for Communication Studies: Gazette* and an adviser on various communication projects for UNESCO, UNRISD, and the International Baccalaureate. He is also honorary president of the International Association for Media and Communication Research and board member of the International Communication Association. Hamelink has authored fifteen books on international communication, culture, human rights, and information technology. Major publications include *Cultural Autonomy in Global Communications* (1983), *Finance and Information* (1983), *The Technology Gamble* (1988), *Trends in World Communication* (1994), *The Politics of World Communication* (1994), and *The Ethics of Cyberspace* (2000).

Nancy Kranich   recently completed a term as president of the American Library Association, where she focused on the role of libraries in democracies, undertaking advocacy, civic-engagement, information-commons, digital-divide, and information-literacy projects in both the United States and abroad. Formerly, she served as associate dean of libraries at New York University. Kranich has appeared on the "Today Show," the C-Span "Washington

Journal," and National Public Radio, and was featured in the *New York Times* and the *Washington Post*. She has made more than 200 presentations and has written extensively on topics related to libraries and information policy, including a book titled *Libraries and Democracy: The Cornerstones of Liberty* (Chicago: American Library Association, 2001). Kranich has a master's degree in public administration from New York University's Wagner School of Public Service, an M.A. in library science from the University of Wisconsin, and a B.A. in anthropology from the University of Wisconsin.

Geert Lovink   is a media theorist, Net critic, and activist based in Sydney, Australia. He studied political science at the University of Amsterdam, where he obtained an M.A., and he received a Ph.D. from the University of Melbourne. He is a cofounder of the Amsterdam-based free community network "Digital City" (http://www.dds.nl) and of the support campaign for independent media in Southeastern Europe, "Press Now." In 1995, together with Pit Schultz, he founded the international "nettime" circle (http://www. nettime.org), which encompasses a mailing list (in English, Dutch, French, Spanish/Portuguese, Romanian, and Chinese), a series of meetings and publications such as zkp 1–4, "Netzkritik" (ID-Archiv, 1997, in German), and "Readme!" (Autonomedia, 1998). He also organized the Tulipomania Dotcom conference, which took place in Amsterdam in June 2000, focusing on a critique of the new economy (www.balie.nl/tulipomania). In early 2001 he cofounded www.fibreculture.org, a forum for Australian Internet research and culture, which has its first publication out, launched at the first fibreculture meeting in Melbourne (December 2001). The latest conference he coorganized is Dark Markets, on new media and democracy in times of crisis (Vienna, October 2002, http://darkmarkets.t0.or.at/). He has coedited two books that document his collaboration with the Dutch designer Mieke Gerritzen: *Everyone Is a Designer* (BIS, 2000) and *Catalogue of Strategies* (Gingko Press, 2001). The MIT Press has published two of his books: *Dark Fiber*, a collection of essays on Internet culture, and *Uncanny Networks*, consisting of collected interviews with media theorists and artists. Online text archives: www.desk.org/bilwet and www.laudanum.net/geert.

Veran Matic   is the editor of Radio B2-92 from Belgrade, which Milosevic's regime had banned four times, yet it always succeeded in continuing to broadcast, using, among other media, the Internet. Besides this radio station, Matic established the Association of Independent Electronic Media

(ANEM), consisting of fifty radio and TV stations, and he is the chair of this association. He also leads the Alternative TV Network, which broadcasts its programs via satellite and through the local stations. In addition, he publishes two progressive magazines and runs a publishing house. He has managed to transfer all of these functions into an Internet department, creating a powerful network of diverse media mutually connected by the Internet, satellite, and conventional distributive systems, which is extremely influential not only in the former Yugoslavia, but in all of Southeastern Europe. He has received numerous awards, including the American Committee to Protect Journalists Award, the Olof Palme Award, and the MTV Award for courage in reporting. In May 2000, the International Press Institute selected him as one of fifty post war press-freedom heroes.

Douglas Morris   is completing a Ph.D. in sociology at Loyola University of Chicago. He has participated in social movements and grassroots publishing projects since the mid-1980s. Morris has cowritten a number of academic papers on activism via the Internet. Writings on the history and processes of Indymedia can be found online at the Indymedia Documentation Site (docs.indymedia.org).

Howard Rheingold   has been an engaged observer and critic of computer technology—particularly computer networking—for over a decade. He has written numerous books, including *The Virtual Community* (1993), *Virtual Reality* (1992), and *Tools for Thought* (1985). Rheingold was also founder of Electric Minds, named by *Time* magazine one of the ten best websites of 1996. He was one of the creators and former founding executive editor of *HotWired*, the online World Wide Web multimedia publication of Wired Venture, and former "Tomorrow" columnist for the *San Francisco Examiner*, syndicated internationally by King Features. Rheingold's books have been translated into French, German, Italian, Japanese, Spanish, and Swedish. His latest book is *Smart Mobs* (2002).

Patrice Riemens   is a footloose cultural activist usually based in Amsterdam.

Scott Robinson   has been involved with networking and the introduction of IT into Mexican rural-producer organizations since 1994, when the Red de Informacion Rural went online (www.laneta.apc.org/rir). He has been involved with the creation of Mexican telecenters since 1997, and has published online about these projects and IT public policies in Latin America. He is currently coordinating the final phase of an IDRC Canada–funded community telecenter project in Morelos state, Mexico (www.telecentros.org.mx). While he prefers producing documentaries, years ago on film, today on video, Robinson's "normal" job is teaching social anthropology at the undergraduate and graduate levels in the Universidad Metropolitana (www.uam.mx), Mexico, D.F.

Douglas Schuler is a former chair of Computer Professionals for Social Responsibility (CPSR) and a member of the faculty of The Evergreen State College. He has been involved with the social implications of technology for twenty years. He has published numerous articles and book chapters and has coedited six books. His *New Community Networks: Wired for Change* (1996), hailed as innovative and indispensable, combined social critique with practical proposals based on his experiences as one of the cofounders of the Seattle Community Network, a free public-access computer network. Schuler has given presentations on civic and community communications in Africa, Asia, Europe, and North America and has been a principal organizer at all nine of CPSR's "Directions and Implications of Advanced Computing" symposia. He is now the program director for CPSR's "Public Sphere Project," which includes the multiyear participatory "Pattern Language for Living Communication" http://www.cpsr.org/program/sphere/patterns/ project. Schuler just completed coediting (with Peter Day) *Community Practice in the Network Society: Local Action / Global Interaction.*

David Silver is an assistant professor in the Department of Communication at the University of Washington. He has written widely on the intersections between computers, the Internet, and contemporary American cultures, and more specifically on the social and cultural construction of cyberspace. He is also the director of the Resource Center for Cyberculture Studies (http://www.com.washington.edu/rccs/), an online, not-for-profit organization he founded in 1996.

Kate Williams is a doctoral student at the University of Michigan and research assistant at U-M's Alliance for Community Technology. She coedited *Job?tech: The Technology Revolution and Its Social Impact* (1995) and has also written on the digital divide, computer literacy, and public computing. In 2001 she convened the digital divide doctoral students workshop.

Index